SCHOOL PLAY

SOURCE BOOKS ON EDUCATION
VOL. 10

GARLAND REFERENCE LIBRARY
OF SOCIAL SCIENCE
(VOL. 331)

Source Books on Education

SCHOOL PLAY
A Source Book

James H. Block
Nancy R. King

GARLAND PUBLISHING, INC. • NEW YORK & LONDON
1987

Library of Congress Cataloging-in-Publication Data

School play.

(Garland reference library of social science ;
vol. 331. Source books on education ; vol. 10)
Bibliography: p.
Includes indexes.
1. Play. 2. Play—Social aspects. 3. Play—
Psychological aspects. I. Block, James H. II. King,
Nancy R. III. Series: Garland reference library of
social science ; v. 331. IV. Series: Garland
reference library of social science. Source books on
education ; vol. 10.
LB1137.S335 1987 371.8'9 86-33491
ISBN 0-8240-8632-5 (alk. paper)

Printed on acid-free, 250-year-life paper
Manufactured in the United States of America

TO OUR PARENTS

CONTENTS

PART III: REVIEW AND COMMENTARY

PART IV: SELECTED BIBLIOGRAPHY

PREFACE

Several years ago, amidst much local media ballyhoo, the Santa Barbara Public Schools joined one national movement--"back to basics"--and led another--"pay to play." Publically and privately, local school officials hoped that their participation in these movements would help to restore credibility and balance to their academic and extracurricular programs. And their hopes were soon met as elective courses of student study gave way to required ones and superfluous extracurricular activities began to disappear. But what local educators perceived as being more basic and balanced schooling, many students soon perceived as being base and boring. So, with the support of their peers, and eventually some parents, these students challenged the school board to reexamine their just initiated policies. And in the spring of 1986, amid much less media fuss, local school officials were directed to return the freedom and fun to schooling with new elective academic offerings and expanded extracurricular ones.

What has happened in Santa Barbara's public schools is now happening in school systems across America. In educators' zeal to make schools excellent and equitable places for students to work, we have made them inhospitable places to play. Especially in the academic arena, we have unnecessarily removed some of the electivity and desirability that has historically made attending class fun. And many students, even our best, are now beginning to give educators the same message. If they cannot find reasonable room for play in school or outside it, they will find room for play despite school.

This book seeks to explore the current state of students' school play. It is addressed, first, to researchers who desire to review the extant literature and to understand the causes, course, and consequences of the various forms of school play. It is addressed, second, to practitioners who desire to apply the extant literature and to maintain some semblance of balance between work and play in the classroom.

The volume is organized into four parts. In Part I, we examine school play from various social science perspectives. The perspectives of a historian, an anthropologist/sociologist, and a psychologist are represented. Then, in Part II, we re-examine school play from various educational perspectives. In particular, the perspectives of preschool, elementary, junior-high, secondary, and special educators are presented.

As one might expect, each author in Parts I and II chose to address the school play literature in somewhat different ways. In Part III, we review and comment on their respective findings and observations. Finally, in Part IV, we present an extensive bibliography of contemporary theoretical, empirical, and applied school play literature.

This four-part organization was guided by three editorial principles. First, we wanted a volume that was *interdisciplinary*. We believed that the study of play in such a complex human context as the school required the insights of a variety of social science and educational disciplines. The different substantive and methodological purposes of each discipline would, we hoped, highlight different facets of school play and, thereby, deepen and broaden the reader's understandings.

Second, we wanted a volume that was *comprehensive*. Although there is a surprisingly large literature on school play, we felt that this literature is unnecessarily difficult to locate and to use. Only part of the problem is that school play studies appear in a wide range of social science and educational disciplines. The larger part is that, in each of these disciplines, the play literature forms a relatively small subset of the issues studied. Consequently, school play findings and ideas are rarely assembled for distribution and dissemination beyond a small group of interested scholars and practitioners.

Third, we wanted a volume that was *original*. Specifically, we wanted a volume that concentrated on play at school and across the schooling period. We believed that too much of the extant interdisciplinary literature on play tended to assume that the school has little or no impact on students' play. We also believed that even the literature that did focus on school play still focussed on only the earliest portions of the school experience.

We hope that the content and organization of this volume will serve to highlight the importance of school play to students. Although school officials emphasize the importance of work in the classroom, play does occur on a daily basis. At times, teachers ignore the play, and, at other times, they may encourage, tolerate, or suppress it. In any case, the play events pose an intriguing contradiction to the growing work orientation of the many American schools. Before school educators attempt to make public elementary and secondary schools more worklike in the future, the nature of this contradiction bears more appreciation and understanding.

James H. Block
University of California
Santa Barbara

Nancy R. King
University of Maryland

ACKNOWLEDGEMENTS

This volume represented a major, new, and often frustrating desk-top publishing undertaking for the editors. Not only did we have to learn much about computer hardware, we also had to learn much about software. Never, in our experience, have so many people made so many technical contributions to the production of a single volume.

We gratefully acknowledge the computer assistance of Gregory Shook at the University of Maryland and the computer/word processing assistance of Dr. Mark Hartwig, Barbara Hamill, and Stanley Nicholson at UCSB. Mark, in particular, has been a godsend. We also gratefully acknowledge the secretarial and administrative assistance of Ruth Pulliam, Candy Stevenson, Barbara Lord, and Jeanne Chambers at UCSB. Ruth was instrumental in getting the project off the ground; Candy and Barbara in providing some invaluable "relief" work; and Jeanne in coordinating people and machines. Mary Rivkin at the University of Maryland, Charles Bacon at UCSB, and Kathy Kair now at the University of Utah provided invaluable research and bibliographic assistance.

Finally, we specially acknowledge three persons without whose quiet competence, personal dignity, and unflagging support this volume would have never been completed. One person is Tricia Mirman. With Ruth's retirement, Tricia assumed full responsibility for not only her first professor but also her first book. The growth of the book in many ways reflects her growth in a new and trying job. The second person is Karen Hearn. It was Karen who shouldered major responsibility for proofreading the penultimate manuscripts and for assembling, under great time pressures, the author and subject index. The third person is Marie Ellen Larcada. Marie Ellen, our editor at Garland, has repeatedly shown an unusual sensitivity to our technical problems and resulting missed production deadlines.

School Play
A Source Book

AN INTRODUCTION TO SCHOOL PLAY

Alyce Taylor Cheska

The authors of this excellent book have two important points to make: Schools are important in the development of children and play is important in the life experiences of these children. These points appear obvious; however, in the current literature, school play as a singular concept is woefully underresearched and underreported. Most books on play focus on human basic development processes, relegating the school to a neutral environmental feature. This volume boldly contends that the school is a major formative institution which structures, sets, and sequences children's play perceptions and behavior.

WHY A BOOK ON SCHOOL PLAY IS NEEDED

A book devoted to school play is long overdue and this volume is a welcome addition to the educational literature for several reasons. First, all peoples play; yet some cultures honor play more than others. Western societies fall somewhere near dishonoring play; for at worst, we depreciate play; and at best, we ascribe utilitarian motives to it, such as dispensing information to the young. Children and youths seem intuitively to recognize that play's major raison d'etre is to satisfy an individual's perceived pleasure, but they go along with the educational uses of play in school possibly because the playful process is satisfying. In children's more discerning moments, they appear to rebel against the utilitarian goals of play. Regarding this rebellion, the authors present a perplexing proposition: Is this rebellion against the inappropriate use of play in the educational process or against the educational process itself?

Second, schooling limits and directs children's play. United States educators have harnessed the energy, excitement, enthusiasm, and ends of play in the pedagogical process. At these times students play *within* the objectives of the school. This is called "instructional" play because teachers and students alike legitimize play in facilitating learning. Instructional play includes, for example, mathematical or social-issue games such as "The Game of Life." At other times students play *with* the objectives of the school. This is called "illicit" play because it illegitimately disenfranchises the schooling process and the teachers from the student's world. Through such activity in the school, e.g., whispering, passing notes, dropping pencils, along with other non-play behavior, students communicate their awareness of being manipulated and isolated from the power structure of the school. Additionally, students play *without* the school. This is called "recreational" play because it is engaged in outside the mission and setting of school. Recess or after-school activities, which occur literally outside the school on the "playground" with minimal or no supervision are examples of recreation.

3

This volume points out the distinct importance of these three types of school play--instructional, illicit, and recreational--in the development of physical, cognitive, and social skills used in children's life experiences. Thirdly, the co-editors and contributors have achieved a worthy purpose in providing a composite panorama of the extant school play literature. Little has escaped their survey. The book divides its information into three parts. The first section frames school play in the social scientific disciplinary perspectives of history, anthropology-sociology, and psychology presented respectively by Barbara Finkelstein, Andrew Miracle, and Debra Pepler. The second section chronologically sequences the educational perspectives of play in preschool, elementary school, junior high school, high school, and special school settings presented respectively by James Christie and E. Peter Johnsen, Nancy King, Robert Everhart, Douglas Kleiber and Glyn Roberts, and Mayer Shevin. In the third section, co-editor, James Block summarizes and applies the above school play research to the school setting. In a controversial commentary on this work, educational psychologist and play researcher Brian Sutton-Smith provocatively derides the romanticizing and taming of play in schools. He argues that play abounds with paradoxical opportunities to try on powers, risks, deceptions and skills and to share these with others, but schools are crushing this spirit of play in our children. For a student, educator, social scientist, or parent, this volume raises substantive issues undergirding school play. It also presents a clear view of the kinds of play which abound in our schools, including illicit play, a barometer of our children's alienation to the school curricular process and to school professionals.

Fourthly, the collective insights of these scholars could change our perception of school play. One realizes, through the writings of these observers, that school play is a potent tool to help children grow beyond developmental physical, social, and cognitive skills to a sense of individual independence, self-esteem, control and creativity. These values, which are so important to children's life experiences, may not adhere to the artificial dependency stressed in schools today, thus alternative strategies are identified. This book looks at play and school from the students' views and shows how they manipulate school through play to gain some sense of control in an alienating setting. For that information alone the book is worth reading. With descriptive explanations of the dilemmas facing the school and its use and misuse of play, the authors present plausible solutions, an aspect of analysis which is frequently missing in social issue surveys.

American schools need evaluation and revitalization in perspective, purpose, program, and personnel. One error may be the marginal status of school play. This book offers reasons for this attitude, suggests ways that play can ameliorate students' alienation, and provides positive applications of play which may help reunite the school with students' life experiences.

SELECTED DISCIPLINARY PERSPECTIVES ON SCHOOL PLAY

The following chapters use two basic perspectives, disciplinary and educational, consistently throughout the volume. The contributors were asked by the co-editors to: (a) identify the major substantive perspectives and methodological techniques that their colleagues have used to study play in schools; (b) illustrate how these perspectives and techniques have been applied in the study of students' school play; (c) summarize what research tells educators about school play, paying special attention to possible school effects; (d) speculate on the nature of these school effects; (e) suggest future substantive and methodological directions for the study of school play; and (f) indicate potential practical applications of play research in schools. To whet the reader's appetite, a few summary morsels of material to be found in the following chapters are offered.

Chapter 1

Barbara Finkelstein, in the opening chapter on historical perspectives on school play, praises the resiliency of play in spite of changing forms and contexts over time, but she claims that the historians unvaryingly study play as instrumental in social change. She further links the historical study of children's play and the emergence of modern institutions--the nation state, the factory and the public school.

Three interpretive traditions provide the foci of play study: (1) play as liberating and creative; (2) play as regulatory and organized; and (3) play as contingent and vulnerable. Some historians have looked at schools as liberating institutions, freeing children to play, while others have thought of schools as regulatory institutions, directing and constraining children's play. The historical impact of these traditions culminated in the work of those who think of the school as a workplace for the young.

Finkelstein wisely notes that in its present stage of development, the historical study of children's play in school tells little about the relative durability of play as a lived experience, about human beings as playing creatures, about schools as play environments, and about children as special keepers of the play capacity. A basic truth is that schools have a capacity to both cultivate and suppress the play of children and children at play.

Chapter 2

Andrew Miracle prefaces his survey of school play with the following eclectic definition : "School play is any play behavior of school-aged children (grades K-12) taking place on school grounds or under the auspices of school personnel". Miracle combines anthropological and sociological perspectives in studying this particular social enterprise of human beings. Both disciplines have tended to use three basic paradigms in studying play: historico-descriptive and evolutionary; functionalism, and structural functionalism and communication.

The main focus of anthropological and sociological studies of school play has been on the socialization of the young in preparation for adult activities. Traditional assumptions stress that children's play is preparatory, while adults' play is prophylactic; that play and games are equivalent; and that play and work are antithetical. The last perception has only recently been challenged, primarily by the work of Csikszentmihalyi (1975, 1981). More recent literature also challenges the second perception by distinguishing games from free play and associating play with creativity.

In the anthropological-sociological literature, play has been defined as an activity, an experience, and a biological process; nevertheless, Miracle believes that play is best defined as behavior and not as state of being: "Play is consummatory behavior, with a genetic basis, that is voluntary and pleasurable, and which results in an altered state of consciousness while leaving one in control of one's actions. Play can only be realized in context to modeling behaviors. The experience of the play state may be sufficient motivation for engaging in play behavior."

Miracle recognizes that school play takes place within two social spheres. One, unstructured play, occurs without the direct intervention of adults and is peer-oriented, occurring, for example, after school or between pedagogical activities. The other, structured play, is supervised by an adult, is adult-oriented and directed, and occurs, for example, in a physical education class. Ethnographic studies show that the greatest number of school play activities appear in structured environments and parallel an acceleration from peer-organized to adult-organized play activities in schools.

Miracle suggests the following practical applications of anthropological-sociological school play literature: (1) Different types of play should be utilized differently in school settings. (2) Play should be used in alternation with other activities as a release. (3) Teachers should utilize play as a management device by ritualizing play activities; e.g., when children are shifting from one lesson to another. (4) Teachers should be aware that cultural variations in play, particularly among different ethnic groups, may lead to misunderstandings. (5) In physical education, teachers should use student desire for free play to motivate them to improve physically.

Chapter 3

"Play in schools and schooled in play" are issues examined by Debra Pepler from the psychological perspective. According to Pepler, the first theoretical psychological inquiry into children's play occurred more than a century ago, but in the past decade a great upsurge has occurred in the study of play in child development. Contrary to the long-held view of Piaget (1962) that play is primarily assimilation (the bending of the outside or "real" world to fit the child's own internal mental schema),children's play is currently viewed as accommodation, helping to consolidate and strengthen the children's newly learned schema.

Because defining play operationally is difficult, psychologists have used various means of identifying play criteria and judging play behavior. One example is the "paradigm case approach" or case studies. Results from this approach suggest that play is typically recognized as being enjoyable, flexible, and frequently involves pretending.

Most psychological investigations of children's play have been conducted from a developmental perspective to determine: (1) how children play at different ages, stages and by gender; (2) why children play as they do as they are motivated to interact with environmental factors; and (3) what impact play has on children's development and how it enhances, facilitates or reflects development. Pepler uses these questions to review psychological research on play and its educational applications. For example, five common themes help explain how play contributes to children's development through: (1) investigation; (2) exercise; (3) experimentation and flexibility; (4) facilitation of the transition from concrete to abstract thought; and (5) social interaction. Sex differences, to take another example, along with environmental factors, such as types of play materials available, kinds of toys present, ratio of girls to boys, teacher's presence, and curricular program, influence how children play.

According to Pepler, the investigation of play functions has just begun. We know that cognitive processes are reflected in the play of children; however, the assignment of cause/effect relationships is premature. Play does provide children a natural vehicle for spontaneous learning; yet the effectiveness of "play training" to improve social cognition and social competence is still uncertain. Whether play training, especially in pretend play, can cause the development of cognitive and social-cognitive skills is uncertain. Pepler concludes that cognitive and social forms of play relate to competencies of young children, but more understanding about the relationships between play and learning for older children is needed.

EDUCATIONAL PERSPECTIVES ON SCHOOL PLAY

Moving from the selected disciplinary reviews of school play literature, Chapters 4 through 8 address the educational perspectives on school play for pre-school, elementary, junior high school, high school, and special school settings.

Chapter 4

James Christie and E. Peter Johnsen, in this chapter on preschool play, point out that the preschool setting is popular for play research for at least five reasons: (1) children are conveniently gathered in one place; (2) more play occurs in preschool than any other school level; (3) an intensified anti-play attitude has accompanied the recent "back to basics" movement in schools; (4) the frequency of play in preschool has generated practical interest in the effect of toy selection and play area arrangements on learning; and (5) constructive play and make-believe (pretend) play peak during preschool years.

Christie and Johnsen define play as follows: "We believe that play...is characterized by pretense, self-generated and pleasurable behaviors, flexibility, and some freedom from the extremes of pressure and anxiety." This rendition is compatible with earlier statements by Finklestein, Miracle, and Pepler that stress play is characterized by behavior and is not simply a state of mind.

Christie and Johnsen treat preschool play as an indicator of development and examine individual differences of age, sex, and social class in how children play. They also examine such ecological factors as arrangements of play space and materials, availability of play materials, and the differential effects of peer and adult presence affecting preschoolers' play. Finally they consider how various curricular factors influence preschoolers' play. Two opposing school curricula, one with "planned variation" directed toward academic achievement and the other with a "traditional" emphasis on social-emotional adjustment, are contrasted in their effects on children's play behavior. Play training curricular experiments such as sociodramatic role tutoring and thematic-fantasy training are also examined. Christie and Johnsen propose, in particular, that future research should study both the child's own disposition, which leads him or her to pick certain play settings and toys, and how play training might prove a rehearsal for the child's self-control and coping mechanisms.

Potential applications of preschool play research offered by Christie and Johnsen include focused observations by teachers of free play behavior, employing social-cognitive scales to gauge preschoolers' developmental progress. Research is also needed, they argue, on how the combinations of environmental setting, manipulation of play materials, peer, teacher influences, and individual differences affect preschoolers' social and cognitive development.

Chapter 5

In this chapter co-editor Nancy King explains elementary school play from the children's point of view. She asked children from three elementary schools what they thought play was, and she found that they defined play as a fun and undemanding activity. Interestingly, all the children identified recess as play. This caused King to look to the context in which play took place rather than the actual activities.

She divided play in elementary school into three main kinds: instrumental, illicit, and recreational. The acts of watching film strips, playing vocabulary games, writing stories, and preparing a Thanksgiving meal all have several things in common. Each is deemed enjoyable by the children, is part of the elementary school curriculum and is identified as *instrumental* play. Such activities are not voluntary or self-directed because they serve the educational goals of the curriculum beyond the purposes of the participants. Yet children enjoy them because they provide physical activity, they may require very little effort, they may allow social contact with other students, they allow for individual expression, and they may have interesting content. An apt axiom for this learning strategy is "keep the fun in fundamentals." Because of the students' increased enthusiasm and increased desire to excel, educators have intuitively thought instructional play a profitable strategy for teaching cognitive skills and enhancing intellectual development. However, the distinction between play and games needs to be recognized. Keeping the game or playful simulation content integrated with the academic content is difficult. In spite of the widespread use of instrumental play, there is little evidence that it increases cognitive skills.

Illicit play is unsanctioned, surreptitious interaction among children during classroom events. Such play takes place in spite of classroom rules and regulations. Teachers think this play is disruptive and try to prevent or control it. The few studies of illicit play have stressed its negative, resistive aspects rather than attempting to explore and understand it. King claims that illicit play provides a sphere of autonomy for children within the curricular environment that is controlled by the teacher. In effect the children exercise a sort of mini-control, allowing disorderly and ridiculing responses to adult norms of conduct. These actions are seldom a serious challenge to authority, for children usually attempt to hide their behavior from their teacher. Nevertheless, these activities can serve as windows to the children's peer culture that a teacher can ill afford not to understand.

Recreational play, e.g., recess, is voluntary, self-directed and pleasurable behavior that ordinarily takes place outside the daily academic schedule and school building. Most playground play research, which has been conducted by anthropologists, linguists, and folklorists, centers about three general types: word play (jingles, rhymes, jokes, riddles), games (peer groups, rules, and adjudication of disputes), and the role of leadership and authority. King emphasizes that the social skills which children practice on the playground are not trivial ("letting off steam") as teachers are prone to believe but serve to strengthen the skills used in adult social settings.

King discusses two major implications of elementary school play. One is the categorization of play--instructional, illicit, and recreational--which develops out of the classroom settings as a response to children's playfulness or the settings' structures. The second is the participants' definitions of school play which are based on the context, not the content of the activities. Thus, if a child's concept of play is to be influenced by the teachers, it must be done through the classroom environmental organization.

Chapter 6

In this chapter, Robert Everhart examines the play of the junior high adolescent. He agrees with King that the dimensions of play are understood within the school organization context and through the cultural patterns created, recreated, and challenged within the school. Building on King's categories, Everhart assumes that because instrumental play and recreational play decline greatly during this school-age period, illicit play takes on relatively greater importance. Everhart treats the illicit play of junior high students as strategies for engaging in play behaviors which oppose, to various degrees, the explicit rules and expectations of school work. Illicit play ranges from parodies and satires expressing aversion to schooling or teachers to staged fights used to trick unsuspecting teachers into thinking they are genuine altercations.

The author contends that rather than being random and unsystematic behavior, illicit play is purposeful and has an internal structure. This is confirmed by Everhart's two-year study of students in junior high school, in which he elicited descriptions of students daily school life and assigned the information to relevant categories. Student responses to the question, "What do you do in school?", included: goofing around, fighting, skipping a period, daydreaming, making time go by, being teacher's pet, shooting things like rubber bands, slamming books down, throwing things, bugging teachers, writing notes. Such illicit play represent conflict, endurance and escape behaviors.

Active conflict between students and teachers seemed to abound in junior high school as students pick on each other, fight, and bug the teacher. Passive conflict, e.g., what a student did--or did not--do in the class, included non-participatory behaviors such as "daydreaming, not doing the work, or sitting on our asses" was also apparent. Ongoing conflict between students and teachers appears even more pervasive than that between students. Rather than enduring classes, students actively "bugged" their teachers or escaped them by skipping class or being the teacher's pet. Such goofing-off behavior opposed and undermined the formal curriculum and the curricular control of the school authorities, namely the teachers. Students seemed to view goofing-off as a symbolic opposi-tional strategy demonstrating their resistance to the forced labor they considered much of their daily classroom work to be. In the eyes of most students, if teachers really understood what kids are like today, then bugging would be unnecessary.

Other researchers (Metz, 1978; Stinchcombe, 1964) besides Everhart, have reported that junior high age students believe school life and the larger culture are significantly out of touch. If this is the case, then illicit play is a barometer measuring the effectiveness of the school's organizational life and providing an opportunity for organizational renewal.

Chapter 7

Douglas Kleiber, developmental psychologist, and Glyn Roberts, sports psychologist, examine the transition of play to sport in the high school. They present the differences among "real play," as an activity which is predominantly enjoyment oriented, "illicit play," represented by drug use, sexual promiscuity, and recreational delinquency, and "instrumental play," sanctioned play, as formally arranged extracurricular activities. They propose that play changes developmentally during the high-school time span and assert that sport best reflects high-school play because it is the most play-like of all the extracurricular activities.

Because high-school youth choose to be in high-school sports, they protect the play quality of the sport experience. This playfulness, however, becomes progressively more sophisticated and adult because school sports are a testing ground for youth's physical and social skills. In this process of transformation or profession-alization, play moves from child-like spontaneity and self-determination toward formalization and standardization, competition and survival, perse-verance and delayed gratification, practice and work values. This growing instrumental quality of high-school sports helps prepare children for the adult work world. Quality of performance and resultant success become more significant factors in organized sports than equity or fairness (Webb, 1969).

The authors review conflicting research on the relationship of sport to such attributes of youth, as success in academic aspiration and attainments, generalized social competencies, social mobility, and personal development. Whether or not an adolescent's personal development is enhanced by sports participation is an unresolved issue. Sport, however, appears to provide a social convoy which selects for and reinforces qualities of persistence, endurance, and interpersonal competence. These qualities may, in turn, be transferred to other educational and organizational contexts.

Kleiber and Roberts conclude their review by arguing that the play values in sports need to be reasserted. Because child's play has become rationalized and professionalized, a bipolarization of play has occurred. On the one hand, play involves elements of mastery--convergent thinking, repetition, accommodation, and practice; on the other hand, it involves elements of enjoyment--divergent thinking, experimentation, and innovation. Ideally, these attributes exist in a delicate balance. When one set of elements is over emphasized, it affects the other. For example, when alienation from enjoyment occurs, it leads to the emphasis on mastery; when alienation from mastery (work) occurs, it leads to immediate gratification without competence. To prevent such disequilibrium in students, Kleiber and Roberts offer several suggestions: (1) study the opportunities for informal "playful" levels of recreation, e.g., co-recreation and intra-mural programs; (2) question athletes who have completed their formal participation to determine effects, if any, of differential treatment; (3) look at the effect sport involvement has on involvement in other school endeavors; and (4) examine the effect of more free time for play experimentation. The authors believe that merging elements of both play and work, both enjoyment and mastery, is an ideal that could well be the basis for providing extracurricular alternatives for all students--and perhaps for reforming classrooms as well".

Chapter 8

Mayer Shevin addresses the conceptualization and utilization of play in special education settings. Because of their perceived deficits and handicaps, students in these classes have traditionally been separated from the rest of the school population.

These children are perceived to exhibit low achievement, have behavior-control problems, and need different social skills. Accordingly, they are trained not to show inappropriate behavior. The insistence on "passive skills" prevents the development of the flexible and divergent skills so essential to play. The implicit definition of play in the world of regular educators in reference to the use of materials, types of settings, or kinds of skills does not carry over into the world of special education. Their play is committed to behavior management, and teachers may perceive free time as dangerous "out of control" time. Instrumental play more resembles work than educators in reference to the use of materials, types of settings, or kinds of skills does not carry over into the world of special education. Their play is committed to behavior management, and teachers may perceive free time as dangerous "out of control" time. Instrumental play more resembles work than play, because in special settings "on-task" behaviors ("what I'm supposed to be doing") are considered positive, while other behaviors, often including play behaviors, are considered "off-task."

In examining research on handicapped children's play, Shevin has distinguished between comparative studies of handicapped and non-handicapped children and intervention studies showing benefits of special treatment in changing behavior in a special population of disabled children. Frequently play in special education is the means by which other objectives are reached, or play may reinforce the desired behaviors. Unfortunately the effect of these uses on either fostering or suppressing play or playfulness in special education settings is not known. Observations of common practices, however, show that play is infrequent and unrelaxed. Because of the step-by-step development of error-free behavior for handicapped children, their play is often disassociated with developmental skills of autonomy and self-direction and does not resemble the types of play available to non-handicapped children. The disabled children's lack of play time and leisure skills creates a serious barrier in interaction with normal children; also, modified games practiced in special education settings do little to prepare the disabled child to participate "in regular games with rules."

The author poses the question, "Can behavior analysis and playfulness co-exist?" He calls for a new conception of the special education teacher as one who empowers, facilitates, validates, negotiates, and advocates rather than the traditional conceptualization of one who analyzes, fragments, pinpoints, refines, manages and evaluates. Making play welcome in the special education classroom includes manipulating the physical environment to create a setting more conducive to play than behavior modification. The following suggestions are made: (1) play should be fostered in relaxed environments where teachers reinforce positive behaviors rather than suppressing inappropriate ones; (2) choice-making environments need to be created that move from locking special education into activities based on passive skills (e.g., compliance and following instructions) to more active skills (e.g., exploration, discovery, problem-solving, playing and making friends); (3) play should be welcomed in familiar environments which make free choice available; (4) play needs to be gendered with real playmates by mainstreaming and role modeling; and (5) play environments should allow a child to check and correct a mistake so that the student makes his or her own assessment of an activity. For some teachers this revitalization of their classrooms presents a total reorientation of approaches and priorities, and for others it may lead to even more profound transformations for the students.

Chapter 9

In his Review chapter, co-editor James Block declares that educators know relatively little about the student career, especially that portion given with suggestions about ways to redesign school work activities along more playful lines.

Block suggests that researchers have tended to focus on school play's resistive properties to the exclusion of its reformative ones and that more study of the dialectic between these aspects of play is needed. One reason for this focus, he suggests, is that opportunities for instrumental play peak in the early school years and subsequently decline. Accordingly older students have fewer chances to perceive school learning activities as fun. They therefore find opportunities for fun outside of instruction (recreational play) or despite instruction (illicit play). However, since older students consider school activities as being either work or play, depending on their particular perceptual mix of electivity, desirability, and pleasure, Block sees no reason that ordinary school learning activities cannot be reformed to be more play-like and hence more fun. Hartwig (1986) has shown play-like learning settings stimulate students' intrinsic motivation to learn, study, and behave.

To this end, Block discusses the importance of the social context of the classroom in shaping student play and suggests that more systematic environmental research designs are needed to test the effects of various classroom settings. Environmental factors include the classroom, the school, and the family, and their links with the societal and cultural environments. Block also regrets that the study of school play, as part of the field of human development, tends to treat the individual as a self-contained entity. School play researchers need to recognize the profound interaction between the individual and the social environment.

Finally, Block further asserts that whether the nature of school play can be commonly defined by experts or not, we must recognize that students perceive school play as a state of mind, not as the varied activities in which they participate. Thus, school play research should help improve the quality of public school instruction by making ordinary school learning activities more perceptually inviting to students.

He suggests that past efforts to make instruction more playful may have failed, not because it cannot be made an integral part of school instruction, but because practitioners lacked the necessary human technology to translate critical play and beliefs and concepts into acceptable and affective practices. Practitioners, he contends, now have the rudiments of this technology and can use it to build on rather than replace teachers' customary strategies. To illustrate his contention, Block suggests five strategies for using the existing school play literature to make school learning activities more playlike

Chapter 10

"Schools aren't particularly good for play, and play isn't particularly acceptable in schools" is the evaluative thrust of the commentary chapter by Brian Sutton-Smith. The acrid criticisms of one of our most insightful play theorists are firmly rooted in common sense and reality. Sutton-Smith is remembered for his bold challenge of the cognitive development theory formulated by the Swiss educational psychologist Jean Piaget. His own "conflict enculturation" theory of children's play has generated great interest among scholars in several disciplines.

Sutton-Smith believes that this volume unfortunately presents play as a contest between socializing adults and the pleasure-bound children. He avows that if the writers of this volume had addressed children's free playground (recreational) play equally as thoroughly as they did instrumental and illicit play, their conclusions might be different.

Calling upon his own experiences and earlier works, Sutton-Smith condemns the common assumption that everything a child does voluntarily is play. He affirms that exploratory behavior and work can be done voluntarily, but neither one is play. He finds a distinction between illicit play and illicit behavior and between instrumental play and instrumental mastery.

Remarking that the romanticism of the volume's authors is reflected in their play definitions and in their emphasis on contextual constraints of the school setting, Sutton-Smith reminds us that this protective viewpoint is specific to Western culture and to the contemporary period. The volume's authors believe that the instrumental manipulation of school children through play in normal classrooms is in direct contrast to the tough-minded behavior control in special education settings; yet both approaches are justified by positive cognitive learning and appropriate social behavior. Sutton-Smith protests that the school's attempts to domesticate and sanctify play denies play's inherent dialectic between mimicry and mockery, modelling and caricature, accepting and inverting, protest and fantasy. Also absent from school play is the similar paradox of malediction, risk, and conflict found in games. Sutton-Smith asserts that if these characteristics of play are excluded from schools, it is at the cost of motivation and vitality. In a parting caveat, Sutton-Smith states, "I really distrust any endeavor to turn *school* play into something that it is not, and I believe we betray children when we take this path."

Seldom do scholars who share their individual ideas about a social issue such as school play agree on all points; and this volume is not an exception. Nevertheless, one point on which all these scholars agree is that none likes what is happening to school play in our society. The following discussion, discourse, and dialectic should stimulate the reader's idea as to what place school play has, if any, in the lives of our youth.

REFERENCES

Csikszentmihalyi, M. *Beyond Boredom and Anxiety.* San Francisco: Jossey Bass, 1975.

Csikszentmihalyi, M. Some Paradoxes in the Definition of Play. In *Play as Context.* Edited by A. Taylor Cheska. West Point, New York: Leisure Press, 1981.

Hartwig, M. The Development and Validation of an Ethnographically-Based Instrument to Elicit Students' Perceptions of Their Classroom. Unpublished Ph.D. dissertation, University of California, Santa Barbara, June, 1986.

Piaget, J. *Play Dreams and Imitation in Childhood.* New York: W. W. Norton & Company, 1962.

Metz, M. *Classrooms and Corridors.* Berkeley: University of California Press, 1978.

Stinchcombe, A. *Rebellion in a High School.* Chicago: Quadrangle, 1964.

Webb, H. Professionalization of Attitudes Toward Play Among Adolescents. In *Aspects of Contemporary Sport Sociology.* Edited by G. Kenyon. Chicago: The Athletic Institute, 1969.

PART I: SOCIAL SCIENCE PERSPECTIVES

HISTORICAL PERSPECTIVES ON CHILDREN'S PLAY IN SCHOOL

Barbara Finkelstein

Historians can make a unique contribution to the study of children's play in school because the study of history can reveal the relative durability or resiliency of one or another form of human behavior, thought, social structure, or culture. This theme, the durability or resiliency of play, constitutes an implicit point of orientation for all historians exploring play, and for those emphasizing children's play in school as well.

Whether they study play as a form of intellectual discourse, or communication, a "mainspring" for human creativity and spirituality, or a reflection of political and economic realities, historians aim to describe, analyze, and explain change over time (see Anchor, 1978; Schwartzman, 1978). Through the transforming power of historical discourse, children's play, like other events--war, revolution, invention--becomes an index of stability or change. Change might be revealed in the forms that play takes or the contexts in which it occurs. Change might emerge in the content of play or in the way that play is understood and described. No matter what their definition of play, or which culture or era they study, historians unvaryingly study play instrumentally--in relation to social change.

The classic historical treatments of adult play, Johan Huizinga's (1955), *Homo Ludens* and Roger Caillois's (1961), *Man, Play and Games* explore play in relation to the economic, political, and intellectual transformations which occurred in Europe over the course of several centuries. For historians of children's play, however, the study begins later--in the mid-seventeenth century when the children of the nobility and commercial middle classes began to attend school and when childhood appeared as a socially distinct stage in the life cycle. It developed further during the eighteenth and nineteenth centuries as more and more children remained in school for protracted periods of time. The study of children's play became a mirror for the whole of society in the twentieth century when schools became compulsory.

Under these social conditions, children of all social classes spent increasingly more time with one another in school and in school-related activities. As schools brought young people together and engaged them in intense activity for sustained periods of time, they contributed effectively to the creation of a distinct world of childhood (Aries, 1962; see, also, deMause, 1974, and Stone, 1977, for general histories of childhood; Finkelstein, 1979, 1985, and Finkelstein and Vandell, 1984, for histories of childhood in the United States; Finkelstein, 1972, Mergan, 1982, and Schwartzman, 1978, for specific historical references to children's play). While structuring common experiences for large numbers of young people, schools also became centers for the cultivation of children and youth cultures.

17

Thus, the historical study of children's play in school links the study of play to the discovery of childhood and the emergence of modern institutions--the nation state, the factory, the public school. History embeds the study of play in the emergence of tutorial institutions for the young, public planning, modern modes of production, and emerging processes of cultural transmission (see Finkelstein, 1984). It is a history that begins when children are gathered together systematically.

THREE INTERPRETIVE TRADITIONS

The work of the historian studying children's play in school is to discover the forms and contents, the location and duration, the limitations and possibilities of the school as a play-generating environment. What effect, if any, have schools on the play preferences and choices available to children over time? Has the school setting influenced the way children play over time? Have the forms of children's play been transformed under the influence of schools? Has the evolution of children's play in school contributed to or detracted from the relationship between generations? What elements of subversion and/or accommodation are to be found in the play of children in school? What sorts of human associations does school play nurture? What social, economic, intellectual, and/or psychological possibilities are organized by children's play in schools? These are the questions that interest historians.

As they approach the study of children's play in school, historians proceed from three distinct, if complementary interpretive postures: one focusing on play as liberating and creative; a second on play as regulatory and organized; a third on play as contingent and vulnerable.

Play as Creative and Emancipatory

The first group, the "play as creative" historians, emphasizes the liberating qualities of play, focusing on its evolution as a form of creativity, an occasion for cognitive and cultural transformation, an expression of imaginative power, and a transforming political event. Some implicitly define play as Johan Huizinga had done fifty years before as an "unconstrained or uncontrolled element of human culture," arising in unregulated social spaces, resistant to, if not subversive of, economic, intellectual, and political authority (Huizinga, 1955). Play, as Huizinga understood it, is fundamental and irreducible, manifesting itself in all spheres of human culture. It is inexplicable as something else, and it can only be defined in terms of its opposite: serious, ordinary, everyday life. It is the very opposite of the instrumental nationality of the modern era. Play is primordial: "...the antithesis of seriousness, a stepping out from real life. It is voluntary and spontaneous. It produces nothing beyond itself" (Huizinga, 1955). It is an activity connected with no material interest. No profit can be gained by it. It involves the player intensely and utterly and proceeds within its own proper boundaries of time and space according to fixed rules and in an orderly manner. Its participants are linked in common understanding of its rules and in opposition to the everyday world. Play lies outside morals, outside material concern, outside common sense. Above all, play is fun. As Stanley Aronowitz (1973) has put it more recently: "...play is the one human activity that is non-instrumental, that is, produced for its own sake." By definition play is the element of culture that is beyond hierarchy, beyond authority. It is fundamental and irrepressible. Rather than reflecting culture, play precedes it. In fact, play provides its redirec-ting motive force (Albin, 1980; Aronowitz, 1973; Gillis, 1974; Keniston, 1971).

Accordingly, "play as creative" historians study places and spaces where spontaneity, fun, regularity, silliness, and nonsense can emerge. For the few who study children's play in school, this sort of definition has led them to focus on the activities of the children, attending to trans-formations in their folklore, sub-cultures, imaginative play, language, activities, play dispositions, and choices. This sort of interest has lead historians to an analysis of classroom and playground rituals, and to the study of misbehavior (e.g., Sutton-Smith, 1981; see, also, Knapp and Knapp, 1976; Mergan, 1982; Opie and Opie, 1969). A very few explore creative play as an element in instrumental activity when the "players" engage in it for sport or theater rather than victory or profit.

There is another type of "play as creative" historian who implicitly defines play as an engine of social transformation and identifies schools as seedbeds of subversive play and revolutionary consciousness. Historians of this sort tend to study youth rather than childhood. They focus their analysis on settings where imaginative play flourishes and where "reversals of the normative order," to use Sutton-Smith's (1981, p.97) phrase, are com-monplace. They pay special attention to the effects of youth cultures in the cultivation of revolution, social change, and/or utopian possibilities. They also study the emergence of high schools and universities as youth-organizing institutions.

Play as Regulated

Other historians, adopting the sociological assumptions of Roger Caillois have implicitly defined play as derivative and instrumental, a re-flection and an instrument of political and economic necessity (Cavallo, 1979, 1981; Goodman, 1979; Rosenzweig, 1983). Not so much an expression of the creative, spiritual side of the human spirit, the "play as regulated" group of historians treats play as a socially constructed reality, an historically defined condition--a product of material and ideological circumstances and transformations.

When historians of this sort study children's play, they rarely study the activities of the children themselves. Proceeding instead on the assumption that children's play mirrors and reflects political and economic conditions, they emphasize the study of play contexts--the social, economic, political, intellectual, and cultural subsoils in which play is embedded.

Indeed, these historians implicitly define play as a context-defined activity and study context rather than children playing when they explore children's play in school.

Play as Contested Terrain: Schools as Political Playfields

A very few historians proceed on an assumption that play is a precarious kind of activity, dependent for its existence and its character on favorable social, political, and intellectual conditions. Like those who regard play as an imposed form of human expression, "play as precarious" historians recognize the importance of the contexts in which play is embedded. These historians proceed on the assumption that there is a dialectical relationship between politics, economics, ideology, and play. They study the development of play over time in an effort to discover the conditions which favor the emergence and development of play as a revolutionary and/or stabilizing form. Some explore the evolution of play forms, play processes, and play concepts; others explore forms of political discourse about play. All study play in school as a political instrument or an agency of political empowerment (Baer,1979; Hearn, 1976-77; Lasch, 1977, 1979).

Some "play as precarious" historians analyze play as a form of political discourse, implicitly defining it as contested terrain over which conflicting cultural and political authorities do battle. The progress of this contest is the subject of an extraordinary essay by Mihai Spariosu (1986) entitled, *Play, Power, Culture.*

As Spariosu tells the story, the concept of play as we know it has been constituted out of a two thousand year old battle for intellectual authority between philosophers and poets. From Plato's time to the present day, their weapons have been literary and linguistic, their battlefields the languages of theoretical and poetic discourse, the two major vocabularies of social vision.

Out of a battle for intellectual preeminence and cultural authority, play became a contested concept, creating its own dialectic. The very definition of play--as nonwork, unserious, imitative, irrational, exuberant--was constituted out of its opposites--work, rationality, calculation, predictability. Arising originally between philosophers and poets, it has been replayed again and again over the centuries in arguments between utilitarians and/or romantics, and between scientists and artists. From the time of its discovery in the sixth century, play was understood to be unreal, a pale imitation of reality, inferior as a way of knowing, trivial, useful only insofar as it contributed to the cultivation of rationality, order, regularity, hierarchy; destructive if it reflected or released irrational, uncontrollable, subversive, or dissonant impulses.

Under the impact of industrialization, play acquired a new dimension. Increasingly understood as ornamental rather than essential--useful if it bound aggression, increased productivity, reduced tension, or motivated work; destructive if it subverted authority, devalued work, induced idleness or sapped energy--the play element was labelled as essentially unproductive. Thus trivialized, play became "leisure," "recreation," or "sport."

Like Spariosu, "play as contingent" historians see the play element as politically defined. Unlike him, however, they also see it as being killed off by a western love of rationality, regulation, productivity, and work in the service of domination and control (Spariosu, 1986).

Whether they focus on the evolution of play as a form of political discourse, an instrument of social transformation, or an agency of political consciousness, one group of "play as contingent" historians, the so-called "critical theorists," emphasize the effects rather than the determinants of play. The few in this group who study children's play in school tend to focus on the fate of subversive play and on the effect of particular play forms on the capacity of individuals to discover inequities, and inequalities, to imagine new social forms, and to empower themselves politically and psychologically.

Whether they identify the development of children's play in school as essentially liberating, constraining, or contingent and precarious, historians exploring children's play in school are relatively new at the attempt. Indeed systematic, historical studies have emerged only over the last quarter century. As a result, the historical literature is more a patchwork of articles and monographs than a well developed sub-genre of historical writing.

In addition to adopting a particular posture toward play as described above, historians of school play also have particular attitudes toward the role of the school in the play lives of children and youth. It is possible to catalogue existing studies roughly under two headings that reflect two different assessments of the role of the school. First, some historians look upon schools as liberating institutions, freeing children to play. Second, there are historians who look upon schools as regulatory institutions, directing and constraining children's play. These two historiographical points of view are not mutually exclusive, though most historians adopt one or another as they discuss play.

FREEING CHILDREN TO PLAY: SCHOOLS AS LIBERATING AGENCIES

Many historians, including Brian Sutton-Smith and Bernard Mergan, the Knapps and the Opies, John Gillis, and Kenneth Keniston among others, proceed on the assumption that schools are play-liberating institutions. From their point of view, schools expand the play repertoires of children beyond any that might have developed before the 1800s when almost all children lived and worked among adults. Some, like Sutton-Smith and Mergan, explore the evolution of schools as play-generating environments. Other historians, like John Gillis (1974) and Kenneth Keniston (1971), explore the emergence of youth cultures (Albin, 1980).

Schools as Play-Generating Environments

Historians like Sutton-Smith, Mergan, the Opies, and the Knapps implicitly root the evolution of children's play in the bedrock of child protection. Consequently, they view schools as protective settings that removed children from the shackles of onerous labor, exploitation, the severities of fundamentalist religion, and social intolerance. Each of these historians documents the evolution of increasingly more tolerant attitudes toward children and play. Taking leaves from the books of childhood historians such as Lloyd deMause, Lawrence Stone, and J.H. Plumb, they define schools as play-generating settings, expanding and cultivating opportunities forever more complex forms of play, and acts of the social and political imagination (deMause, 1974; Plumb, 1975).

Not unexpectedly, these historians are attentive to the cultures of childhood being generated in schools. Though their treatments are not explicitly historical, the work of the Opies and the Knapps, for example, explores children's folklore and implicitly documents the flourishing and diffusion of children's folklore through school playground settings. The Knapps enjoin us not to overlook the education which children offer to one another in "the unsupervised nooks and crannies of their lives where they perpetuate centuries-old folk traditions." (Knapp and Knapp, 1976, p.9)

Commenting on the effect of schooling on children's lore, Bernard Mergan (1982) suggests that schools constituted a specialized environment for cultivation of special kinds of children's lore...and it promoted the diffusion of games. He elaborates the point in an essay exploring the evolution of children's play from the seventeenth to the nineteenth century in the United States.

During the Colonial period, seventeenth century Protestant New Englanders condemned play, regarding it as the the work of the devil. Indeed, they regarded children's play as a subversive activity, "...potentially selfish, irrational, and irresponsible," frivolous, and inimical to the development of salvation and a work ethic. Since children invariably worked, their play was embedded in work. Thus, Mergan concludes, they entered adulthood unaware of any conflict between the two.

By the mid-eighteenth century children found themselves in a more tolerant, less austere society. In the country, they could whittle, run, frolic, and explore the countryside freely. The few living in the city would play in a more sedentary manner--developing semi-sexual parlor games, playing board games. They were "...formal and polite in their word play, relatively free in their games of motion," and, as subsequent achievements revealed, uninhibited in the expression of spatial and visual intelligence. Less likely than their seventeenth century counterparts to be condemned for playing, and, in any case, increasingly free to frolic, eighteenth-century children bequeathed a less Puritanical play legacy of increasing freedom and complexity.

The play of children in the nineteenth century varied in urban and rural environments and among the wealthy and the poor. With few exceptions, however, children of all groups were being liberated from the duties and discipline of preindustrial life. They spent more time in school, less time at work. As Mergan observes, middle class children enjoyed unprecedented opportunities to play freely and fully. Though he did not explicitly argue in this way, Mergan documents the emergence of ever more tolerant attitudes toward children's play and ever more complex and varied environments in which to play freely.

Tolerance for children's play was even further extended during the half-century from 1880 to 1930 when social planners and education reformers "discovered" children's play and made it into an object of study. They constructed and organized school playgrounds--specialized play settings that separated play and work in school--and provided children with supervisable play space.

During the half-century from 1880 to 1930, children's play was reorganized and redefined. Body play became institutionalized into physical education. Team games, and school sports emerged, thus adding to the play repertory of children. As Mergan suggests, the school playground placed boundaries around children and boundaries around their play, but it could not bind their imaginations. Alluding to Sutton-Smith's observation that children's play has become increasingly imaginative, symbolic, and fantasy-rich, he concludes that the physical boundary of the school playground probably induced children to invent new games and to reconstruct traditional behavior on swings and jungle gyms (Mergan, 1982b).

Brian Sutton-Smith (1981) has developed these themes explicitly in his studies of children's play in New Zealand from 1840 to 1950. As he tells the story, children's play evolved in three stages over this period. During the first stage, from 1840-1890, New Zealand children worked more than they played. When boys played, their play was unregulated, spontaneous, inventive, physical, untraditional, harsh, and aggressive.

They hunted, shot, raided orchards and gardens, climbed trees and hills, and subjected themselves to physical dangers. Like the rugged rural environments in which they lived, they were disposed to cruelty, teasing, obscenity, prejudice, and fighting. Even in schools, their play reflected the dog-eat-dog world of which they were a part. Their make-believe play centered on wars--mostly between cowboys and Indians. "Survival in the power struggles of playground and neighborhood required fisticuffs, initiations and torture....There was a vigorous autonomy, a passionate excitement, and a furtive rebelliousness all at the same time, and an almost naive involvement in imaginative play about horses, ploughing matches, circuses, trains, cowboys and Indians, and with grass and flowers." (Sutton-Smith, 1981, p. 137) There were few traditional games, few ordered play spaces.

For girls, the school play yard, separated from that of the boys, not only reinforced gender-segregated play but was a place to play gentler, more egalitarian games, and games of domestic make-believe. The playing of circle games, winding games, line games, and couple games distinguished the play of girls from the more boisterous and aggressive play of young males. Whether they were girls or boys, in school or out, New Zealand children played few traditional games and few singing games in the nineteenth century.

Gradually, however, children came under the control of school authorities and so eventually did their play. As they were ordered into schools, children increasingly played in school yards, where teachers exercised more and more control over their play lives--first through the introduction of gymnastic apparatus and cadet drills, and then, after 1890, through classes in physical education, playground games, and organized sports.

For a short period of time, from 1900 to 1920, New Zealand children, like those in nineteenth-century America, enjoyed a period of unprecedented play opportunity. As they attended school in increasingly larger numbers, they began to develop formal games. Traditional singing, tagging, and skill games came into their own. Not yet fully supervised in school and classroom, nor inundated by pre-packaged materials, radio or television, children created toys and invented games, and "trained themselves in the arts of enterprise" on their playgrounds. They enjoyed a new freedom and a new abundance of play spaces and materials" (Sutton-Smith, 1981, pp.216-17)--at least these historians thought so.

What with school playgrounds, school picnics, commercially produced school books, board games, trinkets, toys, and a new interest in organized games and sports, the period from 1890-1920 may have been the best of all times for children in the variety of games and other recreational possibilities (Sutton-Smith, 1981). The school playground liberated girls to invent new forms of play, and the introduction of physical education and gymnastic equipment encouraged them to incorporate physical activity into their play. In this manner, girls broke the constraints of sedate play, traditionally the only socially and psychologically approved mode available to them.

From 1920 to 1950, school authorities became increasingly involved in the regulation of children's play in school. A reflection of the emergence of "leisure" time as well as more indulgent dispositions among "play masters," the introduction of playground games, organized sports, and physical education necessarily involved teachers in the world of children's play. So too did the organization of school picnics, garden parties, fancy-dress balls, and the emergence of manufactured toys. Taken together, the new curriculum and extracurriculum introduced unprecedented amounts of adult supervision into the world of children's play in schools, even ironically, while they liberated new and imaginative forms. Schools appear to have enhanced children's capacity for symbolic play and feats of the literary imagination.

From 1920 to 1950, children's play in New Zealand schools was rapidly domesticated. Children played fewer rough games, replacing fisticuffs and fighting with competitive games and spectator sports. They substituted quiet for boisterous games, preferring apparently to make scrapbooks, and collect, swap, organize, and use commercial products, postcards, paints, and beads. Riddles emerged as popular folk forms, and girls began to play hierarchical as well as egalitarian games.

In short, children's play in school mirrored the transformation of play into recreation and leisure. Its form and content increasingly depended on commercial products and mechanical contrivances. By 1950, children's play, with few exceptions, had become sophisticated, commercialized, symbolic, and verbal. As physical violence diminished, the number of verbal assaults increased. As Sutton-Smith summarizes, the playground of 1950 mirrored the commercial world of which it was a part--fast paced, domesticated, and free. Girls rather than boys became the keepers of tradition and of playground lore.

In a different study, Sutton-Smith and Rosenberg (1961) used game lists created between 1890 and 1959 in the United States to assess the nature of change in the game preferences of American children. Through a gender-based analysis of game preferences, they concluded that the play repertoire of girls expanded over the sixty years to include leader games, physical skill games, selected organized sports as well as the more traditional singing games, dialogue games, cooperative parlor games, and couple and kissing games. Boys' play repertoires, on the other hand, became more circum-scribed, revealing a preference for rough play and intrusive throwing games of the sort that excluded girls. Implicitly describing the school playground as a gender transforming play-space, they linked children's play in school to historical transformations in the roles of men and women.

As we have seen, the work of Sutton-Smith and his colleagues documents three stages in the evolution of children's play in school. During the first, encompassing the half-century from 1840 to 1890, most children worked. Going to school was a sometime thing, and children's playing time occurred at work. During the second stage, from 1890 to about 1920, children went to school for longer periods of time and expanded their play reperoires--adding formal games, developing game traditions, and continuing older informal forms. Girls, for their part, broke the restraints of sedate play when the school playground became available to them. During a third stage from 1920 to 1950 children's play in school was increasingly supervised, "domesticated," organized, verbal, and commercialized.

Mergan (1982c) has identified a fourth stage in the evolution of children's play, beginning in 1950 and continuing to the present time. During this thirty-year period, fantasy and make-believe have become indispensable elements of children's play repertoires.

New playmasters--child psychologists, physicians, educators--joined with the play manufacturers to influence children's play. Electric toys, educational games, and teddy bears were developed in the first two decades of the twentieth century. World War I brought increases in the numbers of toy guns, soldiers, and heroic and patriotic dolls. The emergence of simple hammer boards, shoelacing toys, and postal boxes with blocks reflects a 1930s emphasis on encouraging independence in children.

The appearance of radio programs and motion pictures, Disney toys, frisbees, and silly putty reshaped the contours of play. Space toys began to appear in the 1940s, and in the 1950s, Barbie dolls made their appearance. In the 1960s and 1970s television dominated the toy markets, and electronic games emerged. While educators continue to influence play, the school itself may no longer be a primary determinant of the content or structure of children's play.

Schools as Settings for the Flowering of Youth Cultures

There is a second approach among "play as creative" historians exemplified in the work of John Gillis (1974) and Kenneth Keniston (1971). Exploring relationships between youth and social change, these historians discovered the seeds of revolutionary consciousness in the game cultures created by youth seeking to make their way in periods of economic transformation. No longer prepared for work from within their families, young men emerged as semidependents, who entered educational institutions, spent more and more time with one another, invented socially disruptive games, and formed cultures of their own. These so called "youth cultures" were later to shape the ideologies of revolution. The French and Italian revolutions, Gillis (1974) argues, originated in economic transformations, educational processes, and the youth cultures of the late eighteenth and early nineteenth centuries. Students also created political protest movements during several decades of the twentieth century (see, also, Fass, 1977).

DIRECTING CHILDREN'S PLAY: SCHOOLS AS REGULATORY AGENCIES

There are historians who reject the foregoing framework of interpretation completely and proceed on the assumption that schools have narrowed rather than expanded the play repertoires of young people. Rather than inviting children to invent new forms of play, the play environment of schools has diminished play possibilities.

Historians like Joel Spring (1974), Cary Goodman, Dominick Cavallo (1979), Paul Boyer (1978), Roy Rosenzweig (1983), Joseph Kett (1977), Stanley Aronowitz (1973), and Nancy King (1985) treat the expansion of schooling and the forming of specialized childhood and youth cultures as providing regulatory opportunities for adults and constraining environments for children.   Following in conceptual pathways originally laid down by Phillipe Aries (1962), these historians view schools as agencies for the regulation and discipline of the young--places of quarantine, rather than liberation and creative expression.

When they explore children's play in school, these historians focus less on children playing than they do on the contexts and ideologies in which play is embedded. They analyze what Clifford Geertz (1973) might call the "hard surfaces" of children's play, the economic, political, and social realities in which children's play is embedded, and play ideologies emerge.   This group of historians documents the emergence of elite social planners, "playmasters," or "boy workers," in the late nineteenth and early twentieth centuries who "discovered children's play," revealed its educational possibilities, tried to confine it to school yards, parks, and recreation facilities, and mold it in classrooms (see Mergan, 1982b).

Fearing the effects of urbanization and industrialization on the quality of urban life for urban children, playmasters in England and the United States created an agenda for the reform of the schools.   They implemented their reforms in the name of child protection, moral reform, and in fear of social disorder. With a passion for social regulation and control, playmasters such as William Wells Newall, Luther Gulick, Henry Curtis, Joseph Lee, Jane Addams, G. Stanley Hall, and Elmer Mitchell, redefined and reorganized children's play in school in the period from 1880 to 1950 (see Hardy and Ingham, 1976, for a superb treatment of differences among historians about the motives of playmasters).

As they document and describe these transformations, some of the "play as regulated" historians focus their analyses on the nature of play spaces within schools. Bernard Mergan calls attention to the reformer's visions of idealized and specialized play areas--parks in the cities, playgrounds in the schools. Through the regulatory spectacles of the playmasters, the school playground was reconceived as a place for pedagogy rather than a place for the invention of new games (Cavallo, 1979; Mergan, 1982). Aronowitz (1973) suggests that playmasters confined children's play to the bathrooms, "...the [only] place where forbidden activity can be undertaken in relative privacy, except for occasional raids by teachers. Smoking, horseplay, exchange of pornographic information through graffiti, novels, and other written material, and talk about sex...provide elements of autonomous interaction" (p.83)

Others of the "play as regulated" group, like Cavallo and Spring focus on the forms as well as the location of children's play as they explore children's play in school during the progressive era. They describe the emergence of organized games and school sports as the institutionalization of imperial dispositions. Successful attempts to introduce adult-controlled intramural and extramural sports, enclose the young in the hammer-lock of muscular Christianity, civilize their political behavior, and to prepare them for life in the modern corporate state (Cavallo, 1981; Mergan, 1982). As they analyze the work of reformers, these historians interpret it as an attempt to suppress children's play in order to socialize, or to "pedagogicalize" it [my word]. As coaches replaced student leaders and teams replaced groups, as organized sports replaced unregulated folk games, as young people became spectators and team players, as fees were charged and athletic associations like the Intercollegiate Athletic Conference and the "Big Ten" emerged, children's play in school both reflected and served the modern corporate state. Through the organization of sporting play, young people in schools and universities became spectators rather than players, rule-followers rather than rule-makers, and fans rather than mobs (Spring, 1974).

Some historians, like Cary Goodman (1979), go even further, suggesting that playmasters entered into a kind of conspiracy with businessmen and government officials to resocialize the children of the urban immigrant poor, and to undermine the authority of their families. This theme, the resocialization of working-class children through the exercise of control over their play, is also an important theme in the work of David Cohen and Marvin Lazerson who document the emergence of two distinct forms of school play for two distinct laboring groups during the progressive era. The children of the upper middle-class were commonly invited to play freely and independently. The children of laboring families in the cities, on the other hand, were exposed to physical and mental regulation on playgrounds and in classrooms, the better to prepare them for the drudgery of unskilled labor in factory and on the assembly line. The preparation of a stratified, docile, and compliant work force is also an important theme in an article by Dominick Cavallo exploring the evolution of kindergarten pedagogy in urban centers from 1860-1930. As Cavallo (1979) tells the story, teachers made use of shame rather than guilt in order to control children's play, to prepare their laboring-class charges to accept the work ethic, to substitute the authority of teachers for that of families, to create public personalities, and otherwise to prepare children for work as laborers (see, also, Baer, 1979).

Thus institutionalized, the planners' visions effectively transformed children's play in schools from authentic folk expressions into forms of vocational education and political socialization. The 1960s movie, *Rollerball*, as James Block insightfully pointed out to me, signalled the transformation of popular culture into spectator sport. While providing entertainment, this form of play could bind imagination, aggression, and political energy as well.

Schools as Workplaces for the Young

There are other "play as regulated" historians--one thinks immediately of Christopher Lasch (1979) and Marvin Lazerson (see, Cohen and Lazerson, 1977)--who explore the evolution of public education and universal schooling as a chapter in the commodification of culture and the transformation of the school into an instrument of the corporate state and of industrial capitalism. The professionalization of team sports, the popularity of competitive play, the disappearance of student-generated, student-controlled games, and the emergence of play masters and professional experts all signal the appropriation of play environments and play processes by imperial intellectuals and corporate interests (see, also, Goodman, 1979).

Nancy King (1985) has identified another kind of attempt to manage children's play in school. In a study of children's play as depicted in elementary school readers from 1900 to 1950, she documents a gradual transformation of children's play into work. During the half century from 1900 to 1950, textbook authors socialized children's play. They portrayed it as bounded in time and space and they associated it with strangers. They judged it as good if it did not interfere with work or if it prepared young people for labor as adults. Over the half century, children's play in books, like children's play in school, became socialized.

The transformation of the school into a workplace for the young, the invention of play spaces designed to bind the impulse and imagination of school children and prepare them for "real work in the classroom," constituted, as Aronowitz (1973) suggests, a means by which the schools could serve as economic sorting machines and instruments of vocational socialization.

Schools as Play-Killing Fields

A few "play as constrained" historians take a dim view of the school as a play-generating, empowering environment for children. As they analyze the evolution of children's play in school, historians like Francis Hearn (1976-77), Neal Baer (1979), Christopher Lasch (1979), and Stanley Aronowitz (1973) tread intellectual pathways originally laid down by Jurgen Habermas (1971) and Herbert Marcuse (1955) who analyzed the limits and possibilities of play in the cultivation of critical sensibility.

As these historians explore the evolution of children's play in schools, they document its transformation into an instrument of social differentiation as well as an instrument of vocational preparation. Frances Hearn (1976-77), for example, in work on school play in England and the United States is sensitive to attempts by nineteenth-century middle class reformers to control the leisure time of immigrant and working class students, the better to moralize and fit them out for docile laboring. Documenting a litany of horrors visited on children of laboring and dependent classes in English and American schools, he concludes that the play impulse was "virtually devitalized by mid-century." In its place came distorted play, escapist leisure, and a vision of alternative realities stripped of emancipatory power. A similar line of argument suffuses in the work of Christopher Lasch (1979), who suggests that the determinacies of industrial capitalism, the pretensions of modern nation states, the emergence of experts, and the psychologizing of schooling have all but destroyed the revolutionary possibilities of school play. Captive of experts and corporations, the schools, Lasch argues, can do two things: contribute to the transformation of play into work on the one hand, or encourage students to venture into escapist, trivialized (i.e., politically disconnected) play on the other. Either way, the revolutionary potential of play becomes muted.

This group of historians has documented the existence of a fundamental irony in the thought and work of modern playmasters (see, e.g., Cavallo, 1981; Curtis, 1917; Lee, 1922; Rainwater, 1929). In an attempt to raise the status of children, of play, and of play experts, playmasters may have contributed to the demise of play in schools. As they rationalized the introduction of athletics, team sports, and competition, and introduced play elements into classrooms and textbooks, playmasters gradually and subtly transformed children's play into work. What is more, they harbored play-killing distinctions between good and bad play. Good play was play that bound impulse and imagination, cultivated team spirit, organized and controlled competition, rewarded merit. Bad play was play that diminished rationality, induced frenzy, detracted from work, and encouraged rule breaking. Good play imitated adult activity. Bad play subverted it. Good play prepared. Bad play did not (Spariosu, 1986).

Beyond trivializing non-instrumental play, playmasters also introduced adults into almost every aspect of children's play, bringing them together as coaches and the coached, and as spectators, team-players, and consumers of athletic contests--co-participants in the passive and supervised play of schools.

As they document the transformation of children's play in school into work and into occasions for adult supervision and shared spectatorship, "play as constrained" historians implicitly locate the development of children's play in school as a chapter in the destruction of the play element in civilization.

Schools as Play-Integrating Institutions

The two visions--of children as inveterate players on the one hand, and objects of manipulation on the other, and of schools as play-liberating and play-constraining environments--reflect two different modes of recovering history. They also reflect the existence of two childhood worlds: a spontaneous, child-controlled, child-generated one, and a dependent, regulated, and supervised one.

An attempt to make sense of these two apparently inconsistent realities is implicit in several new treatments of children's play in school. Historians like Charles Strickland (1984), for example, have documented the appearance, since the late 1960s, of integrated play activities organized through the schools and school-related "leisure" activities--football games, band contests, and the like (see, also, Meyrowitz, 1984). For Strickland, the spectacle of children and adults playing together in school signals the emergence of a new era for children's play in school. It is an era where children's play disappears and where the school becomes an instrument through which the differentiated play worlds of children and adults can once again be integrated. There is no small irony in the fact that schools originally emerged as institutions designed to separate children from adults and to create a protected play world and that they are now being seen as the means to reintegrate the generations.

AN ATTEMPT AT SYNTHESIS AND NEW DIRECTIONS IN THE STUDY OF CHILDREN'S PLAY IN SCHOOL AS A PLAY-INDUCING ENVIRONMENT

In its present stage of development, the historical study of children's play in school tells us little about the relative durability of play as a lived experience, of human beings as playing creatures, of schools as play environments, and of children as special keepers of the play capacity. What the historical literature suggests is that children are both players and objects, and that schools have a capacity to cultivate and suppress children's play. Indeed, a series of double visions emerges from the historical literature.

Children as Players and Objects

First, there is the vision of children as intractable players who will transform any environment into a playground. In the eras before they attended schools, children found ways to turn trees, paths, sticks into objects of fun and to turn each other into combatants, despite the omnipresence of work and adults in their lives. They invented new ways to play when they found themselves on school playgrounds, developing game rituals and team games all but unexperienced by previous generations. Even though play environ-ments in schools were structured and supervised, children nonetheless managed to invent, develop, and transmit a folklore all their own. When manufactured objects, pre-packaged games and toys, radio and television began to litter children's play environments in school and at home, the children found the means to transform them. The emergence and ascendancy of verbal, symbolic, fantasy-rich play can be seen as another expression of the endurance of the play element among children. Subject to increasing regulation, burdened with play objects invented by adults, children have nonetheless found the means to transform and make-over the environment through the development of symbolic, verbal, fantasy-rich play.

A different vision of children's play in school emerges when historians focus on adult intention rather than on children playing. Rather than revealing children as inveterate players, this historical view portrays them as manipulated objects. Stanley Aronowitz (1973) has summarized what historians focusing on the play-regulating qualities of the school reveal about children's play in school. Playmasters created an ideal socializing agent for industrial and postindustrial society. They called the prescribed curriculum work. They assigned play to a special time in the day called recess and they supervised it. Thus the school world would "legitimize play as one of its regular functions, but at the same time, rationalize it as a break from the "real" activity of school. Play in this context was meant to rejuvenate the child in order to make him or her more ready for "learning."

We will need to explore the contents, forms, and locations of children's play and systematically attend to the durability of one or another of its forms in school settings if we are to assess whether schools can kill off the disposition and capacity to play or simply provide a specialized forum for its expression. It is possible that children will give up entirely on playing subversively in school (even in the bathrooms) and cultivate new habitats for the continuing invention of play and games. Or alternatively, the schools might provide an environment that would liberate the play spirits of children.

School Play as Choice or Necessity/Accommodation or Assimilation

A second double vision emerges when we examine historical treatments of the game cultures of children in school. Some historians proceed on the assumption that children's play in school is unvaryingly adaptive, a reflection of the wishes of powerful adults who control the occasions, the objects, and the substance of children's play. Through the transforming definitions of these historians, children's play in school becomes an adaptive mechanism, a way to cope with necessity and accommodate the force of circumstance.

Different indeed is the vision of children's play in school when it is viewed through the lenses of historians who assume that children's play enables children to assimilate rather than accommodate, transform rather than succumb, and escape from rather than adjust to constraint. This group implicitly views children's play in school as the product of choice rather than necessity. This group projects the school as a protected environment, releasing children to engage in new and hitherto unimagined play, enlarging their choices, and enhancing their capacity for fun.

The passion with which historians cling to one or another of these notions makes a merging of the two all the more necessary for future scholars. Explorations of the relative durability of accommodating and assimilative play as reflected in children's play opportunities, game preferences, and play forms would go far to transform the theologies of play historians into inquiries.

School Play as Conserving and Transforming

A third double vision emerges when we explore historical treatments of children's play in school and its relationship to social change. Some historians see play as transformative; others as conservative. Some analyze it as a mirror reflecting economic, social, and psychological arrangements; others as a lamp illuminating new social pathways.

As historians have shown, some play forms--athletic contests, team sports, mating and dating rituals--focus no new visions of social, economic, or political possibilities. If children's play in school were indeed confined to the athletic field, the gym, and the prom, then there would be reason to doubt its capacity to generate social change.

Historians have also documented, however, the nurture of revolutionary consciousness and action in school settings. There is reason, for example, to believe that a transformation in girls' play habits in schools helped to constitute new visions of girlhood and womanhood and to nurture the sort of discontent which generated revolutionary action among women in the nineteenth and twentieth centuries. Indeed, it is possible to argue that school playgrounds provided fertile soil for the flowering of feminist sensibility.

What is more, young people served as shock troops for revolution in the United States, France, and Italy in the eighteenth and nineteenth centuries, and in Russia and Iran in the twentieth. Through the lens of history, children's play and social change appear to be dialectically connected under some circumstances but not under others. It is possible that the emergence of children's play in school enhanced the nurture of political consciousness and revolutionary action or, alternatively, cooled it. It may also be that schools provide both possibilities in varying circumstances yet to be identified. Thus, firm conclusions about children's school play and social change are, as yet, unwarranted.

New Directions

Historians have not as yet explored children's play in school in relation to the evolution of creativity, mentalities, or communication between and among groups. Nor have they analyzed the history of school play as an aspect of the development of the human capacity for bellicosity or friendliness, competition or harmony, hierarchy or equality. There is work to be done on the evolution of children's play in school in relation to play traditions among men and women and people of various ethnic groups, nationalities, and social classes. Links between the evolution of concepts of love, and play are virtually unexplored as well.

The topics yet to be studied are endlessly complex, unvaryingly interesting, creatively challenging. Future studies might focus on the forms and content of play. They might be biographical, demographic, ethnographic, psychological, statistical, or narrative. They might be situated in the first, twelfth, eighteenth, nineteenth, or twentieth centuries.

No matter what aspect or era, systematic studies of play and social change must be relentlessly intergenerational and focus simultaneously on the context, content, and effects of school play. Such studies might focus on the transformation of play over life cycles, linking play patterns of individuals and groups as children to subsequent adult participation in economic, political and social processes. Other studies might focus on relationships between school play and the development of affiliative loyalties, group identities, political styles, and alliances among generational cohorts. Studies might emphasize play cycles of groups--women, laboring people, ethnics, nationals--exploring the nature and effects of school play on the sensibilities of these groups during eras of rapid social change. The array of historical techniques for recovering this history--the uses of material culture, diaries, visual as well as literary sources, and of ethno-methodologies, psychological anthropology, social psychology, psychohistory--are equally stunning, and the subject for another essay.

Historical studies promise new understanding of the school as a play environment, of school children as players, of school play as a cultural, economic, political, and intellectual form, subject to change and even perhaps to extinction. Above all, the historical study of children's play in school provides opportunities to address many of the important dilemmas associated with modern life and to assess its impact on the human capacity for meaningful fun and play. It is a history just waiting to be written.

REFERENCES

Albin, M. *New Directions in Psychohistory.* Edited by M. Albin. Lexington, MA: Lexington Books, 1980.

Anchor, R. History and Play: Johan Huizinga and His Critics. *History and Theory, 17*(1978), 63-93.

Aries, P. *Centuries of Childhood: A Social History of Family Life.* Translated by R. Baldick. New York: Alfred A. Knopf, 1962.

Aronowitz, S. Together and Equal: The Egalitarian Promise of Children's Games. *Social Policy, 4*(1973), 78-84.

Baer, N. The Dynamics of Work and Play: Historical Analysis and Future Implications. Unpublished manuscript, Harvard University, Graduate School of Education, 1979.

Boyer, P. *Urban Masses and Moral Order, 1820-1920.* Cambridge, Massachusetts: Cambridge University Press, 1978.

Caillois, R. *Man, Play, and Games.* Translated by M. Barash. New York: The Free Press, 1961.

Cavallo, D. The Politics of Latency: Kindergarten Pedagogy, 1860-1930. In *Regulated Children/Liberated Children: Education in Psychohistorical Perspective.* Edited by B. Finkelstein. New York: The Psychohistory Press, 1979.

Cavallo, D. *Muscles and Morals: Organized Play-grounds and Urban Reform, 1880-1920.* Philadelphia: University of Pennsylvania Press, 1981.

Cohen, D., and Lazerson, M. Education and the Corporate Order. In *Power and Ideology in Education.* Edited by J. Karabel and A. Halsey. New York: Oxford University Press, 1977.

Curtis, H. *The Play Movement and Its Significance.* New York: The Macmillan Company, 1917.

deMause, L. The Evolution of Childhood. In *The History of Childhood.* Edited by L. deMause. New York: Psychohistory Press, 1974.

Fass, P. *The Beautiful and the Damned.* New York: Oxford University Press, 1977.

Finkelstein, B. *Regulated Children/Liberated Children: Education in Psychohistorical Perspective.* New York: The Psychohistory Press, 1979.

Finkelstein, B. Incorporating Childhood into the History of Education. *The Journal of Educational Thought, 18*(1984), 21-43.

Finkelstein, B. Casting Networks of Good Influence: The Reconstruction of Childhood in Nineteenth Century America. In *American Childhood: A Research Guide and Historical Handbook*. Edited by N. Hiner and J. Hawes. Westport, Connecticut: Greenwood Press, 1985.

Finkelstein, B., and Vandell, K. The Schooling of American Childhood: The Emergence of Learning Communities. In *A Century of Childhood, 1820-1920*. Edited by M. Heininger. Rochester, New York: Margaret Woodbury Strong Museum, 1984.

Geertz, C. *The Interpretation of Culture*. New York: Basic Books, 1973.

Gillis, J. *Youth and History: Tradition and Change in European Age Relations: 1770-Present*. New York: Academic Press, 1974.

Goodman, C. *Choosing Sides: Playground and Street Life on the Lower East Side*. New York: Shocken Books, 1979.

Habermas, J. *Knowledge and Human Interest*. Boston: Beacon Press, 1971.

Halsey, L. *A Philosophy of Play*. New York: Charles Scribner's Sons, 1920.

Hardy, S., and Ingham, A. Games, Structures, and Agency: Historians on the American Play Movement. *Journal of Social History, 7*(1976), 285-297.

Hearn, F. Toward a Critical Theory of Play. *Telos, 30*(1976-77), 145-160.

Huizinga, J. *Homo Ludens: A Study of the Play Element in Culture*. Boston: Beacon Press, 1955.

Keniston, K. *Youth and Dissent: The Rise of a New Opposition*. New York: Harcourt, Brace and Jovanovich, 1971.

Kett, J. *Rites of Passage: Adolescence in America, 1790-1970*. New York: Basic Books, 1977.

King, N. Play as Depicted in Elementary School Readers, 1900-1950. Paper presented at the Annual Meeting of the American Educational Research Association, Chicago, Illinois, March, 1985.

Knapp, M., and Knapp, H. *One Potato, Two Potato. The Secret Education of American Children*. New York: Norton, 1976.

Lasch, C. *Haven in a Heartless World: The Family Besieged*. New York: Basic Books, 1977.

Lasch, C. *The Culture of Narcissism: American Life in an Age of Diminishing Expectations.* New York: W. W. Norton and Company, 1979.

Lee, J. *Play in Education.* New York: The Macmillan Company, 1922.

Marcuse, H. *Eros and Civilization.* New York: Vintage Books, 1955.

Mergan, B. *Play and Playthings: A Reference Guide.* Westport, Connecticut: Greenwood Press, 1982a.

Mergan, B. Space to Play. In *Play and Playthings.* Edited by B. Mergan. Westport, Connecticut: Greenwood Press, 1982b.

Mergan, B. From Play Pretties to Toys: Artifacts of Play. In *Play and Playthings.* Edited by B. Mergan. Westport, Connecticut: Greenwood Press, 1982c.

Mergan, B. Children's Lore in School and Playground. In *Handbook of Children's Folklore.* Edited by B. Sutton-Smith, T. Johnson, and J. Mechling, (in press).

Meyrowitz, J. The Adult-like Child and the Child-like Adult: Socialization in an Electronic Age. *Daedalus,* (Summer, 1984), 19-49.

Opie, I., and Opie, P. *Children's Games in Street and Playground.* Oxford: Clarendon Press, 1969.

Plumb, J. The New World of Children in Eighteenth-century England. *Past and Present, 67*(May, 1975), 64-93.

Rainwater, C. *The Play Movement in the United States: A Study of Community Recreation.* Washington, D.C.: McGrath Publishing Company, 1929.

Rosenzweig, R. *Eight Hours for What We Will: Workers and Leisure in an Industrial City, 1870-1920.* London: Cambridge University Press, 1983.

Schwartzman, H. *Transformations: The Anthropology of Children's Play.* New York: The Plenum Press, 1978.

Spariosu, M. Beyond the Power Principle? Play, Culture, and the Western Mentality. Work in progress, University of Georgia, Athens, Georgia, 1986.

Spring, J. Mass Culture and School Sports. *History of Education Quarterly, 14*(1974), 483-501.

Stone, L. *The Family, Sex, and Marriage in England, 1500-1800.* New York: Harper and Row, 1977.

Strickland, C. The Rise and Fall of Modern American Childhood in the Twentieth Century. *Issues in Education,* 2, no.3(Winter, 1984), 221-228.

Sutton-Smith, B. *A History of Children's Play: The New Zealand Playground, 1840-1950.* Philadelphia: University of Pennsylvania Press, 1981.

Sutton-Smith, B. *The Folkgames of Children.* Austin: University of Texas Press, 1972.

Sutton-Smith, B. *The Folk Stories of Children.* Philadelphia: University of Pennsylvania Press, 1981.

Sutton-Smith, B., and Rosenberg, B. Sixty Years of Historical Change in the Game Preferences of American Children. *Journal of American Folklore,* 74(1961), 17-46.

ANTHROPOLOGICAL AND SOCIOLOGICAL PERSPECTIVES ON SCHOOL PLAY

Andrew W. Miracle

Both anthropologists and sociologists have studied play as human behavior, and a few have focused on school play. The purpose of this chapter is to present an overview of these efforts by first considering the theoretical treatment of play as a general human phenomenon, and then reviewing the specific anthropological and sociological studies of school play. The chapter concludes with a review of the substantive findings of the research on school play and notes on how educators might apply this research-based knowledge.

There are two preliminary questions which need to be addressed in order to explain the structure of this chapter and to provide a framework for understanding certain choices concerning the presentation of the materials. (1) What is the rationale for combining the anthropological and sociological perspectives on play? (2) Given the general treatment of play in the literature, what constitutes school play, as opposed to school-related play and the play of school-aged children?

ANTHROPOLOGICAL VS. SOCIOLOGICAL PERSPECTIVES

While modern anthropology and sociology share some common traditions (e.g., Emile Durkheim), their institutionalization as distinct disciplines has tended to exaggerate differential trends in theory, methodology, and foci (e.g., inductive vs. deductive; qualitative vs. quantitative; nonindustrialized societies vs. industrialized societies). However, none of these distinctions has ever been absolute, and many individuals have successfully moved back and forth across these lines, making contributions recognized by anthropologists and sociologists alike.

Perhaps the most distinguishing characteristic is the degree of anthropology's commitment to holism, the notion that the human condition is best studied as a whole rather than in specialized parts. Traditionally, anthropology has studied the human condition through the union of four basic approaches: (1) the biological (or physical anthropology); (2) the historical (or archaeology); (3) the linguistic; and (4) the social and cultural. While few individual anthropologists successfully integrate two or more of these in their personal research efforts, a dynamic, interactive theoretical frame continues to operate in anthropology.

If the commitment to holism helps to prepare anthropologists as generalists, sociologists benefit from specialization. Sociologists concentrate on the study of human society, that is the social enterprises of human beings. Thus, the efforts of sociologists and social and cultural anthropologists might be expected to overlap to a significant extent. This is certainly the case with the study of play as will be demonstrated in this chapter.

In considering the work of anthropologists and sociologists simultaneously, the most obvious difficulties pertain to the efforts of physical anthropologists, archaeologists and linguists, since there are no counterparts in the discipline of sociology. Thus, only the work of social and cultural anthropologists has been reviewed for this chapter. For information on the play research of physical anthropologists, archaeologists, and linguists, consult Schwartzman's (1978) authoritative review of the anthropology of children's play.

PLAY, SCHOOL PLAY, AND THE PLAY OF SCHOOL-AGED CHILDREN

The second preliminary question centers on the definition of school play. The approach chosen here is to consider the general literature on play, examining its theoretical treatment, before moving to the much more limited body of work on school play. One must define play in order to provide a standard for considering the variety of works claiming to deal with play. While there is no expectation that this definitional attempt will stand for long, it nevertheless seems warranted to begin with a definition, no matter how inadequate it may prove.

Also at issue is the nature of school play. Again, the literature is not helpful in drawing definitional boundaries. Even if a definition of play is stated, there remains the problem of defining school. Is school defined by space, time, or activity? Is any play that takes place on school grounds to be considered school play? Is school play to be bounded by the official hours of the school day? Are we to include play that takes place on summer evenings on the neighborhood school grounds? Is a Saturday Little League game school play if it takes place on a school field but not if it takes place in a city park? Or is school play to be defined by the nature of the activity? Which are to be considered school play: shooting marbles in the school yard before classes begin and without any teacher supervision; a lesson in the rules of kickball by a physical education teacher; a teacher-organized math bee in which the boys contest the girls; or, students flying paper airplanes when the teacher leaves the room?

This chapter will take the widest possible view of school play. Any play behavior of school-aged children (grades K-12) on school grounds or under the auspices of school personnel is considered school play. In addition, other examples of the play of children that might help elucidate the nature of school play also are cited.

DEFINING PLAY

Even a brief review of the theoretical literature on play underscores the lack of definitional consensus among anthropologists and sociologists. Historically, play has been defined from three major perspectives: play as activity; play as experience; and play as biological process. The work of a few theorists is used below to illustrate these varying definitional perspectives.

Play as Activity

Most recent considerations of play begin with the classic definitional treatment by Johan Huizinga.

> [Play is] a free activity standing quite consciously outside "ordinary" life as being "not serious," but at the same time absorbing the player intensely and utterly. It is an activity connected with no material interest, and no profit can be gained by it. It proceeds within its own proper boundaries of time and space according to fixed rules and in an orderly manner. It promotes the formation of social groupings which tend to surround themselves with secrecy and to stress their differences from the common world by disguise or other means (Huizinga, 1955, p.13).

Caillois (1961, pp.9-10) critiques Huizinga's description and then defines play as an activity which is essentially free, separate, uncertain, unproductive, governed by rules, and marked by make-believe. Certainly many anthropologists and virtually all sociologists writing on play in the past two decades have used Caillois and/or Huizinga as a starting point.

Play as Experience

Without equivocation, Csikszentmihalyi (1981) states that "play ultimately is a state of subjective experience" (p.19). Play can only exist because there is an awareness of alternatives. "[W]e play when we know we are playing.... If we could not conceive of acting by a set of rules that are different from those to which we have learned to adapt, we could not play" (p.20). Csikszentmihalyi sees this as a logical extension of principles foreshadowed in Huizinga and Caillois. He believes that they were aware that play is not defined by the form or the content of the activity, but by the experience of the player.

Csikszentmihalyi is best known for the concept of flow, which is related to playfulness. Flow is a process of involvement in a given reality. Playfulness refers to one's attitude towards the reality in which one is involved. However, Csikszentmihalyi has argued that neither flow nor playfulness should be confused with play forms or play behavior. "Although games are designed to produce the experience of flow and the shift in reality necessary for playfulness, playing a game is no guarantee that these experiences will actually be encountered" (p.25).

Play as Biological Process

Norbeck (1974) emphasizes play as a biologically structured adaptive process. He defines play as "behavior, resting upon a biologically inherited stimulus or proclivity, that is distinguished by a combination of traits: play is voluntary, somehow pleasurable, distinct temporally from other behavior, and distinct in having a make-believe or transcendental quality" (p. 1). Norbeck (1979) holds that human play is always culturally molded, varying from society to society, and often is wholly a cultural creation. The adaptive significance of play can be seen in this creative aspect.

A similar approach has been taken by Tipps (1981), who suggests neurological bases for play's adaptive function. He proposes that play is the process by which the brain creates new solutions. However, the most complete formal statement of play as a biologically structured process is that of Laughlin and McManus (1982). They argue that "phenomena such as play and games cannot, in principle, be explained apart from their biological matrix" (p. 42). They assert that Huizinga suffered from such a bias when he defined play as activity without practical end. They conclude that this must necessarily mean no obvious practical end external to the organism since it is perfectly possible, if not probable, that play is activity with a practical internal end.

Summary

Each of the three types of definitions discussed above--i.e., play as activity, experience, and biological process--presents certain conceptual/methodological problems. The activity approach ignores what ought to be obvious--that play is intrinsic to the player, not a set of easily classified observable behavior patterns. However, those who would approach play as an affective state or a biologically structured process present empirical researchers with a significant dilemma. As an observer, one can only detect play indirectly if it is nonbehavioral. If no specific behavior can be equated with play, how can one determine when play is taking place? Laughlin and McManus (1982) note this preoccupation with behavior, calling it understandable but scientifically regrettable since it leads to operationalization delimited by the immediately observable. "This leads to a characteristic paradox: everybody knows the phenomenon when he or she sees it, but nobody can define it noncontroversially" (p.43).

The working definition of play offered here is built on the work of Norbeck (1974, 1979) and Csikszentmihalyi (1975). In fact, the definition is the result of an attempt to meld Norbeck's effort to devise a biologically-based, cross-culturally valid model of play with Csikszentmihalyi's notions of the play and flow experiences:

> Play is consummatory behavior, with a genetic basis, that is voluntary and pleasurable, and which results in an altered state of consciousness while leaving one in control of one's actions. Play can only be realized in contrast to nonplay

behaviors. The experience of the play state may be sufficient motivation for engaging in play behavior.

Conceptual clarity will be improved if we insist on a distinction between the experience of play (as a state of being) and play behaviors as they may be observed in play events. Children observed on a jungle gym or active in a kickball game may be said to be participants in play events. However, while one may assume they are experiencing play, it is unlikely that any observer can verify this assumption. In practical terms, it may make little difference, but theoretically it may be of great significance. All of the positive functions attributed to play (e.g., creativity, learning, adaptation) are associated with play, not with nonplayful participation in a game or other activity.

For the purposes of this chapter, I shall follow Loy's (1968, 1978) definitions of games and sports, viewing them as subcategories of play events. A game is a play event involving competition whose outcome is determined by physical skill, strategy or chance, employed singly or in combination. A sport is an institutionalized game which demands the demonstration of physical prowess.

Such a definitional approach presents a dilemma. If play is a state of being, how can an independent researcher recognize and study this experiential phenomenon? At least since the work of Huizinga, theorists have generally agreed that play was an experience, while observers, both scientists and laypersons, have continued to define play as occurring in fairly predictable behavioral contexts. These contexts might include children's free or unstructured play, game and sport involvement, artistic and esthetic efforts, humor, fantasy and ecstatic psychic states (Norbeck, 1974). As we shall see, there is no easy answer to this methodological problem.

THE STUDY OF SCHOOL PLAY BY ANTHROPOLOGISTS AND SOCIOLOGISTS

After reviewing the general perspectives on play in the anthropological and sociological literature and having made an attempt at definitional synthesis, attention can now be focused on school and school-related play. First, the methodological perspectives and techniques emplloyed by anthropologists and sociologists in the study of school play will be discussed. Then the substantive foci of such studies will be reviewed.

Methodological Perspectives and Techniques

The methods specified in the research literature can be classified into two basic categories: (1) participant observation and ethnography, and (2) survey techniques, including questionnaires and formal interviews. Each of these is discussed briefly.

Participant Observation and Ethnography

A great number of studies of children's play employ participant observation or traditional ethnographic techniques. These include studies by sociologists as well as anthropologists.

The most common observational study involves the researcher as a participant, or as a semi-detached observer, on the playground (e.g., Polgar, 1978) or the playing field (e.g., Miracle, 1981). Sometimes the goal of the research is an ethnographic overview, as in Glassner's (1976) case study of students in the lunchroom and on the playground at an elementary school. This is similar to Suggs' (1981) ethnography of two fourth-grade classes, although Suggs also included classroom observations as well as other techniques.

Certainly the most extensive ethnographic investigation of play is Blanchard's (1981) examination of play among the Mississippi Choctaws. This is the only ethnography that focuses on play in the analysis of a culture. Included in Blanchard's book is information on school sports and physical education classes.

On the other hand, observational techniques also can be used to test specific hypotheses. For example, Evans (1985) used this approach to analyze the process of team selection in children's games as played by students in grades three through six at a single elementary school.

In addition to participant observation, some researchers have used projective tests (e.g., Blanchard, 1981; Tindall, 1973) to elicit information from student players.   Others have developed techniques for recording specific types of behaviors (e.g., Klonsky, 1980) or used video recorders (e.g., Weilbacher, 1981). At least one researcher (Parrott, 1972) employed ethnographic semantic techniques to explore the semantic domains of six boys; this resulted in an ethnography of a second-grade recess. While this study was preliminary in nature, it does provide a model for possible emulation.   Semantic differential techniques also have been utilized (e.g., Beran, 1980).

Finally, one additional genre should be mentioned here--the case study. This would include the ethnographic study of a school (e.g., Henry, 1963), of the youth in a town (e.g., Fischer and Fischer, 1963; Hollingshead, 1949), or even of entire communities (e.g., Lynd and Lynd 1929,1937). Such studies almost always produce considerable information on the play activities of students at school or in school-related situations.

Surveys: Questionnaires and Formal Interviews

Social scientists have been using survey techniques to explore the realm of school play for ninety years or more. In 1896, Croswell (1899) administered questionnaires to "some two thousand children in the public schools of Worcester, Massachusetts" (p.314). His results were presented in tables showing the "Leading Amusements" and "The Favorite Toys." Croswell not only showed difference by sex, but he also had a comparison group from Brooklyn.

McGhee (1900) reported a similar study of children in South Carolina and compared his results to Croswell's findings. McGhee had over 8700 respondents and included a graph showing a "Comparison of Favorite Plays" by sex. His analysis also included a list of "Elements of Interest in Children's Plays" (e.g., surprise, imitation, memory, rivalry).

Two decades later, Foster (1930) surveyed the play activities of elementary school students in Minneapolis. In 1953, there was a report on the leisure time activities of elementary school children in the packing house area of Omaha (Sullenger, Parke, and Wallin, 1953). In the 1960s (Seagoe, 1962; Seagoe and Murakami, 1961) there was a cross-cultural study of play based on the responses of 240 first and sixth graders, half Japanese and half American, which controlled for age, sex and rural-urban differences but not social class. Cheska (1982) reported the results of a survey of 183 Native American youth surveyed at school. The instrument was "The Games and Recreation Activities Opinionnaire," and the results were analyzed statistically for gender differences.

At best, studies such as these yield a rough description of play activity preferences among a set (usually unspecified) of limited options. Nevertheless, such descriptive data can provide a context for understanding play-related social and cultural phenomena. Classic examples would be the work of Coleman (1961) and Gordon (1957).

While early survey studies have some historical interest, inventories of play activities or toys cannot provide much understanding of school play. It makes little difference whether or not such studies employ sophisticated statistical procedures. They cannot be expected to have substantive validity even if there were measures of reliability. Far too many articles appear each year which show little advance over the turn-of-the-century work of Croswell and McGhee. Indeed such crude instruments and primitive sampling techniques are used in many journal articles every year. Oftentimes it seems that the only obvious change in this century has been the modern requirement of statistical manipulation. Data collected without benefit of scientific insight, much less adequate sampling procedures, are subjected to sophisticated statistical tests--as if the presence of formulae would lend validity to the results.

A few recent researchers have been more inventive in their construction and application of survey instruments, as well as more sophisticated in their methodological techniques. For example, Butcher (1985) has recently reported on a longitudinal analysis of adolescent girls' (grades 6-10) participation in physical activity. In examining the variables related to continued participation in physical activity, she examined socializing agents and personal attributes, including the availability of equipment and activity preferences. This type of study has the potential to increase understanding and marks a dramatic advance over simple inventories. While such studies have been attacked for the positivitistic bias they reflect, there can be little doubt that the quantitative study of school play has potential for major advances in the near future.

Summary

Few school play-based studies have been explicitly concerned with methodological questions; those that have perhaps deserve special mention. Lever (1981) used her data on children's play activities to illustrate the problems and advantages of multiple methods of data collection. In studying the consequences of children's leisure activities for sex-role socialization, she utilized four data-gathering techniques: observation of schoolyards, semi-structured interviews, written questionnaires, and a diary record of playtime activities. Comparison of the results led to problems of interpretation since the conclusions generated by the various techniques often varied.

Miracle and Suggs (1981) noted similar problems in the study of friendship among elementary school students. First, observations, especially in the lunchroom and of informal play groups, were employed to develop maps approximating social reality. Second, peer interaction in class settings was quantified to yield a measure of student-student relationships. Third, questionnaires were administered asking students to name their best friends. Not a great deal of association was found among the results of the three techniques. The researchers argued that the ethnographic techniques probably were the most valid (they also were corroborated independently by the classroom teachers), although they also were the most time-consuming and expensive.

Lever (1981), when faced with a similar problem, concluded that there are multiple and contradictory results because of the nature of social reality. "In other words, each method produces truth; it is our job to define just exactly what they are accurate about" (p.208).

This issue is worth consideration because the use of triangulation, multiple methods, and especially the combination of quantitative and qualitative techniques is becoming more widespread. While such approaches may promise to reconfirm findings within the same research project, the fact is they seldom do. The conclusion to be drawn is that what we find through research is, in part, the result of the way we conduct the research, as well as the way we frame the research questions. The decision to define play as behavior, affect, or biological mechanism determines the appropriateness of certain methodological alternatives. In turn, the utilization of those specified techniques will affect the results.

While some might find such an observation discouraging or confusing, others will relish the excitement of the inevitable conflicts which will result. The most appropriate response may be humility and an appreciation of the limits of contemporary social scientific paradigms and methodological techniques.

Substantive Foci

Speculation on play as a heuristic concept has been popular in some pedagogical circles for a long time. In 1907, Johnson expanded his earlier work (1894) on *Education by Plays and Games*. In his book, Johnson quotes sources such as Groos, Gulick, and Hall in describing play as a learning instinct upon which education should be based. Curtis' (1917) book, *Education through Play* pursued similar reasoning. For Curtis, play not only provided for physical training but the training of the intellect and the formation of habits and character.

Sociologists in the early decades of this century also attributed positive educational functions to play. Smith (1924) in a book on Constructive School Discipline stresses the educative value of group play-life and discusses the benefits of school games and athletics. Waller (1932) in his classic treatment on *The Sociology of Teaching* also attributes merit to school athletics and extracurricular activities and discusses the socializing influences of the play group.

In assessing the relationship between play and learning, play sometimes has been viewed as the basis for creativity and artistry, as an exploratory mechanism, as a device for learning and promulgating cultural values, and as a stimulus for thinking (e.g., Scarfe, 1962). Of course, play also has been analyzed as a mechanism for teaching the social processes (e.g., Rose, 1956). Many works on the subject add little to the understanding of play or learning, but they do reflect a concern or an awareness of the relationship and frequently have issued a call for additional research and more understanding.

What is known about school play? With interest in the subject dating back to the nineteenth century and indeed with research on school play dating back to the 1890s, it might be supposed that anthropologists and sociologists have learned a great deal about play by now. Unfortunately, this is not the case.

Actually, few anthropologists and sociologists have studied play in general, and fewer still have studied school play. Moreover, those that have examined play and school play have done so in a limited way, both theoretically and topically.

Theoretical Paradigms

The greatest number of play studies are best categorized as historico-descriptive. Examples would include Culin's (1891) description of "Street Games of Boys in Brooklyn, N.Y." or Volberding's (1948) description of the "Out-of-School Behavior of Eleven-Year-Olds." Most such studies describe play behavior or specific games or sports without offering any theoretically grounded explanation for such occurrences. When explanations are offered to account for the existence of specific play behaviors or events, such explanations are usually attributable to historical antecedents or to social or cultural evolution. In the general literature on play, more studies might be assigned to this category than to any other. However, seldom are descriptions complete enough to allow comparison since the recorder may or may not have included information about the context of the play situation or even detailed information about the players. The descriptions often tell us what the observer thought he or she was seeing or wanted to see.

Evolutionary perspectives are those which adhere to sequential stages of development and would attempt to place specific cultural phenomena into the context of such a schema. Most often evolutionary models assume a notion of direction or progress. Explanation is an attempt to understand a given phenomenon by reference to earlier phenomena, to those historical factors that gave rise to the phenomenon under consideration. Guttmann's (1978) *From Ritual to Record: The Nature of Modern Sport* is an application of an evolutionary paradigm. Guttmann suggests that the evolution of modern sport owes to the breakdown of traditional religious systems in the West and the emergence of pervasive secularity. Many scholars studying sport have taken the position that sport has evolved through several stages from sporting activities through Greek and Roman events, to medieval sport, and eventually to modern sport. Blanchard and Cheska (1985) follow a similar process in describing the sports associated with the various levels in Service's (1962) evolutionary model of culture.

    Functional and structural-functional perspec-tives hold that the parts of any culture have to function to maintain the whole. The goal of functional analysis, then, is to explain how systems maintain themselves.

    In the functional theories of Malinowski, the existence of cultural phenomena are to be explained in relationship to individual human needs. For example, Gmelch (1971) has analyzed the functional use of magic in baseball. The less direct control that rational methods provide an individual, the greater the reliance on magic to relieve the anxiety the individual suffers from such a lack of control. Gmelch argues that outfielders have the most direct control over outcomes and hence exhibit the least amount of magic; batters have the least direct control over outcomes and are found to exhibit the greatest use of magic.

    In the structural-functionalist theories of Radcliffe-Brown, the existence of institutions or social structures is explained in terms of their congruency with other parts of the system, rather than in relationship to individual human needs. Examples would include Fox's (1961) description of "Pueblo Baseball: New Uses for Old Witchcraft" or Heider's (1977) description of flip-the-stick, a noncompetitive game diffused from the Javanese to the Dani of New Guinea. In the process of diffusion, the game underwent a transformation so that it would be congruent with other aspects of Dani culture.

    Another approach to understanding the game/culture relationship is that of John Roberts and his colleagues. They examined games cross-culturally, suggesting that games are expressive cultural activities or models of cultural activities. From this perspective, then, games may be viewed as exercises in cultural mastery. Roberts, Arth, and Bush (1959) conclude that games of strategy are related to social systems, games of chance are related to religious beliefs, and that games of physical skill may be related to environmental conditions. Subsequently, Roberts and Sutton-Smith (1962) proposed a conflict-enculturation hypothesis to explain relationships between types of games, child-training, and cultural variables.

    The *communicative* perspective, that is the combined analysis of play and communication, emerged from the work of Gregory Bateson (1972) and his understanding of metacommunication or the frame which tells the individuals involved that behavior is not to be interpreted in its usual denotative sense. With regard to play, this means that one individual must communicate, "This is play." For playful communication to ensue, another must respond, "O.K., I'll play, too."

For Bateson, the effects of playful communication include creativity and the possibilities of change and growth. By playing, by creating ambiguity and paradoxes about seriousness and play, by creating multiple and potentially conflicting layers of meaning, the likelihood of a creative context is enhanced; novelty and flexibility are likely outcomes. Bateson also notes the relationship of play and learning. In play children not only may learn content, but more importantly they learn how to learn.

Several theoretical perspectives are not well represented in the existing literature. As much as anything, this should be a clue toward uncovering the biases that exist in the work on play. For example there is very little treatment of play by cultural materialists, conflict theorists or Marxists, although there is a growing body of Marxist work in sport sociology.

Symbolic anthropologists sometimes have followed the lead of Victor Turner (1974) in the analysis of play activities as they contrast with normal states of behavior. Perhaps most notable among symbolic anthropologists is Geertz' (1972) piece on the Balinese cockfight. During the cockfight, the usually sober and passive Balinese become aggressive and licentious, illustrating how subordinate cultural themes can find expression. Thus the cockfight is a simulation of the Balinese social matrix, the "crosscutting, overlapping, highly corporate groups, villages, kin-groups, irrigation societies, temple congregations, 'castes'--in which its devotees live" (p.18). Other examples of this approach would include Manning's (1981) analysis of Bermuda's cricket festival, and Turner's (1984) description of Carnival in Rio.

Symbolic interaction is based on the social behaviorism of George Herbert Mead (1934) and is primarily concerned with socialization. Denzin's (1975) article, "Play, Games and Interaction: The Contexts of Childhood Socialization," is the most significant piece in the play literature reflecting this perspective. Recently Snyder (1985) has applied symbolic interaction to an examination of academic and athletic roles and issued a call for additional use of this perspective in sport sociology.

Since the theoretical orientation of a researcher may influence the choice of the subject, the object, and the predicate matter of research (Kenyon, 1986), it is expected that certain areas of play research have been dominated by particular theoretical orientations. This inherent research bias is not only noted in the general literature of play studies but specifically in regard to studies of school play.

Topical Foci

Sociocultural perspectives on play might be divided into four categories. One focus has been on children's play as socialization. This approach has dominated the literature since Meyer Fortes' (1938) study of education in Taleland. Structural-functionalist or preparatory theories are most common for such studies. Such theories suggest that play functions to prepare participants for subsequent roles in life.

A second focus has been on games. Theoretically, the studies of children's games and adult's games are similar, but the games of children usually are viewed as preparatory. For example, Roberts, Arth, and Bush (1959) view games as models of cultural activities and relate them to mastery of the environment, the supernatural, and the social system. However, games of adults usually are viewed as a release. Sutton-Smith (1977) has labeled such theories prophylactic, since they interpret play as protecting the players from the stresses of life.

Sports has been a third focus of investigation. While there are those who view sports as distinct from play (e.g., Edwards, 1973) others such as Loy (1968) and, more recently, Blanchard and Cheska (1985) argue that sport is a type of play event.

The fourth focus has been on the internal structures of play. That such structures can vary even when the external observable forms do not has been demonstrated clearly by several studies of basketball. Tindall's (1973) study of Utes and Anglo-Mormons noted that their cultural goals for playing basketball differed as well as the styles and strategies. This made it virtually impossible for Utes and Anglo-Mormons to play basketball together. Blanchard (1974) drew similar conclusions in his study of basketball as played by the Rimrock Navajo. Wyatt (1976) found that blacks and whites at a southern high school had great difficulty playing pick-up basketball together for the same reasons.

Summary

There are many reasons why the study of play has been limited to certain theoretical perspectives and substantive topics. Paramount, however, is the fact that play has only recently begun to be viewed as a legitimate area of investigation. Moreover, it is still not a popular area for specialization because relatively little prestige is associated with it. The reasons for this may be cultural. Americans, especially, consider play frivolous and nonproductive--unimportant, even unworthy, as a subject for serious scholarship. Perhaps this is so, or perhaps it is simply the case that there are other concerns which seem much more pressing for society and which demand the attention of social scientists to a greater extent.

An interesting outcome of this low level of intensity of research is that the existing studies seem to be grouped around a few topics. It is as if in the lonely world of play scholarship, researchers settle on common questions in order to stimulate an exchange of ideas.

ELEMENTARY SCHOOL PLAY

With few exceptions (e.g., King, 1982; Sieber, 1979), studies of play in elementary schools have focused almost exclusively on play outside the classroom. Moreover, those anthropologists and sociologists studying elementary-school play events have tended to cluster their research endeavors around three questions: (1) What is the nature of the school play environment, and what are the possible outcomes if the environment is altered? (2) Are there any significant gender differences in the play of school-aged children? (3) What is the relationship between play and peer group social structure?

Consequences of the School Play Environment

Many researchers have dichotomized the school play environment into two spheres: play which occurs without direct intervention of adults and play which is initiated, structured, and supervised by an adult. While these are not always distinct categories and elements of the two often are mixed, the dichotomy seems valid enough for the purposes of research.

Polgar (1976) typifies these two settings as free play on school playgrounds with no adult direction and supervised play, such as that in formal physical education classes under the control of a trained physical education teacher. Coakley (1980) categorized his play events into spontaneous play and informal games outside the control of adults and organized team sport events under the direct control of a coach. Elsewhere Coakley (1979) has dichotomized these events into spontaneous play groups and sponsored competitive teams.

Polgar (1976) also has concluded that unstructured play in the peer group context appears to develop egalitarian and consensual models concerned with means, whereas adult-structured contexts promote an authoritarian and imposed model concerned with ends. The extreme case of structured school play is high school athletics.

As might Huizinga, Polgar questions whether activities in the adult-structured, end-oriented contexts constitute play. Polgar (1976) reasons that if "play can be used as a model of behavior, and if adults have a role in the socialization of children different from their peers, then the model of social reality developed in the peer group should differ from that the teacher develops when supervising children's play" (p.266). Polgar, as Podilchak (1982) has for youth sports, concludes that the presence and supervision of an adult change the nature of the play experience. For the sixth-grade boys Polgar studied, "free play was a flexible process of social exchange under consensus," however, under the teacher's supervision play "was an organized structuring of rules, groupings, and activities imposed upon the participants" (p.269).

Gender Differences

The most thorough study of gender differences with regard to the play behavior of elementary school children was conducted by Lever in the early 1970s. Lever (1976, 1978, 1981) studied the play of fifth-grade students. She observed play activities during recess, physical education classes, and after school. In addition, she collected information through semi-structured interviews, written questionnaires, and students, diary records of after-school play activities.

Lever (1976) concluded that there were six notable differences in the play activities of the white, middle-class boys and girls she studied. (1) Boys play outdoors far more than girls. (2) Boys more often played in larger groups. (3) Boys' play occurs in more age-heterogeneous groups. (4) Girls more often play in predominantly male games than boys play in girls' games. (5) Boys play competitive games more often than girls. (6) Boys' games last longer than girls' games.

Lever also notes that while boys' sports continue to be of interest through the teen years and beyond, girls already have dropped out of the game culture by the time they reach age 13 or 14. It may be that this has to do with the complexity and hence the relative challenge of boys' and girls' games. Lever notes that the "ceiling of skill" is higher for boys' games, thus it is likely that boys find their games more challenging. This would account for the fact that boys' games last longer since they can keep one's attention for a longer span of time. It also would help account for the fact that boys continue to play games for years after girls have stopped.

Lever also concluded that boys' play behavior is more complex than girls', as indexed by such attributes as role differentiation, interdependence between players, size of play group, explicitness of goals, number of rules, and team formation. The implication is that "boys' greater exposure to complex games may give them an advantage in occupational milieus that share structural features with those games."

Not only are boys' games more complex, but the structures promote different kinds of skill development than girls' games. Lever (1976) notes that one reason boys' games can continue for a longer period of time than girls' games is because boys are able to resolve their disputes more effectively. Lever speculates that this may owe to the model set by the older boys during age-mixed play. "[W]hen older boys permit younger ones to join them in their games, they in effect teach their juniors a great deal about the setting, not only in terms of the requisite physical skills but the social ones as well" (pp.482-83). Whatever the reasons, Lever states that boys do have a greater consciousness of and experience with rules.

Lever (1976) concludes that differences in leisure patterns of boys and girls lead to the development of particular social skills and capacities. "[B]oys' games may help prepare their players for successful performance in a wide range of work settings in modern society...girls' games may help prepare their players for the private sphere of the home and their future roles as wives and mothers" (p.484). Thus play activities serve to preserve traditional sex-role divisions.

The possible socializing function of play activities has been noted by others. For example, in a study of soccer and ice hockey organizations for eleven and twelve-year old boys, Berlage (1982) asked, "Are children's competitive team sports socializing agents for corporate America?" She concludes that "the attitudes, values and skills inculcated in the training of team athletes more and more mirror the corporate structure, its values and ethic" (p.324). Berlage also observed that parents and coaches accept these values and want children to be socialized according to them, because these values are now seen as basic to American society.

It is obvious in this context that girls do not participate in games and sports to the same degree as boys. Therefore, they do not have the same opportunities to learn these values and social skills. Whether one believes that this is good or bad, there is no denying that the socializing structures are dissimilar. If games and team sports are effective means for socializing youth for participation in the corporate world, lack of participation in these activities might affect females' entry into those careers.

Peer Group Social Structure

Certain relationships between play and peer group would appear obvious. It might be supposed that one would choose to play with friends over nonfriends. Conversely, it would seem that playing with someone would be a means of building a friendship. It also would seem logical to suppose that the play preferences of one's peers would influence one's own notions about play activities. On the other hand, one's own play preferences might be supposed to affect one's choice of friends or peer group with which to play. Research generally confirms these suppositions. Moreover, it would appear that not only are play and friendship interrelated, but these also affect, and are affected by, other variables in the school environment.

In his assessment of informal children's games, Coakley (1980) found that the primary focus in such activities was on the initiation and maintenance of a combination of action, personal involvement, a close contest (challenge), and the reaffirmation of friendships. In a study of fourth-grade peer groups, Suggs (1981) found that the groups he observed were characterized by a common play activity orientation. Thus a student's friendship group is basically a play group. These play groups engage in unique activities and the particular activity of each group is relatively constant over time, i.e., throughout the school year.

In a summary of a year-long study of peer groups in two fourth-grade classes, the following observations were made (Miracle, Rowan, and Suggs, 1984). (1) All of the observed fourth grade peer groups were 100 percent sexually homogeneous. (2) There was a strong tendency toward racial homogeneity in the groups. (3) Within each classroom there was a well-defined pair of social structures, one male, the other female. (4) Both males and females recognized athletic ability and academic superiority as prestigious characteristics. All high-status individuals displayed middle-class dress. Among the males in one classroom, "toughness" was accepted as a route to prestige, while in the other class it clearly was not. Among females, physical attractiveness was an important trait for status attainment.

In this same study, it also was noted that generally the only time and space in which students were allowed to form groups on the basis of free choice was on the playground, after lunch, or during recess. This ecological constraint possibly accounts for the fact that the peer groups tend to be play-oriented. Whatever the cause, it was concluded that one basis for identity and solidarity of these fourth-grade peer groups was the expression and reinforcement of group interests in play activities.

While play activities may define peer groups in elementary school, the selection of friends does not seem to be influenced by some factors known to affect friendship choices of high school students. Fourth graders' friendship choices are affected by racial and ethnic characteristics but not by social class nor prior academic achievement (Hallinan and Tuma, 1978; Suggs, 1981). There is, however, some evidence that these friendship groups, formed largely on the basis of common play interests and activities, have some affect on classroom conduct, study habits, and academic achievement (Rowan and Miracle, 1983).

The racial homogeneity of play groups also was noted by Polgar (1978) in her study of sixth graders, where she examined patterns of social interaction in free play periods. She noted differences in competition in single-color games, color-opposed games, and games between color-mixed teams. In single-color games (blacks only or whites only) and in color-opposed games (blacks versus whites) play continued for long periods, and games were often repeated after one game ended. However, games in which groups or teams were mixed by color took much longer to organize; Polgar presumes this may be because these were not usual groupings. In mixed-color games, Polgar found that more arguments over rules occurred during the progress of the game than in either of the other two types; these conflicts were resolved by reconstituting the game into color-opposed teams, discontinuing the game, or changing the game in a way that resolved the conflict. Polgar observes that a "major problem of mixed groups in free play seems to be a lack of trust on the part of one group (in most cases the blacks) that the game is being played fairly, that the rules apply equally to all players" (p.286). Using games as models, Polgar discusses possible applications to promote racial interaction or the integration of schools as opposed to simple desegregation.

SECONDARY SCHOOL PLAY

Researchers studying play events in high schools have focused almost exclusively on organized sports. Sociologists have been interested in high school athletics for decades and have identified several issues or research questions around which most investigations have centered. Only in the past two decades, beginning with Burnett's (1969) study of the ceremonial importance of high school athletics, have anthropologists paid any attention to high school sports.

The importance of high school sports is undeniable. Talamini (1973) cited eight reasons why any examination of secondary education in American culture must give consideration to the role of sport: (1) It is an integral part of the American system of secondary education (cf. Burnett, 1969). (2) It provides a leisure outlet for the community. As the Lynds (1929) noted for Middletown (Muncie, Indiana): "Today civic loyalty centers around basketball more than any other one thing. No distinctions divide the crowds which pack the school gymnasium for home games...."(p.435). (3) School sport (and its consequences for the development of youth) has long been a center of controversy among American educators. (4) The youth culture is marked by the prominence of athletics. (5) The position of athletic director is often high in the power structure of school systems, giving further credence to the central role of athletics in the school. (6) School athletics have expanded rapidly since the turn of the century. (7) Even in its most highly organized form, school sport contains characteristics of play. (8) Historically, in most times and places, the role of sporting activity in the development of youth has received attention.

What surprised Talamini was the relative lack of serious attention given to school athletics by sociologists concerned with education. For example, in its 45-year history prior to 1971, *Sociology of Education* had never printed an article by a sociologist on school athletics.

Since Talamini's paper, increased attention has been paid to high school athletics by sociologists; the field has yet to attract many anthropologists. Indeed, the entire subdiscipline of sport sociology has experienced considerable growth, as witnessed by the formation of the North American Society for the Sociology of Sport and the publication since 1984 of the *Sociology of Sport Journal*.

An important consideration within the context of this chapter is whether sport is a play event or, more precisely, whether school sports constitute play events. While some theorists who have defined sport as a play form (e.g., Blanchard and Cheska, 1985; Loy, 1968, 1978), others have argued that sport is not play (e.g., Edwards, 1973). While noting that there are limitations to play in the context of sport, Kleiber (1979) argues that the play elements are present in sport and can be increased through manipulation. Not only can play be turned into sport by organization, but sport can be play as long as decision-making power is in the hands of the participants so they can create and modify.

Chalip, Csikszentmihalyi, Kleiber, and Larson (1984) conducted an intriguing experiment involving a sample of high school students who completed self-report forms providing data on social situation, activity, and subjective state at random times during normal waking hours, including once during each class session at school. The results indicate that sport experiences do share characteristics traditionally associated with play:

> For these adolescents, sport is generally experienced more positively than other parts of their lives. Regardless of context, physical activity is associated with significantly higher-than-average challenges. The high challenges are typically paired with high moods and high motivation. This pairing suggests that physical activity can provide a context in which the adolescent may learn to experience challenges as potentially pleasurable. In consequence, physical activity may provide a useful bridge between expressive and instrumental experience (cf. Csikszentmihalyi, 1981b), and may indeed

provide a context in which adolescents can safely explore their capabilities (p.114).

The researchers also found that informal sports offered some particularly attractive features to high school students. The informal sport settings were voluntary, and there was a perceived consonance between demands and skills; a high frequency of such experiences occurs in or near the flow channel, that is, with intense levels of involvement (Chalip, Csikszentmihalyi, Kleiber and Larson, 1984):

> The high positive correlation between challenges and skills in informal sports settings, but not in adult-supervised settings also suggests that the flow experience is easier to achieve when adolescents are in control of the activity, probably because they can manipulate the balance between challenges and skills more easily in an informal setting (p.114).

Snyder and Spreitzer (1981) in an article on "Sport, Education and Schools" argue for a phenomenological perspective in sport research that would build on Csikszentmihalyi's (1975) work. "We suggest that scientific research should take sport seriously in the sense of conceptualizing sport as an immanent, autonomous sphere of human experience. That is, sport should be conceived as a form of human endeavor that begins and ends within the individual and which has its own reason for existence" (p.142).

Csikszentmihalyi (1975) is concerned with the autotelic (from the Greek *auto*, self, and *telos*, goal or purpose), so he does not view sport as some form of external compensation or as preparation for future needs, but rather as an intrinsically satisfying activity whose reward is coterminous with the behavior itself. "To provide intrinsic rewards, an activity must be finely calibrated to a person's skills--including his physical, intellectual, emotional, and social abilities" (p.100).

Most researchers, however, have not been concerned with the experiential state of high school athletes; rather they have tended to concern themselves with empirically verifiable sociological correlates of sport participation. The sociology of high school sports began in earnest with Coleman's (1961) study of ten high schools in Illinois in the late 1950s. Extending the work of Gordon (1957), Coleman concluded that independent of school size, location or socioeconomic composition, athletics dominated school life. Eitzen and Sage (1978) summarize Coleman's findings on athletics as follows:

(1) Membership in a school's leading crowd varied by sex. Girls' status was determined by ascribed characteristics such as parents' achievement, good looks, and possessions. However, status for boys was based on achievement, especially in athletics.

(2) The most important attribute for male popularity was "being an athletic star." This was consistently considered more important than (in order

of importance) being in the leading crowd, being a leader in activities, high grades and honor roll, having a nice car, or coming from the right family.

(3) When asked how they would most like to be remembered, 44 percent of the boys said as an athletic star, 31 percent said as a brilliant student, and 25 percent replied most popular. This contrasted with the parents' response to the same question; three-fourths of them wanted their sons remembered as brilliant students.

Recent research by Thirer and Wright (1985) found that being an athlete was still the foremost criterion for male popularity. For females, being an athlete was ascribed fairly low social status, indicating that in spite of Title IX legislation and changes in women's roles generally in society, athletic performance is still not a valued attribute for female adolescents. This contrasts with the research previously reported on girls in elementary school (Miracle, Rowan, and Suggs, 1984; Suggs, 1981) but is consistent with Lever's (1976) observation that girls stop participating in games by the age of 13 or 14.

A great deal of research has indicated that participation in high school athletics has a positive affect on academic achievement and college aspirations (e.g., Otto and Alwin, 1977; Phillips and Schafer, 1971; Rehberg and Schafer, 1968; Spreitzer and Pugh, 1973). Snyder and Spreitzer (1977) report that the relationship also holds for female as well as male high school athletes.

There is no consensus in the literature explaining why athletic participation affects academic achievement and aspirations. Some research reports that participation in social (nonathletic) extracurricular activities has similar effects (e.g., Hanks and Eckland, 1976; Snyder and Spreitzer, 1977; Spady, 1970). Coakley (1982) presents a good review of the many interpretations of the data.

A few studies have tested the hypothesis that participation in high school athletics also might affect future occupational outcomes. Otto and Alwin (1977) found that high school athletics had a positive effect on occupational prestige and income 15 years after the first survey of 17-year-old males in one Michigan county. Okihiro (1984) also found that athletic and social involvement in extracurricular activities had positive effects on educational and job attainment among a sample of respondents in Ontario six years after completing Grade 12. However, no support for the hypothesis was found by Howell, Miracle, and Rees (1984) in a study utilizing a national survey, Youth in Transition, in which respondents were followed up one year after graduation and again five years after graduation.

There have been some studies of the relationship between high school sports participation and delinquency. Unfortunately, the results of these studies are unclear. Schafer (1969) was the first to report lower delinquency rates for athletes than nonathletes; especially among low achievers from blue collar backgrounds. Landers and Landers (1978) examined the relationship of delinquency and extracurricular participation by type of activity: athletics only, service, and leadership activities, service-leadership activities and athletics, or no form of extracurricular involvement. They found that rates of delinquency were highest for those who engaged in no extracurricular activities. Rates were lower, and approximately the same, for those in athletics or some other extracurricular activity. Rates were lowest for students in both types of activities. In a recent study, Segrave and Hastad (1984) conclude that sports participation is a compelling reason for delinquent youth to stay in school.

There are numerous problems associated with these research efforts. For example, there are difficulties in defining and categorizing delinquent acts. Moreover, neither court records nor self-report accounts are likely to be accurate nor comparable nation-wide. In addition, there is the probable confounding fact that athletes may be conformers, and that athletic involvement is self-selecting in this regard.

There are two additional areas which have received significant attention by researchers: socialization and race relations. The youth sport socialization literature has been reviewed by McPherson (1981, 1986). McPherson looks at the alternative perspectives of socialization through sport as well as socialization into sport. Snyder (1970) has looked at the role of physical education in socialization. Some researchers (e.g., Mantel and Vander Velden, 1974) have focused on attitudes and personality traits, while others have examined the relationship between sport and socialization and social class (e.g., Armstrong, 1984).

The effects of school sports on racial attitudes and interaction have been examined by several sport sociologists (e.g., Chu and Griffey, 1982; Miracle, 1981; Rees and Miracle, 1984). Many others have studied the situation in collegiate and professional settings. This is an area where research results are mixed, perhaps reflecting differences in methodology and conceptualization.

THE INSTITUTIONALIZATION OF PLAY EVENTS

It seems logical to ask how it came about that play events, i.e., recess, physical education, and athletics, were institutionalized in American high schools. Social historians inform us that two apparently independent forces led to this situation: the athleticism movement in the British public schools and the playground movement in America. In both these movements structured physical activity was linked to moral development.

The philosophy of athleticism was exported from British public schools to North America in the nineteenth century. According to Armstrong (1984) team sports fulfilled the same functions on both sides of the Atlantic, specifically, extending institutional control, allowing the students contact with games masters who acted as surrogate parents, teaching "manliness," developing the school leaders, and preparing athletes for elite colleges and universities.

It is interesting to note that during this era there was actually much less adult control of sports in schools than at the present time. For example, many school teams were formed and managed by students. Although "games masters" were found in both British and American boarding schools, their power did not equal that of the modern day coach in American high schools and colleges. Henry Curtis (1917) in *Education Through Play* early bemoaned the fact that athletes were dominated by coaches with a "winning" philosophy rather than a social or educational one. This point is important in light of some current criticism that sport in the American system of education is so organized that spontaneity, enjoyment, and moral development have, for the most part, been removed (Devereux, 1976; Eitzen, 1984; Sage, 1980).

Another independent movement that affected the legitimation of athletics in education was the playground movement in America. Between 1880 and 1920, a group of "play organizers" tried to utilize play as a medium for shaping the moral development of youth, principally in the industrial cities of the East (Cavallo, 1981). It is important to note that, according to the leaders of the "playground movement," this could only be achieved by changing play from an unorganized street activity to an organized activity in the playgrounds. As Cavallo points out children's play was considered far too important to be left to the children.

The leaders of the playground movement of America believed that organized play activities would help teach cooperation, group loyalty, and subordination of self and thus act as a brake to unrestricted capitalism which they viewed as a danger to American society. At the same time it was felt that organized play activities would help to counter juvenile delinquency, perceived to be common in urban areas, and give a sense of moral purpose to youth (Cavallo, 1981).

While the playground movement did not accomplish its primary goals, it was instrumental in shaping the views of the early leaders of physical education, and helped to give impetus to the idea of organized play as an integral part of the American school system. Although some play organizers were ambivalent about the role of the public schools because they felt that the schoool encouraged competition and individualism rather than cooperation and group loyalty, others (notably Luther Gulick and Henry Curtis) felt that play could be incorporated into the school curriculum via physical education courses and extracurricular sports (Cavallo, 1981).

Cavallo notes that the public school did become the focus of organized play after 1920 but not in the form originally envisioned by the playground movement. Play became more and more institutionalized into athletics, which, in turn, became elitist and adult dominated (Spring, 1974). To a great extent the early fears of the play organizers were realized. They wanted active participation by all children, and they discouraged spectatorship (Cavallo, 1981). Yet by the 1920s the issue of spectatorship in public school and college sport was already of great concern (Spring, 1974).

Sports, as highly institutionalized forms of play events, may function positively for schools and communities, quite apart from any effects on the individual players. School sports can serve to integrate various groups and categories of individuals within the school and the community. This is especially important in heterogeneous schools, with a student population drawn from various social strata and ethnic populations. The natural patterning of these diverse elements tends toward voluntary segregation. Organized athletics is one of the few systems that may serve to unite and focus the energies of these disparate elements and thus contribute toward the maintenance of equilibrium within school and community (Miracle, 1978).

School sports also help unite community members at various stages in the life cycle (Precourt, 1976). In a sense, athletics is more than a "coin of communication" (a phrase invented by Gregory Stone; see Cheek and Burch, 1976). For many it is a common experiential bond, a set of behaviors and related sentiments in which they have or will have participated at one level or another, in one or more roles, at various points in the life cycle.

Beran (1981) illustrates this in an article in which she analyzes the Iowa Girls' Basketball State Tournament as a ritual event. She concludes that the ritual of the tournament, as much as the play of the games, "fulfills a collective need for entertainment, allows for reaffirmation of traditional values, acts as an acceptable vehicle for changing social status, ensures the continuation of the organizational structure, and lastly, in the eyes of the viewers and participants, proclaims Iowa's superior high school girls' sport program" (p.157).

CONCLUSIONS

An attempt has been made to review anthropological and sociological studies of play in the school context. Two limitations should be noted. First, only school play in the United States has been analyzed here. The small number of available studies examining school play outside of the United States combined with the large number of contextual variables to be considered, render comparative analyses virtually impossible at this time. Second, while an effort was made to examine studies of play in elementary, middle and high schools, this proved impossible to implement. For the most part, middle schools are not treated separately from the other two levels.

In summarizing the work on school play, however, it can be stated that most studies have dealt with social not individual play. Moreover, most researchers have examined games, not free play. Finally, socialization is assumed to be an important function of school play; that is, a practice or preparatory model prevails.

Additionally, one might note a possible effect of a forced, artificial dichotomy of work/play in schools. Schools tend to be viewed as utilitarian, with school preparation meant for the world of work. Thus the world of school is analogously viewed as work-like.

Suggestions for Future Research

As with the general study of play, no rigorous application of theory has guided most of the studies. In fact, most studies of school play have avoided definitions and operational clarification. Those working in this area assume that everyone knows what play is and thus sidestep these difficult tasks. We need to heed Klaus Meier's (1983) call for definitional clarity and the identification of key variables. Until researchers are more deliberate as to their use of terminology and more precise in their methodology, it will be difficult to advance the understanding of play. For example, whether one defines play as activity, experience, or biological process has implications for applications by educators and other professionals.

Moreover, there is a need for additional, highly focused, theoretically directed research. While the accumulation of accurate ethnographic accounts may continue to be of interest, the field may stagnate without an elaboration of new theoretical paradigms. It is easy to describe play activities, but unless such descriptions contribute to theoretical discussions, they do not move us any closer to understanding what play is and what play does.

A review of the sociological and anthropological literature on play reveals three wide-spread assumptions relevant to school play. First, there is the assumption that children's play is qualitatively and functionally different from adult play. Not only is it rare to find researchers reporting on adults "playing,"but any such behaviors are categorized differently from the same behaviors of children. As noted previously, usually it is assumed that children's play is preparatory while adults' play is prophylactic.

Second, it is often assumed that play and games are equivalent. This is especially true for children. Caillois' (1961) system of classifying games and play probably has contributed to this, since he categorizes mimicry and vertigo-inducing activities, as well as games of chance and agonistic competitions, in a single schema.

Third, until recently it has been assumed that play and work were antithetical. This is due, at least in part, to the influential work of Huizinga (1955), *Homo Ludens*. Huizinga stressed that play "is an activity with no material interest, and no profit can be gained by it" (p.13). Ethnographers have noted the periodic playfulness of workers (e.g., Lancy, 1980), and a few, such as Stevens (1980), have questioned the validity of the work/play dichotomy. This line of thinking has been given impetus in recent years by Csikszentmihalyi and his colleagues (e.g., Csikszentmihalyi and Bennett, 1971).

Finally, review of the literature suggests that the topics of play and development of the individual, as well as play and learning, have not been adequately explored. Two subjects in the area of school play have been ignored for too long. Middle-school adolescents deserve attention. It seems that researchers have a tendency either to group middle-school youth with younger elementary school children or older high school students. The possible influences on play of adolescent development and middle-school institutional structures are seldom recognized. Another ignored topic is nonsport play in high schools. Perhaps it is because high school students are considered adult-like that their play, other than in athletics, has generally been ignored.

Methodological Issues

The primary methodological issue is how to analyze the affective and cognitive elements of play. The work by Chalip, Csikszentmihalyi, Kleiber, and Larson (1984) is exceptional in its innovativeness. In spite of a call by

Stevens (1977), there have been few attempts to link social or cultural issues in play research to physiological or neurological mechanisms. Exceptions would include Laughlin and McManus (1982) and Tipps (1981). Tipps (1981), for example, states that, "Play has a positive emotional quality which enhances experiential exploration and neural alertness to the environment. Exploration results in neurological growth and provides structures for more complex play behaviors" (p.28).

This limited effort to bridge potential physical with social and cultural analyses may be one result of the fact that few physical anthropologists are measuring the parameters and consequences of human play, forcing a reliance on ethologists, physiologists, and motor development specialists. Or, it may be caused by a general reticence to utilize theories with bio-social implications or those which might be vulnerable to attack on the grounds of biological reductionism.

One type of study is a possibility for future efforts, the comparative ethnological study. The cross-cultural work of John Roberts and his colleagues, utilizing the Human Relations Area Files, and the analysis of general field studies by Whiting and Whiting (1975) provide the best examples. While nothing similar has been attempted for school play, it is possible that someone could utilize existing ethnographic descriptions of school play to provide a comparative analysis. Such an effort might prove a valuable contribution.

Applying Research-Based Knowledge

In spite of the need for research, there does seem to be sufficient consensus to inform educators about applications in a few areas. Six of these are suggested here.

(1) Different types of play might be utilized differently. In school settings this is most obvious with reference to the structured play/ unstructured play distinction. Structured play events are considered to be instructive by educators. These events supposedly teach students social rules, authority structures, and role differentiation as well as normative values and ideals. Since this type of play is under the direction of teachers, they can manipulate the process to effect specific goals. On the other hand, more tolerance may be required for unstructured or free play events, which usually are associated with creativity and the learning of social roles. In this type of play, participants are concerned with means rather than ends (Miller, 1973) and with the process of the activity rather than with the outcome (Csikszentmihalyi and Bennett, 1971), while structured play situations are extrinsically motivated activities concerned with ends. However, it is recognized that the teacher's role is so authoritarian and control-oriented, that it may be difficult for teachers to stay uninvolved and to allow children to develop their own patterns of social interaction.

(2) Play might be used in alternation with other activities. Parman (1979) has suggested that play, like sleep, is essential to the organism in providing alternation between systems. That is, play provides a release and prevents overloading certain neurophysiological systems. While the empirical

evidence to support this contention is lacking, it does fit with the folk mythology or conventional wisdom of teachers which allows for short breaks for play between academic lessons. In addition, it might be useful to compare this with traditional theories of play as a release from stress or with the biological process models (e.g., Laughlin and McManus, 1982).

(3) Teachers can utilize play as a device for class management by ritualizing play activities. The ritualized use of play activities might be employed to help students switch paradigms, as when they are shifting from one lesson to another, or from one activity to another. For example, some kindergarten and primary grade teachers have students sing a song or do a circle dance as a transition activity in preparation for lining up to go to lunch. Such activity, because it is used every day in the same way, can serve as a trigger to the desired behavior--walking quietly down the hallway to the lunchroom.

(4) Teachers need to be aware that cultural variations in play may lead to misunderstandings. Rules, styles, and purposes for playing may vary even when the visible forms of play appear to be similar or identical. Still, play may be useful in the acculturation of immigrant children. For example, Robinson (1978) notes that "Vietnamese boys are learning American cultural rules through the informal channel of play" (p.144). However, since few Vietnamese girls participate in play events, Robinson concludes that they will be less prepared to deal with change than the boys.

(5) In physical education, teachers might take advantage of students' motivation for free play. Polgar (1976) has noted that it takes sixth-grade boys only moments to organize themselves for play, but physical education teachers may spend half of the class period simply getting ready to play. To the extent that physical education is meant to improve students physically, i.e., in terms of fitness, perhaps unstructured play should be utilized more frequently since it allows for more time in the physical activity.

(6) There is one additional development which has affected contemporary practices and attitudes toward school play--the professionalization of physical education. Callahan (1962) has described the consequences of the professionalization of educational administrators, and many of his findings also might be applied to physical educators.

Professionalization has isolated physical education from direct community control, since, as experts with years of specialized training, physical educators can claim to know better than parents or other laypersons what is best for children's development through physical activities. Professionalization also has required physical educators and other educators to demonstrate their mastery and control through the implementation of highly structured environments with an emphasis on performance, backed by statistical logs and rationalized by detailed lesson plans. This has culminated recently in the widespread movement toward accountability in education. If schools are to be held accountable for their actions with students, then teachers, including physical education teachers, must be able to demonstrate their absolute control over students and their ability to manipulate students in a purposeful manner.

While explanations for these developments are beyond the scope of this chapter, it should be clear that there has been a progression from peer-organized to adult-organized play activities in schools. In the interests of social control and moral development, physical activity in the schools became highly organized and tightly controlled by adults. The values associated with physical education and athletics were discipline, obedience, and acceptance of the Protestant ethic of hard work within an already-existing moral framework, although self-control, leadership, sportsmanship, and democracy were still presumed to occur. This leads to the idea of sport as work as opposed to play, and serious business as opposed to fun.

The dichotomy between work and play has been criticized for society in general (Csikszentmihalyi, 1975, 1981b), as well as in the context of sport (Devereux, 1976; Kleiber, 1979; Rees, 1980). Research by Chalip, Csikszentmihalyi, Kleiber, and Larson (1984), Polgar (1976), Rees, Hammond, and Woodruff (1986) indicates the value of informal sports contexts in producing challenging and enjoyable activities.

Existing research strongly suggests that there are many positive values, in terms of the development of individual creativity, as well as social skills and values associated with play that children devise and experience outside of the control of adults. Perhaps it is time for educators to seek a restored balance between free, unstructured, peer-constructed play and adult-directed and structured games, sports and other physical activities which provide opportunities for play (cf. Kleiber and Barnett, 1980). Both contexts have much to offer children, and while the lessons to be learned appear to be different, both appear to be essential.

REFERENCES

Armstrong, C. The Lessons of Sports: Class Socialization in British and American Boarding Schools. *Sociology of Sport Journal, 1*(1984), 314-331.

Bateson, G. *Steps to an Ecology of Mind.* New York: Ballantine Books, 1972.

Beran, J. Attitudes of Iowa Children Toward Their Play. In *Play and Culture.* Edited by H. Schwartzman. West Point, New York: Leisure Press, 1980.

Beran, J. The Iowa Girls' High School Basketball Tournament Viewed as an Institutionalized Ritual. In *Play as Context.* Edited by A. Cheska. West Point, New York: Leisure Press, 1981.

Berlage, G.. Are Children's Competitive Team Sports Socializing Agents for Corporate America? In *Studies in the Sociology of Sport.* Edited by A. Dunleavy, A. Miracle, and C. Rees. Fort Worth: Texas Christian University Press, 1982.

Blanchard, K. Basketball and the Culture-Change Process: The Rimrock Navajo Case. *Council on Anthropology and Education Quarterly, 5*, no. 4(1974), 8-13.

Blanchard, K. *The Mississippi Choctaws at Play: The Serious Side of Leisure.* Urbana: University of Illinois Press, 1981.

Blanchard, K. and Cheska, A. *The Anthropology of Sport.* South Hadley, Massachusetts: Bergin and Garvey, 1985.

Burnett, J. Ceremony, Rites and Economy in the Student System of an American High School. *Human Organization, 28*(1969), 1-10.

Butcher, J. Longitudinal Analysis of Adolescent Girls' Participation in Physical Activity. *Sociology of Sport Journal, 2*(1985), 130-143.

Caillois, R. *Man, Play, and Games.* New York: The Free Press, 1961.

Callahan, R. *Education and the Cult of Efficiency.* Chicago: University of Chicago Press, 1962.

Cavallo, D. *Muscles and Morals.* Philadelphia: University of Pennsylvania Press, 1981.

Chalip, L., Csikszentmihalyi, M., Kleiber, D., and Larson, R. Variations of Experience in Formal and Informal Sports. *Research Quarterly, 55*(1984), 109-116.

Cheek, N., and Burch, W., Jr. *The Social Organization of Leisure in Human Society.* New York: Harper and Row, 1976.

Cheska, A. Gender Variations in Game Attraction Factors of Native American Youth. In *Studies in the Sociology of Sport.* Edited by A. Dunleavy, A. Miracle, and C. Rees. Fort Worth: Texas Christian University Press, 1982.

Chu, D., and Griffey, D. Sport and Racial Integration: The Relationship of Personal Contact, Attitudes and Behavior. In *Studies in the Sociology of Sport.* Edited by A. Dunleavy, A. Miracle, and C. Rees. Fort Worth: Texas Christian University Press, 1982.

Coakley, J. Play Group Versus Organized Competitive Team: A Comparison. In *Sport in Contemporary Society: An Anthology.* Edited by D. Eitzen. New York: St. Martin's Press, 1979.

Coakley, J. Play, Games, and Sport: Developmental Implications for Young People. *Journal of Sport Behavior, 3*(1980), 99-118.

Coakley, J. *Sport in Society: Issues and Controversies.* 2nd ed. St. Louis: C. V. Mosby, 1982.

Coleman, J. *The Adolescent Society: The Social Life of the Teenager and Its Impact on Education.* New York: The Free Press, 1961.

Croswell, T. Amusements of Worcester School Children. *Pedagogical Seminary, 6*(1899), 314-371.

Csikszentmihalyi, M. *Beyond Boredom and Anxiety.* San Francisco: Josey-Bass, 1975.

Csikszentmihalyi, M. Some Paradoxes in the Definition of Play. In *Play as Context.* Edited by A. Cheska. West Point: Leisure Press, 1981a.

Csikszentmihalyi, M. Leisure and Socialization. *Social Forces, 60*(1981b), 332-340.

Csikszentmihalyi, M., and Bennett, S. An Exploratory Model of Play. *American Anthropologist, 73*(1971), 45-58.

Culin, S. Street Games of Boys in Brooklyn, N. Y. *Journal of American Folklore, 4*(1891), 221-237.

Curtis, H. *Education Through Play.* New York: Macmillan, 1917.

Denzin, N. Play, Games and Interaction: The Contexts of Childhood Socialization. *The Sociological Quarterly, 16*(1975), 458-478.

Devereux, E. Backyard Versus Little League Base-ball: Some Observations on the Impoverishment of Children's Games in Contemporary America. In *Social Problems in Athletics*. Edited by D. Landers. Urbana: University of Illinois Press, 1976, 37-56.

Edwards, H. *Sociology of Sport*. Homewood, Illinois: Dorsey Press, 1973.

Eitzen, D. School Sports and Educational Goals. In *Sport in Contemporary Society*, 2nd ed. Edited by D. Eitzen. New York: St. Martin's Press, 1984.

Eitzen, D., and Sage, G. *Sociology of American Sport*. Dubuque, Iowa: Wm. C. Brown, 1978.

Evans, J. The Process of Team Selection in Children's Self-Directed and Adult-Directed Games. Unpublished Ph.D. Dissertation, University of Illinois at Urbana-Champaign, 1985.

Fischer, J., and Fischer, A. The New Englanders of Orchard Town, U.S.A. In *Six Cultures: Studies of Child Rearing*. Edited by B. Whiting. New York: John Wiley and Sons, 1963.

Fortes, M. Social and Psychological Aspects of Education in Taleland. *Africa, 11*, no. 4(1938).

Foster, J. Play Activities of Children in the First Six Grades. *Child Development, 1*(1930), 248-254.

Fox, J. Pueblo Baseball: A New Use for Old Witchcraft. *Journal of American Folklore, 74*(1961), 9-16.

Geertz, C. Deep Play: Notes on the Balinese Cockfight. *Daedalus, 101*(1972), 1-37.

Glassner, B. Kid Society. *Urban Education, 11*(1976), 5-22.

Gmelch, G. Baseball Magic. *TransAction, 8*(1971), 39-41,54.

Gordon, C. *The Social System of the High School: A Study in the Sociology of Adolescence*. Glencoe, Illinois: The Free Press, 1957.

Guttmann, A. *From Ritual to Records: The Nature of Modern Sports*. New York: Columbia University Press, 1978.

Hallinan, M., and Tuma, N. Classroom Effects on Changes in Children's Friendships. *Sociology of Education, 51*(1978), 270-281.

Hanks, M., and Eckland, B.   Athletics and Social Participation in the Educational Attainment Process. *Sociology of Education, 49*(1976), 271-294.

Heider, K.   From Javanese to Dani: The Translation of a Game. In *Studies in the Anthropology of Play: Papers in Memory of B. Allan Tindall.* Edited by P. Stevens, Jr. West Point: Leisure Press, 1977.

Henry, J. *Culture Against Man.* New York: Random House, 1963.

Hollingshead, A. *Elmtown's Youth: The Impact of Social Classes on Adolescents.* New York: John Wiley and Sons, 1949.

Howell, F., Miracle, A., and Rees, C.   Do High School Athletics Pay? The Effects of Varsity Participation on Socioeconomic Attainment. *Sociology of Sport Journal, 1*(1984), 15-25.

Huizinga, J. *Homo Ludens: A Study of the Play Element in Culture.* Boston: Beacon Press, 1955.

Johnson, G.   Education by Plays and Games. *Pedagogical Seminary, 3*(1894), 97-135.

Johnson, G. *Education by Plays and Games.* Boston: Ginn, 1907.

Kenyon, G.   The Significance of Social Theory in the Development of Sport Sociology. In *Sport and Social Theory.* Edited by C. Rees and A. Miracle. Champaign, Illinois: Human Kinetics Press, 1986.

King, N.   Children's Play as a Form of Resistance in the Classroom. *Journal of Education, 164*(1982), 320-329.

Kleiber, D.   Limitations to Play in the Context of Sport. *Journal of Physical Education and Recreation, 50*(1979), 18-20.

Kleiber, D., and Barnett, L.   Leisure in Childhood. *Young Children, 35,* no.5(1980), 47-53.

Klonsky, B.   Reinforcement and Helping Patterns in Children's Games. In *Play and Culture.* Edited by H. Schwartzman. West Point, New York: Leisure Press, 1980.

Lancy, D.   Work and Play: The Kpelle Case. In *Play and Culture.* Edited by H. Schwartzman. West Point, New York: Leisure Press, 1980.

Landers, D., and Landers, D.   Socialization via Interscholastic Athletics: Its Effects on Delinquency. *Sociology of Education, 51*(1978), 299-303.

Laughlin, C., Jr., and McManus, J. The Biopsychological Determinants of Play and Games. In *Social Approaches to Sport*. Edited by R. Pankin. East Brunswick, NJ: Associated University Presses, 1982.

Lever, J. Sex Differences in the Games Children Play. *Social Problems, 23*(1976), 478-487.

Lever, J. Sex Differences in the Complexity of Children's Play. American *Sociological Review, 43*(1978), 471-483.

Lever, J. Multiple Methods of Data Collection: A Note on Divergence. *Urban Life, 10*(1981), 199-213.

Loy, J. The Nature of Sport: A Definitional Effort. *Quest, 10*(1968), 1-15.

Loy, J. The Cultural System of Sport. *Quest Monograph, 29*(1978), 73-102.

Lynd, R., and Lynd, H. *Middletown: A Study in Contemporary American Culture*. New York: Harcourt, Brace, 1929.

Lynd, R., and Lynd, H. *Middletown in Transition: A Study in Cultural Conflicts*. New York: Harcourt, Brace, 1937.

Manning, F. Celebrating Cricket: The Symbolic Construction of Caribbean Politics. *American Ethnologist, 83*(1981), 616-632.

Mantel, R., and Vander Velden, L. The Relationship Between the Professionalization of Attitude Toward Play of Preadolescent Boys and Participation in Organized Sport. In *Sport and American Society*. Edited by G. Sage. Reading, Massachusetts: Addison-Wesley, 1974.

McGhee, Z. A Study in the Play Life of Some South Carolina Children. *Pedagogical Seminary, 7*(1900), 459-478.

McPherson, B. Socialization Into and Through Sport. In *Handbook of Social Science of Sport*. Edited by G. Luschen and G. Sage. Champaign, Illinois: Stipes, 1981.

McPherson, B. Socialization Theory and Research: Toward a "New Wave" of Scholarly Inquiry in a Sport Context. In *Sport and Social Theory*. Edited by C. Rees and A. Miracle. Champaign, Illinois: Human Kinetics, 1986.

Mead, G. *Mind, Self, and Society. Volume I*. Chicago: University of Chicago Press, 1934.

Meier, K. On the Assiduous Re-invention of the Wheel. *The Association for the Anthropological Study of Play Newsletter, 10*(1983), 10-23.

Miller, S. Ends, Means, and Galumphing: Some Leitmotifs of Play. *American Anthropologist, 75*(1973), 87-98.

Miracle, A., Jr., Functions of School Athletics: Boundary Maintenance and System Integration. In *Play: Anthropological Perspectives.* Edited by M. Salter. West Point, New York: Leisure Press, 1978.

Miracle, A., Jr., Factors Affecting Interracial Cooperation: A Case Study of a High School Football Team. *Human Organization, 40*(1981), 150-154.

Miracle, A., Jr., Rowan, B., and Suggs, D. Play Activities and Elementary School Peer Groups. In *The Masks of Play.* Edited by B. Sutton-Smith and D. Kelly-Byrne. Oakland: Leisure Press, 1984.

Miracle, A., Jr., and Suggs, D. Studying Friendship Among Elementary School Students: A Comparison of Three Approaches. Paper presented at the 80th annual meeting of the American Anthropological Association, Washington, D.C., December, 1981.

Norbeck, E. The Anthropological Study of Human Play. *Rice University Studies, 60*, no. 3 (Summer,1974), 1-8.

Norbeck, E. The Biological and Cultural Significance of Human Play: An Anthropological View. *Journal of Physical Education and Recreation, 50*(1979), 33-36.

Okihiro, N. Extracurricular Participation, Educational Destinies, and Early Job Outcomes. In *Sport and the Sociological Imagination.* Edited by N. Theberge and P. Donnelly. Fort Worth: Texas Christian University Press, 1984.

Otto, L., and Alwin, D. Athletics, Aspirations, and Attainments. *Sociology of Education, 42*(1977), 102-113.

Parman, S. An Evolutionary Theory of Dreaming and Play. In *Forms of Play of Native North Americans.* Edited by E. Norbeck and C. Farrer. St. Paul, Minnesota: West, 1979.

Parrot, S. Games Children Play: Ethnography of a Second-Grade Recess. In *The Cultural Experience: Ethnography in Complex Society.* Edited by J. Spradley and D. McCurdy. Chicago: Science Research Associates, Inc., 1972.

Philips, J., and Schafer, W. Consequences of Participation in Interscholastic Sports: A Review and Prospectus. *Pacific Sociological Review, 14*(1971), 328-338.

Podilchak, W. Youth Sport Involvement: Impact on Informal Game Participation. In *Studies in the Sociology of Sport.* Edited by A. Dunleavy, A.

Miracle, and C. Rees. Fort Worth: Texas Christian University Press, 1982.

Polgar, S. The Social Context of Games: Or When is Play not Play? *Sociology of Education, 49*(1976), 256-271.

Polgar, S. Modeling Social Relations in Cross-Color Play. *Anthropology and Education Quarterly, 9*(1978), 283-289.

Precourt, W. Basketball, Social Structure, and Cultural Transmission in an Appalachian Community. Paper read at the annual meeting of the American Anthropological Association, Washington, D.C., November, 1976.

Rees, C. Motivation-Hygiene Theory and Sport Participation--Finding Room for the "I" in "Team." In *Sport Psychology: An Analysis of Athlete Behavior, 2nd ed.* Edited by W. Straub. Ithaca, New York: Mouvement Publications, 1980.

Rees, C. Hammond, R., and Woodruff, J. Does the Referee Make a Difference?: An Observational Study of a "Truly" American Game Form. In *The Many Faces of Play.* Edited by K. Blanchard. Champaign Illinois: Leisure Press, 1986.

Rees, C., and Miracle, A., Jr., Participation in Sport and the Reduction of Racial Prejudice: Contact Theory, Superordinate Goals Hypothesis or Wishful Thinking? In *Sport and the Sociological Imagination.* Edited by N. Therbege and P. Donnelly. Fort Worth: Texas Christian University Press, 1984.

Rehberg, R., and Schafer, W. Participation in Interscholastic Athletics and College Expectations. *The American Journal of Sociology, 73*(1968), 732-740.

Roberts, J., Arth, M., and Bush, R. Games in Culture. *American Anthropologist, 61*(1959), 597-605.

Roberts, J., and Sutton-Smith, B. Child Training and Game Involvement. *Ethnology, 1*(1962), 166-185.

Robinson, C. The Uses of Order and Disorder in Play: An Analysis of Vietnamese Refugee Children's Play. In *Play: Anthropological Perspectives.* Edited by M. Salter. West Point, New York: Leisure Press, 1978.

Rose, A. Toward Understanding the Concept and Function of Play. *Educational Theory, 6*(1956), 20-25.

Rowan, B., and Miracle, A, Jr.   Systems of Ability Grouping and the Stratification of Achievement in Elementary Schools.   *Sociology of Education, 56*(1983), 133-144.

Sage, G.   Sport and American Society: The Quest for Success.   In *Sport in American Society.*   Edited by G. Sage.   Reading, Massachusetts: Addison-Wesley, 1980.

Scarfe, N.   Play is Education.   *Childhood Education 39*(1962), 117-121.

Schafer, W.   Participation in Interscholastic Athletics and Delinquency: A Preliminary Study.   *Social Problems, 17*(1969), 40-47.

Schwartzman, H.   *Transformations: The Anthropology of Children's Play.*   New York: Plenum Press, 1978.

Seagoe, M.   Children's Play as an Indicator of Cross-Cultural and Intra-Cultural Differences.   *The Journal of Educational Sociology, 35*(1962), 278-283.

Seagoe, M., and Murakami, K.   A Comparative Study of Children's Play in America and Japan.   *California Journal of Educational Research, 12*(1961), 124-130.

Segrave, J., and Hastad, D.   Interscholastic Athletic Participation and Delinquent Behavior: An Empirical Assessment of Relevant Variables. *Sociology of Sport Journal, 1*(1984), 117-137.

Service, E.   *Primitive Social Organization.*   New York: Random House, 1962.

Sieber, R.   Classmates as Workmates: Informal Peer Activity in the Elementary School.   *Anthropology and Education Quarterly, 10*(1979), 207-235.

Smith, W.   *Constructive School Discipline.*   New York: American Book, 1924.

Snyder, E.   Aspects of Socialization in Sports and Physical Education.   *Quest Monograph, 14*(1970), 1-7.

Snyder, E.   A Theoretical Analysis of Academic and Athletic Roles.   *Sociology of Sport Journal, 2*(1985), 210-217.

Snyder, E., and Spreitzer, E.   Participation in Sport as Related to Educational Expectations Among High School Girls.   *Sociology of Education, 50*(1977), 47-55.

Snyder, E., and Spreitzer, E.   Sport, Education and Schools.   In *Handbook of Social Science of Sport.*   Edited by G. Luschen and G. Sage.   Champaign, Illinois: Stipes, 1981.

Spady, W.   Lament for the Letterman: Effects of Peer Status and Extracurricular Activities on Goals and Achievement. *The American Journal of Sociology, 75*(1970), 680-702.

Spreitzer, E., and Pugh, M.   Interscholastic Athletics and Educational Expectations. *Sociology of Education, 46*(1973), 171-182.

Spring, J.   Mass Culture and School Sports. *History of Education Quarterly, 14*(1974), 483-498.

Stevens, P., Jr.   Laying the Groundwork for an Anthropology of Play.   In *Studies in the Anthropology of Play: Papers in Memory of B. Allan Tindall.*   Edited by P. Stevens, Jr. West Point, New York: Leisure Press, 1977.

Stevens, P., Jr.   Play and Work: A False Dichotomy?   In *Play and Culture.*   Edited by H. Schwartzman. West Point, New York: Leisure Press, 1980.

Suggs, D.   An Ethnographic Approach to the Ecology of Fourth-Grade Peer Groups.   Unpublished M.A. thesis, Texas Christian University, 1981.

Sullenger, T., Parke, L., and Wallin, W.   The Leisure Time Activities of Elementary School Children: A Survey of the Packing House Area of Omaha.   *Journal of Educational Research, 46*(1953), 551-554.

Sutton-Smith, B.   Play as Adaptive Potentiation.   In *Studies in the Anthropology of Play: Papers in Memory of B. Allan Tindall.*   Edited by P. Stevens, Jr.   West Point, New York: Leisure Press, 1977.

Talamini, J.   School Athletics: Public Policy Versus Practice.   In *Sport and Society.*   Edited by J. Talamini and C. Page.   Boston: Little, Brown, 1973.

Thirer, J., and Wright, S.   Sport and Social Status for Adolescent Males and Females.   *Sociology of Sport Journal, 2*(1985), 164-171.

Tindall, B.   Exploration of a "Troublesome Agenda" Based on the Non-Sharing of "Property-Like Information."   Paper presented at the 72nd annual meeting of the American Anthropological Association, New Orleans, Louisiana, November, 1973.

Tipps, S.   Play and the Brain: Relationships and Reciprocity.   *Journal of Research and Development in Education, 14*, no. 3(1981), 19-29.

Turner, V.   Liminal to Liminoid, in Play, Flow, and Ritual: An Essay in Comparative Symbology.   *Rice University Studies, 60*(1974), 53-92.

Turner, V.   Carnaval in Rio: Dionysian Drama in an Industrializing Society.   In *The Celebration of Society: Perspectives on Contemporary Cultural Performance.*

Edited by F. Manning. Bowling Green, Ohio: Bowling Green University Popular Press, 1984.

Volberding, E. Out-of-School Behavior of Eleven-Year-Olds. *The Elementary School Journal, 48*(1948), 432-441.

Waller, W. *The Sociology of Teaching.* New York: John Wiley and Sons, 1932.

Weilbacher, R. The Effects of Static and Dynamic Play Environments on Children's Social and Motor Behaviors. In *Play as Context.* Edited by A. Cheska. West Point, New York: Leisure Press, 1981.

Whiting, B., and Whiting, J. *Children of Six Cultures: A Psycho-Cultural Analysis.* Cambridge, Massachusetts: Harvard University Press, 1975.

Wyatt, D. Pick-Up Basketball: A Case Study of Clique Behavior Variation. Paper presented at the 75th annual meeting of the American Anthropological Association, Washington, D.C., November, 1976.

PLAY IN SCHOOLS AND SCHOOLED IN PLAY:
A PSYCHOLOGICAL PERSPECTIVE

Debra J. Pepler

While children's play has been of long-standing interest to psychologists, there has been a recent increase in the study of play. Rubin, Fein, and Vandenberg (1983), for example, cite approximately 450 different journal articles, books, and conference presentations in their exhaustive review of the psychological literature on children's play; more than half of these were produced after 1975.

This sudden upsurge in the psychological study of play may be related to a rediscovery of how a phenomenon once considered to be developmentally trivial and psychologically irrelevant (Montessori, 1973; Schlosberg, 1947) can actually play a major role in development (Pepler and Rubin, 1982). The Piagetian (1962) view that play reflects "pure assimilation and egocentrism" has been translated into the view that play provides a psychometrically useful reflection of the development of symbolic thinking (e.g., Fenson and Ramsay, 1980; Rubin and Pepler, 1980). Play is currently viewed as consolidating and strengthening newly learned schemas (e.g., Bruner, 1972; Fein, 1979) and as directly eliciting advances in cognitive, social and social-cognitive development (e.g., Burns and Brainerd, 1979; Saltz and Brodie, 1982). This review will examine the psychology of children's school play from this burgeoning developmental perspective.

DEFINING PLAY

Before proceeding with a discussion of play, it has almost become ritual to ponder on certain definitional difficulties. The distinction has been made between exploration and play (e.g., Hutt, 1982; Weisler and McCall, 1976), and many criteria have been considered in the definition of play, including flexibility, positive affect (i.e., pleasurable), nonliterality (i.e., an "as if" or pretend quality), intrinsic motivation (i.e., engaged in for its own sake), attention to means rather than ends (i.e., more concern for the activity than for the outcome) and active engagement (e.g., Ellis, 1973; Krasnor and Pepler, 1980; Rubin, Fein, and Vandenberg, 1983). As yet, there is no consensus on the specific criteria that define play and provide clear distinctions for research. Sutton-Smith and Kelly-Byrne criticize that "...researchers have been more inclined to give the concept support than to define it carefully" (1984, p.29). Faced with the difficulty of defining play, many researchers have avoided the issue and have examined play activity, broadly classified, as it relates to development.

Recently, the problem of providing an *a priori* operational definition of play has been circumvented by moving to empirical tests of judgments of play after experimentation and observation. With this approach, the experimental results are available to guide the categorization of behavior.

This new line of research has been based on the assumption that observers can judge instances of play behavior as play. Matthews and Matthews (1982), for example, addressed the definition of play with a "paradigm case approach." In their study, observers were shown prototypical instances of fantasy play behavior and were subsequently instructed to judge instances of behavior as play if they could say, "This is a case of play, if anything is." Matthews and Matthews found high interobserver agreement in judgments.

Smith and Vollsted (1985) advanced the search for a definition of play by empirically testing a model proposed by Krasnor and Pepler (1980) which postulated that play was best predicted by the observed presence of a combination of defining criteria. Adults were asked to view videotapes of preschool children's play and to note five commonly cited criteria for play. They found that judgments of the occurrence of nonliterality, positive affect, flexibility and attention to means, rather than ends were related to judgments of the occurrence of play. In addition, they found that the more criteria that occurred simultaneously in a child's activity, the more certain were observers in their judgments. Smith and Vollsted concluded that the occurrence of any two of nonliterality, positive affect, and flexibility predicts a judgment of play with near certainty. Apparently, play is typically recognized by untrained observers as being enjoyable, flexible, and frequently characterized by pretend.

Research, such as that of Matthews and Matthews (1982) and Smith and Vollsted (1985), provides a beginning to the search for an empirically based definition of play. It suggests that observers can judge when children are playing, which is the first step in assessing play behaviors as a reflection of development. As we shall see, such initial assessments have important implications for educators and others working with children at play.

THEORETICAL PERSPECTIVES ON CHILDREN'S PLAY

The theoretical inquiry into children's play is more than a century old. Excellent reviews and critiques of play theory can be found in Ellis (1973), Rubin (1982), Rubin, Fein, and Vandenberg (1983), and Sutton-Smith and Kelly-Byrne (1984). Rather than reiterate these reviews in this chapter, I will examine play theories along the dimensions of concern to developmental psychologists. The objectives of developmental psychologists studying play have been to determine: (1) *how children play* (i.e., how they play at different ages; how play reflects developmental stages and sex differences); (2) *why children play as they do* (i.e., what is their motivation to play; how social and non-social environmental factors shape play); and (3) *what impact, if any, play has on children's development* (i.e., does play merely reflect development or does it actually facilitate or enhance it).

How Do Children Play?

The first area of theoretical concern has been to identify qualitative differences in children's play that reflect different developmental stages. Rubin (1982) notes that the proposed hierarchy of play from elementary sensorimotor activity to fantasy play and games with rules originated from descriptions of play by Schiller (1954), Spencer (1873), and Gross (1898, 1901). This and sub-sequently proposed hierarchies presume a linear progression of stages in children's play behavior.

Piaget (1962) proposed a sequence of cognitive complexity from practice play to symbolic play and finally to games with rules. Smilansky (1968) elaborated on Piaget's classification and proposed the progression of cognitive play from functional play to constructive play to dramatic play and finally games with rules. A developmental hierarchy was also proposed for social play by Parten (1932). The social play sequence began with unoccupied behavior and progressed through solitary, parallel, associative, and cooperative play.

Developmental change in play has been one of the primary focuses of play research, and developmental cognitive and social hierarchies have provided the bases for a large number of studies examining age-related changes in children's play. In general, these studies have found that children's play reflects some cognitive and social differences marking developmental changes. Where age differences have been demonstrated, the results tend to support the cognitive hierarchies (e.g., Rubin, Maioni, and Hornung, 1976). The social hierarchy, however, has been called into question. The controversy centers around the interpretation of solitary and parallel play as relatively immature social behaviors. Research indicates that solitary play may be cognitively complex and that children may alternate between solitary and group play rather than proceeding from solitary play through parallel play to group play (e.g., Moore, Evertson, and Brophy, 1974; Rubin, 1982; Smith, 1978).

Why Do Children Play?

A number of classical theories have focused on the motivation of children to play. Their basic assumption is that play is instinctual and that children are predisposed to play. This predisposition has been explained in several ways. For example, the surplus energy theory (e.g., Groos, 1898) proposed that individuals played to dissipate energy not required for survival. In contrast, the relaxation theory (e.g., Patrick, 1916) proposed that individuals played as a result of a need to recuperate from survival activities. These and other classical theories have been criticized on a number of grounds as inadequate explanations for why children play. (For a detailed critique of classical and modern play theories, see Ellis, 1973.)

Modern play theories have also addressed the question of why children play from a biological basis. For example, in his arousal theory of play, Berlyne (1960) proposed that individuals play to achieve an optimal level of arousal: either to decrease arousal and the level of uncertainty or to increase arousal and avoid boredom. Ellis (1973) also cited arousal levels as a motivating factor in play, but in his stimulus-seeking theory, he suggested that individuals play to increase their arousal to optimal levels and glean the optimal level of information from the environment. There has been little research, however, to substantiate or refute these modern theories because levels of arousal as they affect play are extremely difficult to study.

No classical or modern theories specifically address the situational factors that affect play. However, Darvill (1982) did adapt the "general law" of Lewin (1931) for a model relating play behavior and environmental factors. In examining play, Darvill notes that relations among a playing child, the play behaviors, and the play setting must be considered.

What Impact Does Play Have On Development?

A number of modern psychological theories have been presented to explain the link between children's play and cognitive, linguistic, and social development. An examination of these theories reveals five common themes regarding how play contributes to development: (1) play as investigation, (2) play as exercise, (3) play as experimentation, (4) play as a transition from concrete to abstract thought, and (5) social play and social development. The theories relating to each of these themes will now be reviewed.

1. Play as investigation.

Investigation or exploration in play is presumed to contribute to development by allowing children to discover and focus on the objects in their environment. There is a concern throughout the literature with the distinction between play and exploration (e.g., Hutt, 1982; Vandenberg, 1978). Exploration is viewed as a precursor to, rather than a form of play. Be this as it may, the postulations of how a child learns through both investigation and exploration are reviewed here because they are relevant to the discussion of play and education.

Piaget (1952) described the exploration of new objects in the fourth stage of sensorimotor development. He explained that when children are confronted with a novel object, they will try to understand the object by acting on it with each of their schemas. Piaget described the explorations of children as focusing on the object rather than on the children's own activities.

Berlyne (1965) noted that in the face of a novel or complex object, children will inspect, manipulate, and investigate the object to reduce uncertainty about it. Berlyne termed such object-directed activity as specific exploration which has the intent of asking "What is this object and what can it do?"

Hutt (1976) described the characteristic behaviors of investigation observed in her research and extended the definitions of specific and diversive exploration to apply to children's play activities. During specific exploration, which asks "What is this?", children concentrate intently as they manipulate a novel object and actively examine its properties.

In summary, the "play as investigation" position is that children develop a fuller understanding of novel objects through specific exploration or investigation. This understanding is accomplished by visual investigation, manipulation, and concentration on the object and associated activities.

2. Play as exercise.

Play is presumed to contribute to development by allowing children to exercise existing skills and intelligence. Piaget (1962) explained that children are motivated to practice in play by the joy of mastering and showing off to themselves. Piaget contended that when children are engaged in practice play, they are no longer learning or investigating. Instead, children consolidate the skills or schemas that they recently acquired by assimilating them to their own activities and repeating the new skills for their own sake. Piaget (1962) contended that this process of consolidation also occurs in imaginative play in which children reproduce what they have experienced by symbolic representation.

Following Piaget, Smilansky (1968) described the exercise mechanism in several aspects of play. During the elementary type of functional play, children repeat and imitate their manipulations and their actions. Smilansky contended that the practice element in functional play contributes to development by enabling children to gain experience that helps them to know their immediate environment and to practice and learn their physical capabilities. Similarly, through make-believe play, children are able to practice and improve their understanding of representations and roles.

Montessori (1967) also considered the repetitive element of play as a means to consolidate existing intelligence. Montessori described the process underlying a child's play activities as "...working out, [and] making conscious something that his unconscious mind has earlier absorbed" (p.27). During repetitive activities, children practice skills of attention, comparison and judgment. Hence, exercise in play may serve to develop an awareness of the things that children have absorbed by repetition of the experience.

Hutt (1982) described exercise in play as perseverative when an activity is repeated without the introduction of novel elements. She noted that this exercise component of play does not always facilitate development. She stated: "Indeed by being repetitive, play is by definition a highly redundant activity and can usually prevent learning" (1976, p.212). According to Hutt, learning takes place primarily through investigative exploration, hence involvement in playful activities might distract a child from more purposeful exploration. In this respect Hutt agrees with Piaget and Montessori that playful exercise may reinforce acquired skills but does not contribute to new aspects of development.

Bruner (1972), in comparison, recognized a developmental function of practice play in which children exercise the components of a skill. Bruner postulated that the components of a skill are gradually mastered and then require only minimal attention when the skill is performed. Bruner called this process modularization. Attention to the components of a skill is freed after playful practice. These components can be subsequently combined into more complex units which can, in turn, be modularized with practice. This type of practice, which often occurs in play, gradually provides a complex response system that operates smoothly when the child is confronted with a problem.

In summary, the "play as exercise" position is that play involves practice and reproduction; manipulation, imitation, repetition; and attention, comparison, and judgment. There is a disagreement among theorists, however, about the contribution of such exercise development. Montessori (1967) and Piaget (1962) contended that exercise in play does not contribute to new learning but merely consolidates existing motor and mental abilities. Hutt (1982) even suggested that play may prevent learning. Bruner (1972), in contrast, argued in favor of a developmental function of play since children can withdraw focused attention from capacities being exercised and can learn to integrate skills in a pattern.

3. Play as experimentation.

The third mechanism through which play is presumed to contribute to development is by the experimental and flexible nature of play activities. The experimental component of play stems from play as exercise and investigation. Once children have mastered a skill or discovered the properties of an object, they begin to experiment with the action or the object. This experimentation in play is purported to contribute to variability (Sutton-Smith, 1975) and flexibility (Bruner, 1972; 1973) in children's responses.

Experimentation in play is a more advanced activity than the specific investigation of an object. Piaget (1952) noted that experimentation develops from investigation when children repeat movements but vary them slightly to discover different outcomes. These experimental responses subsequently develop into playful activities.

Hutt (1982) also described the progression from investigation to experimentation when children begin to vary responses to an object. She called this diversive exploration, which is action- oriented and has the intent of asking: "What can I do with this object?" In specific exploration, as discussed above, children examine the properties of objects, whereas in diversive exploration, children investigate different ways of using the object. Thus diversive exploration yields information about the potential of children's responses and contributes to the variability and flexibility of these responses. Diversive exploration is characterized by a more relaxed and varied approach to the object and is a component of the mechanism of experimentation and flexibility in play.

Sutton-Smith (1975) proposed that play increases children's repertoires of responses to the environment since play is a form of "variation-seeking." Having engaged in repetitive play with a novel object, children begin to combine their behaviors with the object in a variety of ways and transform the object in imaginative play. Children develop idiosyncratic responses through play that have potentially adaptive functions for subsequent problem solving.

Finally, Smilansky (1968) also referred to the function of variability in play. In constructive play children are engaged in creative activities and thereby learn a variety of uses for play material. In sociodramatic play the variability goes beyond responses to objects and extends to experiences which are varied, combined, and replayed.

The developmental impetus of play is presumed to move from the investigation of novel objects and actions to the exercise of skills and actions with objects and finally to the extension and recombination of these behaviors. The "play as experimentation" position is that play is characterized by trial and error, chance combinations of gestures; intentionally varying responses to an object or testing an object with various routines and combining routings; and finally, forming unique responses. The benefit of this experimental mechanism in play is that it may generate a flexible response set and provide a broad repertoire of skills and routines which can be evoked for more effective problem solving.

4. Play as transition for thought.

A fourth theoretical theme is that play contributes to development by facilitating the transition from concrete to abstract thought. In Piaget's (1962) terms, the transition from sensorimotor schemes to conceptual schemes begins to occur during the second year of life. Representational thinking occurs in play when a symbol takes on the meaning of an object. Piaget noted that children's representational thought develops in close conjunction with symbolic play (assimilation) and imitation (accommodation). The symbolic representations that are produced in play (for example, pretending that a "preemie" doll is a real newborn baby) form part of the process through which children develop abstract thinking.

Vygotsky (1976) clarified the way that the transformation from concrete to abstract thought occurs. He explained that when a child pretends, for example, that a stick is a horse, the stick "becomes a pivot for severing the meaning of horse from a real horse" (Vygotsky, 1976, p.546). It is particularly in play that young children's thoughts are freed from real-life situational constraints and moved from the concrete to the abstract at an age when they may be otherwise incapable of abstract thought.

Smilansky (1968) outlined a similar mechanism in sociodramatic play that facilitates the transition from concrete to abstract thought. She described a sequence in which children first require an object to relate to a role (such as a fireman's hat to pretend being a fireman). Later children are able to pretend that they have the object and enact the designated role (i.e., pretend to put on a hat to designate a fireman). Finally, children are able to use words alone to designate the object and pretend in role-play.

Several researchers have demonstrated a developmental sequence in children's playful transformations from the concrete to abstract. Fein (1975) noted that children initially rely on prototypical objects (e.g., a car that looks like a car), but as their thinking matures, children are able to use less similar objects to symbolize another object in play (e.g., a box to signify a car). A developmental sequence was also described by Watson and Fischer (1977) in the progression from using the self as agent (e.g., being the truck driver) to using objects as agents (e.g., using a doll as the truck driver). Following

Piaget's (1962) formulation, Fenson and Ramsay (1980) discussed this progression as a reflection of decentration, which is the process of gradually becoming less dependent on acts centered on the self.

In summary, theories of "play as a transition for thought" contend that children's thinking can be severed from the concrete and moved into the abstract at an age when they are otherwise incapable of abstract thinking. The mechanism appears to be that an object acts as a pivot or support for symbolic representation. Symbolic play involves using one object to signify another and is, therefore, an elementary form of representational thought. In play, the newly formed capacity to abstract can be practiced and varied. The developmental significance of this process may lie in the opportunity it provides for the child to engage in and practice symbolic thinking, to focus beyond the obvious, and to make novel associations and mental manipulations during play and subsequent problem solving activities.

5. Social play and social development.

Many psychologists have postulated that social play, particularly social pretense, contributes to the development of social skills and social understanding. Based on her research on the sociodramatic play of Israeli children, Smilansky (1968) contended that dramatic play with other children facilitates the development of social-cognitive and social skills. She noted that in order to engage in social pretend play, children are required to utilize role-taking, empathy, sharing, and cooperation. Smilansky claimed that sociodramatic play provides the child with opportunities to exercise and consolidate these social and social-cognitive competencies. This is similar to Piaget's (1962) position, discussed above, that play allows children to practice existing skills and knowledge.

The competencies required to engage in social fantasy play were elaborated by Garvey (1977), based on her research on the sociolinguistic features of sociodramatic play. First, Garvey claimed that social fantasy play cannot occur unless children can distinguish play from reality. Second, children must be able to generate and collectively understand the rules that govern their social play. With the support and feedback from playmates in pretense, children are able to acquire, practice, and refine their understanding of social rules and roles. Examples of the social rules and roles evident in sociodramatic play can be found in a "pretend you are sick" episode cited by Garvey (1976). In this anecdote, the "sick" child momentarily forgot his role when his play partner telephoned for a doctor. The "sick" child answered the call himself. The play partner quickly replied: " No, you're not the doctor, you're sick!" and, thereby, pointed out the violation of the previously accepted roles and rules of the "pretend you are sick" game.

Several other psychologists have cited peer interaction in play as contributing to social development. The impetus appears to come from the conflict, negotiations, and compromise with peers over the rules and roles in a game. Piaget (1932) first cited the function of peer interaction in advancing social skills and understanding. He noted that in order to play formal games with rules, children are required to understand and collectively agree to very stable rules and roles.   According to Piaget, the process of solving disagreements about the rules and roles of a formal game is instrumental in lessening egocentric thought and developing social and social-cognitive competence (Piaget, 1932, 1962).

In summary, social play, particularly social pretense, is presumed to contribute to the development of social skills and social understanding. Participation in social pretend play requires cooperation, sharing, empathy, and role-taking; the ability to distinguish play from reality; and a collective understanding of rules.   By engaging in social play, children exercise and consolidate social skills and understanding and by adapting to the collective requirements of social play, children's tendency to think egocentrically is decreased.

EMPIRICAL PERSPECTIVES ON CHILDREN'S PLAY

The theoretical perspectives on children's play have laid the foundation for play research.   The studies on children's play have covered a wide variety of perspectives.   This review will be limited to the psychological research on play and, in particular, to the research which addresses the developmental issues of concern to educators.   The review will be limited, however, by the available research which is plentiful on the play of preschool and kindergarten children but scarce on the play of children in middle childhood.   The research on older children has likely been limited by the difficulty of observing children of this age in extended bouts of free play.

How Do Children Play?

The starting point for the recent state of research on children's play was to describe play.   The most common methodology for this descriptive research has been to conduct naturalistic observations of children at free play in familiar settings.   An example of a typical observational instrument is that developed by Rubin (Rubin, Maioni, and Hornung, 1976) in which the cognitive play categories of Smilansky (1968) are nested within the social play categories of Parten (1932).   The observations are conducted by first determining whether the child is engaged in play.   If the child is playing, the observer notes whether the play is functional, constructive, dramatic, or a game with rules.   The child's play is subsequently categorized according to its social context as solitary, parallel, or group play activity.   For example, a child playing alone at the water table would be classified as in functional-solitary play; a child building a tower beside another child would be classified as in constructive-parallel play, and a child playing superheroes with another child would be classified as in dramatic-group play.   This observational system is useful in that it provides the observer with a description of both the cognitive and social characteristics of play and indications of individual differences in play behaviors.

Age differences

The results of the descriptive research indicate that the proposed developmental stages are not as clear-cut as the original hierarchies suggested. The cognitive progression from functional to constructive to dramatic play and finally to games with rules (Smilansky, 1968) has been only partially confirmed. Research has shown that functional play decreases during the preschool years, whereas symbolic play increases from age three to approximately age six or seven (e.g., Fein, 1981; Rubin, Maioni, and Hornung, 1976). Piaget's postulation that symbolic play would decrease in middle childhood has not been well documented (Smith, Takhvar, and Gore, 1985). Research has also shown that the proportion of constructive play remains relatively stable over the preschool years (e.g., Rubin, Watson and Jambor, 1978), thus contradicting the prediction that constructive play is an intermediate cognitive stage between functional and dramatic play.

There has been a similar controversy about the progression in social play behaviors postulated by Parten (1932). In particular, several researchers have reported that solitary play is not necessarily an elementary form of play (e.g., Moore, Evertson and Brophy, 1974) but may represent a cognitively complex activity and/or a preference to play alone (Rubin, 1977).

Sex differences

A discussion of how children play would be incomplete without reference to the extensive literature on sex differences in children's play. A comprehensive review of the research in this area can be found in *Social and Cognitive Skills: Sex Roles and Children's Play* edited by Liss (1983). To briefly summarize, research has generally indicated consistent patterns of sex differences in preschool children's play that reflect traditional sex stereotypes. Preschool boys are more active and engage in more rough and tumble play than girls (Blurton-Jones, 1972; Di Pietro, 1981; Smith and Connolly, 1972). Few sex differences have been reported in the level of involvement in social play (e.g., Parten, 1932; Barnes, 1971), although one study indicated that boys were behind girls in this regard (Tizard, Philps and Plewis, 1976a). Similar discrepancies exist in the research on the complexity of pretense play. There is some evidence to suggest that girls are more advanced in pretend play (e.g., Fein and Robertson, 1975) and other evidence to suggest that boys are more advanced in pretense play (e.g., Rubin, Maioni, and Hornung, 1976). A more consistent pattern of sex differences is found in the type of dramatic play activities. Girls tend to prefer domestic themes and roles, whereas boys tend to engage in more active adventure themes and roles (e.g., Connolly, Doyle, and Ceschin, 1983; McLoyd, 1980).

The mixed results of the research on sex differences in children's play may be attributable to situational factors such as teacher behavior, the type of play materials available, and the ratio of girls to boys (Serbin, Connor, Burchardt, and Citron, 1979). For example, both boys and girls tend to increase their participation in sex-typed play in response to the presence of a teacher (Serbin, Conner, Burchardt, and Citron, 1979). In providing for children's play experiences, educators must be attentive to the impact of such situational variables.

Differences in playfulness

Play has been studied in relation to a variety of individual characteristics. Among these, playfulness has received the most attention. Lieberman (1965) first examined playfulness as a trait in relation to divergent thinking. She asked kindergarten teachers to rate their children on five components of playfulness: physical, social, and cognitive spontaneity; manifest joy; and sense of humor. Lieberman found strong correlations between these playfulness traits and concluded that they comprised a playfulness factor in children. These playfulness attributes were also related to three divergent thinking factors: ideational fluency (the ability to generate a large number of ideas or responses), spontaneous flexibility (the ability and disposition to vary responses), and originality (the ability to generate unique responses). In other words, those children who were rated as most playful were also most creative.

The relation between play and divergent thinking was also examined by Singer and Rummo (1973). In a factor analytic study of teacher ratings of play behaviors, they identified a playfulness factor which comprised communicative, curious, humorous, playful, and expressive attributes. These playfulness attributes were directly related to creativity for boys, but the relation between playfulness and creativity was mediated by IQ for girls. A similar relation between inventive play and diversive exploration for boys, but not for girls, was reported by Hutt and Bhavnani (1976). There is no obvious explanation for this sex difference in the relation between playfulness attributes and creativity. Additional support for an individual playfulness attribute has come from a factor analytic study of preschool children's play behavior by Singer, Singer, and Sherrod (1980). They identified a playfulness factor based on behavioral data and found that this factor was relatively stable over a one-year time period.

In summary, there is a considerable body of research describing individual differences in children's play. Age differences in the cognitive and social complexity of play have been demonstrated, but these have not completely supported the hierarchical models of Piaget (1962), Smilansky (1968), and Parten (1932). Sex differences have been observed in children's play that reflect the traditional sex stereotypes. Finally, there is a growing awareness of individual characteristics, such as playfulness, that may affect the interaction between children and their play environments.

Why Do Children Play As They Do?

The factors that affect the play of children represent a second area of concern to psychologists. Children's play environments are multidimensional, and researchers investigating the ecological effects on play must consider both the molar and molecular dimensions of the environment (Darvill, 1982). The molar dimensions of children's environments include general features such as the socioeconomic status of their families. The molecular dimensions of the play environment include general features such as the curriculum and more specific features such as the play materials, play equipment, and playmates. In the following section, the research describing the influence of these environmental factors on children's play will be reviewed.

Socioeconomic status

Socioeconomic status of the child's family is a molar environmental dimension that affects play. The first research on this dimension was Smilansky's (1968) study of Israeli children indicating that both the quantity and quality of play were related to socioeconomic status. Children from low socioeconomic backgrounds engage in sociodramatic play less frequently than their middle-class peers, and their sociodramatic play is less diverse (Griffing, 1980; Rosen, 1974; Smilansky, 1968; Smith and Dodsworth, 1978). Socioeconomic status differences in other types of play have also been documented. Children from lower- class families are more likely to engage in solitary- and parallel-functional play and less likely to engage in constructive and group dramatic play than their middle-class peers (Rubin, Maioni, and Hornung, 1976). These studies indicating that lower- class children engage in less complex cognitive levels of play have instigated research in which lower-class children are trained in sociodramatic play to increase their cognitive functioning.

Preschool curriculum

The effects of a curriculum on children's play is perhaps of greatest import to educators. Preschool curricula have been classified in a variety of ways and compared for their impact on children's play. Comparisons of curricula based on the structure or amount of direction from the teacher yield mixed results.

Huston-Stein, Freidrich-Cofer, and Susman (1977) examined the relation between classroom structure and preschool children's play and social behavior. Classroom structure was judged by the number of teacher-directed activities; ratings of the teachers' warmth, support, and discipline; and program structure. Children in highly structured classrooms engaged in less imaginative play and slightly more positive social interaction than children in less structured classrooms. Similar trends have been reported for observations of Montessori classrooms in which the play tends to be solitary or parallel constructive rather than functional or group dramatic (Rubin and Seibel, 1981). These studies suggest that in structured programs, children are less likely to participate in the more complex form of dramatic play.

There are, however, other studies that suggest the opposite. For example, Johnson, Ershler, and Bell (1980) compared a formal preschool program with a discovery program and reported that the children in the formal program engaged in more complex dramatic play than children in the discovery program although there was no difference in the quantity of dramatic play. The children in the formal program also engaged in more constructive play and less functional play as compared to children in the discovery program. Tizard, Philps and Plewis (1976b) compared children's play activities in language-enriched nursery schools and traditional nursery schools. They reported more symbolic play and dramatic role-play in the language enriched programs and more functional play in the traditional nursery programs.

Play materials and equipment

Another salient feature of the play environment is the quality and quantity of play materials available to the children. First, research indicates that certain types of toys elicit specific types of play. Observations of children's free play in preschools indicate that activities with playdough, plasticine, sand, and water are likely to be functional and non-social; activities with art materials are likely to be constructive and non-social; and activities with dress-up clothes and vehicles are likely to be dramatic and social (Rubin, 1977). One problem with such observations of children's free play is that it is difficult to determine whether the play materials elicited the identified activities or whether the children selected the play materials based on individual differences or preferences (Krasnor & Pepler, 1980).

This problem has been addressed by experimental manipulations of the types of toys available for play. Pulaski (1973) compared children's play with minimally structured materials (e.g., blocks, boxes, ragdolls) and highly structured materials (e.g., realistic play buildings, realistic dolls). The children playing with the minimally structured toys exhibited varied and inventive play, whereas the children playing with the highly structured toys generally played according to the behaviors suggested by the toys. Similar trends were reported by Pepler (1979; Pepler and Ross, 1981) who compared play activities with convergent and divergent play materials. Pepler (1979) provided children in the divergent condition with only wooden pieces (e.g., animals, vehicles); children in the convergent condition were given the wooden pieces with a formboard. Children in the divergent condition exhibited a wide range of constructive and symbolic play behaviors, whereas the children in the convergent condition generally restricted their activity to constructive behaviors directed at solving the puzzle. These studies indicate that the structural quality of play materials affects the type of cognitive play exhibited by children.

The structure of play equipment has also been found to affect the type of cognitive play exhibited by children. Frost and Campbell (1978) observed school-aged children on creative and traditional playgrounds and reported that the creative playground elicited more imaginative play, whereas the traditional playground elicited more functional play.

The availability of play materials may influence the social play of children. Some research on infants indicates that the presence of toys tends to facilitate their social play (Mueller and Brenner, 1977). On the other hand, there is evidence that social interaction between children is more likely to occur when the number of toys is limited (Bjorklund, 1979) or when there are no toys available (Eckerman and Whatley, 1977). Tizard (1977) suggested that older children might engage in more social games with rules in the absence of toys and that a surplus of toys might inhibit extended play activity. As children become more familiar with toys, they will increasingly turn to social play with peers (Scholtz and Ellis, 1975).

Characteristics of children's play partners have been shown to influence play behaviors. First, the familiarity of the play partner affects the complexity of play. Doyle, Connolly, and Rivest (1980) compared preschool children's play with familiar and unfamiliar peers and reported that dramatic play was more likely with a familiar playmate. In a similar comparison, Matthews (1978) found that unfamiliar play partners tend to rely on objects to support fantasy play and with familiarity, children rely more on their imaginations to support fantasy play.

Although a variety of studies address the influence of the age and social competence of a peer on social interaction, there are no studies that examine their effect on play behaviors in particular (Rubin, Fein, and Vanderberg, 1983). The effect of an older and more competent play partner has been examined, however, by observing the play of siblings. Dunn and Dale (1984) reported that a two-year-old can engage in joint role enactment and joint role play with a sibling at an earlier age than normally expected. Rubin, Fein, and Vandenberg (1983) suggest that an older, more socially competent play partner may be better able to initiate, organize, and maintain constructive and fantasy play and, thereby, support a younger partner at a higher cognitive and social level of play. Considerably more research is required to understand the effects of mixed-age groupings on play behavior.

In summary, there are a variety of factors that influence the play behaviors of children. The molar factor, socioeconomic status, has been found to be related to cognitive complexity in play: lower-class children engage in less mature forms of cognitive play activity. Molecular factors such as the available play materials have been shown not only to influence the way that children play with objects but also the way that children play with each other. Darvill stresses that researchers examining the complex influences of the environment on children's play must "be aware of the multidimensional nature of the environment in which children live and play" (1982, p.151). Those responsible for creating children's play environments must also consider the many environmental factors that shape children's play activities.

What Impact Does Play Have On Development?

The final body of research to be reviewed examines the effects of play on development. Theoreticians, psychologists, and educators have long held that play is important for many aspects of children's development (e.g., Bruner, 1972; Piaget, 1962; Smilansky, 1968). Until recently, however, there was a paucity of systematic research to support the causal link between play and development, and there are still many questions to be answered. Play has been studied in relation to both problem-solving and creativity, and pretend play has been specifically examined for its influence on cognitive, social-cognitive, and language skills. This research demonstrating a link between play and development led to a proliferation of play-training studies.

Play and problem-solving

One approach to studying the effects of play has been to provide children with the opportunity to play freely with materials which are later incorporated in a problem solving task. The first research of this type was conducted by Sylva, Bruner, and Genova (1976) using a lure-retrieval problem. They compared the effectiveness of three experiences: play experience with the materials required to solve the lure-retrieval problems, observation of the principle required to solve the problem, and a no-treatment condition. The group with play experience was as proficient at solving the problem as those who had observed the principle and superior to those with no experience. Sylva, Bruner, and Genova reported that children in the play group were persistent and systematic in their problem-solving efforts and did not give up as easily as children in the other conditions. The authors suggested that the superior performance of the children with previous play experience was attributable to the child's activities in play being self-initiated, the opportunity to explore alternative ordering of activities in play, and the focus on means rather than ends in play.

Two other studies have extended the research of Sylva, Bruner, and Genova (1976). Vandenberg (1981) examined a larger age range and variable difficulty tasks and found a similar difference in task performance in favor of a group with play experience, as compared to instructional experience. Smith and Dutton (1979) extended the play versus training paradigm to direct and innovative problem-solving. When the training session related directly to the task of joining two sticks together, the play and training groups were equivalent in their problem-solving performances, and both were superior to a control group. On a more complex task of joining three sticks together, which had not been directly taught to the training group, the play group performed better than both the training and control groups, indicating that play experience may be beneficial for a task that requires innovative transfer.

The link between play and problem-solving was approached with a different paradigm by Pepler (1979; Pepler and Ross, 1981) who examined the effects of play on convergent problem-solving (to a single solution) and divergent problem-solving (to a variety of solutions). Preschool children were provided with one of two types of play experience: play with convergent materials (those that tend to direct play to a single solution, in this case, puzzle-solving) or play with divergent materials (those that facilitate a variety of play activities). Children with play experience were compared to children who had observed or experienced a non-play control condition. The results indicated that children who played with divergent materials performed better on a divergent problem-solving task than the children who played with the convergent materials or the children in the control conditions. The children who played with the convergent materials demonstrated a higher proportion of strategy-based moves in solving the convergent problems but only when the problem- solving task was closely related to the convergent play experience.

A comparison of the effects of play with convergent and divergent materials suggested that the effects of convergent play experiences were very specific, whereas the divergent play experiences transferred more generally. Children who had played with the divergent materials were more flexible and unique in their responses to divergent problems and also appeared to be more flexible in convergent problem-solving by abandoning ineffective strategies.

Play and creativity

Another research direction has been to examine the effect of play on divergent problem-solving or creativity (Dansky, 1980; Dansky and Silverman, 1973, 1975; Li, 1978). These studies emanated from the research of Sutton-Smith (1968), which indicated that children were able to give more alternate uses for toys with which they liked to play. Dansky and Silverman (1973) investigated the effects of play on performance on a divergent, alternate uses table with the play objects. Children who had play experience were superior to an imitation and a control group on the number of nonstandard uses of the objects. In subsequent studies, this result was replicated using different objects in the play and task situations, suggesting that the effects of play generalize to solving problems with unfamiliar objects (Dansky and Silverman, 1975; Li, 1978). Research indicates that fantasy play may be essential to facilitate divergent problem-solving. Li (1978) found that a group directed in make-believe performed better than a free-play group in naming diverse uses for a novel object. In addition, Dansky (1980) found that the beneficial effects of free play were limited to children who typically engaged in make-believe play in school.

Pretend play - a special case

Dansky's, Dansky and Silverman's, and Li's results suggest that the skill required to generate a variety of novel responses on a creativity task may be similar to the cognitive skill of shifting one's thinking from the concrete to the abstract during make-believe play (Johnson, 1976; Singer and Rummo, 1973). Such research as this has elicited special attention to the role of pretend play in development.

Pretend play has been reputed to contribute to a wide variety of developmental outcomes including communicative and sex-role development, cooperation, perspective-taking, creativity, operational thinking, and social problem-solving skills (Rubin, Fein, and Vandenberg, 1983). The theoretical bases for these contributions are: (1) that play, and pretend play in particular, facilitates the transition from concrete to abstract thought and (2) that social play activities enhance social development.

Many of the postulated links between pretend play and development have been supported by research. For example, significant relationships have been found between pretend play and language comprehension (e.g., Fein, 1979b; McCune-Nicolich, 1981), cooperation (e.g., Connolly and Doyle, 1984), perspective-taking (e.g., Rubin and Maioni, 1975), creativity (e.g., Johnson, 1976; Dansky, 1980), and conservation (e.g., Emmerich, and Sigel, 1979). The weakness of these and other correlational results, as Hutt (1977) cautioned, is that it is impossible to determine whether the pretend play experience causes the developmental change or whether a common style or set of skills creates the relations between children's pretend play and developmental indices.

Play training

To test the hypothesis that pretend play causes the development of cognitive, social-cognitive, and language skills, psychologists have employed the "play training" paradigm. This research originated from the work of Smilansky (1968) which indicated that disadvantaged children engaged in less group pretend play than expected for their age. Smilansky used play training to increase the sociodramatic play of these disadvantaged children.

In the typical play training paradigm, preschool or kindergarten children are randomly assigned to experimental and control groups. The experimental group meets with an adult tutor on a regular basis to learn how to engage and sustain social pretense activities. The pretense activities are related either to everyday experiences (sociodramatic) or the enactment of fairy tales (thematic). The control group does not receive play training but, in some cases, meets with an adult to engage in construction activities. The amount of play training varies from three sessions (Golomb and Cornelius, 1977) to three sessions per week for six months (Saltz, Dixon, and Johnson, 1977).

The results of the play training studies indicate that the frequency of group pretend play increases significantly more for the play training group as compared to the control groups (e.g., Feitelson and Ross, 1973; Rosen, 1974; Saltz and Johnson, 1974; Saltz, Dixon, and Johnson, 1977; Smith and Syddall, 1978). There are some data to indicate that play training in thematic fantasy (fairy tales) is more effective in increasing group pretend play than training in sociodramatic fantasy (everyday themes) (Saltz, Dixon, and Johnson, 1977).

This research has been extended to examine other consequences of play training based on the theoretical assumption that symbolic or pretense play facilitates the transition from the concrete to the abstract. It was reasoned that if play training increased pretense activities, it might also promote advancement in cognitive and social-cognitive skills. This was substantiated by a variety of play training studies that found changes in the following cognitive, social, and social-cognitive skills: intellectual performance (Saltz and Johnson, 1974), vocabulary and language development (Lovinger, 1974; Saltz, Dixon, and Johnson, 1977); sequential thinking (Saltz, Dixon, and Johnson, 1977); conservation (Golomb and Cornelius, 1977); cognitive perspective-taking (Burns and Brainerd, 1979; Rosen, 1974; Smith and Syddall, 1978); creativity (Feitelson and Ross, 1973); affective perspective-taking (Burns and Brainerd, 1979; Saltz and Johnson, 1974), impulse control (Saltz and Johnson, 1974; Saltz, Dixon, and Johnson, 1977); and cooperation (Rosen, 1974; Smith and Syddall, 1978).

In summary, although the research demonstrating a link between play and development is still in its infancy, some links have been demonstrated.

Studies on play and problem solving indicate that the effects of play with structured materials may be limited to similar activities whereas the effects of play with unstructured materials may be more general. Similarly, children provided with unstructured play experiences were able to generate more creative responses compared to children with non-play experiences. Some of the research linking play and creativity demonstrated the particular benefits of pretend play in facilitating creative thinking. Other research has supported the link between pretend play and cognitive, social, and language skills. Finally, play training studies have been conducted to test specifically the causal link between pretend play and development; play training was shown to improve a number of skills. The results of the research on play and development should be considered cautiously, however, since there are a number of methodological concerns with this type of research that will be discussed in the following section.

CRITIQUES OF AND FUTURE DIRECTIONS FOR PLAY RESEARCH

The psychological research on children's play has covered a wide range of developmental interests and has begun to answer questions about the nature of children's play and the impact of play on development. The verdict is not yet in on the educational import of children's play. There are methodological problems with the current research paradigms, and there are inconsistencies in the results of various studies. An examination of these problems and inconsistencies should indicate the requisite future directions for research on children's play.

Observational Research On Children's Play

Observing children's play is a complex business; consequently, there are several methodological issues that must be considered for observational research on children's play. First, the time frames have varied considerably among play studies, introducing unknown biases. The time sampling method chosen must be appropriate to the objectives of the research. If a time sample is relatively short (say, 60 seconds), the complexity of the child's play may be underestimated (Krasnor and Pepler, 1980). On the other hand, if the time frame is long, the data will be less independent and difficult to analyze statistically (Smith, Takhvar, and Gore, 1985). A second problem is posed by the difficulty of inferring the imaginary features of play by simply observing the child's behavior. To overcome this difficulty, some researchers have conducted painstaking analyses of children's verbalizations during play to capture any imaginary references. This approach, however, does not completely solve the problem since much imaginative activity takes place inside the child's head and is, thereby, inaccessible to the researcher. Smith, Takhvar, and Gore (1985) have attempted to address this problem by adopting a technique from play therapy and interviewing the child after a play episode to provide richer detail on the imaginary features of play activity. Smith and his colleagues are to be commended for conducting systematic research to address both the methodological and definitional problems plaguing play research. More research of this nature is required to determine the most appropriate methods for identifying and observing spontaneous and complex play behavior.

Research On Ecological Effects On Children's Play

Naturalistic observations of children's play have also been conducted to determine the molar and molecular ecological factors that influence children's play. Socioeconomic status has been cited as one such molar factor. Children from lower- class backgrounds were found to engage in less complex play than their middle-class peers. The research that indicated a developmental lag or deficit in the play of lower-class children has been criticized by Rubin, Fein, and Vandenberg (1983). They suggest that children from lower-class backgrounds may not have a developmental lag but may engage in more elementary exploration and functional play because they are unfamiliar with the materials in a school setting. The children's lack of familiarity with the school setting may also make them more anxious and, therefore, less likely to engage in complex play. Rubin and his colleagues recommend that future research in this area control for: the cultural and familial backgrounds of the children, familiarity with school materials, previous school experience and preference for settings.

Some research on the ecological effects of molecular variables such as the type of play materials and the type of preschool curriculum has also failed to consider all the intervening environmental factors. This may, for example, account for the discrepancies in curricular effects on play. The effects of the educational environment on children's play require further research to address the interaction among variables. For example, the teacher's role in promoting or discouraging certain types of play may comprise a major part of the curricular effects. The types of materials available for play in a preschool curricula should also be documented since they are known to influence the cognitive and social dimensions of play. It is apparent that we have just begun to unravel the complexities of a child's play environment.

Research on Play and Development

Studies of children's play in a more controlled experimental setting have been conducted to avoid some of the difficulties of observing in complex naturalistic settings. The experimental paradigm has been most frequently used in research on the effects of play on problem-solving and creativity. This research has been criticized, however, for methodological problems of design, experimenter bias, and ecological validity (cf. Cheyne, 1982; Rubin, Fein, and Vandenberg, 1983; Smith and Simon, 1984 for incisive critiques of the methodological issues). In light of these criticisms, conclusions about the beneficial effects of spontaneous play on convergent problem-solving are premature, and conclusions about the effects of play on divergent problem-solving and creativity should be tentative.

Several recommendations and directions have been suggested for future research on the contribution of play to development. Since children's play is seldom a one-shot 10 to 15 minute experience, the research should incorporate more repetitions of experimental play sessions to improve ecological validity (Smith and Simon, 1984). In addition, to improve the relevance of research to everyday life, the conditions and tasks should be appropriate to the play and/or educational activities of children (Smith and Simon, 1984). More data should be gathered on the children's behaviors during the play and problem-solving sessions to provide information on the mechanisms that underlie any effect of play on problem-solving. The research on the effects of play should be extended to include older children (Rubin, Fein, and Vandenberg, 1983). Finally, play should not be considered as a unitary construct (Rubin, Fein, and Vandenberg, 1983). Research should continue to examine the relations between specific types of play (e.g., make-believe) and specific developmental outcomes (e.g., more flexible problem-solving).

Play Training Research

Studies using a play-training paradigm have produced an impressive list of skills showing improvement. These include: intellectual perfor-mance, vocabulary and language development, sequential thinking, conservation, perspective-taking, creativity, impulse control, and coop-eration. There are, however, several problems with this research that cast doubt on the strength of the causal effects of pretend play.

First, the children's exposure to the experimenter and, therefore, familiarity and rapport with the experimenter have not been equivalent for the experimental and control groups in some studies (Saltz and Brodie, 1982). For example, Rosen's experimental group was given 40 training sessions, whereas the control group met with the adult for only 10 sessions. Such a discrepancy raises questions of an attention effect that might have contributed to the advantage of the group receiving play training. Other studies, however, have controlled for an attention effect and demonstrated superior performance by the group receiving play training.

A second problem is that play training involves a high level of verbal stimulation for the children that might not be present for comparison groups such as a construction group (Smith and Syddall, 1978). The verbal stimulation received by the play training group, not the experience in pretense activities, may account for the improvement in intellectual and language functioning. Smith and Syddall(1978) conducted an experiment to examine this alternative hypothesis and found that when verbal stimulation was equated for a play training and a skills training group, there were no differences in intellectual performance although the play training group performed better on role-taking measures.

A third problem with this research is the inconsistency across studies of effects following sociodramatic play training (Brainerd, 1982). For example, Burns and Brainerd (1979) reported gains in affective perspective-taking in favor of a sociodramatic play training group, whereas Saltz, Dixon, and Johnson (1977) did not find this improvement in affective perspective-taking following sociodramatic play training. The effects of play training studies on perspective-taking are also difficult to compare and assess because of problems with some measures of perspective-taking (Rubin, 1980).

Finally, Brainerd (1982) identified three other concerns with the results of play training studies. He noted that the effects of play training within a study are sometimes inconsistent. For example, in a study that he conducted (Burns and Brainerd, 1979), play training elicited superior performance in one of two cognitive tasks and one of two affective tasks. Brainerd (1982) also noted that the improvement of the play training group, although significantly greater than that of the comparison group, is often quite small. Finally, Brainerd (1982) voiced concern that play training is sometimes more effective with kindergarten children than with preschool children. He suggested that the play training learning effect may actually be a performance effect: the kindergarten children make fewer performance errors following exposure to the experimental conditions.

The methodological problems and inconsistencies in the results of the play training studies elicit cautious conclusions. Although Brainerd (1982) laments that the pretend play training studies have not produced results that justify its adoption, its applications for education have been suggested. These have been based on the presumed causal link between pretense play and cognitive, social and social-cognitive development and the relative success of the play training studies. Among others, Saltz (Saltz and Brodie, 1982) and Singer (1973) have recommended that similar teacher-directed group pretense activities be incorporated into the preschool and kindergarten curricula. Rubin (1980) was more cautious in concluding that children enjoy pretend play with peers, pretend play reflects perspective-taking and other cognitive skills, and pretend play training seems to be pleasurable, productive, and didactive.

Play and Learning?

In light of the growing body of research on the effects of play on development, it is important to note that there is a controversy as to whether learning, particularly social learning, actually occurs during play. According to a number of psychologists (e.g., Garvey and Berndt, 1977; Rubin, 1980) social play is "framed" or punctuated by negotiations required to initiate play activity and conflicts that pull the players out of the play picture and back to the real world. The argument, therefore, is that any learning or adaptation that occurs during such peer interaction takes place outside the play frame during these negotiations, conflicts, and compromises. Hence, it cannot be said that play itself contributes to social development since it is the social interaction required to support play that enhances social learning. Whether social and social-cognitive learning actually take place within the play frame or outside it appears to be a moot point for educators. What is important to note is that social play and its associated activities have beneficial consequences for children and there is considerable research to support this position.

IMPLICATIONS AND APPLICATIONS OF PLAY RESEARCH FOR EDUCATION

This review of psychological theories and research on children's play highlights many aspects of children's play environments that influence play activities and indicates relations between play and cognitive, social, and social-cognitive develop-ment. The task now facing us is to step back from the theories and research to consider the implications and applications of the ecological effects and the presumed link between play and development.

Before proceeding with a discussion of the role of play in schools, the expectations for play must be clarified. While some might propose that play is the best medium for learning, particularly during the preschool years, this is not my stance. Play researchers have not set out to prove that play is the best way to learn problem-solving skills, perspective-taking, or other competencies but to ascertain whether the spontaneous play of children contributes to their development. This process has involved first understanding the nature of play, then examining the factors that shape the play experience, and finally demonstrating the links between play and development. Our task is far from complete. We have begun to understand the nature of play and its developmental underpinnings, and we have begun to understand the environmental effects on play activities. The investigation of the function of play has barely begun, but we are beginning to see where some of the answers may lie (Cheyne, 1982).

What, then, can we tell educators about play? The extant research seems to have implications for: (1) observing the play of children as a reflection of their development; (2) designing the environment to enhance play activities; and (3) providing children with the opportunity to learn through play.

Play as a Reflection of Development

The cognitive and social play hierarchies (Parten, 1932; Piaget, 1962; Smilansky, 1968) were developed to reflect changes in the nature of play over the childhood years. Piaget (1962), in particular, described the cognitive processes that were reflected in the play of children from infancy through middle childhood. The research on how children play has contributed further to the understanding of the changing nature of play as a reflection of development. An application that has emerged from this research is the assessment of development through observations of play. For example, given that symbolic play and language are both dependent on the development of representational capacities, McCune-Nicolich and Fenson (1984) suggest that symbolic play may be a valuable tool for assessment and intervention with language-delayed children. They illustrate this application with a comparison of two language-delayed children, one with age-appropriate symbolic play and the other with a lag in symbolic play. McCune-Nicolich and Fenson suggest that the first child requires language training, whereas the second child may need another form of cognitive intervention to address the more general deficit in representational capacities. They suggest that, in this case, symbolic play training may be an appropriate form of intervention. The development of assessment instruments and appropriate intervention techniques may be one application of the research on the nature of play. Caution should be advised, however, as considerably more research is required. In addition, the results of descriptive research suggest that practitioners should refrain from making judgments of developmental status based on the traditional hierarchies of cognitive and social play. Models for assessment are required that are based upon fine-grained distinctions of cognitive complexity and social participation (Krasnor and Pepler, 1980).

Designing the Play Environment

The research on the environmental factors that influence children's play provides more clear-cut guidelines for educators. First, the type of materials that are provided for play influence the type of play that will occur. Highly structured materials, such as puzzles and stacking toys, tend to direct and restrict children's play activities (Pepler, 1979; Pulaski, 1973). Simple forms of non-social functional play are associated with playdough, sand, and water (Rubin, 1977). Art materials elicit constructive, non-social activities, whereas dress-up clothes and vehicles elicit more complex social dramatic activities (Rubin, 1977). The materials in a play environment should be chosen for their age-appropriateness, interest, and challenge for the children. The play materials can be varied to elicit social or non-social activity and different levels of cognitive complexity in play according to the goals of the educational setting.

Characteristics of the play partner have also been shown to influence play activities. Although there is minimal research on the play of children in mixed-age groups, descriptions of sibling play suggest that the play of the younger child in a dyad can be enhanced by an older play partner (Dunn and Dale, 1984). The play of children in schools might be similarly enriched if there were opportunities to play with older children.

The role of the teacher or adult in the educational play environment is central in establishing a milieu for play. Not only do teachers provide the materials for play, but they can provide the initiation, clarification, and elaboration required to support it. For example, Sylva (1984) suggests that teachers can enhance children's problem-solving in play by encouraging children to experiment when a problem arises, suggesting alternatives when children run out of ideas, and reflecting on the achievements of the children when they have solved the problem. Teachers can also facilitate fantasy play by suggesting, clarifying, and elaborating themes and roles for the children. A teacher may even occasionally join the play to help initiate the pretense activities. The degree of intrusiveness required of the teacher will vary according to the characteristics of the children, activity, and situation as well as the goals of the educational setting.

Research has shown that children's play differs according to the curriculum. Constructive play is encouraged by teacher instruction and the availability of appropriate materials, such as in a Montessori program (Johnson and Ershler, 1982). Functional and dramatic play are more likely to occur under a curriculum that poses minimal structure on children's behavior (Johnson and Ershler, 1982). Finally, dramatic play is likely to be found in a program where the teacher models and encourages make-believe play and provides a variety of play materials to support dramatic activities (Johnson and Ershler, 1982).

Providing the Opportunity to Learn Through Play

In considering the implications and applications of play research for educators, it is important to remember that play is not being posited as the best or most efficient means of acquiring problem-solving skills, creativity, language, or social competence. Play is, however, an intrinsically motivated, pleasurable, and engaging activity for children and, as such, provides a natural vehicle for spontaneous learning. Although research on the impact of play on development is still in its infancy, some directions can be provided to educators responsible for creating a play environment to enhance learning.

First, convergent problem-solving skills can be practiced and enhanced by providing children with highly structured convergent materials. This is the basis of the Montessori program, for example, in which the materials provide strong direction for children's activities, and consequent learning. Second, divergent problem-solving or creativity may be enhanced by providing a variety of play materials that capture the interests and imaginations of individual children. The most successful attempts at enhancing creativity through play will likely come by building on and diversifying each child's interests. Finally, social-cognitions and social competence are likely to be exercised and enhanced by the provision for and perhaps training of social pretend play.

CONCLUSION

Psychological theories and research on children's play have not developed to the extent that they can provide clear directions for the incorporation of play in educational programs. Initial guidelines have been presented for the types of materials and activities that encourage cognitive and social forms of play. These cognitive and social forms of play have, in turn, been shown to reflect and relate to a variety of competencies of young children. Considerably more understanding is required about these relations between play materials and play activities and learning for older children. An example of a research application for older children might be to examine play with computers (Simon, 1985). To expand our knowledge of the importance of play, researchers must now start to examine the processes that underlie the links between play and development. The role of educators will be to continue to provide children with a variety of play experiences to facilitate learning and to prepare children to face the divergent problems of everyday life.

REFERENCES

Barnes, K. Preschool Play Norms: A Replication. *Developmental Psychology, 5*(1971), 99-103.

Berlyne, D. *Conflict, Arousal, and Curiosity.* New York: McGraw-Hill, 1960.

Berlyne, D. *Structure and Direction in Thinking.* New York: Wiley, 1965.

Bjorklund, G. The Effects of Toy Quantity and Qualitative Category on Toddlers' Play. Paper presented at the meeting of the Society for Research in Child Development. San Francisco, California, March, 1979.

Blurton-Jones, N. Categories of Child-Child Interaction. In *Ethological Studies of Child Behavior.* Edited by N. Blurton-Jones. Cambridge, England: Cambridge University Press, 1972.

Brainerd, C. Effects of Group and Individualized Dramatic Play on Cognitive Development. In *The Play of Children: Current Theory and Research.* Edited by D. Pepler and K. Rubin. Basel, Switzerland: Karger AG, 1982.

Bruner, J. The Nature and Uses of Immaturity. *American Psychologist, 27*(1972), 687-708.

Bruner, J. Competence in Infants. In *Beyond the Information Given.* Edited by J. Anglin. New York: Norton, 1973.

Burns, S., and Brainerd, C. Effects of Constructive and Dramatic Play on Perspective Taking in Very Young Children. *Developmental Psychology, 15*(1979), 512-521.

Cheyne, J. Object Play and Problem-Solving: Methodological Problems and Conceptual Promise. In *The Play of Children: Current Theory and Research.* Edited by D. Pepler and K. Rubin. Basel, Switzerland: Karger AG, 1982.

Connolly, J., and Doyle, A. Relation of Social Fantasy Play to Social Competence in Preschoolers. *Developmental Psychology, 20*(1984), 797-806.

Connolly, J., Doyle, A., and Ceschin, F. Forms and Functions of Social Fantasy Play in Pre-Schoolers. In *Social and Cognitive Skills: Sex Roles and Children's Play.* Edited by M. Liss. New York: Academic Press, 1983.

Dansky, J. Make Believe: A Mediator of the Relationship Between Play and Associative Fluency. *Child Development, 51*(1980a), 576-579.

Dansky, J. Cognitive Consequences of Sociodramatic Play and Exploration Training for Economically Disadvantaged Preschoolers. *Journal of Child Psychology and Psychiatry, 20*(1980b), 47-58.

Dansky, J., and Silverman, I. Effects of Play on Associative Fluency in Preschool-Aged Children. *Developmental Psychology, 9*(1973), 38-43.

Dansky, J., and Silverman, I. Play: A General Facilitator of Associative Fluency. *Developmental Psychology, 11*(1975), 104.

Darvill, D. Ecological Influences on Children's Play: Issues and Approaches. In *The Play of Children: Current Theory and Research*. Edited by D. Pepler and K. Rubin. Basel, Switzerland: Karger AG, 1982.

DiPietro, J. Rough and Tumble Play: A Function of Gender. *Developmental Psychology, 17*(1981), 50-58.

Doyle, A., Connolly, J., and Rivest, L. The Effect of Playmate Familiarity on the Social Interactions of Young Children. *Child Development, 51*(1980), 217-223.

Dunn, J., and Dale, N. A Daddy: 2-Year-Olds' Collaboration in Joint Pretend With Sibling and With Mother. In *Symbolic Play: The Development of Social Understanding*. Edited by I. Bretherton. New York: Academic Press, 1984.

Eckerman, C., and Whatley, J. Toys and Social Interaction Between Infant Peers. *Child Development, 48*(1977), 1645-1656.

Ellis, M. *Why People Play*. Englewood Cliffs, New Jersey: Prentice-Hall, 1973.

Emmerich, W., Cocking, R., and Sigel, I. Relationships Between Cognitive and Social Functioning in Preschool Children. *Developmental Psychology, 15*(1979), 495-504.

Fein, G. A Transformational Analysis of Pretending. *Developmental Psychology, 11*(1975), 291-296.

Fein, G. Play and the Acquisition of Symbols. In *Current Topics in Early Childhood Education*. Edited by L. Katz. Norwood, New Jersey: Ablex, 1979.

Fein, G. Pretend Play: An Integrative Review. *Child Development, 52*(1981), 1095-1118.

Fein, G., and Robertson, A. *Cognitive and Social Dimensions of Pretending in Two-Year-Olds*. Detroit: Merrill-Palmer Institute, 1975.

Feitelson, D., and Ross, G. The Neglected Factor - Play. *Human Development,* *16*(1973), 202-223.

Fenson, L., and Ramsay, D. Decentration and Integration of the Child's Play in the Second Year. *Child Development, 51*(1980), 171-178.

Frost, J., and Campbell, S. Play and Equipment Choices of Conserving and Preconserving Children on Conventional and Creative Playgrounds. Paper presented at the Seventh World Congress of the International Playground Association, Ottawa, 1978.

Garvey, C. Some Properties of Social Play. In *Play: Its Role in Development and* *Evolution.* Edited by J. Bruner, A. Jolly, and K. Sylva. New York: Penguin, 1976.

Garvey, C. Play With Language. In *Biology of Play.* Edited by B. Tizard and D. Harvey. Philadelphia: Lippincott, 1977.

Garvey, C., and Berndt, R. Organization of Pretend Play. Paper presented at the meeting of the American Psychological Association, Chicago, Illinois, 1977.

Golomb, C., and Cornelius, C. Symbolic Play and Its Cognitive Significance. *Developmental Psychology, 13*(1977), 246-252.

Griffing, P. The Relationship Between Socio-Economic Status and Sociodramatic Play Among Black Kindergarten Children. *Genetic* *Psychology Monographs, 101*(1980), 3-34.

Groos, K. *The Play of Animals.* New York: Appleton, 1898.

Groos, K. *The Play of Man.* New York: Appleton, 1901.

Huston-Stein, A., Friedrich-Cofer, L., and Susman, E. The Relation of Classroom Structure to Social Behavior, Imaginative Play, and Self-Regulation of Economically Disadvantaged Children. *Child Development,* *48*(1977), 908-916.

Hutt, C. Exploration and Play in Children. In *Play: Its Role in Development and* *Evolution.* Edited by J. Bruner, A. Jolly, and K. Sylva. New York: Penguin, 1976.

Hutt, C. Towards a Taxonomy and Conceptual Model of Play. In *Developmental Processes in Early Childhood.* Edited by S. Hutt, D. Rogers, and C. Hutt. London: Routledge and Kegan Paul, 1982.

Hutt, C., and Bhavnani, R.   Predictions From Play.   In *Play: Its Role in Development and Evolution*.   Edited by J. Bruner, A. Jolly, and K. Sylva. New York: Penguin, 1976.

Johnson, J.   Relations of Divergent Thinking and Intelligence Tests Scores with Social and Nonsocial Make-Believe Play of Preschool Children. *Child Development, 47*(1976), 1200-1203.

Johnson, J., and Ershler, J.   Curricular Effects on the Play of Preschoolers.   In *The Play of Children: Current Theory and Research*.   Edited by D. Pepler and K. Rubin.   Basel, Switzerland: Karger AG, 1982.

Johnson, J., Ershler, J., and Bell, C.   Play Behavior in a Discovery-Based and a Formal Education Pre-School Program.   *Child Development, 51*(1980), 271-274.

Krasnor, L., and Pepler, D.   The Study of Children's Play: Some Suggested Future Directions.   In *Children's Play*.   Edited by K. Rubin.   San Francisco, California: Jossey-Bass, 1980.

Lewin, K.   Environmental Forces in Child Behavior and Development.   In *A Handbook of Child Psychology*.   Edited by A. Murchison.   Worcester: Clark University Press, 1931.

Li, A.   Effects of Play on Novel Responses of Preschool Children.   *Alberta Journal of Educational Research, 24*(1978), 31-36.

Lieberman, J.   Playfulness and Divergent Thinking: An Investigation of Their Relationship at the Kindergarten Level.   *The Journal of Genetic Psychology, 107*(1965), 219-224.

Liss, M.   *Social and Cognitive Skills: Sex Roles and Children's Play*.   Edited by M. Liss.   New York: Academic Press, 1983.

Lovinger, S.   Sociodramatic Play and Language Development in Preschool Disadvantaged Children.   *Psychology in the Schools, 11*(1974), 313-320.

Matthews, W.   Sex and Familiarity Effects upon the Proportion of Time Young Children Spend in Spontaneous Fantasy Play.   *Journal of Genetic Psychology, 133*(1978), 9-12.

Matthews, R., and Matthews, W.   A Paradigm Case Approach to the Study of Fantasy.   In *The Play of Children: Current Theory and Research*.   Edited by D. Pepler and K. Rubin.   Basel, Switzerland: Karger AG, 1982.

McCune-Nicolich, L.   Toward Symbolic Functioning: Structuring of Early Pretend Games and Potential Parallels With Language.   *Child Development, 52*(1981), 785-797.

McCune-Nicolich, L., and Fenson, L. Methodological Issues in Studying Early Pretend Play. In *Child's Play: Developmental and Applied.* Edited by T. Yawkey and A. Pellegrini. Hillsdale, New Jersey: Lawrence Erlbaum, 1984.

McLoyd, V. Verbally Expressed Modes of Transformation in the Fantasy Play of Black Preschool Children. *Child Development, 51*(1980), 1133-1139.

Montessori, M. *The Absorbent Mind.* New York: Dell, 1967.

Montessori, M. *The Montessori Method.* Cambridge, Massachusetts: Bentley, 1973.

Moore, N., Evertson, C., and Brophy, J. Solitary Play: Some Functional Reconsiderations. *Developmental Psychology, 10*(1974), 830-834.

Mueller, E., and Brenner, J. The Origins of Social Skills and Interaction Among Play Group Toddlers. *Child Development, 48*(1977), 854-861.

Parten, M. Social Participation Among Preschool Children. *Journal of Abnormal Psychology, 27*(1932), 243-269.

Patrick, G. *The Psychology of Relaxation.* Boston: Houghton-Mifflin, 1916.

Pepler, D. Effects of Convergent and Divergent Play Experience on Preschoolers' Problem-Solving Behaviors. Unpublished Ph.D., University of Waterloo, 1979.

Pepler, D., and Ross, H. The Effects of Play on Convergent and Divergent Problem-Solving. *Child Development, 52*(1981), 1202-1210.

Pepler, D., and Rubin, K. Current Issues in the Study of Children's Play. *Human Development, 25*(1982), 443-447.

Piaget, J. *The Moral Judgment of the Child.* New York: Free Press, 1932.

Piaget, J. *The Origins of Intelligence in Children.* New York: International Universities Press, 1952.

Piaget, J. *Play, Dreams, and Imitation in Childhood,* New York: Norton, 1962.

Pulaski, M. Toys and Imaginative Play. In *The Child's World of Make-Believe.* Edited by J. Singer. New York: Academic Press, 1973.

Rosen, C. The Effects of Sociodramatic Play on Problem Solving Behavior Among Culturally Disadvantaged Children. *Child Development, 45*(1974), 920-927.

104 *Pepler*

Rubin, K. The Social and Cognitive Value of Preschool Toys and Activities. *Canadian Journal of Behavioral Science, 9*(1977), 382-385.

Rubin, K. Fantasy Play: Its Role in the Development of Social Skills and Social Cognition. In *Children's Play*. Edited by K. Rubin. San Francisco, California: Jossey-Bass, 1980.

Rubin, K. Early Play Theories Revisited: Contributions to Contemporary Research and Theory. In *The Play of Children: Current Theory and Research*. Edited by D. Pepler and K. Rubin. Basel, Switzerland: Karger AG, 1982.

Rubin, K., Fein, G., and Vandenberg, B. Play. In *Handbook of Child Psychology. Volume 4. Socialization, Personality, Social Development*. Edited by E. Hetherington. New York: Wiley, 1983.

Rubin, K., and Maioni, T. Play Preference and Its Relationship to Egocentrism, Popularity, and Classification Skills in Preschoolers. *Merrill-Palmer Quarterly, 21*(1975), 171-179.

Rubin, K., Maioni, T., and Hornung, M. Free Play Behaviors in Middle and Lower Class Pre-Schoolers: Parten and Piaget Revisited. *Child Development, 47*(1976), 414-419.

Rubin, K., and Pepler, D. The Relationship of Child's Play to Social-Cognitive Development. In *Friendship and Childhood Relationships*. Edited by H. Foot, T. Chapman, and J. Smith. London: Wiley, 1980.

Rubin, K., and Seibel, C. The Effects of Ecological Setting on the Cognitive and Social Play Behaviors of Preschoolers. Proceedings of the Ninth Annual International Interdisciplinary Conference on Piagetian Theory and the Helping Professions, 1981.

Rubin, K., Watson, K., and Jambor, T. Free Play Behaviors in Preschool and Kindergarten Children. *Child Development, 49*(1978), 534-536.

Saltz, E., and Brodie, J. Pretend-Play Training in Childhood: A Review and Critique. In *The Play of Children: Current Theory and Research*. Edited by D. Pepler and K. Rubin. Basel, Switzerland: Karger AG, 1982.

Saltz, E., Dixon, D., and Johnson, J. Training Disadvantaged Preschoolers on Various Fantasy Activities: Effects on Cognitive Functioning and Impulse Control. *Child Development, 48*(1977), 367-380.

Saltz, E., and Johnson, J. Training for Thematic-Fantasy Play in Culturally Disadvantaged Children: Preliminary Results. *Journal of Educational Psychology, 66*(1974), 623-630.

Sanders, K., and Harper, L. Free Play Fantasy Behavior in Preschool Children: Relations Among Gender, Age, Season, and Location. *Child Development, 47*(1976), 1182-1185.

Schiller, F. *On the Aesthetic Education of Man.* New Haven, Connecticut: Yale University Press, 1954.

Schlosberg, H. The Concept of Play. *Psychological Review, 54*(1947), 229-231.

Scholtz, G., and Ellis, M. Repeat Exposure to Objects and Peers in a Play Setting. *Journal of Experimental Child Psychology, 19*(1975), 448-455.

Serbin, L., Conner, J., Burchardt, C., and Citron, C. Effects of Peer Presence on Sex-Typing of Children's Play Behavior. *Journal of Experimental Child Psychology, 27*(1979), 303-309.

Simon, T. Play and Learning With Computers. *Early Child Development and Care, 19*(1985), 9-78.

Singer, D., and Rummo, J. Ideational Creativity and Behavioral Style in Kindergarten Aged Children. *Developmental Psychology, 8*(1973), 54-161.

Singer, J. (Ed.) *The Child's World of Make-Believe.* New York: Academic Press, 1973.

Singer, J., Singer, D., and Sherrod, L. A Factor Analytic Study of Preschoolers' Play Behavior. *American Psychology Bulletin, 2*(1980), 43-156.

Smilansky, S. *The Effects of Sociodramatic Play on Disadvantaged Preschool Children.* New York: Wiley, 1968.

Smith, P. A Longitudinal Study of Social Participation in Preschool Children: Solitary and Parallel Play Re-Examined. *Developmental Psychology, 14*(1978), 17-523.

Smith, P., and Connolly, K. *Patterns of Play and Social Interaction in Preschool Children. Ethological Studies of Child Behavior.* Edited by N. Blurton-Jones. Cambridge: Cambridge University Press, 1972.

Smith, P., and Dodsworth, C. Social Class Differences in the Fantasy Play of Preschool Children. *Journal of Genetic Psychology, 133*(1978), 183-190.

Smith, P., and Dutton, S. Play and Training in Direct and Innovative Problem-Solving. *Child Development, 50*(1979), 830-836.

Smith, P., and Simon, T. Object Play, Problem Solving and Creativity in Children. In *Play in Animals and Humans.* Edited by P. Smith. Blackwell: Oxford Press, 1984.

Smith, P., and Syddall, S. Play and Non-Play Tutoring in Preschool Children: Is It Play or Tutoring Which Matters? *British Journal of Educational Psychology, 48*(1978), 315-325.

Smith, P., Takhvar, M., and Gore, N. Play in Young Children: Problems of Definition, Categorization, and Measurement. *Early Child Development and Care, 19*(1985), 25-41.

Smith, P., and Vollsted, R. On Defining Play: An Empirical Study of the Relationship Between Play and Various Play Criteria. *Child Development, 56*(1985), 1042-1050.

Spencer, H. *Principles of Psychology (Vol.2)*. New York: Appleton, 1873.

Sutton-Smith, B. *Novel Responses to Toys*. Merrill-Palmer Quarterly, 14(1968), 151-158.

Sutton-Smith, B. The Useless Made Useful: Play as Variability Training. *School Review, 83*(1975), 197-214.

Sutton-Smith, B., and Kelly-Byrne, D. The Phenomenon of Bipolarity in Play Theories. In *Child's Play: Developmental and Applied*. Edited by T. Yawkey and A. Pellegrini. Hillsdale, New Jersey: Lawrence Erlbaum, 1984.

Sylva, K. A Hard Headed Look at the Fruits of Play. *Early Child Development and Care, 15*(1984), 171-183.

Sylva, K., Bruner, J., and Genova, P. The Rule of Play in the Problem-Solving of Children 3-5 Years Old. In *Play: Its Role in Development and Evolution*. Edited by J. Bruner, A. Jolly, and K. Sylva. New York: Penguin, 1976.

Tizard, B. Play: A Child's Way of Learning? In *Biology of Play*. Edited by B. Tizard and D. Harvey. London: Heinemann, 1977.

Tizard, B., Philps, J., and Plewis, I. Play in Preschool Centers. I. Play Measures and Their Relation to Age, Sex, and IQ. *Journal of Child Psychology and Psychiatry, 17*(1976a), 251-264.

Tizard, B., Philps, J., and Plewis, I. Play in Preschool Centers. II. Effects on Play of the Child's Social Class and the Educational Orientation of the Center. *Journal of Child Psychology and Psychiatry, 17*(1976b), 265-274.

Vandenberg, B. Play and Development From an Ethological Perspective. *American Psychologist, 33*(1978), 724-738.

Vandenberg, B. The Role of Play in the Development of Insightful Tool-Using Strategies. *Merrill-Palmer Quarterly, 27*(1981), 97-109.

Vygotsky, L. Play and Its Role in the Mental Development of the Child. In *Play--Its Role in Development and Evolution*. Edited by J. Bruner, A. Jolly, and K. Sylva. Middlesex, England: Penguin Books, 1976.

Watson, M., and Fischer, K. A Developmental Sequence of Agent Use in Late Infancy. *Child Development*, 48(1977), 828-836.

Weisler, A., and McCall, R. Exploration and Play. *American Psychologist*, 31(1976), 492-508.

PART II: EDUCATIONAL PERSPECTIVES

PRESCHOOL PLAY

James F. Christie

E. Peter Johnsen

Ever since play first became the object of serious inquiry around the beginning of this century, preschools have been a favorite setting for play research. A modest estimate would be that more than one hundred studies have been conducted on preschool play. As is evident in a recent historical survey of the play literature (Sutton-Smith, 1983), most of this research has taken place within the past two decades.

There are several reasons for the popularity of preschools as a site for researching children's play. First, there is a convenience factor. Because schools offer preassembled groups of children, it is much easier to study play in school than in nonschool settings. Second, far more play occurs in preschools than at any other school level. From the beginning of the early education movement in eighteenth-century Europe, play has been an integral part of most preschool programs (Spodek, 1974). Third, it has become difficult to study play in school settings beyond the preschool level. Public schools have been biased toward goal-oriented behavior and have been, on the whole, antithetical toward play and other nonacademic forms of activity. This anti-play attitude has intensified in recent years with the advent of the "back to basics" movement and has even filtered down to the kindergarten level (Glickman, 1984). Fourth, the frequency of play in preschools has generated interest in practical problems such as the selection of toys and the arrangement of play areas. These concerns have in turn prompted a considerable amount of preschool-based play research. Finally, constructive play and make-believe play, considered by many to have important roles in social and intellectual development, are at their peak during the preschool years. Researchers interested in studying these forms of play are naturally drawn to preschools.

This chapter will attempt to summarize the voluminous literature on preschool play. We begin by identifying the major perspectives and methodologies that have been used to study play in preschool settings. Next, the research is reviewed and major findings are highlighted. Finally, recommendations are made for future research, and practical applications are extrapolated from studies that were reviewed.

MAJOR RESEARCH PERSPECTIVES

The problems involved with defining play are legion, as is well documented in the literature (Christie and Johnsen, 1983; Rubin, Fein, and Vandenberg, 1983). Some argue that play must involve pretense and positive feelings and be flexible and goalless (Krasnor and Pepler, 1980). Others have argued that, rather than being a discrete category of behavior, play is a characteristic of many activities, including some goal-oriented pursuits (Blanchard, 1984). This controversy notwithstanding, we believe that play, in the fullest sense of the term, is characterized by pretense, self-generated and pleasurable behaviors, flexibility, and some freedom from the extremes of pressure and anxiety.

In this chapter, we hope to rotate the prism slightly and look at this enigmatic concept in terms of three perspectives which characterize most of the research on preschool play. In these perspectives, play is viewed as: (1) an indicator of development, (2) an outcome of the environment, and (3) a skill subject to training effects. Undoubtedly, viewing play in terms of these three perspectives adds to the complexity of an already complicated concept. But it allows some organization of the massive literature on play during the preschool period and may help to clarify the many different research questions that have been asked and the assumptions upon which those questions rest.

By limiting our review to research emanating from these three perspectives, we have deemphasized research primarily concerned with psychological theory and play's role in development. Many of these studies have been conducted with preschoolers, usually in laboratory settings. Included in this group are the many correlational studies that have examined relationships between play and creativity, intelligence, and other aspects of social-intellectual development, and experimental studies that have investigated causal links between play and associative fluency and problem solving. These investigations are discussed in some detail in Debra Pepler's chapter.

Play as an Indicator of Development

Those who argue that play reflects development focus attention on systematic changes in play behavior and their underlying correlates in children as they mature. Fein (1979) has called these scholars *structural-developmentalists*, indicating their interest in the symbolic nature of pretense and their concern for orderly changes with maturity. The central force behind this approach is Piaget (1962), who maintained that play is reflective of changes in young children's symbolic skills and an index of their growing maturity. Play's contribution to the developmental process itself, according to Piaget, is limited; a position which runs counter to the beliefs of other theorists (e.g., Vygotsky, 1976).

Structural-developmentalists are more concerned with the influence of experience (i.e., the cumulative intellectual history of children) on play than with the here-and-now environment of toys, space, and teacher presence (Fein, 1979). The research conducted by these investigators is descriptive in nature. They systematically observe children while they play and code their behaviors, using different observation scales. Rubin's research on social and cognitive play levels is exemplary of this line of inquiry (e.g., Rubin, Maioni, and Hornung, 1976; Rubin, Watson, and Jambor, 1978).

Play as an Outcome of the Environment

Other researchers view play as an effect of setting variables. These scholars, who are concerned about the relationship between the child and stimulus characteristics of the immediate environment, can be referred to as *functionalists* (Fein, 1979). Their focus is on what gains the child's attention in a play environment, how children respond to settings that vary in apparatus, space, the presence of adults and peers, and the geography of the play setting itself. Functionalists use both descriptive and experimental designs, at times observing the effects of naturalistic settings which differ in terms of a given variable (e.g., amount of play equipment) and at other times manipulating the variables in question. Smith and Connolly's (1980) extensive study of the preschool ecology is an example of this type of research.

Play as a Trainable Skill

Play can also be viewed as a skill that is acquired or learned. Functionalists and some structuralists are concerned with play as a behavior that can be influenced. These scholars, whom we will refer to as *interventionists,* argue that not only can play be increased via training, but that such training is associated, perhaps casually, with changes in other intellectual, social, or creative-imaginative processes (Athey, 1984; Rubin, Fein, and Vandenberg, 1983). As a result, a number of experiments have been conducted in which preschoolers were directly trained or encouraged to engage in different types of play, particularly make-believe play. The effects of the training are then monitored, not only on the children's play behavior but also on aspects of their cognitive performance. Saltz, Dixon, and Johnson's (1977) three-year-long play training study is an example of this tradition.

RESEARCH REVIEW

Each of the above perspectives has generated a large volume of research. Viewing play as an indicator of development has led to research on *individual differences* in preschoolers' play behavior. Investigations of age, sex, and social-class differences in play compose the bulk of this area of research. The perspective of play as an outcome of the environment has resulted in studies of *ecological factors* and their impact on children's play. Included in this group are investigations of play materials, indoor and outdoor settings, peer and adult presence, and school curricula. Finally, researchers who view play as a trainable skill have conducted a series of *play training* experiments in which preschoolers were either taught or encouraged to engage in pretend play.

Individual Differences

A discussion of individual differences in play during the preschool years requires, first of all, an explanation of the two main components of play: social factors and cognitive factors. Over fifty years ago, Parten (1932) developed a scheme for classifying the social aspects of play which, with minor modifications, is still in use today. She suggested that play patterns move developmentally from solitary to parallel to various forms of group play. Much later, Smilansky (1968), working from Piaget's (1962) statements on play, developed a system of classifying the cognitive components of play into four categories: (a) functional (sensorimotor), (b) constructive, (c) dramatic, and (d) games with rules. As in Parten's system, these categories were ordered sequentially from least to most mature. The definitions of the social and cognitive components appear in Figure 1 with examples.

In the following sections, we review the research on individual differences in play with respect to sex, social class, and age. We will focus on gender differences, social class effects, and age trends in the social and cognitive components of play.

Sex

One of the most obvious differences among children is that of gender. The concept of sex differences and the biological and social influences that promote or discourage sex-typing (the masculine and feminine labels which a culture assigns to events, practices, and characteristics) has generated hundreds of studies in psychology. Because most samples of preschool children involve both boys and girls, studies employing naturalistic observations typically examine differences in play outcomes in terms of gender. One of the most obvious findings is that male children engage in more large muscle, highly active play and in more rough-and-tumble play that involves mock aggression than girls (Blurton-Jones, 1976; DiPietro, 1981).

In general, many studies have found that girls are more likely than boys to engage in constructive play (Rubin and Krasnor, 1979; Rubin, Maioni, and Hornung, 1976; Rubin, Watson, and Jambor, 1978). Boys, on the other hand, are reported to engage in more solitary functional play and perhaps more dramatic play. Rubin, Fein, and Vandenberg (1983) note that sex differences in the overall amount of pretend play appear to be sensitive to ecological factors such as the availability of sex-typed props and whether the play takes place indoors or outdoors (e.g., Sanders and Harper, 1976).

A finer analysis of these findings helps to clarify these differences. Girls' constructive play appears to be similar to what other authors have called "educational" play (e.g., Moore, Evertson, and Brophy, 1974), involving goal-directed activities such as block building, art construction activities, and challenging puzzles. In addition, girls' dramatic or pretend play is more likely to involve role playing (Sanders and Harper, 1976) and to use fantasy processes involving imaginary objects and people than boys' play (Hetherington, Cox, and Cox, 1979). Rubin, Fein, and Vandenberg (1983)

FIGURE 1

DEFINITIONS OF PLAY COMPONENTS

Smilansky's Cognitive Play Levels

1. *Functional play* involving repetitive muscle movements with or without objects. Examples include: (a) running and jumping, (b) gathering/dumping and stacking/knocking down, (c) manipulating objects (stringing beads, rolling a toy car, putting, etc.) or materials (sand, playdough, water, etc.)

2. *Constructive play* involving using objects (blocks, legos, tinkertoys, etc.) or materials (sand, playdough, etc.) to make something.

3. *Dramatic play* involving role playing and/or make-believe transformations. Examples include:

   a. Role playing: pretending to be a parent, baby, firefighter, shark, or monster.
   b. Make-believe transformations: pretending to drive a car (arm movements), sound a horn (vocalization), or give an injection with a pencil (object use). Behaviorally indicated use of imaginary objects is also included.

4. *Games with rules* involving the recognition, acceptance, and conformity with preestablished rules. Categories include: chasing games (tag), leader games (Mother May I), singing games (London Bridge), games of individual skill (marbles), board games (checkers), and sports (kickball) (Sutton-Smith and Rosenberg, 1971).

Parten's Social Play Levels

1. *Solitary play* involving playing alone with materials different from those of children within speaking distance; no conversations with others.

2. *Parallel play* involving playing with toys or engaging in
activities similar to those of other children who are in close
proximity; however, there is no attempt to play with the other
children.

3. *Group play* involving playing with other children; roles may or
may not assigned. Group play subsumes Parten's associative
and cooperative play categories.

---

interpret such findings as indicating a somewhat more rapid development of
the cognitive aspects of play in girls. Most researchers report that the themes
expressed in pretend play are sex stereotyped (Cramer and Hogan, 1975;
Sutton-Smith, 1979; Tizard, Philps, and Plewis, 1976a). Boys tend to role
play typical male roles, male occupations, and active, aggressive characters
such as superheroes. Girls prefer feminine roles with domestic overtones
(Johnson and Roopnarine, 1983).

Children's toy preferences also appear to be stereotyped. Huston
(1983) points out that, by age three, children show sex-typed choices of toys
in free play and in controlled laboratory environments. Girls were found to
reject male type toys, and boys rejected female-type toys. She attributes these
early toy choice patterns to early socialization by adults. However, girls
seemed tol be less intensely prohibited in the selection of toys than boys; thus,
boys are less likely than girls to violate a taboo of cross-sexed selection of
play materials (Sutton-Smith, 1979). As society changes its views of
women's roles and as work patterns encourage the growing participation of
fathers in the child-rearing process, these patterns of toy preference may
become less stereotyped.

Social Class

The relationship between social class and play is an arena of
controversy. Smilansky's (1968) original investigation of Israeli children laid
the foundation for this debate. She summarized her research outcomes to
suggest that lower socioeconomic-status (SES) children evidenced deficits in
the quality and quantity of their sociodramatic play. Subsequent studies by
American, British, and Canadian researchers have tended to confirm these
findings (Feitelson and Ross, 1973; Rosen, 1974; Rubin, Maioni, and
Hornung, 1976; Saltz and Johnson, 1974; Smith and Dodsworth, 1978).

Because such findings mirror recent controversies over similar
research on the issue of differences between SES groups in language and
thought, and because race is frequently embedded in this debate, some
attention to critical commentary on this research is warranted. McLoyd
(1982, 1983a) has criticized these studies for lack of control groups and for
other confounds. She also has suggested that the measurement of verbal
exchanges in group play was affected by situational factors which rendered

depressed findings for low-SES children. Finally, she and Smith (1983) questioned the importance of group dramatic play for the development of competence in young children. Smith suggests that these findings reflect differences in the means whereby experience may be gained, not deficits in incorporating experiences into long-term developmental changes. Schwartzman (1984) argued in a similar vein, citing limited evidence from ethnographic studies in cross-cultural settings. She argues that neither SES nor cultural differences support a deficiency model.

Sutton-Smith (1983a), Udwin and Shmukler (1981), Griffing (1980), and a particularly astute study by Fein and Stork (1981) temper these criticisms of the research. All of these works argue for the continued appearance of differences between SES groups in sociodramatic play. The contribution of these studies lies in the fact that the differences are more specific. It appears that children in both SES groups almost always engage in some pretend play and that the key difference between groups is the amount of language produced during pretense. Further, Fein and Stork (1981) speculated on the theoretical meaning of these differences, noting that, in addition to the deficit model of SES differences, another position is tenable. Such differences may suggest a deficit of opportunity. Lower-SES children may be socialized to restrict play to settings where researchers fear to tread (e.g., playgrounds and city neighborhoods). Furthermore, the emotional uncertainty of unfamiliar school settings may depress such children's advanced dramatic interactions.

Other research suggests that social class differences in group pretend play may be confounded not only with research settings but also with sex. Griffing (1980) reported that, among low-SES children, boys engaged in higher quality sociodramatic play than girls. The situation was reversed with middle-class children.

Age

We end our review of research on individual differences in play behavior with studies on age-related changes in the social and cognitive aspects of play. By focusing on the three cognitive play categories-- functional, constructive, and dramatic--we will attempt to describe the changing patterns of play across the preschool and early kindergarten years.

Functional Play

Functional play, the least mature form of play in terms of cognitive functioning, declines over the preschool period (Hetherington, Cox, and Cox, 1979; Rubin and Krasnor, 1979; Rubin, Watson, and Jambor, 1978; Tizard, Philps, and Plewis, 1976a). This generally seems to be the case regardless of the social aspect of functional play (i.e., whether it is solitary, parallel, etc.). Because functional play does not depend on the use of imagination or symbol manipulation, it is the type of play which appears first in the life cycle, but it is attenuated as intellectual processes become more symbolic.

Constructive Play

Constructive play is the modal or most prevalent form of play during the preschool years, occupying more than 50 percent of free play time by age four (Rubin, Fein, and Vandenberg, 1983). The evidence concerning age changes in the social aspects of constructive play is mixed. While some studies did not detect significant changes in the amount of parallel or solitary constructive play during the preschool years (e.g., Rubin and Krasnor, 1979), other studies indicate that parallel constructive play increases as children leave preschool and enter kindergarten (e.g., Rubin, Watson, and Jambor, 1978). On the other hand, Hetherington, Cox, and Cox (1979) reported a decline in parallel constructive play from four to six years of age. Constructive play, by its very nature, depends on the availability of appropriate construction materials. Variations in the amount of such materials may account for these contradictory findings.

Interest in the changes in constructive play have been stimulated by Rubin's (1982) suggestion that for preschoolers at age four, parallel constructive play is strongly associated with other indices of social and intellectual competence. This is useful information because parallel play has generally been considered less mature than group play. A combined examination of the social and cognitive scales suggests that parallel play of a constructive nature may have an important role in development.

Dramatic Play

Pretend or dramatic play has received the most attention in the research literature. The general finding has been that pretend play increases relative to other forms of cognitive play classifications during the preschool period (Hetherington, Cox, and Cox, 1979; Iwanaga, 1973; Johnson and Ershler, 1981; Rubin and Krasnor, 1979; Rubin, Watson, and Jambor, 1978; Sanders and Harper, 1976). Hetherington, Cox, and Cox, for example, found that dramatic play rose from 12 percent of all play at age four to about 25 percent at age six. As Rubin, Fein, and Vandenberg (1983) note, this generalization is limited to middle-class children in intact family situations. In addition, dramatic play is characterized by two developmental changes during the preschool years: (a) children's capability for fantasy emerges as pretend episodes become less dependent on props and their degree of realism or verisimilitude (Copple, Cocking, and Matthews, 1984) and (b) play becomes influenced by children's abilities to create frames, i.e., to negotiate and plan the *modus operandi*, roles, and settings in which play episodes occur (Garvey, 1979).

How do the social aspects of dramatic play clarify the changing aspects of pretense during these years? Rubin, Fein, and Vandenberg (1983) provide the most cogent summary of relevant studies. Solitary dramatic play remains relatively consistent, occupying a quite small percentage of total pretense during the preschool years, with some evidence of small increases after five years of age. Parallel dramatic play increases to about 20 percent of pretend activities by age five. In comparison, group dramatic play (often referred to as sociodramatic play) peaks at age four, constituting 75 percent of all pretense in school environments, and declines slightly thereafter.

Summary

Preschool boys and girls do play differently. The evidence is clear that, in terms of the cognitive component of play, girls engage in more constructive play while boys remain more functional. Boys are more physically active and more constrained to restrict their toys and play themes to stereotyped categories. In terms of the social component of play, boys may be somewhat more social, involving themselves in more group functional play and perhaps in more group dramatic play. These findings on social play differences are more tentative. Finally, males seem more dependent on concrete props than females, who appear to be more capable of detached imagination and fantasy (Matthews, 1977). The general suggestion arising from these findings is that girls mature more rapidly during the preschool years and that play differences reflect this acceleration.

While SES differences in the most cognitively advanced form of social play continue to appear in the literature, the meaning of these differences is debatable and perhaps, by now, somewhat politicized. Some evidence suggests that environmental variables, such as, setting and location, produce such differences (Tizard, Philps, and Plewis, 1976b). Researchers are subsequently warned to exercise caution in drawing conclusions about training low-SES children in group dramatic play or in formulating deficit theories to explain differential outcomes.

Several age trends in the cognitive play levels have been consistently reported. Although constructive play is the modal ludic activity during the preschool years, dramatic play, especially in social groups, not only increases but matures in character to represent fantasy less dependent on the immediate environment and more organized and controlled by the participants. Functional play, on the other hand, declines with increasing age.

One qualification to which authors repeatedly refer is that these studies have used schools as the setting for their descriptions of play. Many of the typical materials found in preschools may suggest to children the relevance of construction activities and thereby "pull" for constructive play. More information is needed on the patterns of social-cognitive play in other settings, however, before we can infer or estimate school effects on constructive play.

Ecological Factors

During the 1930s, a considerable amount of research was conducted on the effects of materials and settings on children's play. This early ecological research was primarily motivated by practical concerns such as finding better ways to design and equip preschool classrooms. The observational instruments employed in these studies tended to be imprecise and subjective (Smith and Connolly, 1980). Interest in the relationship between school ecology and play waned during the 1940s but rebounded during the late 1960s with the resurgence of interest in child development. Recent ecological studies of preschool play are, for the most part, motivated by developmental theory and employ more sophisticated methods of data collection and analysis than those used in earlier research.

Our review focuses on four categories of ecological variables: (a) settings, (b) peers and adults, (c) curriculum, and (d) play materials. The setting section reviews research on how features of preschool settings, such as the density and arrangement of space and materials, affect children's play patterns. The section on peers and adults examines how play is affected by people who inhabit preschool settings. Topics include the age, sex, and familiarity of playmates, and teacher:child ratios. The curriculum section focuses on the relationship between play and the amount of structure in preschool programs. Finally, the section on play materials examines research on age and sex differences in toy preferences. Other topics include the social value of different play materials and the effects of toy realism and complexity on play levels.

Settings

A number of studies have investigated the effects of different aspects of school settings on preschoolers' play. Setting variables include: the amount of space and materials, how the space and materials are arranged, and differences between school areas (e.g., block area, housekeeping corner, etc.). Most research on preschool settings has been conducted indoors. However, several studies have been conducted in playgrounds and some others have investigated differences in preschoolers' play patterns in indoor and outdoor locations.

Spatial Density

Spatial density refers to the amount of space per individual in a setting and is an index of crowding. Several studies have investigated the effects of spatial density on preschoolers' play behavior, focusing on levels of aggression and social interaction exhibited during free play. McGrew (1972) found that spatial densities ranging from 37 to 86 square feet per child had little impact on either variable. Loo (1972) reported that preschoolers exhibited less aggression and less social interaction (boys only) in a 15-square-feet-per-child setting than in a less crowded 44-square-feet-per-child setting. Fagot (1977) compared the play of children in three preschools in the Netherlands (average density of 13 square feet per child) with that of children in two American preschools (25 and 113 square feet per child). She found that, while there were no differences in aggressive behavior, the children in high-density Dutch preschools exhibited more positive social interaction than those in the less-crowded American schools.

Smith and Connolly (1980) have pointed out a number of problems which may account for these studies' contradictory findings. McGrew, for example, varied the amount of space and number of children while the amount of play equipment remained constant. Differences in equipment density (amount of equipment per child) may therefore have affected the children's behavior.   Loo kept equipment density stable across different spatial densities, but she failed to distinguish between rough-and-tumble play and true aggression.   Finally, Fagot's results may have been influenced by differences between the U.S. and Dutch cultures.

In order to separate the effects of space, play equipment, and number of children, Smith and Connolly (1980) conducted an extensive series of studies with two separate groups of preschoolers over a period of three years. Spatial densities of 75, 50, 25, and 15 square feet per child were examined. Results showed that, when amount of space and equipment are both varied, less space per child reduces the amount of gross motor activity (e.g., running, chasing, and rough-and-tumble play) during play but has little effect on children's social behavior until spatial density reaches 25 square feet per child.   Beyond this threshold, increased crowding results in increased aggression and reduced group play.

Amount of Play Materials

In an early study, Johnson (1935) varied the amount of equipment on three preschool playgrounds.   The amount of equipment was reduced at one playground, whereas additional equipment was added to the other two. Results showed that when equipment was removed, there were more social contacts and more aggressive behavior during play.   On the other hand, when the amount of equipment was increased, the children engaged in fewer social games and less aggression.

Smith and Connolly (1980), as part of their series of studies on spatial and play equipment density, reported similar results in indoor settings.   They found that less play material per child resulted in less solitary play, more parallel play, more sharing, and more aggressive behavior, whereas more materials per child resulted in the opposite.   The overall amount of group play was not affected.   However, as the amount of materials decreased, the mean size of play groups increased.

Scholtz and Ellis (1975) increased the "complexity" of an indoor play setting by attaching ladders, ropes, and panels to several trestles and by adding several wooded cubes.   Results showed that preschoolers engaged in less peer interactions in the high complexity condition.   Because the high-complexity setting contained more materials than the low-complexity setting, the results may be attributable to differences in amount of equipment rather than complexity.   Viewed from this perspective, Scholtz and Ellis' findings are identical to those of the previous studies: less equipment resulted in more social interaction.

Arrangement of Space and Materials

Surprisingly little research has been done on the effects of arrangement of space on preschool play.   The few studies that have been conducted have dealt with the issue of open versus partitioned space.

Several studies suggest that small, partitioned areas result in higher quality play than large, open areas. Sheehan and Day (1975) found that dividing a large day-care classroom into smaller areas with shelves and partitions reduced the amount of unruly behavior and increased the amount of cooperative interaction during free play. Field (1980) observed the play of preschoolers in four classrooms with differing spatial arrangements and teacher:child ratios. Large open-spaced rooms were compared with equal sized rooms containing partitions, and high (1:4) and low (1:12) teacher:child ratios were also compared. She found that the highest social and cognitive levels of play occurred in the classroom with small, partitioned areas and low teacher:child ratios and that the lowest quality play occurred in the class with a large open area and a high teacher:child ratio. It is not clear if a single factor--partitioned space or the low teacher:child ratio--was primarily responsible for the enhanced play quality, or whether this was an interaction effect of space and ratio.

Kinsman and Berk (1979) found that "opening up" a classroom by removing a barrier between the block and housekeeping areas had some beneficial effects on preschool and kindergarten children's play. Removing the barrier resulted in more mixed-sex play, particularly in the housekeeping area. Play integrating materials from the two areas also increased but only with the kindergartners. Arrangement of materials is another potentially important ecological variable. In a playground study, Bruya (1981) found that preschoolers spent more time playing on wooden platforms when the structures were linked together rather than separated. The linked arrangement also resulted in more peer contacts.

School Areas

Research has also been conducted to determine if children prefer playing in different preschool areas and if these areas have differential effects on play. In terms of preference, boys and older children have been found to spend more time playing outdoors than girls and younger children (Harper and Sanders, 1975; Omark and Edelman, cited in Sanders and Harper, 1976). Within indoor settings, girls have been found to play more than boys in the housekeeping, art, and book areas, whereas boys spend more time in the block area (Shure, 1963).

Indoor and outdoor settings appear to affect the type of play in which children engage. Roper and Hinde (1978) and Smith and Connolly (1972) both report that preschoolers engage in more gross motor play outdoors than indoors. Neither study found any differences in the social quality of children's play across the two settings. In addition, evidence indicates that indoor and outdoor settings may have differential effects on play, depending on social class. Tizard, Philps, and Plewis (1976b) reported that, unlike middle-class children, low-SES preschoolers engaged in more symbolic play and considerably longer play sequences outdoors than indoors. This finding reinforces Fein and Stork's (1981) contention that setting is a factor that needs to be taken into account in studies of social-class differences in play behavior.

Several other findings relate to areas within indoor settings. Shure (1963) found that solitary play was the most common form of play in game areas, whereas group play predominated in the block and housekeeping areas. Parallel play and onlooking behavior were exhibited most often in the art and book areas. Vandenberg (1981) reported that preschoolers exhibited more solitary and parallel play in a "fine motor" room equipped with paint, scissors, crayons, and other art materials and more associative play in a room containing large motor equipment such as a jungle gym and slides. Results of a series of studies by Pellegrini (1982, 1984) indicate that preschoolers' language varies when they play in different areas of the classroom. Children were found to use more imaginative, explicit, and cohesive language in the housekeeping corner than in block, art, or water and sand areas.

Peers and Adults

Physical features of the environment such as space and materials are not the only ecological variables that affect play. The people who inhabit a setting can also exert considerable influence on children's play behavior. The studies reviewed below have focused on the effects of peers and adults. The adult studies are limited to those that have investigated the effects of adult presence of preschoolers' play. Studies featuring direct adult involvement in children's play will be reviewed later in the section on play training.

Peers

The age of children in a setting appears to affect, at least to a degree, the social level of preschoolers' play and their choice of playmates. Goldman (1981) compared the play of three and four year-old children in same- and mixed-age classes. She found that the children engaged in more solitary play and less parallel play in mixed-age groups than in same-age groups. However, the amount of positive interaction (including group play) did not differ between the two conditions. Within the mixed-age classes, sex rather than age appeared to be the major factor influencing playmate selection. Roopnarine and Johnson (1984), on the other hand, report that age was more important than sex in determining choice of playmates in a mixed-age class containing three to eight year-old children. These findings suggest that the relative influence of sex and age on playmate selection depends on the age range of the children involved. If the age range is small, sex is the more important factor. As the age range gets larger, age becomes increasingly important.

Peer familiarity is another potentially important ecological variable that needs to be controlled in studies of social and cognitive play levels. Doyle, Connolly, and Rivest (1980) reported that preschoolers exhibited more group play and more dramatic play with familiar peers than with unfamiliar ones.

The presence of peers appears to effect children's play with objects. Rabinowitz, Moely, Finkel, and McClinton (1975) discovered that peers spent more time playing with a novel toy and less time with familiar toys when in the presence of a same-sex peer than when alone. Scholtz and Ellis (1975) reported that children's preference for playing with objects and peers changes with time. They found that play with objects declined with repeated exposures, the rate of decline being a function of the complexity of the objects. Conversely, play with peers increased as a result of repeated exposures. These findings are attributable, according to Ellis (1984), to the fact that peers have more stimulus/information generating potential than even the most complex objects.

A final group of studies have examined the play of different groups of children in homogeneous and heterogeneous combinations in an attempt to determine if the play of one group affects the play of the other. Tizard, Philps, and Plewis (1976a) found evidence of a "brush off" effect in their study of low- and middle-class preschoolers play. Results showed that play of low-SES children attending predominantly middle-class preschools was more mature than that of children who attended predominantly low-income schools.

Field, Roseman, DeStefano, and Koewler (1981) observed handicapped and nonhandicapped children playing separately and in a combined group. The handicapped children were found to engage in more peer-directed and less teacher-directed play in the integrated condition than in the nonintegrated groupings. However, because the square footage per child was halved in the integrated condition, the gain in peer interaction may have been caused by increased spatial density rather than by the presence of nonhandicapped peers. Guralnick (1981), in a similar study, did control for spatial density and found no difference between the social quality of handicapped preschoolers' play in integrated and nonintegrated groupings. The handicapped children, however, did exhibit less socially inappropriate play in the presence of nonhandicapped children.

Adult Presence

Several studies have investigated the effects of adult presence on play behavior. These studies have focused on teachers. Paraprofessionals and parents are also often present during preschool play periods, but we were unable to find any research on their effects on children's play patterns.

Field (1980), in a study reported earlier in the section on spatial arrangements, found that preschoolers engaged in higher social and cognitive levels of play in classes with low teacher:child ratios than in ones with high ratios. This conflicts with the findings of a large-scale study of British preschools conducted by Sylva, Roy, and Painter (1980). In this study, nineteen observed preschools were divided into two groups: those with high ratios, ranging from 1:5 to 1:7, and those with lower ratios, ranging from 1:8 to 1:10. Sylva, Roy, and Painter found that children in the school with the higher teacher:child ratios engaged in more elaborated play than those in schools with the lower ratios, a finding directly opposite that of Field's study. It should be remembered that Field's results were confounded with whether or not the classrooms were partitioned. Furthermore, the range of ratios in the Sylva, Roy and Painter study fall in between the extreme ratios used by Field

(1:4 and 1:12), and both studies used different measures of play quality. The issue of the impact of teacher:child ratios on play is far from resolved.

Sylva, Roy, and Painter also examined the effects of teacher proximity on play. They found that preschoolers engaged in longer play sequences when adults were close to them, even if the adults were passive and did not interact with the children. The average length of a play bout with no adult nearby was 1 1/2 minutes, whereas with adults close at hand, the bouts lasted twice as long. Bruner (1980), commenting on this study, speculated that the increased persistence in play was attributable to the adults acting as a buffer against distraction. An examination of transitional probabilities revealed that the children were also more likely to move toward higher levels of play and stay there when adults were nearby or interacting with them. The facilitating effect of adults on play was particularly strong for older preschoolers.

Curriculum

Partly due to conflicting educational philosophies and partly as a result of Project Follow Through and its principle of *planned variation*, large differences currently exist among early childhood education curricula (Evans, 1975). Some programs, such as the one developed by Bereiter and Engelmann (1966), place a high value on academic achievement and put much emphasis on direct teacher instruction. Other programs, often referred to as traditional, focus on social and emotional adjustment and feature large amounts of child-initiated activity. Such programs vary greatly in terms of their provisions for play, raising the possibility that they may have differing effects on children's play behavior.

Most of the research on curricular effects on play has focused on structure, a rather nebulous construct which refers to the amount of control that adults exert over children's activities. The Bereiter-Engelmann program is classified as a high structure because it features large amounts of teacher-led instruction. The Montessori (1964) method is also usually considered to be high structure, not because it features a great deal of direct instruction by teachers (which it does not), but because the children are expected to interact in a specified manner with an organized, coordinated set of materials. Traditional preschool programs, on the other hand, are low in structure because the children have considerable choice in choosing activities and in their utilization.

Several researchers have reported that classroom structure is negatively related to the amount of make-believe play exhibited by preschoolers (Rubin and Bryant, cited in Rubin and Seibel, 1979; Huston-Stein, Freidrich-Cofer, and Susman, 1977; Smith and Connolly, 1980). Other investigators, however, have found more pretend play in higher structure classrooms than in lower structure ones (Griffing, 1980; Johnson and Ershler, 1981; Tizard, Philps, and Plewis, 1976b). The findings concerning social aspects of play are equally mixed. Several studies have found that classroom structure has a negative impact on prosocial interaction and the social level of play (Rubin and Bryant, cited in Rubin and Seibel, 1979; Huston-Stein, Freidrich-Cofer, and Susman, 1977; Smith and Connolly, 1980), whereas others have reported no differences in these variables between higher- and lower-structure classrooms (Murphy and Goldner, 1976; Johnson, Ershler, and Bell, 1980; Tizard, Philps, and Plewis, 1976b).

These contradictory results are due, in part, to variations in the definition of structure. For example, Smith and Connolly's (1980) high- and low-structure programs differed only in the amount of adult involvement in children's play, while the formal and discovery-based programs studied by Johnson, Ershler, and Bell (1980) had radically different educational orientations. Differences in other ecological variables such as spatial density, play materials, and teacher/child variables may also have contributed to the conflicting findings. Attempts have been made to control some of these variables *within* studies, particularly in Smith and Connolly, but variations undoubtedly exist *across* studies.

Toys and Other Play Materials

Early childhood educators have long realized that children's play is affected by the types of toys and materials that are available. It is not surprising, therefore, that toys have been a popular topic for play research. Early studies were primarily concerned with toy preference and the social value of different toys. While these topics are still being investigated, the focus of recent research has shifted to the effects of toy attributes such as realism, novelty, and complexity. Many of the toy-attribute studies have been conducted in rooms separate from preschool classrooms, with the children being studied individually or in small groups. These studies are included in this review because the play materials that were investigated are an important part of the preschool setting.

Toy Preference

Much of the early research on play materials focused on age and sex differences in toy preference. Van Alstyne (1932) and Parten (1933) found that two and three year-old children spent more time playing with locomotor toys (e.g., wagons, kiddy-cars, etc.), sand, and housekeeping toys than older children. The older children were found to prefer playing with art construction materials and blocks more than the younger ones. Van Alstyne also found a number of sex differences. Boys preferred playing with blocks and locomotor toys, whereas girls played more with housekeeping toys, dolls, and art construction materials.

Several recent studies indicate that the sex differences in toy preference discovered a half century ago still persist today. Tizard, Philps, and Plewis (1976a) and Rubin (1977) reported that preschool boys were more likely to play with vehicles and blocks, whereas girls preferred cutting and pasting, paints, and puzzles. We were unable to find any recent studies on age differences in toy preference, so it is unknown if Van Alstyne's and Parten's age trends are still valid.

Social Value

In addition to toy preference, Parten and Van Alstyne also investigated the effects of different types of toys on the social level of children's play. Parten (1933) used her social play scale (Parten, 1932) to assign social participation scores to the toys used by the preschoolers in her toy preference study. Housekeeping toys, dolls, and vehicles were associated with the highest levels of social play. Beads, trains, sand, paint, and scissors received the lowest social participation scores. Van Alstyne (1932) found that wagons, dishes, blocks, and doll corner toys were related to high levels of cooperative play, whereas scissors, painting, beads, and puzzles tended to elicit parallel play (which she referred to as "passive cooperation").

Recent studies by Hendrickson, Strain, Tremblay, and Shores (1981) and Stoneman, Cantrell, and Hoover-Dempsey (1983) have found a similar relationship between toy types and social play. Vehicles, blocks, and dramatic play materials (dolls, housekeeping toys, dress-up clothes) were found to be associated with group play. Fine motor toys (puzzles, beads, Legos, peg boards) and art construction materials (paints, crayons, cut and paste) were associated with solitary and parallel play.

Toy Realism

Another group of studies has investigated the effects of the realism of toys on make-believe play. The first of these studies was conducted by Phillips (1945), who observed the play of three to five year-olds with high- and low-realism toys. The high-realism materials consisted of a set of detailed dolls and dollhouse furnishings. The low-realism toys were identical in size and shape but had less detail. Results revealed that, while more theme changes occurred with the low-realism props, there were no differences in the amount of make-believe with the two sets of materials.

Interest in the realism/make-believe issue has been rekindled by recent research on children's representational skills. This research has revealed a developmental progression in the type of toys needed to sustain symbolic play: two-year- olds require realistic props, whereas three-year-olds do not (Elder and Pederson, 1978; Fein, 1975). In addition, Pulaski (1973) found that realistic props may actually interfere with the imaginativeness of kindergartner's pretend play.

Results of recent toy realism investigations, on the whole, go along with this developmental trend in representational abilities. Olszewski and Fuson (1982) found that realism of play materials did not affect the level of preschoolers' make-believe play. However, as in Phillips' study, the high- and low-realism toys were very similar. Other studies have used sets of materials that were more dissimilar and have found differences in the materials' impact on make-believe. Jeffree and McConkey (1976) found that two-1/2-year-old nonhandicapped children and older handicapped children with comparable mental ages both engaged in more make-believe with high-realism toys. Johnson (1983), on the other hand, reported that three- and four-year-old middle-class preschoolers exhibited more representational activity with low-realism props. McGhee, Ethridge, and Benz (1981) found that low-realism toys resulted in higher levels of pretend play with three-to-five-year old low-SES black males and in a greater variety of pretense with middle-class males. McLoyd (1983b) discovered that high-realism objects prompted more solitary make-believe in three-1/2-year-old low-SES preschoolers but not in five-year-olds. Group make-believe was not affected. Both the younger and older subjects exhibited more representational activity with low-realism objects.

These findings suggest that realistic props facilitate make-believe in younger preschoolers but not in older preschoolers. There were, however, some differences between studies as to the precise age at which this change occurs. It is likely that subject differences (e.g., social class) combined with differences in the functional definition of realism to cause the discrepant results.

It is interesting to note that McGhee, Ethridge, and Benz, (1981) found that, while the low-income and middle-class males exhibited more make-believe with low-realism toys, both groups preferred playing with the high-realism toys. This suggests that the realism level of toys that is most conducive to make-believe is not the level at which preschool boys prefer to play.

Novelty and Complexity

Considerably less research has been conducted on the effects of other toy attributes such as novelty and complexity. Hutt (1971) found that preschoolers typically explore novel toys prior to playing with them. The results of this and other research suggest that play and exploration are similar but distinctly different behaviors (see Weisler and McCall, 1976). Switzky, Haywood, and Isett (1974) investigated the effects of toy complexity on four-to-seven-year-old children's play and exploratory behavior. They found that, as toy complexity increased, exploration increased and play decreased. This finding points out the importance of distinguishing between the two behaviors when conducting toy research.

Rabinowitz, Moely, Finkel, and McClinton (1975) investigated three-to-five-year-old children's interactions with a novel toy (a large, colorful clown figure) and familiar toys (dolls, trucks, and puzzles). They found that the children spent more time engaged with the familiar toys. The children did, however, spend more time with the novel toy when in the presence of a same-sex peer than when alone. In addition, boys interacted with the novel toy more than girls. Unfortunately, Rabinowitz, Moely, Finkel, and McClinton, did not distinguish between play and exploration, so it was not clear in which type of activity the children were engaging. Also, novelty and toy type were confounded.

Summary

Settings

Evidence from Smith and Connolly's (1980) extensive study of preschool settings indicates that spatial density has little effect on the social quality of children's play until the space available per child is less than 25 square feet. Beyond this threshold, increased crowding results in more aggression and less group play. Reducing the amount of equipment per child, on the other hand, appears to increase both aggression and positive social interaction.

Several studies indicate that the arrangement of space and materials can affect play patterns. Researchers have reported that adding partitions to large indoor areas and removing barriers between the block and housekeeping areas have had a positive impact on play levels. Linking outdoor play equipment also have been found to facilitate certain types of play. More research is needed, however, to determine the generalizability of these findings.

Other research has revealed sex and social-class differences in setting preference. Boys and low-SES children tend to spend more time playing outdoors than girls and middle-class children. In addition, children have been found to engage in different types of play indoors and outdoors, but it appears that the social quality of their play does not differ across the two settings.

There appears to be a negative correlation between the amount of equipment and materials available in preschool settings and the amount of social interaction in children's play. As the amount of play materials decreases, there is increased social interaction of both a positive (e.g., sharing) and negative (e.g., aggression) nature.

Children appear to engage in different levels of play in different areas of the preschool classroom, with the highest levels of group play occurring in the block and housekeeping areas. These findings generally agree with the results of the research on the social value of toys: blocks and dramatic play materials tend to be associated with high levels of social interaction.

Peers and adults.

Research has shown that the people who occupy preschool settings can also affect children's play. Preschoolers exhibit higher social and cognitive levels of play when playing with familiar peers. They are also more likely to play with novel objects when peers are present. Limited evidence suggests that the play of less mature children improves when they are given opportunities to play with more mature children. Additional research is needed to determine if a "brush off" effect exists and how to control this effect.

Adult presence has been found to lengthen the duration of preschoolers' play sequences and to increase the probability that children will move to higher levels of play. The effects of teacher:child ratios on play, however, is not clear.

Curriculum

Of the four categories of ecological variables reviewed in this chapter, least is known about curricula. Findings on the effects of program structure on play are equally split, half favoring high-structure programs and half favoring low-structure programs. Until agreement is reached on a precise definition of structure and a way is discovered to control the multitude of confounding variables, this situation is unlikely to change.

Play materials

Research has revealed enduring sex differences in toy preference, with boys preferring vehicles and blocks and girls being partial to dramatic play materials (housekeeping, toys, dolls, and dress-up clothes) and art construction materials. Vehicles, blocks, and dramatic play materials have been found to be associated with high levels of group play, whereas fine motor toys and art materials appear to encourage solitary and parallel play. These two sets of findings may help explain why boys tend to be more social in their play than girls. Both of the boys' favorite playthings pull for social play, while one of the girls' favorites, art material, does not.

Evidence from toy attribute studies indicates that realistic props promote make-believe play in younger preschoolers but may inhibit pretense in older children. Little is known about how play is affected by other attributes of toys such as novelty and complexity.

Changing Play Through Training

During the past two decades, a number of studies have investigated the effects of training on preschoolers' play patterns. This research was prompted by Smilansky's (1968) pioneering study in which low-SES Israeli children were successfully trained to engage in sociodramatic play. Results showed that Smilansky's training procedure not only resulted in gains in the amount and quality of the children's group dramatic play but also appeared to improve some aspects of their cognitive performance.

Smilansky's findings led researchers in the U.S., Britain, Canada, and South Africa to investigate the impact of play training on children in their countries. Most of these studies used lower-SES preschoolers as subjects. The basic goal was to improve the children's make-believe play skills, allegedly facilitating their cognitive and/or social development.   In summarizing the results of this research, we have grouped the studies by the type of training employed.

Most researchers have used variations of Smilansky's original play training procedure. This method of tutoring, which we will refer to as sociodramatic play training, attempts to help children incorporate elements such as role playing, object transformations, and social interaction into their play. Adults do this by supplying theme-related props, suggesting play themes and activities, and by joining in the children's play and modeling the desired play behaviors.

Other studies have used thematic-fantasy training, a procedure originally developed by Saltz and Johnson (1974). This type of training involves helping children to enact fairy tales (e.g., Three Billy Goats Gruff) or stories. The teacher reads a story, assigns roles to the children, and helps them enact the story by prompting and at times by taking a role in the dramatization. The stories that are enacted in this type of training tend to have a higher degree of fantasy than the themes that are used in sociodramatic play training. Thematic-fantasy training is also very structured. In contrast, sociodramatic play training encourages children to work together to assign their own roles and to plan their own story lines. It is more demanding because the children have to create their own play frame.

The results of play training research, on the whole, have been quite positive. Findings indicate that sociodramatic play training is very effective in enhancing preschoolers' group dramatic play abilities (Christie, 1983; Dansky, 1980; Lovinger, 1974; Saltz, Dixon, and Johnson, 1977; Smith, Dalgleish, and Herzmark, 1981; Smith and Syddall, 1978). In addition this type of training has been found to lead to gains in some measures of intellectual and social development (see Pepler's chapter). Results show that thematic-fantasy training is also effective in promoting group dramatic play (Saltz and Johnson, 1974; Shmukler and Naveh, 1980; Udwin, 1983). In fact, evidence indicates that it is just as effective as sociodramatic play training in facilitating this type of play (Shmukler and Naveh, 1980). Like sociodramatic play training, thematic-fantasy training has also been found to lead to gains in a variety of psychological test outcomes.

Unfortunately, these findings have been substantially limited by a number of methodological weaknesses (see Brainerd, 1982, and Christie and Johnsen, 1985, for discussions of these issues). While these limitations preclude attributing gains to training per se, they do not diminish the fact that most studies found increases in group dramatic play. One common problem has been the failure of experimenters to control for the effects of peer interaction and adult tuition which accompany play training (Rubin, 1980; Smith, Dalgleish, and Herzmark, 1981). The possibility therefore exists that the social and cognitive benefits of play training were caused by social interaction rather than by the play component of the training.

Another important limitation has been the lack of follow-up assessments to establish the permanency of training effects. Fortunately, both of these limitations are beginning to be addressed. Gains in play and changes in other variables have been maintained on posttests administered 4 weeks (Udwin, 1983), 8 weeks (Smith, Dalgleish, and Herzmark, 1981), and 12 weeks (Christie, 1983) after play training has ceased. These findings suggest that play training has lasting effects on some aspects of children's behavior.

In summary, research has shown that play training can have a positive impact on preschoolers' play behavior. There is some question, however, as to which aspect of the training--play, peer conflict, or adult tuition--is responsible for its facilitative effects. From a theoretical perspective, this is a serious weakness because it prevents the findings of play training research from being used as conclusive evidence that play has a causal role in determining behavior. From an applied perspective, perhaps this limitation is less serious. Educators are likely to be content with the finding that play training has been found to be an useful intervention strategy with some preschool children, not only fostering increased sociodramatic play but frequently producing changes in patterns of selected cognitive and social variables.

FUTURE DIRECTIONS FOR RESEARCH

We have seen that play itself may be influenced by differences between children, such as age, sex, and social background. In addition, the environment in which play occurs and the materials available appear to influence how much and what kind of play transpires. However, Krasnor and Pepler (1980) have pointed out that the studies in which toys or settings were found to "pull" for characteristic play patterns may have been confounded with unknown preferences *within* individuals, i.e., the children's own dispositions which might have led them to pick out such settings or toys. So we have a "chicken-and-egg" situation in which we are unable to determine how the psychological differences between players interact with the varying situations and materials that surround play activities.

Factorial studies which examine the possible interactions between organismic characteristics like predisposition to play and a variety of situational variables under the control of the experimenter (e.g., toy types, spatial arrangements, density variables) would provide some very interesting beginnings. Training research studies which have at times concluded that play leads to selective improvement in cognitive and social outcomes have to be evaluated in light of additional research which raises some doubts about these effects. When control groups are expanded to examine possible confounds (e.g., Simon and Smith, 1985), it appears that training enhances play but that its role as a causal agent is still in doubt. In addition, some authors have sagely suggested that instigating play in experimental environments is itself a difficult task and that validating the treatment should be a priority in designing training studies (Dansky, 1985).

Some additional attention in the training literature should also be given to psychological outcomes, particularly those involving prosocial behavior. Even though it may not be possible to attribute such outcomes solely to play, teachers will no doubt be interested in how play training might serve as a rehearsal for the emergence of self-control and coping mechanisms (Johnsen, 1984).

Finally, as many authors have emphasized, problems with definitions, as noted above, have led to difficulties in researching play. While observation scales have improved as combinations of the various aspects of play have been used (e.g., the social and cognitive levels), researchers sometimes approach play's definition slightly differently. Thus, what constitutes sociodramatic play for one investigator might not qualify for another. What is obviously needed is improved continuity in research definitions and testing techniques, with a wide variety of replications using many different samples of children.

Play then, like many other complex research concepts, needs both experimental and descriptive efforts in concert with one another to examine the complex and cumulative relationships between play and the many other variables with which it interacts. Therefore, a number of standard recommendations--careful definitions, systematized measurement techniques, the expansion of variables beyond those familiar in the literature, especially those connected to social behavior, and careful control over the many potential confounds--all seem appropriate to research on preschool play (Brainerd, 1982; Christie and Johnsen, 1985).

PRACTICAL APPLICATIONS

A number of potential applications emerge from the research on preschool play. Research on individual differences in play behavior has revealed consistent age trends in cognitive and some social aspects of play. Observation of free play behavior is therefore an excellent means for for teachers to gain insights into preschoolers' developmental progress. We recommend that teachers use a two-dimensional scale such that developed by Rubin, Watson, and Jambor (1978). This scale allows a simultaneous view of both the social and cognitive components of play, yielding nine possible categories of play and three game categories. The play categories, sans the three game ones, are illustrated in Figure 2.

FIGURE 2

SOCIAL-COGNITIVE COMPONENTS OF PLAY: NINE CATEGORIES

	Solitary	Parallel	Group
Functional	solitary-functional	parallel-functional	group-functional
Constructive	solitary-constructive	parallel-constructive	group-constructive
Dramatic	solitary-dramatic	parallel-dramatic	group-dramatic

When interpreting the results of free play observations, teachers should keep the following age trends in mind. First, solitary play appears to occupy a limited proportion of play time at every age level and may be irrelevant to questions of social maturity (Smith, 1978). Second, it is not clear whether all children move through a sequence of parallel play, so the significance of this form of play is difficult to interpret. Third, all forms of functional play appear to be indicative of immaturity, whereas group-dramatic play and constructive play reflect mature cognitive and social development. Older preschoolers who exhibit a preponderance of functional play may therefore benefit from additional diagnosis and intervention (Krasnor and Pepler, 1980).

Teachers also need to take children's gender and their social class into account when interpreting play patterns. One should expect the social and cognitive level of girls' play to generally be more mature than that of boys'. In addition, it appears necessary to observe low-SES children playing in both indoor and outdoor settings in order to gain a true picture of their play competence.

Finally, evidence indicates that peer familiarity affects the level of preschoolers' play, suggesting that play observations should not be conducted until children have had time to become well acquainted. By delaying systematic observation until the third or fourth week of school, teachers will likely obtain a more accurate picture of their students' play capabilities.

It is important to remember that preschoolers' play patterns are not just the result of individual differences. Environmental factors also affect the social and cognitive level of children's play. Preschools traditionally have an open, spontaneous atmosphere which is in sharp contrast to the more structured environment found in most public schools. Preschools tend to be person and process oriented, placing heavy emphasis on social development and learning through activity. The flexible structure of most preschool curriculums allows considerable time for free-choice activities, including play. In addition, preschools' person/process orientation has resulted in many classrooms being equipped with materials which encourage constructive and group dramatic play. Thus, the nature of the preschool makes it possible--in fact, relatively easy--for teachers to influence children's play patterns by manipulation of ecological variables and by selective involvement with children during free play periods.

The research on ecological factors suggests several ways in which early childhood educators can influence the type of play that occurs in their classrooms. Results of studies on play materials and indoor areas indicate that group play can be encouraged by providing blocks, vehicles, and dramatic play materials such as housekeeping props, dolls, and dress-up clothes. Sociodramatic play can be fostered by adjusting the ratio of realistic to nonrealistic props to match children's representational abilities. Younger preschoolers appear to require a high proportion of realistic materials in order to engage in make-believe play. With older preschoolers, however, pretend play is encouraged when the balance is shifted toward a preponderance of nonrealistic props.

Smith and Connolly's (1980) research on indoor play settings indicates that a minimum space of 25 square feet should be available per child. Below this threshold, increased crowding leads to reduced amounts of group play and increases in aggression. Other results suggest that teachers can influence the social quality of play by limiting the amount of available play materials. Sharing can be increased by reducing the amount of equipment available per child. This should be done cautiously, however, because reducing play equipment density also results in increased aggression. Conversely, aggressive behavior can be reduced by making more materials available.

Considerable controversy surrounds the practice of play training. Some researchers have questioned whether low-SES children really need to be trained to engage in sociodramatic play (e.g., Fein and Stork, 1981), and others have argued that peer conflict or adult tutoring rather than play are responsible for the gains attributed to play training (Christie and Johnsen, 1983; Rubin, 1980; Smith and Syddall, 1978). The fact remains, however, that studies have shown that training can enhance the frequency and the quality of play episodes, any other effects notwithstanding. Play itself has at least two distinct advantages. It involves social interaction as group constructive and dramatic activity become more frequent with age. A variety of authors argue for the importance of social interaction between children as a source of stimulation for development (Hartup, 1983). Play is also inherently satisfying and pleasurable. Schools that are moving toward structured experiences and the use of technological aids that abet isolation might reconsider the importance of social "fun" and its role in guaranteeing children's' rights to childhood. This reason alone may warrant the inclusion of play in preschool programs.

In conclusion, the research reviewed in this chapter has enhanced our knowledge about preschool play. Marked progress has been made in understanding the complexities of individual differences in play behavior during the preschool years. We also know more about the effects that play materials, spatial density, and peers have on children's play. Much, however, remains to be learned about the effects of other environmental variables and play training. Spatial arrangements, teacher:child ratios, and curricula appear to have an impact on children's play patterns, but the findings of past studies have been equivocal. More research is needed before any firm recommendations for practice can be made concerning these important issues. Nevertheless, the information currently available should better enable educators to plan for play and enhance its quality.

134   *Christie and Johnsen*

REFERENCES

Athey, I. Contributions of Play to Development. In *Child's Play: Developmental and Applied.* Edited by T. Yawkey and A. Pellegrini. Hillsdale, New Jersey: Erlbaum, 1984.

Bereiter, C., and Engelmann, S. *Teaching Disadvantaged Children in the Preschool.* Englewood Cliffs, New Jersey: Prentice-Hall, 1966.

Blanchard, K. Play as Adaptation: The Work-Play Dichotomy Revisited. Paper presented at the Annual Meeting of The Association for the Anthropological Study of Play, Clemson, South Carolina, 1984.

Blurton-Jones, N. Rough-and-Tumble Play Among Nursery School Children. In *Play: Its Role in Development and Evolution.* Edited by J. Bruner, A. Jolly, and K. Sylva. New York: Basic Books, 1976.

Brainerd, C. Effects of Group and Individualized Dramatic Play Training on Cognitive Development. In *The Play of Children: Current Theory and Research.* Edited by D. Pepler and K. Rubin. Basel, Switzerland: Karger, 1982.

Bruner, J. *Under Five in Britain.* Ypsilanti, Michigan: High/Scope, 1980.

Bruya, L. Observed Motor Behavior on Linked and Non-Linked Play Structures. Unpublished Paper, North Texas State University, 1981.

Christie, J. The Effects of Play Tutoring on Young Children's Cognitive Performance. *Journal of Educational Research, 76*(1983), 326-330.

Christie, J., and Johnsen, E. The Role of Play in Social-Intellectual Development. *Review of Educational Research, 53*(1983), 93-115.

Christie, J., and Johnsen, E. Questioning the Results of Play Training Research. *Educational Psychologist, 20*(1985), 7-11.

Copple, C., Cocking, R., and Matthews, W. Objects, Symbols, and Substitutes: The Nature of the Cognitive Activity During Symbolic Play. In *Child's Play: Developmental and Applied.* Edited by T. Yawkey and A. Pellegrini. Hillsdale, New Jersey: Erlbaum, 1984.

Cramer, P., and Hogan, K. Sex Differences in Verbal and Play Fantasy. *Developmental Psychology, 11*(1975), 145-154.

Dansky, J. Cognitive Consequences of Sociodramatic Play and Exploration Training for Economically Disadvantaged Preschoolers. *Journal of Child Psychology and Psychiatry, 20*(1980), 47-58.

Dansky, J. Questioning a Paradigm Questioned. *Merrill-Palmer Quarterly,* *31*(1985), 279-284.

DiPietro, J. Rough and Tumble Play: A Function of Gender. *Developmental Psychology, 17*(1981), 50-58.

Doyle, A., Connolly, J., and Rivest, L. The Effect of Playmate Familiarity on the Social Interactions of Young Children. *Child Development, 51*(1980), 217-223.

Elder, J., and Pederson, D. Preschool Children's Use of Objects in Symbolic Play. *Child Development, 49*(1978), 500-504.

Ellis, M. Play, Novelty, and Stimulus Seeking. In *Child's Play: Developmental and Applied.* Edited by T. Yawkey and A. Pellegrini. Hillsdale, New Jersey: Erlbaum, 1984.

Evans, E. *Contemporary Influences in Early Childhood Education.* (Second edition). New York: Holt, Rinehart, and Winston, 1975.

Fagot, B. Variations in Density: Effect on Task and Social Behaviors of Young Children. *Developmental Psychology, 13*(1977), 166-167.

Fein, G. A Transformational Analysis of Pretending. *Developmental Psychology, 11*(1975), 291-296.

Fein, G. Play and the Acquisition of Symbols. In *Current Topics in Early Childhood Education.* Volume II. Edited by L. Katz. Norwood, New Jersey: Ablex, 1979.

Fein, G., and Stork, L. Sociodramatic Play: Social Class Effects in Integrated Preschool Classrooms. *Journal of Applied Developmental Psychology, 2*(1981), 267-279.

Feitelson, D., and Ross, G. The Neglected Factor: Play. *Human Development, 16*(1973), 202-223.

Field, T. Preschool Play: Effects of Teacher/ Child Ratios and Organization of Classroom Space. *Child Study Journal, 10*(1980), 191-205.

Field, T., Roseman, S., DeStefano, L., and Koewler, J. Play Behaviors of Handicapped Preschool Children in the Presence and Absence of Nonhandicapped Peers. *Journal of Applied Developmental Psychology,* 2(1981), 49-58

Garvey, C. Communicational Controls in Social Play. In *Play and Learning.* Edited by B. Sutton-Smith. New York: Gardner Press, 1979.

Glickman, C. Play in Public School Settings: A Philosophical Question. In *Child's Play: Developmental and Applied.* Edited by T. Yawkey and A. Pellegrini. Hillsdale, New Jersey: Erlbaum, 1984.

Goldman, J. Social Participation of Preschool Children in Same- Versus Mixed-Age Groups. *Child Development, 52*(1981), 644-650.

Griffing, P. The Relationship Between Socioeconomic Status and Sociodramatic Play Among Black Kindergarten Children. *Genetic Psychology Monographs, 101*(1980), 3-34.

Guralnick, M. The Social Behavior of Preschool Children at Different Developmental Levels: Effects of Group Composition. *Journal of Experimental Child Psychology, 31*(1981), 115-130.

Harper, L., and Sanders, K. Preschool Children's Use of Space: Sex Differences in Outdoor Play. *Developmental Psychology, 11*(1975), 119.

Hartup, W. Peer Relations. In *Handbook of Child Psychology: Volume IV. Socialization, Personality and Social Development* (Fourth edition). Edited by P. Mussen. New York: Wiley, 1983.

Hendrickson, J., Strain., P., Tremblay, A., and Shores, R. Relationship Between Toy and Material Use and the Occurrence of Social Interactive Behaviors by Normally Developing Preschool Children. *Psychology in the Schools, 18*(1981), 500-504.

Hetherington, E., Cox, M., and Cox, R. Play and Social Interaction in Children Following Divorce. *Journal of Social Issues, 35*(1979), 26-49.

Huston, A. Sex-typing. In *Handbook of Child Psychology: Volume IV. Socialization, Personality, and Social Development* (Fourth edition). Edited by P. Mussen. New York: Wiley, 1983.

Huston-Stein, A., Friedrich-Cofer, L., and Susman, E. The Relation of Classroom Structure to Social Behavior, Imaginative Play, and Self-Regulation of Economically Disadvantaged Children. *Child Development, 48*(1977), 908-916.

Hutt, C. Exploration and Play in Children. In *Child's Play.* Edited by R. Herron and B. Sutton-Smith. New York: Wiley, 1971.

Iwanaga, M. Development of Interpersonal Play Structure in Three, Four, and Five year-old Children. *Journal of Research and Development in Education, 6*(1973), 71-82.

Jeffree, D., and McConkey, R.   An Observation Scheme for Recording Children's Imaginative Doll Play.   *Journal of Child Psychology and Psychiatry, 17*(1976), 189-197.

Johnsen, E.   Play and the Positive: What About the Lighter Side?   Paper presented at the Annual Meeting of The Association for the Anthropological Study of Play, Clemson, South Carolina, March, 1984.

Johnson, J.   Context Effects on Preschool Children's Symbolic Behavior. *Journal of Genetic Psychology, 143*(1983), 259-268.

Johnson, J., and Ershler, J.   Developmental Trends in Preschool Play as Function of Classroom Program and Child Gender.   *Child Development, 52*(1981), 995-1004.

Johnson, J., Ershler, J., and Bell, C.   Play Behavior in a Discovery-Based and a Formal-Education Preschool Program.   *Child Development, 51*(1980), 271-274.

Johnson, J., and Roopnarine, J.   The Preschool Classroom and Sex Differences in Children's Play.   In *Social and Cognitive Skills.*   Edited by M. Liss. New York: Academic Press, 1983.

Johnson, M.   The Effect on Behavior of Variation in the Amount of Play Equipment.   *Child Development, 6*(1935), 52-68.

Krasnor, L., and Pepler, D.   The Study of Children's Play: Some Suggested Future Directions.   In *Children's Play.*   Edited by K. Rubin.   San Francisco, California: Jossey-Bass, 1980.

Kinsman, C., and Berk, L.   Joining the Block and Housekeeping Areas: Changes in Play and Social Behavior.   *Young Children, 35*(1979), 66-75.

Loo, C.   The Effects of Spatial Density on the Social Behavior of Children. *Journal of Applied Social Psychology, 2*(1972), 372-381.

Lovinger, S.   Sociodramatic-Dramatic Play and Language Development in Preschool Disadvantaged Children.   *Psychology in the Schools, 11*(1974), 313-320.

Matthews, W.   Modes of Transformation in the Initiation of Fantasy Play. *Developmental Psychology, 13*(1977), 212-216.

McGhee, P., Ethridge, O., and Benz, N.   Effect of Level of Toy Structure on Preschool Children's Pretend Play.   Paper presented at the Meeting of The Association for the Anthropological Study of Play, Fort Worth, Texas, April, 1981.

McGrew, W.   *An Ethological Study of Children's Behavior.*   New York: Academic Press, 1972.

McLoyd, V.   Social Class Differences in Sociodramatic Play: A Critical Review.   *Developmental Review, 2*(1982), 1-30.

McLoyd, V.   Class, Culture, and Pretend Play: A Reply to Sutton-Smith and Smith.   *Developmental Review, 3*(1983a), 1-17.

McLoyd, V.   The Effects of the Structure of Play Objects on the Pretend Play of Low-Income Preschool Children.   *Child Development, 54*(1983b), 626-635.

Montessori, M.   *The Montessori Method.*   New York: Schocken, 1964.

Moore, N., Evertson, C., and Brophy, J.   Solitary Play: Some Functional Reconsiderations.   *Developmental Psychology, 10*(1974), 830-834.

Murphy, M., and Goldner, R.   Effects of Teaching Orientation on Social Interaction in Nursery School Children.   *Journal of Educational Psychology, 66*(1976), 725-728.

Olszewski, P., and   Fuson, K.   Verbally Expressed Fantasy Play of Preschoolers as a Function of Toy Structure.   *Developmental Psychology, 18*(1982), 57-61.

Parten, M.   Social Participation Among Preschool Children.   *Journal of Abnormal and Social Psychology, 27*(1932), 243-269.

Parten, M.   Social Play Among Preschool Children .   *Journal of Abnormal and Scoial Psychology, 28*(1983), 136-147.

Pellegrini, A.   The Construction of Cohesive Text by Preschoolers in Two Play Contexts.   *Discourse Processes, 5*(1982), 101-108.

Pellegrini, A.   The Effects of Classroom Ecology on Preschoolers' Functional Uses of Language.   In *The Development of Oral and Written Language in Social Contexts .*   Edited by A. Pellegrini and T. Yawkey.   Norwood, New Jersey: Ablex, 1984.

Phillips, R.   Doll Play as a Function of the Realism of the Materials and the Length of the Experimental Session.   *Child Development, 16*(1945), 123-143.

Piaget, J.   *Play, Dreams and Imitation in Childhood .*   New York: Norton, 1962.

Pulaski, M. Toys and Imaginative Play. In *The Child's World of Make-Believe: Experimental Studies of Imaginative Play*. Edited by J. Singer. New York: Academic Press, 1973.

Rabinowitz, F., Moely., B., Finkel, N., and McClinton, S. The Effects of Toy Novelty and Social Interaction on the Exploratory Behavior of Preschool Children. *Child Development, 46*(1975), 286-289.

Roopnarine, J., and Johnson, J. Socialization in a Mixed-Age Experimental Program. *Developmental Psychology, 20*(1984), 828-832.

Roper, R., and Hinde, R. Social Behavior in a Play Group: Consistency and Complexity. *Child Development, 49*(1978), 570-579.

Rosen, C. The Effects of Sociodramatic Play on Problem-Solving Behavior Among Culturally Disadvantaged Preschool Children. *Child Development, 45*(1974), 920-927.

Rubin, K. The Social and Cognitive Value of Preschool Toys and Activities. *Canadian Journal of Behavioral Science, 9*(1977), 382-385.

Rubin, K. Fantasy play: Its Role in the Development of Social Skills and Social Cognition. In *Children's Play*. Edited by K. Rubin. San Francisco: Jossey-Bass, 1980.

Rubin, K. Nonsocial Play in Preschoolers: Necessarily Evil? *Child Development, 53*(1982), 651-657.

Rubin, K., Fein, G., and Vandenberg, B. Play. In *Handbook of Child Psychology: Volume IV. Socialization, Personality, and Social Development*. (Fourth edition). Edited by P. Mussen. New York: Wiley, 1983.

Rubin, K., and Krasnor, L. Changes in the Play Behaviors of Preschoolers: A Short-Term Longitudinal Investigation. Paper presented at the Meeting of the American Educational Research Association, San Francisco, California, April, 1979.

Rubin, K., Maioni, T., and Hornung, M. Free Play Behaviors in Middle- and Lower-Class Preschoolers: Parten and Piaget Revisited. *Child Development, 47*(1976), 414-419.

Rubin, K., and Seibel, C. The Effects of Ecological Setting on the Cognitive and Social Play Behaviors of Preschoolers. Paper presented at the Meeting of the American Educational Research Association, San Francisco, California, April, 1979.

Rubin, K., Watson, K., and Jambor, T. Free-Play Behaviors in Preschool and Kindergarten Children. *Child Development, 49*(1978), 534-536.

Saltz, E., Dixon, D., and Johnson, J. Training Disadvantaged Preschoolers on Various Fantasy Activities: Effects on Cognitive Functioning and Impulse Control. *Child Development, 48*(1977), 367-380.

Saltz, E., and Johnson, J. Training for Thematic-Fantasy Play in Culturally Disadvantaged Children: Preliminary Results. *Journal of Educational Psychology, 66*(1974), 623-630.

Sanders, K., and Harper, L. Free-Play Fantasy Behavior in Preschool Children: Relations Among Gender, Age, Season, and Location. *Child Development, 47*(1976), 1182-1185.

Scholtz, G., and Ellis, M. Repeated Exposure to Objects and Peers in a Play Setting. *Journal of Experimental Child Psychology, 19*(1975), 448-455.

Schwartzman, H. Imaginative Play: Deficit or Difference? In *Child's Play: Developmental and Applied*. Edited by T. Yawkey and A. Pellegrini. Hillsdale, New Jersey: Erlbaum, 1984.

Sheehan, R., and Day, D. Is Open Space Just Empty Space? *Day Care and Early Education, 3*(1975), 10-13,47.

Shmukler, D., and Naveh, I. Modification of Imaginative Play in Preschool Children Through the Intervention of an Adult Model. *South African Journal of Psychology, 10*(1980), 99-103.

Shure, M. Psychological Ecology of a Nursery School. *Child Development, 34*(1963), 979-992.

Simon, T., and Smith, P. Play and Problem-Solving: A Paradigm Questioned. *Merrill-Palmer Quarterly, 31*(1985), 265-277.

Smilansky, S. *The Effects of Sociodramatic Play on Disadvantaged Preschool Children.* New York: Wiley, 1968.

Smith, P. A Longitudinal Study of Social Participation in Preschool Children: Solitary and Parallel Play Reexamined. *Developmental Psychology, 14*(1978), 512-516.

Smith, P. Differences or Deficits? The Significance of Pretend and Sociodramatic Play. *Developmental Review, 3*(1983), 6-10.

Smith, P., and Connolly, K. Patterns of Play and Social Interaction in Preschool Children. In *Ethological Studies of Child behavior*. Edited by N. Blurton-Jones. Cambridge, England: Cambridge University Press, 1972.

Smith, P., and Connolly, K.. *The Ecology of Preschool Behavior*. Cambridge, England: Cambridge University Press, 1980.

Smith, P., Dalgleish, M., and Herzmark, G. A Comparison of the Effects of Fantasy Play Tutoring and Skills Tutoring in Nursery Classes. *International Journal of Behavioral Development, 4*(1981), 421-441.

Smith, P., and Dodsworth, C. Social Class Differences in the Fantasy Play of Preschool Children. *Journal of Genetic Psychology, 133*(1978), 183-190.

Smith, P., and Syddall, S. Play and Non-Play Tutoring in Preschool Children: Is It Play or Tutoring Which Matters? *British Journal of Educational Psychology, 48*(1978), 315-325.

Spodek, B. The Problem of Play: Educational or Recreational? In *Play as a Learning Medium.* Edited by D. Sponseller. Washington, D.C.: NAEYC, 1974.

Stoneman, Z., Cantrell, M., and Hoover-Dempsey, K. The Association Between Play Materials and Social Behavior in a Mainstreamed Preschool: A Naturalistic Investigation. *Journal of Applied Developmental Psychology, 4*(1983), 163-174.

Sutton-Smith, B. The Play of Girls. In *Becoming Female: Perspectives on Development.* Edited by C. Kopp and M. Kirkpatrick. New York: Plenum, 1979.

Sutton-Smith, B. Commentary on Social Class Differences in Sociodramatic Play in Historical Context: A Reply. *Developmental Review, 3*(1983a), 1-5.

Sutton-Smith, B. One Hundred Years of Change in Play Research. *TAASP Newsletter, 9*(1983b), 13-17.

Switzky, H., Haywood, H., and Isett, R. Exploration, Curiosity, and Play in Young Children: Effects of Stimulus Complexity. *Developmental Psychology, 10*(1974), 321-329.

Sylva, K., Roy, C., and Painter, M. *Childwatching at Playgroup and Nursery School.* Ypsilanti, Michigan: High/Scope Press, 1980.

Tizard, B., Philps, J., and Plewis, I. Play in Pre-school Centers - I. Play Measures and Their Relation to Age, Sex, and I.Q. *Journal of Child Psychology and Psychiatry, 17*(1976a), 251-264.

Tizard, B., Philps, J., and Plewis, I. Play in Pre-school Centers - II. Effects on Play of the Child's Social Class and of the Educational Orientation of the Center. *Journal of Child Psychology and Psychiatry, 17*(1976b), 265-274.

Udwin, O.   Imaginary Play Training as an Intervention Method with Institutionalized Preschool Children.   *British Journal of Educational Psychology, 53*(1983), 32-39.

Udwin, O., and Shmukler, D.   The Influence of Sociocultural, Economic, and Home Background Factors on Children's Ability to Engage in Imaginative Play.   *Developmental Psychology, 17*(1981), 66-72.

Van Alstyne, D.   *Play Behavior and Choice of Play Materials of Pre-School Children*.   Chicago: University of Chicago Press, 1932.

Vandenberg, B.   Environmental and Cognitive Factors in Social Play.   *Journal of Experimental Child Psychology, 31*(1981), 169-175.

Vygotsky, L.   Play and Its Role in the Mental Development of the Child.   In *Play: Its Role in Development and Evolution*.   Edited by J. Bruner, A. Jolly, and K. Sylva. New York: Basic Books, 1976.

Weisler, A., and McCall, R.   Exploration and Play: Resume and Redirection.   *American Psychologist, 31*(1976), 492-508.

ELEMENTARY SCHOOL PLAY: THEORY AND RESEARCH

Nancy R. King

Play may seem a peculiar issue to study in the context of the elementary school. Parents assume that their children work in school; teachers try to keep the children working throughout the school day, and the curriculum includes messages emphasizing the importance of work. Further, success in school depends as much on the display of appropriate work habits as on the mastery of the curricular content. For example, in addition to being graded on their academic achievements, children are also evaluated in terms of their abilities to focus on academic lessons in the midst of potentially distracting surroundings and to complete assigned tasks that may not be particularly interesting to them.

Although work is emphasized in elementary school classrooms, play does occur during the school day. Classrooms include play because most participants in elementary schools are young children, and young children are often playful. Many elementary school teachers tolerate or encourage children's playfulness because they believe that play is a natural mode of learning for young children. Play, then, is not an unlikely topic for serious consideration by elementary school researchers and practitioners.

There are two possible approaches to the study of play in the elementary school. First, play can be studied from the perspective of an outside observer. This is the typical approach of adults who study children's play and derive descriptions and explanations of play activity based on their perceptions as non-participating adult researchers. The second approach involves studying play from the perspective of an insider, that is, that of the players themselves.

Though rarely the preferred orientation of researchers, studying play from the insiders' perspective seems to be the more appropriate approach because play is widely understood to be an *insider's* phenomenon. Only those who are actually involved in a given activity can be certain that they are "playing." Observers may mistake enjoyable work activities, for example, for play. A serious attempt to derive and understand play from the participant's perspective, then, is the approach likely to produce a valid description grounded in actual play experiences.

In the case of children's play, this approach requires defining and understanding play activity from the *children's* point of view; and in order to understand how children define play, it is necessary to ask the children themselves. Studies of children's play from an insider's perspective, then, must use multiple research methodologies, including interviewing as well as observation, to capture as much as possible of the phenomenon in the words of children and to avoid intruding on the play experiences or shaping them in any way. Such methodologies allow a rich description of play as the players experience it to emerge.

This chapter will focus on play in the elementary school primarily from the children's perspective. It is important to emphasize the fact that the play discussed here takes place in school and that this setting influences the definitions and descriptions of the play activities themselves. This chapter, then, is about *school* play.

The discussion to follow has three sections. First, children's definitions of play will be described and discussed. The changes in their definitions as they move through the elementary grades and the categories of play which evolve will also be presented. Second, using the children's definitions, the educational research relevant to each category of play will be examined. In this section, the research from the outsider's perspectives will be organized and discussed according to the insider's approach to school play. Finally, the usefulness of this research to both practitioners and theorists will be explored.

CHILDREN'S DEFINITIONS OF PLAY IN SCHOOL

The Studies

In a series of three related studies involving 94 children in three elementary schools, children were asked to define and discuss work and play in school. The children were enrolled in fifteen different classrooms, kindergarten through the fifth grade, and represented predominantly white, middle-class populations (King, 1979, 1983).

In order to describe the insider's perceptions, the data were collected using a combination of non-participant observation and interviewing. Each classroom was observed for a minimum of two consecutive school days, and the children's activities were noted in detail. This record included "official" activities such as participating in reading lessons, singing with the class, completing seat work, and participating in kickball during physical education. The children's "unofficial" activities were also noted; these included activities such as looking out the window, passing notes, whispering to friends, chatting with the teacher, silly laughing, and clowning around.

With the help of the teachers, three boys and three girls from each classroom were chosen so that each group of six children represented a range of academic accomplishment and classroom behavior. Each of these children was interviewed individually in a quiet area in the school building. After a number of open-ended questions which permitted the children to offer examples of work and play in school, each child was read a list of activities in which he or she had been observed to participate during the preceding two days. In each case, the child was asked to categorize the activity as either work or play, and, in some cases, children were asked why they had placed an activity in the category they chose.

The Findings

The findings of these studies indicate that elementary school children of all ages have no difficulty categorizing their school experiences into examples of work and examples of play. In fact, the children see work and play as entirely separate categories and the differences between them as altogether obvious.

While their ability to differentiate work from play is stable throughout the elementary grades, the children's criteria for their categorizations change dramatically. Kindergarten children rely on the social context of their activities to distinguish between work and play. If the teacher requires the children's participation in an activity, that activity is labeled work. Kindergartners do not label assigned tasks play no matter how much they may enjoy participating. Activities are labeled play only when the children believe that their participation is voluntary and free of direct supervision by the teacher.

The remarkable consistency of the kindergartners' responses can be explained by their focus on the social organization of their activities. Activities required for one child in the observed classrooms were ordinarily required for all of the children. Consequently, their categorizations of particular activities are uniform.

In contrast, there is only one school activity upon which all upper elementary school children agree: they all define recess as play. Most responses with regard to particular activities, however, vary from child to child. It appears that older children apply criteria that kindergartners do not consider.

The criterion which the children introduce in the primary grades and which gradually emerges as the single most important quality differentiating between work experiences and play experiences is that of pleasure. As children move through the elementary grades, the psychological context of activities becomes increasingly important and eventually supplants the social context as the primary criterion used by the children in categorizing their activities.

Because activities which some children enjoy may not be enjoyed by others, the categorization of specific activities becomes more idiosyncratic and less uniform in the upper grades. By the fifth grade, children draw fine distinctions and offer reasons for their categorizations that are numerous and complex. An activity may be play if the child is "in the mood" or work if the child "doesn't feel like it." Further, what is fun for one child may be tedious or difficult for someone else, and an activity a child enjoys on one day, may not be enjoyed on another. The application of the criteria or the relative importance of the criterion, then, rely on the individual orientation of each child. The criteria themselves, however, are uniform and stable.

As an increasingly diverse number of activities is labeled play, the category of work becomes narrowed to include only those activities which are required, evaluated, and difficult or tedious. The category of play, on the other hand, includes all activities which are fun and/or undemanding. Play in elementary school thus becomes a broad category which includes dissimilar activities and apparently contradictory elements.

CATEGORIES OF PLAY IN ELEMENTARY SCHOOL

A closer examination of the children's responses reveals that, within the large category of play, there are three distinct types of classroom play in elementary school. These sub-categories are produced by the fact that the children are playing in school; and they can be organized and discussed in terms of the teachers' reactions to children's classroom play(King, 1982b). Teachers often incorporate play into the academic curriculum; this play becomes the category of instrumental play. Classroom play they cannot incorporate, teachers try to suppress. The suppression of play forces children to conceal their playfulness, and these activities belong to the category of illicit play. Finally, what teachers cannot suppress they place outside the school building and the daily schedule. These activities make up the category of *recreational* play.

The first category of play includes activities which are organized and evaluated by the teacher but which older elementary school children label play if they enjoy participating. Examples of instrumental play include watching a filmstrip, playing vocabulary games, writing stories, making pictures of wildlife, listening to the teacher read a story, and preparing a Thanksgiving mural. Children enjoy instrumental play for many different reasons. These activities may permit physical activity; they may be undemanding and require little effort; they may permit social contact among children, encourage individual expression, or include interesting content.

Although upper-elementary school children call these activities play, there are numerous differences between instrumental play activities and the spontaneous play activities usually associated with children. Most importantly, instrumental play activities are not voluntary or self-directed, and they serve goals beyond the purposes of the participants. Teachers organize these activities so that playful elements are included, but the teacher maintains control of the situation and the playful elements are not permitted to obscure the academic messages.

The second category of play includes all unsanctioned, surreptitious interaction among children during classroom events. Whispering, passing notes, and silly laughing are examples of illicit play. Such play is intrinsically motivated and takes place in spite of the rules and regulations of the classroom; teachers ordinarily view illicit play as a disruptive nuisance and they take steps to prevent and control it. The children realize that their illicit play is unwelcome in the classroom, and they are usually careful to hide these activities from the teacher.

The final category of play, recreational play, includes activities which are voluntary and self-directed as well as pleasurable. These activities meet both the social and the psychological criteria of play, and all elementary school children define such experiences as examples of play in school. Activities during recess are the best examples of this type of school play.

In summary, all the classroom activities identified by the children as play fall into one of these three categories of school play. Taken together, they encompass the meaning of play in elementary school from the children's perspective. It is not difficult to use the children's definitions to organize recent research about elementary school play and to explore what researchers have learned about each category. In other words, the insider's understandings can be used to organize and discuss research produced from the outsiders' perspective.

RESEARCH ABOUT ELEMENTARY SCHOOL PLAY

Instrumental Play

The belief that play is a natural mode of learning for young children has a long history in the field of education, and instructional strategies based on play activities have often been popular with classroom teachers. At the turn of the century in this country, for example, the play-school movement captured the attention of many educators and spawned numerous experiments and curricular innovations (Hetherton, 1914; Pratt, 1948; Winsor, 1973). Currently, both the theories of developmental psychologists and the observations of early childhood educators support those who believe that children at play are learning important cognitive and social skills. It is not surprising, then, that play continues to be an important element in the instructional repertoire of elementary school teachers.

Play activities used to teach academic lessons are examples of instrumental play in school. This category of play is the one most widely researched and discussed by educators. Every academic content area can and, according to many, should include academic experiences which are organized as instrumental play. For example, logical reasoning skills and social studies concepts can be taught using a variety of games and play experiences (Van de Walle and Thompson, 1981; Shears and Bower, 1974). Simulation games that permit children to work on an assembly line are easily developed and organized in classroom settings. Activities such as this introduce children to economic concepts, social relations skills, and the work reality of many adults (Palermo, 1979).

Language arts lessons can also be organized as games. Riddles and activities involving dramatic play are recommended for the teaching of reading (Gentile and Hoot, 1983; Tyson and Mountain, 1982). Singing games to teach spelling and physically active games to develop reading vocabulary are also recommended (Wharton-Boyd, 1983; Dickerson, 1982). In addition, teachers are encouraged to take advantage of the children's natural interest in play to facilitate learning and engender positive attitudes in math and science. Active games, puzzles, and brain teasers are examples of activities that are typically suggested or recommended (Hollis and Felder, 1982; Kraus, 1982; Hounsell and Trollinger, 1977). Finally, there is a growing interest in the ways in which computers can be used in instrumental play (Malone, 1980). Computers which offer children a wide variety of experiences with simulations and games in many curricular areas and lessons in programming that are designed as games are examples of instrumental play. (Goodman, 1984; Kraus, 1981)

Although there are many books and articles exhorting teachers to provide instrumental play in their classrooms, the literature includes little evidence that instrumental play increases learning. In fact, most authors are forced to admit that the evidence that does exist is fragmentary and inconclusive. Still, there are studies comparing the outcomes of lessons organized as games to the outcomes of lessons which used traditional instructional strategies. For example, Zammarelli and Bolton (1977) studied 24 children who were 10 to 12 years of age and concluded that those who had used a toy designed to teach a mathematical concept achieved greater insight into the nature of the concept and exhibited greater short-term memory of the concept than did children who had not used the toy.

Bright, Harvey, and Wheeler (1979) studied the effects of games on the academic achievement of upper elementary children in mathematics. These authors found an overall improvement in the post-test scores of children who had played games that required them to practice multiplication and division. They concluded that instructional games are an effective way to retrain math skills. However, the study did not include a control group, and the authors were unable to conclude that instructional games are preferable to other instructional strategies.

A number of studies also indicate that instrumental play environments are *not* conducive to learning cognitive skills. For example, a study of ten primary grade classrooms showed that the play-based curricular programs used by some of the teachers were less successful in teaching reading and math skills than the traditional programs used by other teachers (Evans, 1979). Baker, Herman, and Yeh (1981) also found that the use of play materials in academic lessons was negatively correlated with pupil achievement. They conclude that play activities distract children and impede academic growth.

In spite of the lack of conclusive supporting evidence, many educational researchers and theorists continue to encourage teachers to use games and play activities to enhance and enliven academic lessons (Cruickshank and Telfer, 1980; Hollis and Felder, 1982; Schoedler, 1981). The most frequent reasons for using instrumental play have more to do with the children's attitudes than with their achievement. It is usually argued that children who are given the opportunity to play participate more willingly and more energetically in classroom events. Their whole-hearted participation seems, to many, to justify the use of play in the classroom (Avedon and Sutton-Smith, 1971; Block, 1984).

Unfortunately, few researchers recognize or acknowledge the distinction between play and games, and they usually equate instrumental play with classroom games. Play and games are actually separate concepts which may or may not include common characteristics (Makedon, 1984). Games, for example, are not playful if the children do not enjoy participating. In such cases, children would categorize the games as examples of classroom work in spite of the teacher's intent to organize the lessons as play. Classroom games must include a substantial element of enjoyment and playfulness to qualify as examples of instrumental play.

Developing excellent instructional games is not an easy task. Teachers must take care that the game or simulation integrates the playful elements with the academic content (Makedon, 1984). If playful elements dominate, children may fail to attend to the academic aspects of the lesson; if the academic focus curtails playfulness, the children may not participate with enjoyment. In the latter case, it is likely that the children will see the game as an example of classroom work.

Teachers must also remember that different children have different reactions to the same experience. Therefore, the children's personal characteristics, attitudes toward learning, levels of achievement, and abilities to play games must be considered when designing instructional games for them (Bredemeier and Greenblatt, 1981). Teachers must be particularly careful to assess the impact of competitive games. Cooperative experiences may have more positive cognitive and social outcomes than competitive situations for young children, and cooperative games may be a better choice for the elementary school teacher (Sapon-Shevin, 1978). Finally, teachers must also be aware that the school environment imposes constraints on play situations (Saegesser, 1984). It may be difficult at times to protect the playful elements of an academic lesson from the influences of the work orientation of the elementary school structure.

In summary, instrumental play is a major concern for both practitioners and theorists interested in play in school. It is particularly clear in the case of instrumental play that the classroom context influences the nature of the play itself. The school creates and sustains such play, and educational researchers legitimate the importance of instrumental play by studying and discussing it at length. In spite of a considerable body of literature, however, we actually know very little about the contribution instrumental play makes to the children's cognitive growth and intellectual development.

Illicit Play

In contrast to the abundance of research about instrumental play, illicit play is a category for which we have few formal research studies and about which we have little information. Studies that do exist often start from the premise that illicit play behaviors are aberrant and dysfunctional. Consequently, the focus of the researcher is on controlling or eliminating, rather than on exploring and understanding the children's play.

The fact that educators rarely study illicit play does not diminish the significance of this play phenomenon. Illicit play is important to the children because it provides them a sphere of autonomy within the structure of the classroom. Though they realize that such play involves risk to the participants, children use illicit play activities to avoid assigned tasks or to make contact with peers during periods of classroom work.

Children's illicit play in the classroom is evident in individual acts such as doodling, playing with small toys, or sneaking a piece of candy. Pairs of children or small groups may pass notes, whisper, make faces, or giggle together. Illicit play may also appear on the playground when groups of children huddle together to sing new words to familiar tunes and thus to challenge authority, ridicule adults, and satirize established norms of behavior (Jorgensen, 1983). Such parodies are particularly popular in ele- mentary schools; they enable children to express their disdain for schooling in general and their resentment of individual teachers in particular. These satirical songs as well as written notes and ritual insults often require verbal fluency and social skills ordinarily admired by school officials. In the context of illicit play, however, these competencies become offensive (Gilmore, 1983).

These examples demonstrate that illicit play is heavily influenced by the fact that it takes place in school. It is clear, for example, that the teacher's organization of the curricular environment, the nature of classroom work, and the teacher's leadership style are important factors which influence the children's illicit play (Bossert, 1979). For example, in classrooms where children were grouped by ability for academic lessons, Schwartz observed that each ability group developed a distinctive form of illicit play (1981). The most academically able students interacted covertly and quietly during teacher-directed lessons. They also established a variety of subtle procedures for passing notes and maintaining peer contacts although the teacher openly discouraged such interaction. When the teacher did permit peer interaction, their covert network dissolved and the children substituted an open system of informal peer contact.

Children who were in the least academically able group, on the other hand, participated in overt, disruptive, illicit play during classroom work. Their illicit play distracted the teacher and disturbed the other children; it was a substitute for academic tasks rather than an accompaniment to classroom lessons. These children were described as disruptive and uncooperative by the teacher, and, although the form of their play may not be indicative of their academic competence, the appropriateness of their placement in a low ability group was confirmed by their behavior during periods of school work.

Spencer-Hall (1981) also observed intermediate grade children hiding their illicit play from their teachers. Her data show that potentially disruptive behavior is often quietly and carefully concealed. Children who are accomplished at avoiding detection are seen as compliant and cooperative by teachers, though their illicit play activities are as numerous and as varied as those of other pupils who are less clever at concealing their play. The children teachers consider disruptive are those who are caught playing, not those who play more frequently.

Occasionally, illicit play is a group effort. For example, Melvin Williams (1981) observed a group of students stage a mock fight. The other children in the classroom knew that the fight was not serious, but they reacted with fear, horror, and partisan comments nonetheless. The teacher did not recognize the fight as play and devoted considerable time and effort stopping the "fight," quieting the children, and reestablishing order in the classroom. The children laughed together later at the teacher's gullibility.

Examples of group illicit play are unusual, and the disorders caused by illicit play are rarely a serious challenge to the authority of the teacher. Still, the opportunity to be disorderly with regard to adult norms of conduct may be one of the principle attractions of illicit play. During illicit play children deny the relevance of the school's agenda and create a peer community that excludes the teacher. Children thus assert their control over both their loyalties and their activities at school.

Although teachers find illicit play to be disruptive, annoying, and exhausting, such play has value for them as well. The children's social life, ordinarily hidden from teachers, becomes visible during episodes of illicit play. Further, illicit play activities are conducted in an area easily observed by teachers and researchers alike. The serious study of illicit play, then, could provide the opportunity to observe both children's peer culture and the nature of play in school.

Recreational Play

The third category of play includes those activities which the teacher ordinarily places outside the daily academic schedule and the school building. The classroom context, consequently, has a less immediate and obvious impact on the content and organization on these play experiences than it does on instrumental or illicit play activities. Perhaps because the link to the official goals of the classroom is not established in the case of recreation, educators study this category of school play less often than they study instrumental play. Those studying recreational play are more likely to be anthropologists, linguists, or folklorists. These researchers ordinarily focus on playground activity and neighborhood play groups, though there are also a small number of studies focused on classroom activities.

Sylvia Polgar (1976) is one of the few researchers to compare play in a teacher controlled situation to play which is initiated and directed by children. Polgar studied sixth grade boys during physical education classes and during recess. Though the activities in which the boys participated were similar in the two settings, the experiences the boys had during their play were quite different.

The teacher organized the games during physical education classes; these games had many rules and regulations stipulated by the teacher, and they focused on goals beyond those of the participants themselves. In contrast, the games that developed informally on the playground had fewer rules and were played simply because the children enjoyed them. The differences Polgar found convinced her that the experiences children have during play are heavily influenced by the context in which they participate.

John Evans (1985) also studied the play experiences of boys in the upper elementary grades during physical education classes and contrasted this play to the experiences of the same group of boys on the playground during recess. He found major differences in the selection of teams for group games. In the physical education classes teachers assigned children to teams in order to begin the games without undue delay. On the playground, however, the boys selected teams themselves; they used intricate procedures based on cooperation and negotiation to create teams they considered "fair." Both athletic prowess and friendship patterns were taken into consideration. Evans argues that playground games provide children opportunities to develop and practice important social skills; such opportunities are not available during games directed and controlled by teachers.

Polgar and Evans highlight the essential differences between recreational and instrumental play. These studies also indicate some reasons why researchers studying recreational play ordinarily observe playground activity. In most schools, recess is the only time of the school day when children are not subject to the direct supervision and guidance of teachers. Consequently, it is the time of the school day when spontaneous play activities are most likely to occur.

Children participate in a wide variety of activities during recess. Many play active games such as tag, soccer, races, and hopscotch; others prefer quiet games such as fingerplays or jacks. Children also chat with friends, observe the activity around them, or romp and shout in an apparently unorganized and boisterous display of energy.

The research about recreation emphasizes three major categories of playground activity. First, there are studies of children's word play; these focus on aspects of storytelling as well as on childhood jingles, rhymes, jokes, and riddles. Second, researchers focus on the games children play during recess. The games themselves, the children's strategies for solving disputes and adjudicating rules, and the nature of the groups which evolve during playground activity are some of the areas researchers study. Finally, researchers explore the exercise of leadership and the nature of authority on the playground. The role of dominant children and aspects of children's culture are included in such studies. We will now turn to a consideration of the literature in each of these areas.

Word Play

The most famous study of children's word play is *The Lore and Language of Schoolchildren* by Iona and Peter Opie (1959); it was carried out in England and had a tremendous influence on studies that followed. Opie and Opie collected numerous examples of word games and organized them into categories such as witty responses, rhymes, riddles, jeers and torments. Mary and Herbert Knapp (1976) also studied children's word play. They found that word play often provides the framework children use to play tricks, choose teams, and create games. Singing games and word plays create a sense of community among children of differing ages and abilities and are an important element in the culture of a play group.

John McDowell's study of the speech play of fifty Chicano children also documents the ways in which children's word play creates and reveals their peer culture (1979). In addition, his research emphasizes the importance of understanding both the children's peer culture and the larger ethnic culture in which it was embedded. In the case of word play, for example, it is necessary to know how various groups play with language before the children's speech play can be properly understood (Kirschenblatt-Gimblett, 1979). This is particularly true when the children use their ethnic heritage as an immediate source and foundation of such play.

Recent studies of word play activities among Chicano and black children in Texas (Bauman, 1982) and among black and white children in an urban school setting (Levanthal, 1980) highlight the impact of culture on speech play. Connie Levanthal's study, in particular, demonstrates the need for participants as well as researchers to understand cultural aspects of word games. Levanthal observed black children in four third- grade and two fifth-grade classrooms playing a game called "Sounding" or "Playing the Dozens." This game involves the ritual exchange of insults; success depends on the creativity and wit expressed in the formulation of the insult. When white boys who did not understand the peer culture of the black children attempted to join the game, they failed to recognize its playful aspects and interpreted the situation literally. Their insults were overt expressions of hostility, and the interaction between players became a form of argumentation. The game as played by the white boys no longer qualified as word play.

Although most studies focus on playground interaction, Stuart Reifel (1984) found examples of spontaneous word play in an elementary school cafeteria. Because the children were required to remain seated and expected to focus on their eating, the opportunity to play was limited. In spite of the constraints of the setting, Reifel observed many examples of word games such as riddles, teasing, dramatic play, and clever repartee based on themes which had to do with food. Those children who initiated play events emerged as group leaders and were admired for their ability to amuse themselves and others. The adults in the cafeteria seemed largely unaware of the children's play. If the children were reasonably quiet and appeared to be eating reasonably quickly, the adults paid little attention to other aspects of their cafeteria behavior.

Games

The study of active games is the second major category explored by researchers. These studies focus on playground activities and investigate the content of the games themselves and the nature of the peer groups which develop during game activity.

Recess is the only time during most school days when children are permitted to create and maintain self-initiated peer groups. Since recess is also the only time when most school children are permitted to play spontaneously, it is not surprising that play activities are ordinarily the basis for the formation of peer friendships. Peer groups are, for the most part, based upon and maintained by the children's interest in common play activities.

Beth-Halachmy (1980) observed children's social interactions during recess and analyzed the data in terms of the size of the groups that developed. The data showed that boys and girls in the primary grades play with an average of four or five other children; in the intermediate grades, girls play in groups which are slightly smaller, and boys play in groups of approximately six children. All children observed spent the greatest amount of time in small groups and the least amount of time alone.

Since peer groups at the elementary level are, for the most part, divided along the lines of game preferences, they are also divided by sex. By the intermediate grades, most children play exclusively with children of the same sex. The play groups of fourth graders in one elementary school of a large urban school district, for example, were observed to be 100 percent sex homogenous (Miracle, Rowan and Suggs, 1984).

The games played by boys' groups differ from those played by girls' groups. Most researchers find that boys' groups tend to play more active games, and girls tend to play more quiet games. Janet Lever (1975-1976) studied 181 white middle-class fifth-grade children enrolled in one suburban and two urban schools. She found that boys play competitive games more often than do girls; these games provide boys with opportunities to adjudicate disputes and settle quarrels within the constraints of established, agreed-upon rules. Lever links the social skills boys practice during games to the social skills many people use in adult work settings.

The number and the types of disputes that arise during boys' games may be influenced by the racial characteristics of the play group. Sylvia Polgar (1978) observed black and white sixth grade boys on a school playground and found that single-color play groups experienced few disputes concerning game rules. Color-opposed games organized so that the teams were selected by color also experienced few arguments. The boys tended to state the rules clearly and to strive for fairness in the competition. The cross-color competitive situation allowed solidarity among team members and clear rules for interaction between the races during the game. The least stable game situation involved mixed-color teams. These games took longer to start, involved many arguments, and disintegrated most frequently.

The content of children's playground games is an important aspect of recreational play in the elementary school. Researchers who have closely observed children at play relate that the experience of participating in a game is not to be confused with a description of the game rules. Children involved in games shape the rules to suit their needs; throughout the play activity the situation remains under the children's control (Opie and Opie, 1969). Although the games children choose are clearly influenced by adult society (Sutton-Smith, 1972), adults are rarely involved in organizing and directing children's activities during recess. Playground games are not, however, leaderless, chaotic, or confused. Even very young children organize games which include clear rules concerning participants' behavior.

During recreational activities the children negotiate game rules to suit the skills and desires of the players involved. Some games, such as jacks and tether ball, ordinarily include variations, and negotiating these variations is required by the rules themselves. However, even during games such as soccer and baseball, which have rules established by adults, participants find or create opportunities to introduce changes. Sometimes initiating a playground activity requires little discussion; at other times, establishing the rules for an activity requires lengthy debate (Hawes, 1974).

Observations of first-grade, urban Appalachian children playing hopscotch on the playground of an inner-city elementary school revealed that they have well-developed procedures for supporting their game activity and promoting the participation of the children involved. The children negotiated patterns of turn rotation and remained engaged in the progress of the game even when they were not actively participating. Further, the players successfully pursued their game in spite of interference from the sidelines and successfully protected their play space from numerous intrusions, both purposeful and inadvertent (Borman, 1979).

Linda Hughes' (1983) study of a group of children playing the ball game, four square, illustrates the ways in which children manipulate and negotiate game rules to accomplish their goals. Among the variations of this game these players devised was one known as "Rooie Rules" in honor of the child, Rooie, who initiated it. Although the children knew how to play according to Rooie rules, none of them could list these rules. They did share, however, a tacit understanding that Rooie rules involved being nice to other players and being particularly lenient with young and unskilled participants. When Rooie rules were invoked, *deliberate* confrontations were not condoned, though "accidental" infractions were tolerated. It was obvious when the children's play was carefully observed that the flow of the game depended upon a flexible linking of rules and action rather than on a strict adherence to one rigid interpretation of the rules.

Foursquare, as played by these children, was a rich communal activity dominated by relationships rather than by rules. Hughes' findings thus indicate that an adequate interpretation of the playground experiences of young children requires an understanding of the interpersonal context in which their games proceed.

Although K. S. Goldstein's research was not carried out on a school playground, the game Goldstein studied is often played by children during recess. The game, known as "Counting Out," has numerous variations and is often used to assign roles or create teams. Goldstein found that young children learn counting out rhymes such as "One Potato, Two Potato," from older children and believe that the outcome of any counting out activity depends solely on chance. Still, some of the younger children interviewed were perplexed when it seemed to them that the counter was in control. In one case, for example, they noticed that the counter's brother was never chosen to be "It."

Older children also described counting out as a game of chance, but Goldstein's observations did not support their idealized versions of game conduct. In fact, older children were observed to use a variety of techniques to control the outcome of counting out games, and, in the hands of a sophisticated counter, counting out was anything but a game of chance. Counters controlled the game by selecting a rhyme based on the number of children in the group, by extending the rhyme, or by deciding anew where to start each successive round. Counters used various methods to conceal their strategies, and the children admired their skill in controlling the game while maintaining the illusion that the outcomes were a matter of luck alone (Goldstein, 1971).

While some playground games require complex social or cognitive skills, many games require considerable physical strength or agility. Rough-and-tumble play and play fighting are examples of the active physical play of some children during recess, though these games are ordinarily discouraged by the supervising adults. Most episodes of play fighting last only a few seconds and follow a clearly observable pattern. It is clear that even participation in this seemingly haphazard play involves the recognition and acceptance of established rules of etiquette (Aldis, 1975).

Ginsburg (1980), for example, observed symbolic appeasement gestures among third, fourth, and fifth-grade boys that served as mutually understood indicators that aggressive play should stop. Uninvolved children rarely interfered in a play fight unless one child exhibited an appeasement gesture that was ignored. In such a case, aid was likely to be offered to the child who had submitted (albeit in a face-saving, symbolic way) by a third child who was usually bigger than the aggressor.

Children's Culture

Play fights and other playground games reveal aspects of the exercise of leadership and the nature of status on the playground. These are important elements of the peer culture which flourishes during recess.

Barry Glassner's study (1976) of playground interaction documents the capacity and willingness of elementary-school children to develop and maintain their peer culture. In a more detailed study, Sluckin (1981) studied children's culture by systematically observing and interviewing children on two playgrounds in Great Britain for a period of two years. Sluckin observed organized games, quiet conversations, fights, teasing, scatalogical taunts, crude rhymes, and power struggles.

Sluckin asked children why their playground activities are important, and he quotes the particularly insightful response of one five year old child, on:

Author:	What do you think playtime's for ?
Jon:	I think it's to make me grow up a bit.
Author:	How?
Jon:	Well, I think running around and playing hopscotch and lying down make me grow up a bit. Well, I mean I get a bit more excited in the playground.
Author:	You say it helps you to grow up?
Jon:	No, that doesn't mean anything. I can't think of anything else what it's for.
Author:	What about playing hopscotch, do you think it's a very grown-up thing to do?
Jon:	No, of course not.
Author:	I thought you said playing hopscotch makes you grow up?
Jon:	It doesn't make you grow up right to the ceiling!

Author: What does it do?
Jon: It makes me grow up extremely slowly.
(Sluckin, 1981, 1)

Other children answered similarly; they recognized the intrinsic merit of play time, but they also indicated a connection between the skills they use on the playground and the skills that adults use in social settings. Sluckin also acknowledges this link and points to the combination of regulated competition, voluntary participation, and negotiated rules as particularly relevant to the social and economic reality these children will encounter in adulthood.

When Sluckin asked teachers the purpose of playground activity, they responded by pointing out that children need opportunities to "let off steam" and relax. They also stressed the importance of the social skills that children practice on the playground. When pressed for details, however, the teachers had very little idea what children actually do during play time. A study such as Sluckin's permits these teachers and other adults to become aware of both the children's activities and the meaning of those activities in the context of the children's social culture.

Studies of playground interaction indicate that elementary school age children are capable of creating and maintaining their own sub-cultures complete with rituals, traditions, rules, loyalties, and values. During recreation the children's willingness and ability to develop their own cultural context can be realized. Research into the nature of playground activity enables educators to become aware of the value of these play experiences to the children. Children's games also teach the astute observer about the larger cultural context in which the children live (Farrer, 1977).

Summary

The three categories of play evident in the elementary school are differentiated by the impact of the classroom environment on the context and organization of the play activities. When teachers use activities traditionally associated with children's play to serve the academic goals of the classroom curriculum, the category of instrumental play emerges. This category is most intimately organized and controlled by teachers.

When classroom play escapes the control of teachers and becomes part of the children's resistance to adult intervention in their social interactions, illicit play results. Teachers attempt to suppress such play and reassert control. Teachers have least control over recreation which is considered to be a sort of "time-out" from the important business of the school and, therefore, is rarely scrutinized by teachers or seriously investigated by educators.

For each category of play, researchers have gathered and shared evidence concerning the experience and meaning of the play activities to the children and to the educational enterprise. The majority of the work by educators has been in the area of instrumental play. There are extremely few studies of illicit play although these activities occupy teachers' time and attention daily in the classrooms. And there are fewer, yet, studies of recreational play except for anthropologists and folklorists have investigated children's culture and the nature of recreational activities. .

Though there are fewer studies of illicit and recreational play than there are of instrumental play, the studies we do have are more detailed, more descriptive, and more informative. We may learn more about children and their experiences because they are freer to express themselves during recreation than they are during instrumental play. It may also be that the research agenda of most researchers of recreation encourages a close look at the play phenomenon itself without the need to evaluate or prescribe.

CONCLUSION

Play was once thought to include nothing but frivolous and trivial activity. In Colonial times, adults believed that playfulness indicated a tendency toward moral laxity, and they admonished children to avoid the frivolity of play by turning to work and study. A textbook published in 1839 repeated this message in the following warning:

> "...if you waste your schoolboy years in indolence and play...in all probability, you will not be successful in any business in which you may engage, and you will live and die in poverty and obscurity." (Abbott, 1839)

Attitudes toward play had changed by the late nineteenth century. Some adults tolerated children's play because the young continued to insist on playing in spite of efforts to prevent their play. Others came to see the play of children as an expression of a youthful zest for living, an innate curiosity, and a naive innocence. Current attitudes toward play avoid both the image of play as a dark influence and the romantic ideal of play as the quintessence of childhood purity.

Play is now believed to be a natural activity of both children and adults. Educators stress particularly the importance of play to the cognitive, psychological, and social development of young children. Play activities are used to motivate children to become involved in classroom experiences, to reinforce and consolidate academic gains, and to enrich learning experiences. Recently there has been an upswing in the number of studies about play and in the interest in play displayed by educational researchers and other social scientists.

Largely because of the instrumental attitude educators have toward nearly all school activities in general and toward school play in particular, the category of instrumental play is of overriding interest to educational researchers. Those who advocate play in the elementary school extol play as a powerful motivator or a meaningful reward. Classroom play thus becomes one in a range of possible instructional alternatives; it is intended to be controlled by adults in the interest of adult goals.

While the focus on instrumental play may not be surprising, it *is* surprising that in spite of the large number of studies, most findings are suggestive and inconclusive, and researchers actually know little about instrumental play. Further, since the purpose of most studies is to establish a causal relationship between classroom play activities and academic achievement, the nature of the participants' experiences is rarely examined in detail. Consequently, this body of literature is seriously flawed as a source of understanding about play in the elementary school. This does not, however, prevent educators from praising the contribution of play and encouraging teachers to include play experiences in academic lessons.

When they focus their research solely on instrumental play, educators deny themselves the opportunity to learn about play situations controlled by children. Although they are not designed or supervised by teachers, playground activities, for example, are not without educational significance. The opportunity to organize and control their own play experiences permits children to acquire, and requires them to practice, a range of interpersonal skills in a variety of social situations. As they use social skills to accomplish immediate purposes, they also practice skills they will use as adults.

An exclusive focus on teacher-controlled play may also lead to an idealization of children's play. Unpleasant, anti-social, and uncouth elements are ignored or controlled, and only "good" play comes to the researcher's attention. "Excessive" playfulness becomes a form of deviant behavior (Sutton Smith, 1983). Researchers thus narrow and purify the play they choose to study; since they ignore disorderly or unsavory aspects of play, they present a picture that is inevitably incomplete and distorted (Sutton-Smith, 1982). While it is certainly important to study instrumental play, it is equally important to understand the categories of children's play which adults find difficult to appreciate and condone.

IMPLICATIONS

This discussion of elementary school play has implications for both practitioners and researchers. The most important implication for researchers is that elementary school play can not be narrowly equated with instrumental play. Both recreation and illicit play deserve the attention of the educational community. The serious study of all categories of classroom play will require researchers to extend the range of research methodologies they use to include anthropological and ethnographic techniques. The benefits to researchers and teachers alike will be an enhanced understanding of children's culture as expressed in their play and a heightened awareness of the meaningfulness of play as expressed by children.

This discussion also has implications for school practitioners including curriculum developers, instructional supervisors, and classroom teachers. Two implications stand out; first, the categories of play which emerge in the elementary school are created by the organization of the classroom setting. Each is a response of the setting to the children's playfulness or a response of the children to the setting's structure. The impact of the setting on the children's definitions of play emphasizes the fact that these definitions are socially constructed in particular contexts; they are not simply the result of maturation.

The second implication is closely tied to the first. Participants' definitions of school play are based on the contexts of activities, not on the content of the activities themselves. If teachers want to influence children's definitions of play, they must do so through the organization of the classroom environment. The organization of events in most elementary school classrooms creates a sharp differentiation between work and play. As a consequence, by the fifth grade, work activities no longer include experiences which the children enjoy, and play is no longer defined to include activities which the children believe to be valued by school officials.

If teachers want to integrate work and play experiences in the elementary school, they must create contexts which include dimensions of both work and play. For example, teachers may design academic activities which are required but which include opportunities for autonomy and self-expression. It is also possible to design play experiences for students that are pleasureful and voluntary and that teachers consider important within the framework of the official daily schedule.

The definitions of play which are developed during the elementary school years have a continuing impact on children's play throughout school and into their adult years. Educational practitioners may not recognize the school's impact on these emerging perspectives. Once their influence is recognized, however, educators must assume responsibility for their role in shaping school children's definitions of and orientation toward play.

REFERENCES

Abbott, J. *The School-Boy or a Guide for Youth to Truth and Duty.* Boston, Massachusetts: Crocker and Brewster, 1839.

Aldis, O. *Play Fighting.* New York: Academic Press, 1975.

Avedon, E., and Sutton-Smith, B. (Eds.) *The Study of Games.* New York: John Wiley and Sons, 1971.

Baker, E., Herman, J., and Yeh, J. Fun and Games: Their Contribution to Basic Skills Instruction in Elementary School. *American Educational Research Journal, 18*(1981), 83-92.

Bauman, R. Ethnography of Children's Folklore. In *Children In and Out of School.* Edited by P. Gilmore and A. Glatthorn. Washington, D.C.: Center for Applied Linguistics, 1982.

Beth-Halachmy, S. Elementary School Children's Play Behavior During School Recess Periods. In *In Celebration of Play.* Edited by P. Wilkenson. New York: St. Martin's Press, 1980.

Block, J. Making School Learning Activities More Play-Like: Flow and Mastery Learning. *Elementary School Journal, 85*(1984), 65-75.

Borman, K. Children's Interactions on Playgrounds. *Theory into Practice, 18*(1979), 251-257.

Bossert, S. *Tasks and Social Relationships in Classrooms.* New York: Cambridge University Press, 1979.

Bredemeier, M., and Greenblatt, C. The Educational Effectiveness of Simulation Games. *Simulation and Games, 12*(1981), 307-332.

Bright, G., Harvey, J., and Wheeler, M. Using Games to Retain Skills with Basic Multiplication Facts. *Journal for Research in Mathematics Education, 10*(1979), 103-110.

Cruickshank, D., and Telfer, R. Classroom Games and Simulations. *Theory Into Practice, 19*(1980), 75-80.

Dickerson, D. A Study of Use of Games to Reinforce Sight Vocabulary. *The Reading Teacher, 36*(1982), 46-49.

Evans, J. The Process of Team Selection in Children's Self-Directed and Adult-Directed Games. Unpublished Ph.D. Dissertation, University of Illinois at Urbana-Champaign, 1985.

Evans, M. A Comparative Study of Young Children's Classroom Activities and Learning Outcomes. *British Journal of Educational Psychology, 49*(1979), 15-26.

Farrer, C. Play and Inter-Ethnic Communication. In *The Study of Play: Problems and Prospects.* Edited by D. Lancy and A. Tindall. West Point, New York: Leisure Press, 1977.

Gentile, L., and Hoot, J. Kindergarten Play: The Foundation of Reading. *The Reading Teacher, 36*(1983), 436-439.

Gilmore, P. Spelling 'Mississippi': Recontextualizing a Literacy-Related Speech Event. *Anthropology and Education Quarterly, 14*(1983), 235-256.

Ginsberg, H. Playground as Laboratory: Naturalistic Studies of Appeasement, Altruism, and the Omega Child. In *Dominance Relations: An Ethological View of Human Conflict and Social Interaction.* Edited by D. Omark, F. Strayer, and D. Freedman. New York: Garland STPM Press, 1980.

Glassner, B. Kid Society. *Urban Education, 11*(1976), 5-21.

Goldstein, K. Strategy in Counting Out: An Ethnographic Folklore Field Study. In *The Study of Games.* Edited by E. Avedon and B. Sutton-Smith. New York: John Wiley and Sons, Inc., 1971.

Goodman, F. The Computer as Plaything. *Simulation and Games, 15*(1984), 65-73.

Hawes, B. Law and Order on the Playground. In *Games in Education and Development.* Edited by L. Shears and E. Bowers. Springfield, Illinois: Charles C. Thomas, Publisher, 1974.

Hetherton, C. *The Demonstration Play School of 1913.* Berkeley: University of California Publications, 1914.

Hollis, L., and Felder, B. Recreational Mathematics for Young Children. *School Science and Mathematics, 82*(1982), 71-75.

Hounshell, P., and Trollinger, I. Games for Teaching Science. *Science and Children, 15*(1977), 11-14

Hughes, L. Beyond the Rules of the Game: Why Are Rooie Rules Nice? In *The World of Play.* Edited by F. Manning. West Point, New York: Leisure Press, 1983.

Jorgensen, M. Anti-School Parodies as Speech Play and Social Protest. In *The World of Play.* Edited by F. Manning. West Point, New York: Leisure Press, 1983.

King, N. Play: The Kindergartner's Perspective. *Elementary School Journal,* *80*(1979), 81-87.

King, N. School Uses of Materials Traditionally Associated with Children's Play. *Theory and Research in Social Education, 10*(1982a), 17-27.

King, N. Classroom Play as a Form of Resistance in the Classroom. *Journal of Education, 164*(1982b), 320-329.

King, N. Play in the Workplace. In *Ideology and Practice in Schooling.* Edited by M. Apple and L. Weis. Philadelphia: Temple University Press, 1983.

Kirschenblatt-Gimblett, B. Speech Play and Verbal Art. In *Play and Learning.* Edited by B. Sutton-Smith. New York: Gardner Press, Inc., 1979.

Knapp, M., and Knapp, H. *One Potato, Two Potato.* New York: W.W. Norton and Company, Inc., 1976.

Kraus, W. Using a Computer Game to Reinforce Skills in Addition Basic Facts in Second Grade. *Journal for Research in Mathematics Education, 12*(1981), 152-155.

Kraus, W. Math Learning Games: Simple vs. Complex. *School Science and Mathematics, 82*(1982), 397-398.

Leventhal, C. Afro-American Speech Play in Integrated Schools: Some Preliminary Comments. In *Play as Context.* Edited by A. Cheska. West Point, New York: Leisure Press, 1980.

Lever, J. Sex Differences in the Games Children Play. *Social Problems, 23*(1975-1976), 478-487.

Makedon, A. Playful Gaming. *Simulation and Games, 15*(1984), 25-64.

Malone, T. What Makes Things Fun to Learn? In *A Study of Intrinsically Motivating Computer Games.* Palo Alto, California: Xerox, 1980.

McDowell, J. *Children's Riddling.* Bloomington: Indiana University Press, 1979.

Miracle, A., Rowan, B., and Suggs, D. Play Activities and Elementary School Peer Groups. In *The Masks of Play.* Edited by B. Sutton-Smith and D. Kelly-Byrne. New York: Leisure Press, 1984.

Opie, I., and Opie, P. *The Lore and Language of Schoolchildren.* Oxford: The Clarendon Press, 1959.

Opie, I., and Opie, P.   *Children's Games in Street and Playground.*   Oxford: The Clarendon Press, 1969.

Palermo, J.   Education as a Simulation Game: A Critical Hermeneutic. *Journal of Thought, 14*(1979), 220-227.

Polgar, S.   The Social Context of Games: Or When Is Play Not Play? *Sociology of Education, 49*(1976), 265-271.

Polgar, S.   Modeling Social Relations in Cross-Color Play.   *Anthropology and Education Quarterly, 9*(1978), 238-289.

Pratt, C.   *I Learn from Children.*   New York: Simon and Schuster, 1948.

Reifel, S.   Play in the Elementary School Cafeteria.   Paper presented at the Annual Meeting of The Association for the Anthropological Study of Play, Clemson, South Carolina, April 1984.

Saegesser, F.   The Introduction of Play in Schools.   *Simulation and Games, 15*(1984), 75-96.

Sapon-Shevin, M.   Cooperative Instructional Games: Alternatives to the Spelling Bee .   *The Elementary School Journal, 79*(1978), 81-87.

Schoedler, J.   A Comparison of the Use of Active Game Learning with a Conventional Teaching Approach in the Development of Concepts in Geometry and Measurement at the Second Grade Level.   *School Science and Mathematics, 81*(1981), 365-370.

Schwartz, F.   Supporting or Subverting Learning: Peer Group Patterns in Four Tracked Schools.   *Anthropology and Education Quarterly, 12*(1981), 99-120.

Shears, L., and Bower, E.   (Eds.)   *Games in Education and Development.* Springfield, Illinois: Charles C. Thomas, Publishers, 1974.

Sluckin, A.   *Growing Up in the Playground.*   Boston: Routledge and Kegan Paul, 1981.

Spencer-Hall, D.   Looking Behind the Teacher's Back.   *The Elementary School Journal, 81*(1981), 281-289.

Sutton-Smith, B.   *The Folkgames of Children.*   Austin: University of Texas Press, 1972.

Sutton-Smith, B.   Play Theory of the Rich and for the Poor.   In *Children in and out of School.*   Edited by P. Gilmore and A. Glatthorn. Washington, D.C.: Center for Applied Linguistics, 1982.

Sutton-Smith, B. Play Theory and Cruel Play of the Nineteenth Century. In *The World of Play.* Edited by F. E. Manning. West Point, New York: Leisure Press, 1983.

Tyson, E., and Mountain, L. A Riddle or Pun Make Learning Words Fun. *The Reading Teacher, 35*(1982), 170-173.

Van de Walle, J., and Thompson, C. Fitting Problem Solving into Every Classroom. *School Science and Mathematics, 81*(1981), 290-297.

Wharton-Boyd, L. The Significance of Black American Children's Singing Games in an Educational Setting. *Journal of Negro Education, 52*(1983), 46-56.

Williams, M. Observations in Pittsburgh Ghetto Schools. *Anthropology and Education Quarterly, 12*(1981), 211-220.

Winsor, C. *Experimental Schools Revisited.* New York: Agathon Press, Inc., 1973.

Zammarelli, J., and Bolton, N. The Effects of Play on Mathematical Concept Formation. *British Journal of Educational Psychology, 47*(1977), 155-161.

PLAY AND THE JUNIOR HIGH ADOLESCENT

Robert B. Everhart

The purpose of this chapter is to examine the nature of junior high school play by focusing on a particular play form that characterizes so much of students' daily routine: goofing off. To analyze goofing off and its complexities is to understand an important aspect of the complex social interaction in which perspectives of play are socially constructed. Dimensions of play, as we shall discuss, must be understood within the organizational context in which they exist and through the cultural patterns created, re-created, and challenged within the school. In this chapter, I will examine junior high school play as an activity heavily patterned around the regularities which are part of the junior high's organizational life. I will show how junior high school play is integral to the making of the student cultures so characteristic of junior high school life.

It is useful, first, to realize that while play may take many forms, junior high school play is of a particular genre. King (1981, 1982a, 1982b), in her studies of elementary school children's play, has categorized school play into its *instrumental, recreational*, and *illicit* components. Instrumental play is incorporated within the practice of school work and enhances that work's goals and objectives. Viewing films, class contests, or science projects might be considered as forms of instrumental play because they are planned and engaged in for the purposes of pursuing the objectives of work. Recreational play also exists within the work context but constitutes a planned respite from work within the school's formal objectives: Recess games fit this category of play. Illicit play is characterized by those strategies of play wherein students engage in play behavior that oppose, to various degrees, the explicit rules and expectations of work.

At the junior high school, the first two forms of school play are either absent or relatively rare. Opportunities for instrumental play decline in junior high as teachers prepare students for the more content-oriented instructional practices of high school. Opportunities for recreational play also virtually disappear with the cessation of recess as a central programmatic activity. Whatever recreational play that exists is present in after-school extra-curricular activities in which only a minority of students participate. Junior high play, then, is largely of an illicit nature.

Illicit play takes on a number of different dimensions in junior high schools, yet as King notes, illicit play is a type of play on which we have little information, and this in formation comes from the level of the elementary school. Jorgensen (1983) and Gilmore (1983), for example, have discussed how elementary school children use parodies and satire of instructional activities as a form of expressing aversion to schooling or teachers. Similarly, Lancy (1976) has noted that elementary school students often see themselves "fooling around" and "bugging" (defined as bothering someone, either another student or the teacher). Williams (1981), too, has discussed how illicit play

167

can take the form of group activities such as staged "fights," meant to trick unsuspecting elementary teachers into thinking the act was in fact a real fight.

Yet, by the time of adolescence, illicit play has become an essential form of junior High school play, taking on a number of guises. With few exceptions, however, the nature and function of this form of play are minimally understood. There is a tendency to view it as generalized "fooling around" (Lancy, 1976)--that is, as somewhat random and unsystematic behavior lacking a complex inner logic. Moreover, when attempts are made to understand illicit play, they usually are done under rubrics other than play. Woods (1979) for example, discusses humor, or "having a laugh" as a "life saving response to the exigencies of the institution - boredom, ritual, routine, regulations, oppressive authority" (p.120). Likewise, Cusick (1973) and Willis (1977) point to other forms of oppositional activity in which adolescents engage in order to create a sense of purpose and meaning to their school career.

In this chapter, we will see that the illicit play of junior high school adolescence is not only purposeful but has an intricate internal structure. We shall summarize portions of a two-year field study in one junior high school (Everhart, 1983). The study was based upon first hand observation of student life in that school and described how illicit play was understood by participants.   One way to tap this level of understanding was through approaches developed by cognitive anthropologists (Spradley, 1979), which can be used with any cultural group. While the specific approach used in this study is detailed in my earlier work, my basic procedure was to elicit from students culturally relevant categories descriptive of their daily life.

First, I will describe what students in Harold Spencer Junior High said they did in school. Next, I will single out "goofing off" as a primary student activity and report on its social context. Then, I will turn to the patterned regularities of goofing off and show that such activity is not random but organized around interactional, temporal, and spatial routines. Finally, I will discuss the consequences of goofing off, the manner in which such forms of illicit play can be seen organizationally and culturally, and raise for review the conceptual tools which we might consider to further such analyses. Implications for educational practice conclude the chapter.

STUDENT ACTIVITIES IN THE JUNIOR HIGH SCHOOL

In Table 1, I have outlined the school activities in which students said they engaged. The list represents a picture, a 'map' if you will, of the school as seen by a cross-section of the students themselves. In the rest of this section, I will point to some major "intersections" on the map, places where students' self-described activities came together, in order to understand better the total milieu into which goofing off fits. Overall, I will show that conflict, endurance, and escape characterize the bulk of activities mentioned by students.

Table 1

What Students Do In School.

Go to the cans.	*Smoke joints or cigarettes, shit.*	
Work.	*Do tests, math assignments, write essays, take notes.*	
Pick on kids.	*Give them flat tires, harass or threaten them, pick on Mike and Kathy, throw their books on the floor, steal their food.*	
Get busted, fight, mess or goof around.		
Skip.	*To the park or mall, at home, a period.*	
Go to class.	*Daydream.*	
	Make time go by.	*Goof off, push the clock, daydream, bug the teacher.*
	Be teacher's pet.	*Grade papers, pass out books, take out attendance slips, record stuff in grade book, go to office, get out of class or spelling tests.*
	Get in trouble, sit on our asses, don't do much, do as little as I can, sit and rot, sleep, get detention	

	and points.	
Go to lunch.	*Goof around.*	*chase kids to courtyard, go to lockers, wait outside classes.*
	Eat lunch, talk, scrounge.	
Goof off.	*Shoot things.*	*Rubber bands, paper clips or wads.*
	Slam books down, break pencil points, have pencil fights, throw apper in wastepaper basket, borrow paper from someone, hack a loogey, do anything you're not supposed to, talk.	
	Throw things.	*Chalk, erasers, gym bags, books, mike.*
	Bug teachers.	*Talk, bug substitutes, do your push-ups screwy, chew gum, defy them, be late on purpose, pretend you are chewing gum, pass notes with nothing on them, talk about them and/or let them hear you, tap pencils or feet, laugh, kid them, flip intercom switch or lights on and off, flip teacher off, ask teacher to repeat questions, not do work, wear hats or coats in class, be late and don't bring slip, laugh*

when they yell at
you, move slow
when they tell you
to do something,
not be in seat
when bell rings,
lay your head on
the desk.

Write notes,
crawl behind
chairs, take
someone's books
and have them
chase you, punch
other kids
around.

Conflict

A perusal of Table 1 supports the notion that varying degrees of conflict are indeed descriptive of the life of junior high students. Conflict seems to abound as kids "pick" on each other, "fight," and "bug" the teacher.

While "picking on kids" was one form of conflict with other students, "fighting" was probably the most physical and, in some respects, the most serious expression of conflict. Fights were not that significant in terms of numbers of people who fought but because everyone heard about them, talked about them, and discussed the issues. Friends of the fighters lined up with one party or another, making the competition between groups of people rather than simply between the antagonists themselves.

Yet, the underlying and ongoing conflict between the student and the teacher, in many respects the two prime antagonists in the conflict arena, was even more pervasive than the conflicts between students. According to Table 1, there were two main student-teacher interactions. Somewhat passive interactions occurred when students daydreamed, did not do their work, or sat on their "asses." More conflict oriented interactions happened when students "bugged" their teachers.

The term "conflict" immediately conjures up visions of the "blackboard jungle," vicious fights, continual challenge of teachers' authority, and other images of outright warfare. Nothing could be further from the truth with the students at Harold Spencer Junior High. I never once saw a knife fight of any kind. And although there were occasional bloody noses from fights in the hall, these fights were no different or worse than the ones I witnessed in my own days as a student or I broke up as a junior high teacher. Yet that does not change the fact that teachers had dominance over students in a forced environment, and this situation guaranteed some degree of resistance by students against the all-encompassing authority of the teacher. Accordingly, conflict, in terms of "bugging the teacher" and its part in the ideational system of the students' world, seemed a preordained consequence of the formal organization of the school.

Endurance

There are two reasons why it is useful to review the subject of "work" and "classes" as something that students say they do in school. One reason is that work was not often discussed, and thus students did not view it as an important element in their collective existence. A second reason is that there are indications that classes were something students usually endured. Terms such as "daydream," or "do as little as I can," or "don't do much" were signals of how students saw classes as something with which to put up. While not all classes were seen in the same way, even those minimally approved of classes were regarded cautiously. Thus, for most students, life in classrooms necessitated a passive resignation of that which was seen to be their fate, most specifically, to accept their role as receivers of knowledge and then to hold out or endure until the period or day was over.

Escape

Some students attempted to circumvent the need to endure classes by "skipping" or "being teacher's pet." Skipping involved various strategies to absent oneself from portions of the school day; most of these strategies were violations of school procedures. To be a pet meant getting out of class work and thereby doing something more than enduring. Being a pet also meant participation in additional classroom activities that set the pet apart from the other students who had to be involved in only teacher-required activities. Being a pet thus meant the possession of some control over the scope of involvement in the activities of the school. For some students such control was worth the ridicule from other students, since pets were ridiculed if they actively solicited favors from the teacher. Other students could be held in high regard by fellow students if the frequency of such favors was low and if the student did not seek them out. The important fact is that being a pet was but one of a number of strategies used by students to escape some of the formalized imperatives of classroom life. In subsequent examinations of "goofing off," other forms of such escape will be examined.

GOOFING OFF

The themes of conflict, endurance, and escape provide the backdrop for one activity students saw as central to their role in the school--that of "goofing off," and it is to an analysis of that activity which we now turn. I have chosen to examine goofing off primarily because it is so uniformly perceived by students as the raison d'etre for their presence in school.

We can begin our understanding of goofing off by examining a social studies class taught jointly by Mr. Richards and Mr. Bruce. While most students tolerated Bruce, few students liked Richards, in part because he appeared excessively authoritarian, unbending, and insistent on exactness for every paper or project. It had to be done his way ("right") or not at all, and most of the students resisted such an uncompromising position by reacting against it.

One day's experience was typical of this class:

> We entered the room and sat down in the assigned seats. The bell rang and the aide, Mrs. Rose, stood at the front taking attendance by seat number. After attendance, Richards said: "On your desks you will see textbooks. The first thing you will do is turn to page 204. That is where the section on Bulgaria begins. I want you to read carefully pages 204?- 210, and when I say carefully, I mean carefully! For those who have poor memories and forget the assignment, it is also written on the board to your right. I will pass out worksheets on which are listed ten questions from the reading, and what I want you to do is to answer the questions, being sure to write in complete sentences, capitalizing the first word of each sentence. Are there any questions? Well, if there are not, there shouldn't be any excuse for not doing a good job."
>
> Marty and Chris (two boys with whom I had established a close relationship) started reading, Chris finishing the six pages in about ten minutes. By that time, Richards had passed out the mimeographed sheets with the question on them. Chris looked at them, then put them down and began thumbing though the book looking at the pictures.
>
> "No good pictures, looks like they're from the Dark Ages," he mumbled.
>
> Looking at the front of the book, Marty said, "No wonder, look when the son of a bitch was printed, 1963."
>
> "Neat," Chris acknowledged as he began to work on the questions, but not too energetically. He intermittently doodled on the desk, being careful to wipe it off after completing a design or picture. Chris finished the questions in about fifteen minutes, and Richards, seeing that some students had finished, told them to "find something to do" until everyone finished because they were going to review the answers in class. Chris pulled out a copy of Eric Von Daniken's *Chariot of the Gods* and began reading it.
>
> After about ten minutes, Richards asked how many were not done. About ten people raised their hands, and Richards said that he would give them five more minutes to finish. "I think some of you people better spend more time on the assignment and less time fooling around," he said. "It shouldn't be taking you forty minutes to do this assignment."
>
> Richards then told the class to get out their papers and he started reviewing the answers to the ten questions. He asked for volunteers for each question, but volunteers were few despite the presence of eighty people in the class. Slowly, Richards elicited answers to all the questions. Richards then asked everyone to pass in their papers. It was about five minutes before the end of the period.

"All right, keep it quiet till the bell rings, or I'll find something for you to do. Martin, turn around."

Richards started walking around the room. He was a stickler on people being quiet before the bell rang, and sometimes had the whole class sit straight for twenty seconds before he would let them go. As the bell rang, Chris and Martin vaulted out of their seats, walked rapidly to the door, and hurried to lunch.

After lunch, John, Chris, and I ambled over toward the "A" building for fifth-period English with Mr. Von Hoffman. The assignment today was to give oral reports which were assigned almost one week ago. The reports were to be short (two to three minutes) and Von Hoffman stood near his desk recording grades as each student finished his report.

A girl began by giving a report on photography, but it was clear that few people were paying attention.

Von Hoffman interrupted the girl giving the report. "People, have some courtesy for those giving reports and stop your talking. I'm sure you wouldn't want to be giving a report with half the class talking and not paying attention."

"I don't care," chipped in Mike on the other side of the room.

Chris stated, "Hey, Mr. Von Hoffman. If everybody talks we shouldn't have to give our reports, right?"

The girl continued. John had to give his report in about fifteen minutes, so he turned around to Chris sitting behind him.

"Chris, Chris."

"Yeah."

"Tell me something I can do for a report."

"I don't know. How about Hickory, Dickory Dock?"

"No, I'm serious, what should I do?"

"Hey, I know. Why don't you tell some story about your rabbits? Like raising rabbits and how you do that. You could fake that for a few minutes."

"That sounds, yeah, why not. Just about raising rabbits, something like that will keep him happy." John then turned around and jotted a few notes on a scrap of paper.

After listening to reports on "My Trip to Glacier (National Park)" and a slide show on Japan, it was then John's turn. He walked up to the front of the room, turned to face the class, caught Chris's eyes, and started laughing.

"Come on, John, give your report or sit down," Von Hoffman directed. John started but began laughing again.

"Great report, Mr. Von Hoffman," said Mike, clapping, "give him an A."

"Outstanding," Chris said, adding his support. "Best report of the year."

"OK, John, sit down please."

"No, no. I'll give it. Tell Chris to stop laughing."

Von Hoffman then walked to the back of the room, stood next to Chris's seat and said to John, "Begin! I have some pet rabbits at home and I'd like to tell you about raising them. First, you have to feed them, and I feed them food that rabbits eat."

Chris raised his hand. "What kind of food do rabbits eat?"

John replied, "They eat rabbit food which I buy at the rabbit food store (everyone in the class laughed). They also eat food which comes from our table." He went on, "Rabbits do not like the cold ground so you have to build cages for them. The cage I have is off the ground so they don't get wet, and it is made of wire."

Chris raised his hand again. "John, where did you get the cage?"

John said that he had built it "with scrap lumber and special materials that one gets from the rabbit store." From then on, every time John spoke, Chris raised his hand and asked in a very serious and studious manner a question about something that John had said. Finally, Von Hoffman, irritated by Chris constantly raising his hand, asked him to not interrupt and let John finish his speech.

"But Mr. Von Hoffman," Chris said innocently, "I'm just trying to find out more about rabbits and the only way I can learn is to ask questions of someone who knows."

John continued, describing what rabbits like to do for entertainment and how even in winter if it gets cold, you have to put a heater in their cage. Finally, John ended his report by saying that "rabbits are also kind of stupid animals, in fact they are so stupid I butchered all of them last week, and they do make very good stew." With this, he sat down.

John, Chris, and Mike snickered to each other from across the room. I overheard some of the girls in the class saying "Yuk," or "How could you kill those soft little bunnies." One girl turned around to John and said, "None of that is very funny." Chris continued to laugh and volunteered, "Good speech, old boy. Mr. Von Hoffman, I think he deserves an A."

Von Hoffman was obviously irritated. "An A like mad. Just sit down and be quiet, both of you. I don't know why you can't take anything seriously enough to do a good job on it. I ask you to give one oral report a term and you have to make a big joke out of it."

"Did you give John an A, Mr. Von Hoffman?"

"Chris, shut up. No more out of you for the period or you'll be down to visit Mr. Pall."

John turned around to Chris and said, "What a sorehead."

As the class was ready to leave, Von Hoffman told me that he was tired of "that group always goofing off in here." He said that they took nothing seriously and that even though John, Chris, and Mike were "good students," they seemed to think it was more fun to "fool around" and be rude than it was to do their work. "I can't understand why they have to act that way. There are some students in here who never give me any trouble. It's the same ones all the time."

Von Hoffman's question, basic as it was, was a good one. Why was it that Von Hoffman always had trouble with "that group" fooling around while

Richards (in the class I described earlier) seemed to experience relatively little harassment from Chris, John, Mike, or Marty? Certainly, there was little doubt that Richards ran a much more regimented class; consequently, it was difficult to get away with very much. Still, for Chris or John or others such was not necessarily a deterrent because, as individuals, they were often quite passive in classes that were equally as "loosely" operated. For example, John basically put up with music during fifth-period and Chris was untypically quiet in his second-period art class.

The antics of Chris, John, and their friends are quite typical of junior high students and, although usually not considered as such, are representative of the genre we are terming "illicit play." Students did seem to pick and choose the classes in which they goofed off, this selectivity being a point raised by others who have examined various facets of student life (Allen, 1982; Stinchcombe, 1964; Werthman, 1971). This context of selectivity helps us understand goofing off more completely.

For John, Chris, Mike, and a few others (all were B students), one of the most important determinants of whether or not they goofed off was having friends in the class. Friends were important because they provided people with whom to interact, either about subjects of importance or in activities that symbolized the significance of the group, a point made clear in a variety of studies on adolescent activities in schools (Coleman, 1974; Cusick, 1973; Epstein, 1983; Schlechty, 1976). Goofing off with friends was a way of acting in class in the same way that one did in informal situations when the person could choose his own associates. Later in the year, Bill, a person who knew Chris but was not really good friends with him, told me, "If you don't have anybody to talk to, you just sit through the whole class, duh! And you don't get interested in the class. But if you have friends, you can goof off with your friends." I asked him if this made the class more interesting, and he replied, "Sure, you can goof off more."

Since friends were so important in the goofing off process, then, by definition, there were people with whom Chris and his group either did not goof off with or who, to their way of thinking at least, did not goof off at all. Because goofing off occurred largely with friends, the students' perceptions of who goofed off, and actualization of those perceptions into behavior, provided what appeared to be a consistent and reliable way by which they drew boundaries around their own group of friends. Goofing off did not cause, but was associated with the boundaries that had been drawn and were being drawn around the membership of relevant peer groups.

WAYS TO GOOF OFF

Thus far we have established that goofing off is an activity that students saw occurring among friends or, at least, among compatible people. While everyone goofed off, different groups of students did it in their own way and qualitative differences existed between the types of goofing off and conditions affecting its practice. In this section, we will review the different ways to goof off, examining goofing off as a form of social interaction. Also in this section, we will see that goofing off is somewhat regularized by spatial considerations within the classroom as well as by student perceptions as to the timeliness for different goofing- off activities.

Goofing-off as Student-Student Interaction

Table 2 provides an overview of ways to goof off. It illustrates that students consciously perceived goofing off not to be a solo event but one that involved explicit interaction among friends.

The interactional dimensions of goofing off are best illustrated if we can return to the classes of Richards, the social studies teacher, and Von Hoffman, the English teacher. Remember that Von Hoffman was quite frustrated over the course of the year as he witnessed John, Chris, Mike, and others playfully shoving each other over desks, into lockers, and on to lawns before, after, and during classes. Richards thought that such behavior was "disruptive" and "juvenile" and said that he would never tolerate it in his class - and he usually did not. His objections did not, however, change the nature of "punching your friends" as a significant category describing social interactional ways students used to goof off.

Table 2

Interactional Ways For Students To Goof Off.

Write Notes.
Shoot Things:

Paper Wads
Rubber Bands.
Paper Clips.

Break Pencil Points.
Throw Paper in Wastebasket.
Borrow Paper from Someone.
Throw Things:

Chalk.
Erasers.
Books.
Gym Bags.

Talk.
Punch Friends Around.

I asked Chris one day if there was any difference between picking on Larry or Dan before math class and the hitting and shoving he did with John before and after (sometimes even during) Von Hoffman's English class. Chris told me that there were two kinds of punching and hitting around, one was the "kidding" kind and the other the "serious" kind (cf. Glassner, 1976).

The serious kind was related to "picking on kids," that is, students not liked or ones considered to be "weird." The "kidding" kind was reserved directly and specifically for friends, and, for Chris, that meant the kind he did with John, Mike, and others in his group.

Table 2 also shows that much of goofing off consisted of throwing or shooting things; chalk, erasers, paper clips, rubber bands, or paper wads. One particular incident serves well to illustrate the social interactional patterns of shooting things:

> Dave, Steve, and Don, and a few other students were engaged in a paper wad fight with straws; I was sitting directly behind Dave on the right-hand side of the room near the windows. As before, when Marcy, the English teacher, was not looking or was preoccupied, the group began their usual barrage of paper wads across the room. But this time I, too, was getting hit with paper wads, and it became apparent that I was the target for both Steve and Don who were sitting on the left-hand side of the room. At about that time, a boy named "Wolfie," who was *persona non grata* with Don and his friends, began rolling his own paper wads, shooting them back to Steve and Don, neither of whom were at all interested in returning paper wads to Wolfie. Wolfie shot a few more wads toward Steve and Don, but they continued to ignore him as they shot wads toward Dave and me.
>
> One of the basic tenets of spit wad fights seemed to rest in having an adequate supply of projectiles on hand because, in the heat of battle, it took too much time if one had to roll wads while others were shooting. There were two ways of obtaining a supply: making a supply in advance or having friends provide a supply by making them or picking up missiles from the floor. Wolfie had not made any wads in advance, and he tried to pick some up from the floor to replenish his dwindling supply. Immediately, however, other students sitting near where the paper wads were landing began to pick them up and hand them to Dave in front of me.
>
> "Come on, you guys, give me some of those," Wolfie pleaded with Jim, who had been handing Dave paper wads. Jim ignored him and nonchalantly continued to lean over on the floor as Marcy turned her back.
>
> "Bug off, will ya," Jim said curtly as he tried to shake Wolfie away.
>
> Dave continued to have a ready supply but Wolfie, having to roll his own and having his requests for more ammunition ignored, was limited to muzzle-loading speed. Since nobody was shooting back at him, he was effectively limited from the non-verbal interaction of shooting spit wads and soon quit.

All such similar events now made more sense to me. I had seen eraser and chalk fights before class where Don and his group had been throwing erasers and where Yaeger had tried to join the festivities. But Yaeger, too, was denied participation in these activities by virtue of being ignored and eventually shoved out of the room. Don and his friends simply had no time for involvement with someone not part of their group. Yaeger was excluded because he had attempted to break into what was essentially an intricate and tightly closed communication system that existed between members of a social group. Because of the social characteristics of such activities as throwing and shooting things, they took on an important meaning to those who engaged in them (see, also, Allen, 1982; Glassner, 1976; and Licata and Willower, 1975). While "disruptive" to teachers, they formed another strand in the activities of goofing off, representative of the complex culture of junior high students who actively created elements of their own culture.

Goofing Off as Student-Teacher Interaction

I have discussed goofing off as a form of social interaction among students. We have examined the meaning system shared among members of the group as it pertains to the activities of the group. Reference to Table 1 demonstrates, however, that much goofing off was directly or indirectly related to someone other than students--teachers --in the form of "bugging the teacher." The variety of categories of "bugging the teacher" represents still another way by which groups of students were cemented together via the goofing off process.

Bugging took many *forms* but one of the more common ones was to say something about a teacher so that he or she would overhear, but be unable to do much about it. Numerous "Christie Love" incidents illustrated this.

> In an attempt to reduce some of the problems with girls at the lunch hour, Mr. Edwards, the principal, had released one of the women teachers to patrol rest rooms and halls during the lunch hour in order to catch smokers and break up minor disturbances ("Hawkeye" served in a similar capacity for boys). Many of the students dubbed the woman "narc," Mrs. Hanslenski, as "Christie Love," (after the television show starring a black policewoman). If Hanslenski approached a specific group at lunch, a member of the group almost invariably said "here comes Christie" because they knew she disliked the label.

"Flipping the intercom switch" and "flipping lights off and on" are two more illustrations of the interactional aspects of ways to bug the teacher. Flipping the intercom switch was perhaps the most "exciting" of these two individual bugs in that it caused the teacher the most surprise. Don, Dave, and Steve were experts at this:

> Leaving the room at the end of class, Steve or Don pulled the "call" button down on the intercom, located adjacent to the door. Marcy, at the front of the room organizing papers and putting away books, did not recognize what had happened (pulling the "call" button signaled someone in the main office that the teacher wanted information for some reason). The office would then call back to the room, "office."
> "I didn't call the office."
> "Well, someone called the office from your room, Mrs. Marcy."

Marcy muttered, "It must have been those boys again. Oh why didn't they put that switch somewhere else?"

Bugging the teacher had two basic forms: one was socially initiated (that is, initiated by two or more people), as indicated in Table 3. These activities included those just discussed.

Table 3

Socially Initiated Ways To Bug The Teacher

Bug substitutes.
Talk about them.
Talk about them and let them hear you.
Tap feet.
Tap pencils.
Laugh.
Wear hat/coat in class.
Pass notes with nothing on them.
Flipping lights off and on.
Flipping intercom switch.

There were also "individual" ways of bugging the teacher (see Table 4). These forms did not require the direct participation of others to carry out the bug, but they were still socially significant and provided another interdependent link that helped to bind students together.

Table 4

Individually Initiated Ways To Bug The Teacher

Chew gum.
Pretend to chew gum.
Be late on purpose.
Be class joker.
Flip teacher off
Talk back.
Be late and don't bring slip.
Move slow when they tell you to do something.
Not be in your seat when the bell rings.
Lay your head on the desk during films.
Not do work.
Tap feet.
Tap pencils.

Gum chewing, as well as many of the other categories in Table 4, illustrates the importance of group solidarity, participation, and support in bugging the teacher, even for activities that were done by individuals. Bugging the teacher was an act of "brinksmanship" (Licata and Willower, 1975) that cemented those involved in, or supportive of, the act into a common framework or bond. There was nothing more exhilarating to the group than to act in unison on a bug started by one or a few other students. Consequently things such as "tapping pencils" or "tapping feet" were euphoric activities when picked up by a large number of students. These were activities that united the group in one of the few ways it could be united, in an alliance against a commonly perceived force--the teacher.

Why did students bug teachers? Such activities were not always initiated for reasons of social solidarity, though that certainly was a consequence. Other more basic issues undergirded the initiation of bugging the teacher.

Certain teachers were bugged almost incessantly; others were bugged less. Whether a teacher was the target of this particular form of goofing off was, at least from the point of view of the students, dependent on two things; whether they thought they could get away with bugging him or her (or more accurately, the degree of bugging they could get away with) and the personal relationship they had with that particular teacher. Very often, complex factors affected these two conditions.

For example, the teachers who were most bugged were not liked for various reasons. Some, such as Hackett, "are not nice to us," which meant that "they talk down to us" or "treat us like babies." Most teachers who were bugged seemed, to the students, to be distant and to reflect a sense of superiority. Additionally, they were "mean" because they had lots of "stupid rules" which did not make any sense: rules such as having to print instead of write your name, writing your name in the right-hand corner of your paper rather than in the left hand corner, or doing "stupid exercises" in grammar books.

Conversely, teachers who were liked were bugged infrequently. Again, this did not mean that students did not goof off in their class, simply that they did not do it to bug the teacher as frequently. Usually, if a teacher was considered "good," he or she was not bugged as much. To be a good teacher in the eyes of most students meant to be "understanding" or "to know a little about what kids are like today." A good teacher did not do "just the same old thing" all the time. In these classes students were permitted to sit together, talk while working on projects, and walk around the room.

Yet just because students did not goof off to bug the teacher, that did not necessarily mean they liked the class or the teacher; it often meant that the teacher was too strict or observant to allow many activities to occur. Mr. Richards probably had the most efficiently run classes in the school. Papers were turned in in a uniform manner; books were stacked in a consistent way; he could leave the room for five minutes and rarely would there be a peep from anyone (some students always suspected that he was waiting around the corner to "catch us"). But Richards was also one of the more disliked teachers in the school and that made students want to goof off far more than they did.

Yet it was difficult because he watched the class very carefully, gave out detentions with considerable liberality, and usually had an aide to help supervise. This made it doubly hard to bug him, and bugs were restricted to individually initiated bugs, as Dave said, "Just to piss him off," things like smiling at him, purposefuly piling the books the wrong way on the counter, and tapping feet.

From the comments of most students, there were more teachers whose classes were "boring" than not, and "bugging the teacher" had to take a subtle form because many of these teachers were fairly strict and had "good control" over their classes. Consequently, the bugging had to be phased in at opportune moments: between events, intermittently so as not to draw too much attention, subtly so as not to indicate conspiracy. Yet this did not seem to alter too significantly the comment made by Steve about almost all his classes: "Class is so boring and you wanna have something to do that is fun, so you bug them as much as you can."

Bugging the teacher then had a dimension to it that reflected the collective nature in which it was defined and the consequences that grew out of it for the students who engaged in it. Involved in "boring classes" in which "there is nothing else to do," students viewed the nature of goofing off as an oppositional strategy to demonstrate symbolically their resistance to estranged labor which they experienced in much of their daily life within the classroom. While this separation from control may have been differentially experienced by individual students as to time and place, it appeared to be a universal experience. When experienced in those places and times where individual experiences coalesced into collective realization, bugging the teacher became largely socially initiated or sustained. This phenomenon of periodic collective manipulation of teachers by students is more generally discussed by Mehan (1980) and McDermott (1976).

Time, Timing, and Tempo

While interactional factors predominated in the patterns of goofing off, two other characteristics helped define the parameters of goofing off. These characteristics--those of time and space--were so omnipresent and pervasive that on first consideration they seemed barely worthy of mention. But like other aspects of the student world, it would be a mistake to take too much for granted (see Mehan, 1979).

I reported earlier in this chapter how Dave once told me that goofing off to bug the teacher involved a sense of timing. His exact words were: "You have to know the right time." Knowing the sequencing of events, the timing, and the tempo was very important in maintaining the delicate equilibrium between not doing anything and continually being in Pall's office(the assistant principal's). Students recognized that there were certain definite times during a class when goofing off was more effectively carried out than other times; there were also types of goofing off that were better suited to different times.

There were, for example, times to talk to your friends. Karen said "When Hackett is working with a group is a good time to talk, but if you're laughing too loud and he hears you he really gets pissed." In Von Hoffman's class, John told me that a good time to talk was when he was passing out an assignment or worksheet because he never seemed to do much if you talked then. Likewise, films provided opportune times to talk in social studies because the room was so dark and so big, but you had to be careful that you knew where Richards was or else he would sneak up behind you and slap you with a ruler. Marcy's class was a particularly good class in which to talk because she always gave two or three different assignments in class, and she was too busy collecting papers or sorting materials to closely watch the entire class. She did not seem to mind much if students talked as long as they did not throw things.

Times of changing activities provided opportunities for throwing or shooting things with friends or talking. Don, Dave, and Steve quite often took advantage of these interstitial times to lob paper wads, rubber bands, and other assorted missiles.

Seatwork was another good time to goof off in a variety of ways, particularly talking, bugging students, shooting and throwing things. That was why sharpening pencils, throwing paper in the wastebasket, borrowing paper, and such other activities were so important. These activities provided a rationale to be out of the seat, something necessary if you had a friend "you just have to talk to."

Most teachers tolerated goofing off to a certain degree but then took measures to stop it once that limit had been reached. The secret for the student was to know the limit and then be able to switch to another form of goofing off once the limit had been reached or exceeded. Thus, strategies of bugging the teacher often changed because of an almost subconscious realization by the students that there was a need to move into a new form of bugging. The timing of such moves was partially dependent on the student awareness that timing of acts was correlated with the probabilities of being caught and the resulting consequences. For example, Terri frequently arrived late to chorus without an "admit slip" because it provided her with an excuse to get a smoke in the girl's restroom in the middle of the morning. It was relatively easy to do this because she said, "All they do in the office is give me an admit slip and tell me not to do it again." In other classes, she said she'd never try that, because "the first thing you get is thirty minutes from some guy like Jenkins." Similarly, "group stares" (where everyone stared at the teacher to make him or her nervous) or laughing at the teacher were not attempted in some places because the consequences were too severe--for example, more work. According to Chris and John, they rarely did either in Richards's class because "He's so sensitive, he gets so flustered then really piles it on." But the word was that everyone did them in Franks' class; he was really "too dumb to know the difference."

Bugging the teacher, then, was a learned activity that changed to some degree every time the student went to a new class. There was a folklore among the students about what kind of bugs worked with which teachers and what times to use them. This folklore (the general existence of which is described by Fein, 1979) spread among the students and was acted upon and tested daily. It was known to be fairly easy to get away with nearly everything in Von Hoffman's class, and even students who never had him for classes would lean their head in the room and yell "Hi Buzzard," mocking his nose and thatchy haircut. Similar activities were not attempted in math or social studies, nor were they tried if things got "hot," that is, if there was a crackdown on particular actions. In such cases, the students merely moved on to another form of activity, one that was calculated to bug the teacher.

If the times to goof off were contextually influenced, so were the strategies of goofing off temporally related. For example, students perceived time in terms of their consciousness of how fast it went:

> I asked Robin and Terri if some classes went faster than others.
>
> "Social studies drags."
>
> "How does it drag?" I inquired.
>
> Robin answered, "Sixth period. Are you kidding, you've been in there."
>
> "The reading program, those reading machines" (referring to teaching machines where reading tapes were flashed on a screen and the student was tested for speeed and comprehension). Terri said she had that third period.
>
> "You mean that drags?"
>
> "Oh, God, man does it drag," Robin said. "If I had a choice between kissing Bob Boyd, who is the "dog" of the school, and doing reading..."
>
> Barry indicated that he, too, saw time "dragging" in some of his classes. I asked which classes dragged. He looked around and said:
>
> "This one [English]. We sit here and we do the same thing over and over, prepositional phrases, prepositional phrases, and we just do it over and over and over and everyday it gets boring. We sit there and do assignments three and four times. This class really drags because I know we are going to do the same thing again and again."

Students, with whom I associated, attempted to adapt to subjectively different lengths of time by creating their own agenda to make the time pass more rapidly. I asked Phil what he did to make time go faster:

> "Shoot paper wads, shoot people with paper clips, get everybody riled up because then you're all ready to go. Then all of a sudden time is over."
>
> "So that makes the time go fast?"
>
> "Yeah, sure does help."
>
> "Do you ever get bored goofing off?"
>
> "Sometimes, if nobody is paying attention."
>
> "Nobody is paying attention; what do you mean?"
>
> "Like we're always cracking jokes in Von Hoffman's class and, you know, sometimes people will stop laughing or won't join in, then it starts to get boring."

As Phil indicated, the key to making time go by in a boring class was to maintain the momentum (Kounin, 1970; Smith and Geoffrey, 1968), and to anticipate events in the future that provided something to which to look forward. But especially important was to involve one's peers in the goofing off process, for then the collectivity made time go by even faster. Little wonder, then, that goofing off with friends was so highly valued, for it removed, to some extent, the alienative dimensions of student labor in the school.

Space

The physical arrangement of the classroom and the effect on student interaction never appeared influential in the amount and type of goofing off until one day I overheard Dave talking to Chris, mentioning how math was so boring because he was not located near any friends that were "fun." After this, I began to look more closely at how varying spatial arrangements affected the patterns of goofing off and learned that the physical layout of the school and the location of the students were important factors affecting patterns of goofing off (Allen, 1982).

With few exceptions, classrooms at Harold Spencer were arranged in a standard physical arrangement--rows of movable desks lined up facing the teacher at the front of the room. Some rooms had tables lined up across the room with seats at each table, again facing the front. Two notable exceptions were the math "lab," into which about 40 percent of the students were scheduled, and the "big room" that housed some of the social studies and science classes. The math lab consisted of individual "study carrels" along the perimeter of the room, together with individual tables seating three or four students in the middle of the room. In the "big room," a large college-style lecture room, students sat in long somewhat concave rows of tables with permanently fixed seats at the table. This room held about eighty students, the math lab about sixty.

Perhaps the most important classroom spatial factor influencing the pattern of goofing off was where the student sat. Obviously, the further removed the student was from the teacher's line of vision, the greater the probability that goofing off could occur with minimal intrusion from the teacher. Accordingly, at the beginning of the year, there usually was a jockeying for seats at the rear of the room and on the outside perimeter--those areas most marginal to the teacher's line of vision. Soon, however, seating charts altered these arrangements of peers.

Despite the implementation of seating charts, however, goofing off was still a way to mediate the effect of seat location. Marcy once mentioned in the teachers' lounge that Karen and Lisa seemed to pass a lot of notes, but Mr. Miller, the math teacher, said he never had a problem with that, just the fact that every time he turned around they were talking. Similarly, Marcy mentioned once that Don, Steve, and Dave were always "throwing stuff" in her class, but Crealey told me he never had problems with them in science. Marcy said that she could never figure out why Don, Steve, and Dave always "acted up" in class and why she had trouble getting them to take their work seriously.

The answer to this paradox was quite simple. Don, Steve, and Dave had learned to work around the structure of the school in order to carry out their agenda. Marcy continually remade the seating chart in order to prevent what was so important to these three--their social interaction about issues important to them and their group. While she attempted to disperse the boys in order to preclude that interaction, minimization of their talking simply led to other forms of goofing off--"shooting things," "throwing things," and "bugging the teacher." Often, attempts to discourage one form of social interaction resulted in the appearance of other forms of interaction.

This does not explain precisely why the actions of Don, Steve, and Dave did not frustrate Crealey in science. Part of the answer is found in how the classes were arranged and the way students were dispersed throughout them. In fact, if we compare where the students sat in two classes--the math lab and social studies--we can better understand the patterns of goofing off as strategies of illicit play.

Students in the math lab told me they goofed off a lot but almost always in the form of talking among each other. Either they talked at the tables where they sat in groups or they left their seats to meet at the pencil sharpener or on the way to the wastebasket or while checking answers at the table where the answer keys were kept. All of these were legitimate forms of behavior, that is, forms of activity sanctioned by the organization of the class. Students who sat at tables or carrels were supposed to get up and move around to check answers, get new math packages, take tests, and so on. Because this was a permissible activity, students did not have to use as many circuitous ways to communicate; interpersonal communication was built into the instructional process itself.

The social studies class was completely different from the math lab. Students were not permitted to walk around during class; they were not permitted to speak during class; they were not granted the luxury of talking informally among themselves during the time in which the class was in session. In addition, Richards was known for his propensity to give out numerous detention notices. John told me that "he's got enough paper in there [meaning detention notices] that he'd write out a detention notice for everybody if he thought he had a reason. I saw him give five of them out in one day in ten minutes - just for chewing gum."

But the fact that Richards "watches us like a hawk" did not deter goofing off in social studies. It was just a different kind of goofing off. Most of the girls told me that they passed more notes in social studies than in any other class, and from my observations, I would say they were right. Another type of goofing off in social studies was a form of shuffleboard along the tables, using wads of paper with pencils as the "pusher" (a practice especially popular during the many films). And activities to "bug the teacher" were more obvious in the class--tapping pencils, slamming books shut, laying heads on desks during films, and sleeping, tapping feet, and the like. Such activities were easy to disguise in a large room with between seventy and eighty students (as one person said, "they can't really pay attention to every single person"), and students took advantage of the anonymity provided by the spatial arrangement.

SUMMARY AND CONCLUSIONS

Goofing off constituted the very essense of illicit play among students at Spencer. The activity itself was largely under the control of students and, more specifically, certain clusters of students from whom the behaviors were generated out of the bonds of friendship and collegiality. A special communication system evolved as students came into contact with an ongoing system of social relations emanating out of their somewhat predefined, but still developing, world of activity.

Illicit play, then, while it is an activity in which junior high students frequently engage, was also a form of knowledge production--that is, it produced, as does curriculum, knowledge relevant to behavior, attitudes, and values in the students' work environment--the school. Yet, as we have seen, activities such as goofing off were not erratic or randomly acted out but were quite purposeful and emerged out of the context within which the junior high student role was defined and created as the student lived out his or her career. Goofing off, as a form of illicit play, was quite descriptive of the junior high organizational structure and culture within which it exists.

The dynamics, the actual constitutive processes whereby goofing off takes on particular meaning for students in the junior high school, are relatively clear. Even if we trace only the somewhat benign series of events leading from Richard's class, to lunch, and then on to Von Hoffman's class, we see clearly the defining thread of collectivity weaving its way through these events. These events culminated in John's report about raising rabbits and the "understanding" that friends backed each other in situations where teachers challenged the "credentials" of a fellow colleague. Moreover, these events, together with other forms of direct social interaction (see Table 2), cemented certain groups together while, at the same time, serving to exclude others from group interaction.

The activities of, knowledge created, and dynamics within goofing off formed the basic building blocks of a system of understanding that is the essential process that makes for the collective nature of groups such as Don's and Chris'. Strikingly present in the illicit play characterized by goofing off is the great extent of initiatory behavior through which students attempt to define and control relevant spheres of influence. This initiatory behavior opposes and undermines both the formal curriculum and the curricular control of those in the authority structure of the school, especially that of teachers.

A number of studies address, to various degrees, the structural conditions within the school and larger society that are associated with student oppositional behavior. Stinchcombe (1964), for example, discusses the phenomenon of adolescent "rebellion" (and along with it the many behaviors and perspectives that I have described as "goofing off") as resting in the minimal level of articulation that exists between the formal activities of the school in relation to the workplace. Stinchcombe concludes that students' "rebellion" is in part caused by the mismatch between how student activities are organized and the understanding of students as to what will be required of them when they enter the work world. Cusick (1973) describes the cultural regularities of student peer groups along similar lines. He pays particular attention to the manner in which much of the student-initiated routine within school is, in part, based on the student perspective that they are relatively non-involved in most of the formal activities of the school. Thus, student allegiance to peer-generated norms is, in part, a response to the minimal participation afforded by the formal organization of learning. Similarly, Metz (1978) has described the process of "expressive alternatives" in schools where students believe that the activities of their life in school and conditions of the larger culture are significantly out of touch with one another.

The analysis pursued in this chapter, while acknowledging the dysfunctions between the structure of schooling and the larger environment, attempts to understand student activities and knowledge as an illicit play form. Such an analysis raises both theoretical as well as pragmatic questions.

First, we must take note that illicit play is part and parcel of the world of work described by Roy (1958) and more recently Burawoy (1979) and Willis (1977). Just as there are resistances and oppositional forms which develop in the workplace and which serve as a potential counterforce to minimal worker control of the productive process, so the same oppositional forms are present in the junior high school in the strategies of illicit play. Forms of illicit play such as goofing off can be seen as "school effects" in the sense that they are generated by certain structural conditions within the school. Illicit play, in this regard, is the outcome of schooling process where students have little control over the formal curriculum. By turning to activities such as goofing off, students maintain some semblance of control over at least part of the school's informal curriculum.

It is also useful to examine the term "illicit play" as a generic category in which a range of activities such as goofing off exist. On the one hand, instrumental and recreational play are supported and legitimated by schools because they further the explicit purposes of the school. They extend and integrate the formal routines to the extent that they serve as an "earned recess from the dreariness of work and life" (Hearn, 1976-1977, p.156). In this sense, activities that are part of this play are incorporative of the leisure industry in our society because they are activities to be "consumed," credits earned for participation in the alienative aspects of work. They are, then, instrumental for, rather than in contradiction to, the manner in which schooling continues elements of the social order.

Illicit play, on the other hand, contradicts basic organizational processes as perceived by those in organizational authority. To see illicit play as contradicting basic organizational processes creates a dilemma for educators. To suppress illicit play because it challenges formal organizational routines can lead to a tightening of the very authority which illicit play emerges to oppose. One would thus predict that such a tightening process would give rise to other, possibly more radical, forms of illicit play such as explosive defiance or elements of violence (Gouldner, 1954). Yet to acknowledge the nascent qualities of illicit play, to use it as an educative form so to speak, means understanding the play form as regenerative and itself the form of more participatory and critical educational practices--ones which, while educatively desirable, could at the same time serve to diminish the formal authority within our educational structures. Obviously, the route one choses is highly dependent upon the fundamental premises guiding educational practice.

For educators, illicit play, then, must be seen in a different light than typically viewed. Rather than viewing it only as disruptive, random, and senseless, educators must view its practices as expressive, somewhat ordered, and purposeful. Illicit play represents the single most prevalent aspect of student life wherein students can control and define their presence within an organizational culture whose fundamental purpose is to control and define its clients. As such, illicit play can be seen as both a measure of organizational life as well as an opportunity for organizational renewal.

This renewal can occur in teacher preparation programs where illicit play can be seen to be representative of the classroom ecology over which prospective teachers have some measure of influence. It would be helpful, for example, for prospective teachers to understand illicit play as a symbolic form of expression rather than as behavior to be managed (Everhart, 1983b). The forms of student illicit play and their respective roles in classroom instructional organization could then be used as a diagnostic activity providing teachers with still another measure of classroom climate. Such an activity would help prospective teachers come to a more critical understanding of the manner in which school life and student life intersect.

The main point is to realize that the symbolic messages communicated by illicit play forms, such as goofing off, are too important for educators to pass off any longer as "normal" for junior high school life. They are "normal" only to the extent we have accepted them as a natural dimension of school life. To the extent those premises are challenged, then illicit play can be useful in assisting educators to be actively involved in personal, organizational, and cultural renewal.

REFERENCES

Allen, J. Classroom Management: A Field Study of Students' Perspectives, Goals, and Perspectives. Unpublished Ph.D. Dissertation, University of California, Santa Barbara, 1982.

Burawoy, M. *Manufacturing Consent.* Chicago: University of Chicago Press, 1979.

Coleman, J. *Youth: The Transition to Adulthood.* Chicago: University of Chicago Press, 1974.

Cusick, P. *Inside High School.* New York: Holt Rinehart, and Winston, 1973.

Epstein, J. Choice of Friends over the Life Span: Developmental and Environmental Influences. Report #345, Center for the Social Organization of Schools, Johns Hopkins University, 1983.

Everhart, R. *Reading, Writing, and Resistance.* London: Routledge and Kegan Paul, 1983a.

Everhart, R. Classroom Management, Student Opposition, and the Labor Process. In *Ideology and Practice in Schooling.* Edited by M. Apple and L. Weis. Philadelphia: Temple University Press, 1983b.

Fein, G. Small Groups and Culture Creation: The Idioculture of Little League Baseball Teams. *American Sociological Review, 44*(1979), 733-745.

Gilmore, P. Spelling 'Mississippi': Recontextualizing a Literacy Related Speech Event. *Anthropology and Education Quarterly, 14*(1983), 235-256.

Glassner, B. Kid Society. *Urban Education, 11*(1976), 5-22.

Gouldner, A. *Patterns of Industrial Bureaucracy.* Glencoe: Free Press, 1954.

Hearn, F. Toward a Critical Theory of Play. *Telos, 30*(1976-1977), 145-160.

Jorgensen, M. Anti-School Parodies as Speech Play and Social Protest. In *The World of Play.* Edited by F. Manning. WestPoint, New York: Leisure Press, 1983.

King, N. Play: The Kindergartener's Perspective. *Elementary School Journal, 80*(1979), 80-87.

King, N. School Uses of Materials Traditionally Associated with Children's Play. *Theory and Research in Social Education, 10*(1982a), 17-27.

King, N. Classroom Play as a Form of Resistance. *Journal of Education, 164*(1982b), 320-329.

Kounin, J. *Discipline and Group Management in Classrooms.* New York: Holt, Rinehart, and Winston, 1970.

Lancy, D. *The Beliefs and Behaviors of Pupils in an Experimental School: School Settings.* Pittsburgh: Learning Resource Development Center, 1976.

Lancy, D. The Classroom as Phenomenon. In *The Social Psychology of Education.* Edited by D. Bar-Tal and L. Saxe. New York: Halsted Press, 1978.

Licata, J., and Willower, D. Student Brinkmanship and the School as a Social System. *Educational Administration Quarterly, 11*(1975), 1-14.

McDermott, R. Kids Make Sense: An Ethnographic Account of the Interactional Management of Success and Failure in One First Grade Classroom. Unpublished Ph.D. Dissertation, Stanford University, 1976.

Mehan, H. *Learning Lessons.* Cambridge: Harvard University Press, 1979.

Mehan, H. The Competent Student. *Anthropology and Education Quarterly, 11*(1980), 131-152.

Metz, M. *Classrooms and Corridors.* Berkeley: University of California Press, 1978.

Roy, D. Banana Time: Job Satisfaction and Informal Interaction. *Human Organization, 18*(1959-1960), 158-168.

Schlechty, P. *Teaching and Social Behavior.* Boston: Allyn and Bacon, 1976.

Smith, L., and Geoffrey, W. *The Complexities of the Urban Classroom.* New York: Holt, Rinehart, and Winston, 1968.

Spradley, J. *The Ethnographic Interview.* New York: Holt, Rinehart, and Winston, 1979.

Stinchcombe, A. *Rebellion in a High School.* Chicago: Quadrangle, 1964.

Werthman, C. Delinquents in Schools: A Test of the Legitimacy of Authority. In *School and Society.* Edited by B. Cosin, I. Dale, G. Esland, D. MacKinnon, and D. Swift. London: Routledge and Kegan Paul, 1971.

Williams, M. *On the Street Where I Live.* New York: Holt, Rinehart, and Winston, 1981.

Willis, P. *Learning to Labour.* Teakfield: Saxon House, 1977.

Woods, P. *The Divided School*. London: Routledge and Kegan Paul, 1979.

HIGH SCHOOL PLAY:
PUTTING IT TO WORK IN ORGANIZED SPORT

Douglas A. Kleiber and Glyn C. Roberts

The course of adolescence in the United States follows almost invariably through some kind of public or private high school. Since the primary task of high schools is to prepare adolescents to be participating and contributing members of adult society, it seems reasonable for schools to focus on providing students with the cognitive and intellectual skills needed for the work place and public life more generally. It may seem surprising, then, that play and activities oriented toward immediate gratification would find any sanctioned place in the high school day. But, in fact, a substantial amount of school time (i.e., that involving school officials and the scheduling and accommodation of activities) and student energy is devoted regularly to clubs, sports, and other organized purposes not directly related to the formal educational curriculum. Furthermore, there is considerable evidence that such extracurricular activities, particularly sports, play a central role in the social reward system of adolescents (Coleman, 1961, 1979).

What about these extracurricular activities, organized as they are by adults for adolescents? Are they actually play or, rather, to what extent are they play? Is the fact that extracurricular activities are so important to students the reason why they are sanctioned by school officials? Or do they serve other functions? Are they recognized as extensions of childhood play, with unique emotional and social benefits, or as a means of reducing the pain of compulsory attendance and boring classes? Alternatively, how much are such activities conceived of literally as an extra curriculum, preparing adolescents only somewhat differently for adult opportunities? Perhaps there is some truth in each of these suggestions or in some combination. And, finally, what difference does it make to schools and to the individual students involved? These we take as our research questions.

The following is a preliminary analysis of the subject of play and sport in the high school. Our focus is on the changing nature of play that accompanies American adolescence and on the influence of play and sport experience on other developmental processes. High school is considered as a social context that affects play and sport behavior in complex but somewhat predictable ways.

We will consider "play" rather inclusively, at first, as activity which is predominantly enjoyment oriented, and following King's lead (in this volume), we will differentiate "sanctioned play" from "illicit play" and "real play." Illicit play in high school might be well represented in drug use, sexual promiscuity, and recreational delinquency (Anson, 1977; Csikszentmihalyi and Larson, 1978) as well as in the divergent class activities (e.g., whispering, teasing, joking) that King identified in elementary schools. The nonchalant horseplay and socializing in school corridors could be seen as manifestations of "real play," as would informal games at noon breaks and other free periods. Formally arranged extracurricular activities might well be regarded as "sanctioned play," and we will restrict our attention here primarily to that form, examining both its conditions and its effects on other behavior within school and afterward.

We will also restrict ourselves to a focus on sports rather than considering all extracurricular activities though comparisons with other activities will be made where appropriate. Our justification for this restriction is largely pragmatic; there is simply more research done on sport than on any other "sanctioned play" activity. But it can also be argued that sport is the most "playlike" of all extracurricular activities. It is not tied explicitly to vocational tracks to the degree that other organizations, such as a science club, are, and it evolves in large part from more primitive physical play impulses and from activities, namely, games, which have themselves been the focus of the play of earlier periods. And, while there is a considerable literature that questions the existence of play in sport (e.g., Kleiber, 1983; Lueschen, 1967; Mergen, 1981; Sack, 1977), sport activities do often invoke a "play spirit," i.e., intense and serious action with a sense of distance and "separateness" from "the real world" (Csikszentmihalyi, 1975; Huizinga, 1955). Thus, we are interested in sport as it reflects a transformation of play. Sport experience may offer the last vestige of play for a substantial number of high school students. And this may apply not only to those who participate actively but also to those who identify closely with the athletic events of a high school.

Before we begin our analysis of sport and play, however, one additional point about the conceptual relationships of extracurricular activities to both play and work needs to be made. Sanctioning extracurricular activities in school may make them more instrumental than personally expressive. Such activities may allow a participant to court the favor of particular groups of friends or teachers or even to secure a college scholarship. Play-like activities such as games and voluntary social groupings contain an implicit set of conditions which function instrumentally to maintain interrelatedness, afford social acceptance, and even offer the requisite experiences for being well-rounded in the eyes of those who determine selection into subsequent occupational and educational roles. Such factors led Noe (1969) to regard almost all of leisure in adolescence as more instrumental than expressive.

A relatively greater emphasis on extrinsic rewards rather than intrinsic satisfaction, then, would make such activities inconsistent with commonly accepted notions of play (see Ellis, 1973; Piaget, 1962; Schwartzman, 1978). The adult direction of such activities and their use to control students would further reduce their play-like qualities; a lack of self-direction is also antithetical to play. Thus, while some semblance of play is maintained by keeping such activities separate in the "extra" curriculum, the meaning of play is consequently reconditioned for many, if not most, high school students. Following is a more elaborated model of the changes which occur in the course of high school years.

THE TRANSFORMATION OF PLAY IN ADOLESCENCE

In the course of childhood, play evolves from a singular activity to a social one. Early research (Parten, 1932) establishing a sequence from solitary to parallel to associative to group game play has been generally accepted (see also Piaget, 1962). And this pattern of socialization has implications for the nature of play itself. The spontaneity and self-determination so essential to play are challenged when others are involved. Cooperation and compromise are required. Defining and arranging are always necessary in social play and it is frequently a frustrating process for children. Still, children come to see such social construction as a part of the play itself, and this process, difficult and confused as it may be at any given time, is thought to contribute substantially to social and moral development (Devereux, 1976; Piaget, 1962). But such effects are not sought by the children; playing the game is their only reason for such social engineering. Arranging a game or forming a club is just the first in a two-part process.

These social skills which evolve in later childhood (from eight to twelve mostly) also correspond with a growing interest in demonstrating competence to others. School becomes one testing ground; but expanding physical competence, along with the social skills to which we have just referred, often shape a growing interest in sport. As an institutionalized form of game playing (Loy, Kenyon, and McPherson, 1978), sport offers children standards of comparison and a stage for demonstration. Furthermore, it provides a great number of systems and agents of instruction for children as they enter what Erik Erikson (1963) referred to as the "age of instruction" (p.259). But it is important to note that children *choose* to be instructed by coaches, while in schools and homes that prerogative falls to teachers and parents, respectively. This choice protects some of sport's play quality.

Nevertheless, the formalization and standardization that sport brings to a game, such as baseball, which was initially played only with friends, inevitably transforms it. In a classic study, Webb (1969) presented evidence to suggest that "playing fair" becomes less important than winning and performing well as children get more deeply involved in sport. He described this pattern as the "professionalization" of play (see also Mantel and Vander Velden, 1974). The demands for competence and excellence in sports promote a product orientation that is antithetical to most play values and, in fact, leads those who are less able, whatever their interest, to drop out (Orlick and Botterill, 1977; Roberts, 1984; Tutko and Bruns, 1976). And for those who stay involved, the values which insure their success within the sport system are consistent with those of the parent economic system. Perseverance and delay of gratification in the course of demanding practice, for example, are certainly more consistent with the values of work than with play. This, then, becomes an important justification for such "extracurricular" activities while at the same time signifying a transformation of play.

We submit that the conditions supporting the adoption of sports in secondary schools in the United States have also led to a *bifurcation* of play in American adolescence. As children's play has become rationalized historically (Miracle, 1985, this volume; Finkelstein, this volume) and as it becomes professionalized, ontogenetically, it is more a matter of work. But play also exists as abandonment and, perhaps as a reaction to the transformation of other play forms, may find alternative expression in unsanctioned, illicit, and deviant activities. Figure 1 illustrates the separation of these two components of play in adolescence.

It is important to recognize an inherent bipolarity in play that makes the expression of extreme responses, still within the realm of play, possible. Earlier in childhood, play has elements both of serious effort and pleasurable repetition--what might be called a "mastery" orientation--and of imagination and pretense or an orientation toward "divergence." These two separate components can be found in playing "house," "Dungeons and Dragons," and in self-directed games of all sorts. The dialectic of play involves convergent thinking, repetition, accommodation, and practice on one hand and divergent thinking, experimentation, and innovation on the other. As Sutton-Smith and Kelly-Byrne (1984) point out, most theories of play incorporate this bipolarity although any given play activity may emphasize one or the other aspect. So sport reflects more of the convergent, repetitive, mastery-oriented aspects of play while containing some measure of divergence and separation from the "real world." Our premise is that the bipolarity is forced to extremes where games and sports become rationalized within a social reward system that emphasizes the outcomes of supposedly playful activities and serves the cause of achievement and production while degrading the process itself (Lasch, 1979). As play loses its character of being both dynamically innovative and conservatively mastery oriented, the choice of expressive styles may be forced. Bipolar play loses a central place in the lives of adolescents and is transformed for some into a means of direct acculturation to adult values and for others into a pattern of deviance. Only rarely is the fluctuation between experimentalism and mastery effectively preserved.

This bifurcation of the two fundamental components of play transforms its fundamental character. And while we offer the model as a metaphor for heuristic purposes, our suggestion is that the play impulse is forced in one direction or the other for many, and perhaps most, American adolescents. What seems clear additionally is that one direction represents deviation from social and cultural norms and values while the other seeks some accommodation with them. Thus, the movement toward sanctioned play forms is justified or rationalized by presumed benefits to socialization and acculturation. But is this "professionalization of play" in school justified? What exactly do those involved gain by participating? And what are the implications for the student body as a whole? More broadly we may ask, is there a place for play in sport and in school? Let us first examine the evidence regarding the educational and psychosocial benefits of involvement in organized sport in high school.

Figure 1.

THE BIFURCATION OF PLAY IN ADOLESCENCE

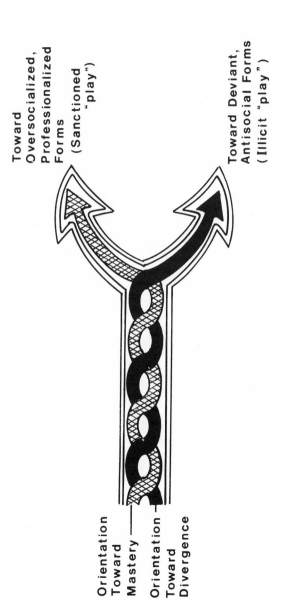

Toward
Oversocialized,
Professionalized
Forms
(Sanctioned
"play")

Toward Deviant,
Antisocial Forms
(Illicit "play")

Orientation
Toward
Mastery

Orientation
Toward
Divergence

SPORT, EDUCATION, AND ACHIEVEMENT

Organized sport has become a major part of secondary school life. The most frequent mention of a high school in a newspaper communication will be through the sports pages; and it is a truism that sporting contests form a major portion of "mass public entertainment" for communities, especially rural ones. This celebration of high school sports is not without its critics. Sport is considered by some (e.g., Coleman, 1961) to be a diversion of energy and creativity that might be better put into academic pursuits. The proponents of sport have argued, however, that sport actually helps students in that it fosters pride for the school and helps athletes focus upon academics, if only to maintain eligibility. Given the status accorded high school athletics, it is little wonder that research has been conducted to investigate the relationship of sport to academic orientation and achievement.

The literature on sport, education, and achievement is considerable and may be broken down into three broad categories. The first deals with sport participation and its influence on academic expectancies, with the underlying assumption that heightened expectancies lead to heightened achievement. The second deals with sport and academic achievement, and the third focuses on athletic experience as a source of social mobility. At this stage, it is best to consider each category separately.

Sport and Educational Orientation

One of the first studies to investigate the relationship of academic orientation to athletic participation was done by Schafer and Armer (1968). They found that athletes had higher expectations of going to college than nonathletes and had higher expectations of completing four years of college even when factors such as intelligence (IQ), type of curriculum, and socioeconomic status (SES) were controlled. Evidently, athletic participation enhances academic orientation.

Spady (1970) also investigated the effect of athletic participation on academic orientation and found a positive relationship. Participation was related to higher academic goals. However, Spady found that participation appeared to be beneficial only when combined with other extracurricular activities such as service or leadership activities. Indeed, as a consequence of a follow-up study four years later, Spady did nothing but "lament" the athlete who did not engage in other forms of extracurricular activities. A specific study of the academic attainment of athletes versus athletic, service-oriented students by Landers, Feltz, Obermeier, and Brouse (1978) confirmed Spady's feelings.

There is other evidence that athletic participation is associated with academic orientation (Buhrmann and Bratton, 1977; Otto and Alwin, 1977; Phillips and Schafer, 1971; Picou, 1978; Rehberg, 1969; Rehberg and Cohen, 1975; Schurr and Brookover, 1970; Spreitzer and Pugh, 1973). And while these studies focused on males almost exclusively, the limited research conducted on female athletes leads one to conclude that athletic participation may be associated with academic aspiration for them as well (Hanks, 1979; Hanks and Eckland, 1976; Landers, Feltz, Obermier, and Brouse, 1978; Snyder and Spreitzer, 1977). For example, Snyder and Spreitzer looked at both music and sport to determine whether participation in extracurricular activities affected aspiration in academics. Their findings revealed that both sport and music enhanced academic aspiration for females.

Clearly, from the research reported above, sport involvement relates to academic orientation. Many factors may be responsible: athletics may foster relationships with achievement-oriented peers; athletics may transfer achievement attitudes; or athletes may receive more vigorous counseling to attend college (Phillips and Schafer, 1971; Rehberg, 1969). However, there are two caveats to the general conclusion that sport positively affects academic orientation. One is the effect of socioeconomic status (SES), and the other concerns the academic climate of the school.

Several studies have investigated the SES phenomenon. Rehberg and Schafer (1968) found SES to be a factor in academic orientation toward college regardless of whether one was an athlete or not. Ninety-five percent of high school students of high social status who received parental encouragement to attend college and who were high academic performers planned to attend college for four years. But students who had high social status and low academic performance had different expectations. High status, low-achieving athletes, in particular, expected to go to college to a greater degree than low-achieving nonathletes (68 percent versus 49 percent). Students who had low social status and were high or low in academic attainment also had different college expectations than high status, high academic students. Generally, athletic participation led to higher expectations of attending college than nonparticipation, regardless of academic performance.

Picou and Curry (1974) criticized previous research in that only white males from the Northeast had been sampled. Thus, they used 3,245 rural and urban youth from the "deep South" to investigate the relationship of athletic participation and academic aspirations. Picou and Curry found that athletes from low SES backgrounds who received little encouragement from parents to continue past high school and who had low grade point averages (GPAs) had higher educational aspirations than similar nonathletes, especially in rural schools. Participation in high school athletics had a moderate relationship with educational aspirations in all schools, but GPA and parental educational encouragement were stronger predictors of academic aspiration.

Feltz and Weiss (1984) examined female students who were either athletes only, athlete-service oriented, or students who were engaged in neither athletics nor service activities. They found no differences in academic orientation among the groups. The variable that accounted for the most variance in academic orientation was SES--high SES athletes scored higher than low SES athletes.

When considering the effect of sport on academic orientation, SES is obviously an important mediating construct. The other important mediating variable in the relationship of athletics and academic orientations is school climate. In those studies that have taken the academic value orientation of the school into account, the more academic prowess is valued in the school, the more negative the relationship of academic orientation to athletic participation. For example, Start (1967) investigated the sporting attainment of 2,500 secondary school boys (aged eleven to fifteen years) in Britain. She found that in grammar schools, where there is a high academic press on children, most athletes came from the "B" streams rather than the "A" ones. However, the amount of participation decreased with each stream lower than "B". In comprehensive schools, where there is less academic press, most athletes were found in the higher streams of the school. Indeed, the lower 25 percent of the academic streams in the comprehensive streams were barely represented on athletic teams. These general findings have been corroborated by Rehberg and Schafer (1968), Spreitzer and Pugh (1973), and Spady (1970).

Those schools having an academic press on students seem to devalue athletics, and athletes in such schools have a lower academic orientation and attainment. Likewise, the more that athletics is valued, athletes have higher academic aspirations and attainment (Buhrmann, 1972; Landers, Feltz, Obermeier, and Brouse, 1978; Rehberg and Schafer, 1968; Start, 1967). Thus, the academic versus sport orientation inherent in the school is an important consideration in determining the effects of athletics on academic variables.

Of course, this brings up the matter of national and cultural differences as well. It should be reiterated that the focus here is on high schools in the United States. In addition to Start's (1967) investigations in Britain, studies in other countries (e.g., Jerome and Phillips, 1971; Kandel and Lesser, 1972) tend not to find a positive relationship between involvement in athletics and academic orientation.

The extant literature supports the general contention that participation in interscholastic athletics is strongly associated with enhanced academic orientation. However, two variables, SES and academic climate of the school, seem to mediate the impact of the athletic experience on academic orientation.

Sport and Academic Attainment

Buhrmann (1972) has investigated the relationship of athletic participation to academic performance directly. He studied 158 boys from two junior high schools over the years 1959 to 1965 and concluded that athletes were considerably more successful than nonathletes in terms of grades and standardized tests. Buhrmann did find that the higher the SES of a boy, the more likely he was to participate in athletics, but even when holding SES constant, the relationship between athletic success and academic achievement remained. Buhrmann states that athletics may be the most important avenue for low SES students to gain status which leads to academic aspiration and higher scholarship.

Eidsmoe (1963) compared the GPA of high school varsity basketball and football players to their classmates and found that athletes had higher GPAs. Schafer and Armor (1968) found similar results. Athletes had higher GPAs than nonathletes even when intelligence, type of curriculum, and SES were controlled.

Despite some qualifications, and some contradictory evidence (e.g., Hauser and Lueptow, 1978; Lueptow and Kayser, 1973, 1974), there is considerable evidence that athletic participation is strongly associated with academic expectations and academic attainment (Buhrmann, 1972; Buhrmann and Bratton, 1977; Hanks, 1979; Hanks and Eckland, 1976; Landers, Feltz, Obermeier, and Brouse, 1978; Otto and Alwin, 1977; Picou, 1978; Picou and Curry, 1974; Rehberg and Schafer, 1968; Schafer and Armor, 1968; Schurr and Brookover, 1970; Snyder and Spreitzer, 1977; Spreitzer and Pugh, 1973). The interesting question is why? Several investigators have attemped to address this issue.

Rehberg (1969) and Phillips and Schafer (1971) have reviewed the literature on the positive effects of athletic participation on academic orientation and attainment and consider five plausible explanations. First, athletics may facilitate association with achievement oriented peers, which enhances achievement in academics. Second, athletics may transfer skills such as persistence, effort, self-improvement, and so on. Third, self-esteem and aspirations are positively related, and the increased attention bestowed on athletes leads to higher self-esteem and enhanced aspirations. Fourth, the athlete is expected to maintain a consistent image with respect to athletics and academic performance. This image entails increased striving in academics. Fifth, the athlete may be a recipient of vicarious scholastic and career counseling which may enhance academic expectations and attainment.

These explanations are only speculative and need testing. Some work, however, has attempted to examine them empirically. Otto and Alwin (1977), for example, in an extensive study to investigate the reasons *why* athletes are generally higher in academic aspiration and achievement, attempted to determine whether significant others or peer status served as the mediating variable.   Significant others may encourage an athlete to an academic orientation in order to continue athletics or through the socialization of valued attributes; or athletic prowess may enhance peer status, which enhances academic orientation and makes the athlete wish to maintain the peer status(see Spady, 1970; Rehberg and Schafer, 1968). Otto and Alwin found that athletic participation had a significant effect upon educational aspiration and academic attainment and also on occupational aspiration, attainment, and income. However, no evidence was obtained for peer status functioning as the mediating variable. Rather, the evidence favored significant others as having a strong influence upon aspiration and attainment. Otto and Alwin concluded that the effect of athletics is mediated by significant others who teach appropriate goal structures and attainment strategies that are beneficial in establishing academic directions and aspirations.

Picou (1978) found similar results to Otto and Alwin. Athletic participation in Picou's study led to increased contact with achievement-oriented peers, teachers, and coaches, which had a positive impact upon educational orientation. However, Picou only found this strong relationship for white athletes. Only a modest relationship was found for black athletes, leading Picou to conclude that the competitive sport experience may be different for blacks and whites. Hanks (1979), on the other hand, using a nationwide sample of black and white male and female athletes, presented evidence to suggest that while athletic participation led to academic orientation through increased encouragement from significant others and contact with college-bound peers, there were no differences according to race or sex. Thus, the research seems to suggest that athletes in general are reinforced from the increased attention given to them by peers, teachers and parents toward enhanced educational goals and achievement striving.

In summary, athletic participation seems to enhance educational expectations and achievement, but the evidence is not conclusive. We have already cited evidence showing that in schools which emphasize academic prowess, athletic participation does not lead to enhanced academic orientation. Further, athletes who participate in athletics to the exclusion of other extracurricular activities have enhanced aspirations, but do not typically show enhanced attainment (Landers, Feltz, Obermeier, and Brouse, 1978; Rehberg and Cohen, 1975; Spady, 1970). Moreover, given the importance of sport in most American public high schools (Coleman, 1961), enhanced academic orientation may be more a function of the attention and encouragement focused upon athletes rather than the sport experience per se. The possible generalization of particular self-evaluations, motivational orientations, and work habits from sport to the classroom remains to be fully assessed in more rigorous investigations. But the empirically established relationship between sport involvement and academic orientation seems to be largely attributable to the social economy of athletics in the communities in which school sports are embedded.

Sport and Social Mobility

The influence of sport on educational orientation, albeit mediated by other social factors, may have a positive effect on long-term educational and occupational success as well. While the evidence provided so far leaves open the question of the particular dynamics of the relationship between sport and subsequent success, there is additional evidence on social mobility to be considered. Several researchers have identified a relationship between participation in high school sports and subsequent occupational attainment and economic payoff (Howell and Picou, 1983; Otto and Alwin, 1977); but the intervening influences have only been suggested. Certainly staying in school longer is one possible influence (Howell, Miracle and Rees, 1984; Snyder and Spreitzer, 1983). Those involved in sports are less likely to leave school early (Hendry, 1978) and, as was suggested before, more likely to go to college. Still, it may be the education, then, rather than the sport experience that contributes to subsequent occupational attainment (e.g., Haerle, 1975).

Where there is a relationship between sport involvement and social mobility, it may also be that success in sport raises the visibility of participants. This visibility marks them for success in other areas thereby raising general expectations and, directly or indirectly, creating greater opportunities beyond, as well as before, graduation.

A more popular interpretation of the positive relationship between athletic participation and socioeconomic success is that the skills learned are transferable or are at least assumed to be (Otto and Alwin, 1977). The persistence and general social competence one learns in the context of sport may be generalizable to other settings, essentially preparing a high school athlete for the work roles of the future. Or it may be that would-be employers simply perceive this to be the case and afford special opportunities. The extent to which the development of such generalizable skills and personal characteristics is a product of sport has, of course, been the subject of another circumscribed area of research.

SPORT AND PERSONAL DEVELOPMENT

The impact of the sport experience on the development of attributes pertinent to success in later life has long been debated. The proponents argue that organized sports provide a forum for the teaching of responsibility, cooperation, subordination of self to the greater good, and the shaping of motivation and achievement behaviors. There is certainly a logic to the argument, if not much evidence (see Stevenson, 1975). The assumption that sport builds character does not set well with the critics of competitive sports who view the consequences of sport experience as being mostly negative (e.g., Ogilvie and Tutko, 1971). Critics view the cost in human relations attributed to an overemphasis upon winning (Tutko and Bruns, 1976), the increase in incidents of aggression as a consequence of competition (Berkowitz, 1972) and the social stigma attached to being rejected or "cut" from sport teams (Orlick and Botterill, 1977) as too high a price to pay. We have devoted a good bit of attention ourselves to the "effect of sport" question (Kleiber, 1983; Kleiber and Roberts, 1981; Roberts, 1984; Roberts, Kleiber and Duda, 1981). Obviously, the subject of sport and personal development is complex. One way of simplifying the issue is to consider personality development and social development separately.

Personality Development

According to Erik Erikson (1963) the period just preceding adolescence is one in which a child establishes competence and a sense of industry while being especially vulnerable to social conditions that would reflect negatively and reveal inferiority. Some avoid competitive situations for that reason. Others seek them out as opportunities for demonstrating competence. Still others select sports specifically as a domain of special expertise--oftentimes as a refuge from the classroom where inadequacies may be more in evidence.

Although we have more to learn about children and youth of all ages, it appears that athletic participation for children is associated with higher perceived competence, both physical and general, and with higher self-esteem (Bowlsby and Iso-Ahola, 1980; Roberts, Kleiber, and Duda, 1981). Where there is a relationship to self-esteem, though, we must ask if it is mediated as much by the influence of participation as by social status. The strong relationship that Coleman (1961) and Eitzen (1976) found between athleticism and popularity among adolescents has been established with elementary students as well (Buchanan, Blankenbaker, and Cotton, 1976).

The link between sport and social success must itself be examined critically. The primary task of adolescence according to Erikson (1963) and others is to establish an identity. And while this process benefits from the feedback of adults and peers alike and perhaps even from commitment to the "career" direction of sport, reducing behavioral alternatives through conformity to the mores of the sport establishment may ultimately limit identity achievement. Erikson saw the potential for danger in the years immediately preceding adolescence of overemphasizing the employment of skills and becoming thereby "the conformist and thoughtless slave of one's technology and of those who are in a position to exploit it" (p.216). Former professional basketball player Bill Bradley implied this in reflecting on his own experience of "entering the tunnel of narrowing perspective at age 14" (Lipsyte, 1976).

We have suggested elsewhere (Kleiber, 1983; Kleiber and Rickards, 1985) that such a pattern of overaccommodation may offer only temporary salutary effects for identity development, acting instead as a kind of identity "foreclosure" (Marcia, 1980) that may lead to psychological difficulties for the athlete when the school, college, or professional sports career is over. Such is suggested by the research of Malmisur (1975, 1976) on the ego development of university athletes. Using Loevinger's interview method for measuring ego maturity, he found that athletes mostly reflected a lower level of ego development than nonathletes, a more "conformist" maturity concerned primarily with prestige, appearance, status, material possessions, and rules and obligations. Fewer than 20 percent reflected the higher stages of conscientious, autonomous, or integrated maturity. Others (e.g., King and Chi, 1979; Sage, 1978; Snyder and Spreitzer, 1983) have found ample evidence to indicate that athletes are indeed more conventional and conservative than nonathletes.

This pattern of overaccommodation in sport may be less problematic for girls. Ironically, while girls find it hard to get into sports, they may be less vulnerable to the particularly co-opting circumstances just described. Because they are likely to be involved in sport in spite of rather than because of sex-role prescriptions, they are probably better able to separate their experience in sports from the rest of their social existence and operate with more autonomy. In fact, female athletes are more likely than male athletes to show higher levels of autonomy than nonathletes (cf. Kleiber and Hemmer, 1981).

More research is obviously needed. There would appear to be justification for examining such conventionality at psychological as well as ideological levels. Schafer (1971), for example, argued that the conventionality and failure to mature may be the result of the dependency that athletes come to have on coaches and the sport establishment more generally. And such dependency becomes doubly difficult in adolescence, a time when identity depends to a great extent on individuation and the separation process.

Social Development

Separating personality from social development is difficult if not altogether arbitrary. Among the psychological skills thought to be developed in games and sports are strategic competence (Sutton-Smith and Roberts, 1964), negotiation and conflict resolution (Lever, 1976, 1978), cooperation, leadership and even "gallantry" (Goffman, 1967). All of these have social consequences. In fact, very few aspects of personality do not. Athletics, especially team sports, call upon personal resources in the interest of collective success. It must be recognized that cooperation and association are as important to sport as competition (Lueschen, 1970). Indeed, there is evidence that sport facilitates community relations, even racial integration (Miracle, 1981). So, the earlier-mentioned implications of conformity and conventionality notwithstanding, it is reasonable to project a positive effect of athletic experience on general social and organizational competence.

Still, the competitiveness of sport can be destructive. A preoccupation with outcomes, i.e., when "winning is the only thing," often justifies any means of success. Earlier ideas about the relationship between sport and aggression have proved to be too simplistic. There is very little evidence that one either releases aggression from playing sport (the catharsis theory) or is more likely to be aggressive as a result (theories of frustration-aggression and social learning). A more convincing argument is that through well-regulated contests, one may even learn to control aggressive impulses (Scott, 1970). Indeed, learning to be "tough, daring and courageous while still friendly" may be one of the greatest values of sport (Winer,1979). But the continuing importance of winning has a cultural impact. American children are among the most "irrationally rivalrous" in the world (Kagan and Madsen, 1972). In a field experiment of our own (Kleiber and Roberts, 1981) we involved children in a "kick soccer world series" and found that participants were somewhat more likely to be rivalrous in a subsequent opportunity for gift giving than were nonparticipants. And there is additional evidence, although mostly from laboratory situations, for the negative impact of competition on prosocial behavior (e.g., Barnett and Bryan, 1974).

Such possible negative effects must be contrasted with another alleged benefit of sport, the deterrence of delinquency. There is, in fact, considerable evidence of a negative association between athletic involvement and delinquent behavior (see Landers and Landers, 1978, for a review). But closer examination suggests that, as with other associated benefits, the relationship may be more a matter of preselection into sport than the effect of sport per se. As Hendry (1978) and Roberts (1983) have both established with British samples, athletes are typically those who would conform most closely to the standards of the school while those rejecting school values would reject sport. Furthermore, the possibility that delinquency and antisocial behavior is at least as common among athletes needs to be considered in light of the general tolerance that preferred status may grant them. And the possibility of a propensity for generalizing aggressiveness, sensation-seeking, and risk-taking behavior beyond sport contexts needs to be examined further as well.

Finally, with regard to sport participants, it should be reiterated that "the value of fair play" is steadily less important as years of participation go by (Mantel and Vander Velden, 1974; Webb, 1969), and there is evidence that athletes endorse fewer of the values of "sportsmanship" than nonathletes (Kroll and Peterson, 1965). Bend (1971) goes so far as to argue that sport is commonly associated with antisocial norms--cheating, violence, and winning at all cost. Of course, the spectators are still another story. The potential for aggression and violence among those who are not dealing directly with "conflict" but who may have just as much invested psychologically in the outcome is also a subject for serious investigation (see, for example, Gaskell and Pearton, 1979). But here we confine ourselves to the players themselves.

We would also suggest that the formation of divisive social cliques in high schools may be related to the bifurcation of play discussed earlier. In the social economies of adolescence, the capitalization of skills for status leaves little room for one who would experiment with new skills and forces such play impulses outside the realm of school. And, while the advantages would appear then to fall to those who are "on the bus" versus those who are not, the rationalization of play for its institutional values not only undermines the experimental aspects of play but may reduce its identity-creating properties to a narrowing of vocational and avocational alternatives or, in the case of sport, to becoming a "jock."

To summarize, it would appear that sport provides a social convoy for many athletes, encouraging and enabling them while perhaps leaving them somewhat deluded with respect to the lasting validity of an athlete identity. Nevertheless, the demands of training and team involvement generally select for and reinforce qualities of persistence, endurance and interpersonal competence, and these abilities may be transfered into other educational and organizational contexts. What remains to be considered are the conditions under which sport may be developmentally adaptive rather than simply conformist and socially insulating. We will argue that the reassertion of play values in sport will contribute to that effect.

MOTIVATION, PERFORMANCE, AND ENJOYMENT

It is a common misconception that suffering must accompany anything worthwhile. "No pain, no gain" is the expression. But it is equally limiting to equate enjoyment with pleasure. If we let pleasure be used to signify immediate sensation, enjoyment is more the experience of freely committed attention or the result of intense involvement (Csikszentmihalyi, 1975, 1982, 1985). We talk about people being really "into" something as a reflection of this kind of enjoyment. Csikszentmihalyi and his colleagues (Csikszentmihalyi, 1975, 1981, 1982, 1985; Csikszentmihalyi and Larson, 1984) use the word "flow" to describe the experience of enjoyment, a word used frequently by participants in describing their experience of intense involvement in such apparently disparate activities as chess, rock dancing, and heart surgery.

In the flow expierience there is total concentration, little or no self-consciousness, and a sense of self-transcendence resulting from the merging of consciousness and action. The activities which afford such experience provide clear feedback and are sufficiently challenging to engage a full measure of the actor's skill but not so demanding as to be anxiety-provoking.

The matching of challenges and skills is critical; if challenges are greater than skills, anxiety results, while a lack of challenge in relation to available skills is likely to be experienced as boredom. When one is not experiencing "flow" but desires that type of intense involvement, the options involve manipulating the challenges and/or developing higher skills, and that is what makes this a *growth* model of enjoyment.

Sport has many of the conditions conducive to flow--clearcut demands and feedback from the environment. And the importance of winning may even heighten the intensity of involvement and provide a goal structure which restricts attention. Sport is recognized as one of the most potentially flow-producing activities (Chalip, Csikszentmihalyi, Kleiber, and Larson, 1984; Csikszentmihalyi, 1975; Csikszentmihalyi and Larson, 1984). But the significance of winning in sport may be distracting, and the more consequential winning and even participation are in terms of such extrinsic rewards as social status, recognition, scholarships, etc., the more likely that intrinsically rewarding aspects of sport will be undermined (see also Lepper and Greene, 1978). The characteristic of sport as play is similarly threatened when its separateness is violated (Huizinga, 1955; Kleiber, 1983). So, for sport to maximize its flow-producing potential, its play values--especially separateness and deemphasis of extrinsic consequences and constraints--must be reestablished.

Interestingly, though, this reassertion of play values would have the effect of enhancing rather than diminishing performance. When one is in "flow," however relaxed and "playful," full attention is committed to the task at hand. Recent work on achievement motivation describes such behavior as "task-oriented" (Maehr, 1984; Maehr and Nicholls, 1980; Nicholls and Miller, 1984; Roberts, 1984). By focusing on the task at hand and ignoring the outcome, one's goal is to perform to the best of one's ability, and more effective concentration is the result.

Perhaps more importantly, the experience of "flow" is available at any level of ability, as long as the challenge is appropriate. Those of lower ability may thus find a level of sport involvement which provides flow experience. A contest loss or task failure is never humiliating under such circumstances. It leads rather to adjustments necessary for renewed investment.

In summary, then, sport must have a "be here now" imperative to be play in the fullest sense. Otherwise it is a vehicle of normative socialization, at best, or a distraction from more important concerns, at worst. Extrinsically reinforced sport involvement appropriated in service of social status and social mobility, offers a work-culture of "play" for those in high school. Those who are not sports participants are forced to seek enjoyment in escape from the social controls of school. Those who do "make the most of" sport opportunities, however, run the risk of narrowing their personality in such a way that short-term gains are lost in "the inevitable metathesis of the retiring athlete" (Hill and Lowe, 1974). Without a diversification of interests and with an orientation toward recognition and status, even the most accomplished athlete may experience a downward slide when playing days are over (see also McPherson, 1977; Spady, 1970).

An intrinsically motivated orientation to the game itself and to the skills involved, on the other hand, is likely to insulate an athlete somewhat from the compromising effects of sports institutionalization. And, more importantly, it is reasonable to hypothesize that the pattern of enjoyment-based learning that leads a person of any skill level to be "experimental" while mastering increasingly complex task demands will serve him or her well in nearly any context.

IMPLICATIONS

Most of this chapter is conjectural. Its purpose is to establish theoretical premises for further research. But at the risk of overstating the case, several courses of action for school programs would be indicated if the relationships we have suggested are, in fact, true. We have presented school as a social variable that contributes to the bifurcation of play in adolescence. Nevertheless, the school may be restructured to significantly reduce that effect. Our first two suggestions make school sport activities less professionalized, while the latter two offer to make them more inherently playlike.

1. In a study of students who chose not to participate in extracurricular activities, Vornberg (1983) found that the most common reason was "lack of relevance." One inference to be drawn from this study is that extracurricular activities are judged according to their fit with one's particular set of skills. Another inference, however, is that extracurricular activities are rarely seen as opportunities for students to be involved at less formal, more "playful," levels. Somehow reducing the skill-to-participation-to-status association would seem important. In an interesting study of the impact of a 1954 report on "School Athletics" by the Educational Policy Commission of the National Education Association, Talamini (1973) found that the proposed reemphasis of play-type extramural co-recreation and "carryover" intramurals had been mostly ignored by high school administrators. A reconsideration of the recommendations of that report would seem in order.

2. Program expansion is not the only recourse. More free time might well be made available to allow for the playful experimentalism which is so natural to adolescents, if somewhat foreign to school. Free time alone is often a rare and valued commodity in high schools and junior high schools. Expanding such periods might create some interesting effects--creatively constructive as well as challenging ones. But education itself needs to be reconsidered in the waning of the industrial era. What kinds of skills will enable people to live and be happy and constructive off the job? Education for leisure has been recognized as a paramount need for quite some time now (Green, 1968). Many adolescents will not be employed upon leaving school.

Education should concern itself with helping such individuals make the most of their "freedom."

3. Those in sports themselves might well be treated differently. Abolishing post season tournaments was one 1954 Education Policy Committee's recommendation which deserves further consideration, but it is not likely that the external significance of sport in the community and society more generally can be reduced any time soon. Nevertheless, a school policy that allows athletes to focus on sport to the exclusion of other aspects of life should be reexamined. The practice of "redshirting" athletes, watering down coursework, and allowing them to avoid academic preparation--while exploiting their athletic talents--can hardly be condoned in light of the comments of ex-athletes who obviously regret their misspent "education." This is true of those who are successful in sports and afterward (Kleiber and Greendorfer, 1984) as well as those who show evidence of a "downward slide." "Life after sports" should be considered jointly by athletes and school personnel.

4. Sport involvement may even serve as a template for involvement in other endeavors. Beyond just studying to "stay eligible," the development of a task orientation in sport may be readily transferred to the classroom. Learning to read in high school may require a commitment to intellectual task mastery (as well as a good dose of humility!) for someone who has been reinforced for concentrating only on physical task mastery.

Finding activities that are enjoyable as well as enhancing to development might well be taken as a mandate for high schools. Sports and the arts have been called "transitional" activities because they have structures which "demand discipline and engage adolescents in cultural systems" (Csikszentmihalyi and Larson, 1984, 95). Not only do they thus serve to prepare adolescents for an adult future, they also serve as templates for comparison in the examination of occupational alternatives. Combining elements of both play and work in merging enjoyment and mastery is an ideal that could well be the basis for providing extracurricular alternatives for all students--and perhaps for reforming classrooms as well.

REFERENCES

Anson, R. Recreation Deviance. *Journal of Leisure Research, 8*(1977), 177-180.

Barnett, M., and Bryan, J. Effects of Competition with Outcome Feedback on Children's Helping Behavior. *Developmental Psychology, 10*(1974), 838-842.

Bend, E. Some Potential Dysfunctional Effects of Sport Upon Socialization. Paper presented at the Third International Symposium on the Sociology of Sport, Waterloo, Ontario, 1971.

Berkowitz, L. Sport Competition and Aggression. *Fourth Canadian Symposium on the Psychology of Motor Learning and Sport.* Edited by I. Williams and L. Wankel. Ottawa: University of Ottawa Press, 1972.

Bowlsby, R., and Iso-Ahola, S. Self-Concepts of Children in Summer Baseball Programs. *Perceptual and Motor Skills, 51*(1980), 1202.

Buchanan, H., Blankenbaker, J., and Cotton, D. Academic and Athletic Ability as Popularity Factors in Elementary School Children. *Research Quarterly, 47*(1976), 320-325.

Buhrmann, H. Scholarships and Athletics in Junior High School. *International Review of Sport Sociology, 7*(1972), 119-131.

Buhrmann, H., and Bratton, R. Athletic Participation and Status of High School Girls. *International Review of Sport Sociology, 12*(1977), 57-67.

Chalip, L., Csikszentmihalyi, M., Kleiber, D., and Larson, R. Variation of Experience in Formal and Informal Sport. *Research Quarterly for Exercise and Sport, 55*(1984), 109-116.

Coleman, J. *The Adolescent Society.* New York: Free Press, 1961.

Coleman, J. *The School Years.* London: Methuen, 1979.

Csikszentmihalyi, M. *Beyond Boredom and Anxiety.* San Francisco: Jossey-Bass, 1975.

Csikszentmihalyi, M. Leisure and Socialization. *Social Forces, 60*(1981), 332-340.

Csikszentmihalyi, M. Toward a Psychology of Optimal Experience. In *Annual Review of Personality and Social Psychology, Volume 3.* Edited by L. Wheeler. Beverly Hills, CA: Sage, 1982.

Csikszentmihalyi, M. Emergent Motivation and the Evolution of Self. In *Motivation and Adulthood*. Edited by D. Kleiber and M. Maehr. Greenwich, Connecticut: JAI Press, 1985.

Csikszentmihalyi, M., and Larson, R. Intrinsic Rewards in School Crime. *Crime and Delinquency*, 24(1978), 322-330.

Csikszentmihalyi, M., and Larson, R. *Being Adolescent*. New York: Basic Books, 1984.

Devereux, E. Backyard Versus Little League Baseball: The Impoverishment of Children's Sports. In *Social Problems in Athletics*. Edited by D. Landers. Urbana, Illinois: University of Illinois Press, 1976.

Educational Policies Commission. *School Athletics*. Washington, D.C.: National Education Association, 1954.

Eidsmoe, R. High School Athletes Are Brighter. *School Activities*, 35(1963), 75-77.

Eitzen, S. Sport and the Social Status in American Public Secondary Schools. *Review of Sport and Leisure*, 1(1976), 139-155.

Ellis, M. *Why People Play*. Englewood Cliffs, New Jersey: Prentice-Hall, 1973.

Erikson, E. *Childhood and Society*. New York: W. W. Norton, 1963.

Feltz, D., and Weiss, M. The Impact of Girls Interscholastic Sport Participation on Academic Orientation. *Research Quarterly*, 55, No.4(1984), 332-339.

Gaskell, G., and Pearton, R. Aggression and Sport. In *Sports, Games, and Play: Social and Psychological Viewpoints*. Edited by J. Goldstein. New York: Wiley, 1979.

Goffman, E. *Interaction Ritual*. Chicago: Aldine, 1967

Green, T. *Work, Leisure, and the American Schools*. New York: Random House, 1968.

Haerle, R. Education, Athletic Scholarships and the Occupational Career of the Professional Athlete. *Sociology of Work and Occupations*, 2(1975), 373-403.

Hanks, M. Race, Sexual Status and Athletics in the Process of Educational Achievement. *Social Science Quarterly*, 60, No.3(1979), 482-496.

Hanks, M., and Eckland, B.   Athletics and Social Participation in the Educational Process. *Sociology of Education, 49*(1976), 271-294.

Hauser, W., and Lueptow, L.   Participation in Athletics and Academic Achievement: A Replication and Extension.   *The Sociological Quarterly, 19*(1978), 304-309.

Hendry, L. *School, Sport, and Leisure.* London: Lepus Books, 1978.

Hill, P., and Lowe, B. The Inevitable Metathesis of the Retiring Athlete. *International Review of Sport Sociology, 9*, No. 3-4(1974), 5-29.

Howell, F., Miracle, A., and Rees, R. Do High School Athletics Pay?: The Effects of Varsity Participation on Socioeconomic Attainment.   *Sport Sociology Journal, 1*(1984), 15-25.

Howell, F., and Picou, S. Athletics and Income Achievements. Paper read at the Annual Meeting of the Southwestern Sociological Association, Houston, Texas, March, 1983.

Huizinga, J. *Homo Ludens.* Boston: Beacon Press, 1955.

Jerome, W., and Phillips, J.   The Relationship Between Academic Achievement and Interscholastic Participation: A Comparison of Canadian and American High Schools. *Journal of the Canadian Association for Health, Physical Education, and Recreation, 37*(1971), 18-21.

Kagan, S., and Madsen, M. Experimental Analyses of Cooperation and Competition in Anglo-American and Mexican-American Children. *Developmental Psychology, 6*(1972), 49-59.

Kandel, D., and Lesser, G. *Youth in Two Worlds.* San Francisco: Jossey-Bass, 1972.

King, J., and Chi, P.   Social Structure, Sex-roles, and Personality: Comparisons of Male/Female Athletes/Nonathletes.   Edited by J. Goldstein. In *Sports, Games, and Play: Social and Psychological Viewpoints.* New York: Wiley, 1979.

Kleiber, D. Sport and Human Development: A Dialectical Interpretation. *Journal of Humanistic Psychology, 23*(1983), 76-95.

Kleiber, D., and Greendorfer, S. Social Reintegration of Former College Athletes.   Unpublished manuscript, University of Illinois, Urbana-Champaign, 1984.

Kleiber, D., and Hemmer, J. Sex Differences in the Relationship of Locus of Control and Recreational Sport Participation. *Sex Roles, 7*(1981), 801-809.

Kleiber, D., and Rickards, W. Leisure and Recreation in Adolescence: Limitation and Potential. *In Constraints on Leisure.* Edited by M. Wade. Springfield, Illinois: C. C. Thomas, 1985.

Kleiber, D., and Roberts, G. The Effects of Sport Experience in the Development of Social Character: An Exploratory Investigation. *Journal of Sport Psychology, 3*(1981), 114-122.

Kroll, W., and Peterson, K. Study of Values Test and Collegiate Football Teams. *Research Quarterly, 36*(1965), 441-447.

Landers, D., Feltz, D., Obermeier, B., and Brouse, T. Socialization via Interscholastic Athletics: Its Effect on Educational Attainment. *Research Quarterly, 49*(1978), 475-483.

Landers, D., and Landers, D. Socialization via Interscholastic Athletics: Its Effects on Delinquency. *Sociology of Education, 51*(1978), 299-301.

Lasch, C. The Degradation of Sport. *In Culture of Narcissism.* New York: W. W. Norton, 1979

Lepper, M., and Greene, D. (Eds.). *The Hidden Costs of Rewards.* New York: Wiley, 1978.

Lever, J. Sex Differences in Games Children Play. *Social Problems, 23*(1976), 478-487.

Lever, J. Sex Differences in the Complexity of Children's Play and Games. *American Sociological Review, 43*(1978), 471-483.

Lipsyte, R. Interview with Bill Bradley. In *Play and Leisure.* Edited by J. Fiscella. Detroit: Wayne State University, 1976.

Loy, J., Kenyon, G., and McPherson, B. In *Sport and Social Systems.* Reading, Massachusetts: Addison-Wesley, 1978.

Lueptow, L., and Kayser, B. Athletic Involvement, Academic Achievement and Aspiration. *Sociological Focus, 7,* no. 1 (1973-74), 24-36.

Lueschen, G. The Interdependence of Sport and Culture. *International Review of Sport Sociology, 2*(1967), 127-141.

Lueschen, G. Cooperation, Association, and Contest. *Journal of Conflict Resolution, 14*(1970), 21-35.

Maehr, M. Meaning and Motivation: Toward a Theory of Personal Investment. In *Research on Motivation in Education, Volume 1: Student Motivation.*

Edited by R. Ames and C. Ames. New York, New York: Academic Press, 1984.

Maehr, M., and Nicholls, J. Culture and Achievement Motivation: A Second Look. In *Studies on Cross-Cultural Psychology.* Edited by N. Warren. New York: Academic Press, 1980.

Malmisur, M. Social Adjustment Differences Between Student Athletes and Student Nonathletes as Measured by Ego Development. *Sport Sociology Bulletin, 4,* no.2(1975), 2-12.

Malmisur, M. Ego Development of a Sample of College Football Players. *Research Quarterly, 47*(1976), 14-153.

Mantel, R., and Vander Velden, L. The Relationship Between Professionalization of Attitude Toward Play of Preadolescent Boys and Participation in Organized Sport. In *Sport in American Society.* Edited by G. Sage. Reading, Massachusetts: Addison-Wesley, 1974.

Marcia, J. Identity in Adolescence. In *The Handbook of Adolescent Psychology.* Edited by J. Adelson. New York: Wiley, 1980.

McPherson, B. The Occupational and Psychological Adjustment of Former Professional Athletes. Paper presented at the American College of Sports Medicine Annual Meeting, Chicago, Illinois, May, 1977.

Mergen, B. Riesman Redux: Football as Work, Play, Ritual, and Metaphor. In *Play as Context.* Edited by A. Cheska. West Point, New York: Leisure Press, 1981.

Miracle, A. Factors Affecting Interracial Cooperation: A Case Study of a High School Football Team. *Human Organization, 40*(1981), 150-154.

Miracle, A. Corporate Economy, Social Ritual, and the Rise of High School Sports. Paper presented at the Annual Meeting of the North American Society for the Study of Sport, Boston, Massachusetts, November, 1985.

Nicholls, J., and Miller, A. Development and Its Discontents--The Differentiation of the Concept of Ability. In *The Development of Achievement Motivation.* Edited by J. Nicholls. Greenwich, Connecticut: JAI Press, 1984.

Noe, F. An Instrumental Conception of Leisure for the Adolescent. *Adolescence, 4*(1969), 385-400.

Ogilvie, B., and Tutko, T. If You Want to Build Character, Try Something Else. *Psychology Today, 5,* no. 5(1971), 61-63.

Orlick, T., and Botterill, C. *Every Kid Can Win.* Chicago: Nelson Hall, 1977.

Otto, L., and Alwin, D. Athletics, Aspirations and Attainments. *Sociology of Education, 50,*(1977), 102-113.

Parten, M. Social Participation Among Preschool Children. *Journal of Abnormal and Social Psychology, 27*(1932), 243-269.

Phillips, J., and Schafer, W. Consequences of Participation in Interscholastic Sports. A Review and Prospectus. *Pacific Sociological Review, 14*(1971), 328-338.

Piaget, J. *Play, Dreams and Imitation in Childhood.* New York: W. W. Norton, 1962

Picou, J. Race, Athletic Achievement and Educational Aspiration. *The Sociological Quarterly, 19*(1978), 429-438.

Picou, J., and Curry, G. Residence and the Athletic Participation-Educational Aspiration Hypothesis. *Social Science Quarterly, 55*(1974), 768-776.

Rehberg, R. Behavioral and Attitudinal Consequences of High School Interscholastic Sports. A Speculative Consideration. *Adolescence,* Spring, (1969), 69-88.

Rehberg, R., and Cohen, J. Athletes and Scholars: An Analysis of the Compositional Characteristics and Images of These Two Youth Cultures. *International Review of Sport Sociology, 10*(1975), 91-107.

Rehberg, R., and Schafer, W. Participation in Interscholastic Athletics and College Expectations. *American Journal of Sociology, 73*(1968), 732-740.

Roberts, G. Achievement Motivation in Children's Sport. In *The Development of Achievement Motivation.* Edited by J. Nicholls. Greenwich, Connecticut: JAI Press, 1984.

Roberts, G., Kleiber, D., and Duda, J. An Analysis of Motivation in Children's Sport: The Role of Percieved Competence in Participation. *Journal of Sport Psychology, 3*(1981), 206-216.

Roberts, K. *Youth and Leisure.* London: Allen-Unwin, 1983.

Sack, A. Sport: Play or Work? In *Studies in the Anthropology of Play.* Edited by P. Stevens. West Point: Leisure Press, 1977.

Sage, G. American Values and Sport: Formation of a Bureaucratic Personality. *Leisure Today,* October(1978), 10-12.

Schafer, W. Sport, Socialization, and the School: Toward Maturity or Enculturation. Paper presented at Third International Symposium on the Sociology of Sport, Waterloo, Ontario, 1971.

Schafer, W., and Armor, J. Athletes Are Not Inferior Students. *Transaction,* *6*(1968), 21-26, 61-62.

Schurr, T., and Brookover, W. Athletes, Academic Self-Concept, and Achievement. *Medicine and Science in Sports, 2*(1970), 96-99.

Schwartzman, H. *Transformations: The Anthropology of Children's Play.* New York: Plenum, 1978.

Scott, J. Sport and Aggression. In *Contemporary Psychology of Sport.* Edited by G. Kenyon. Chicago: The Athletic Institute, 1970.

Snyder, E., and Spreitzer, E. Participation in Sport as Related to Educational Expectations Among High School Girls. *Sociology of Education, 50*(1977), 47-55.

Snyder, E., and Spreitzer, E. *Social Aspects of Sport.* New Jersey: Prentice-Hall, 1983.

Spady, W. Lament for the Letterman: Effects of Peer Status and Extracurricular Activities on Goals and Achievement. *American Journal of Sociology, 75*(1970), 680-702.

Spreitzer, E., and Pugh, M. Interscholastic Athletics and Educational Expectations. *Sociology of Education, 46*(1973), 171-182.

Start, K. Sporting and Intellectual Success Among English Secondary School Children. *International Review of Sport Sociology, 2*(1967), 47-54.

Stevenson, C. Socialization Effects of Participation in Sport: A Critical Review of the Research. *Research Quarterly, 46*(1975), 287-301.

Sutton-Smith, B., and Kelly-Byrne, D. The Phenomenon of Bipolarity in Play Theories. In *Child's Play: Developmental and Applied.* Edited by T. Yawkey and A. Pellegrini. Hillsdale, New Jersey: Lawrence Erlbaum, 1984.

Sutton-Smith, B., and Roberts, J. Rubrics of Competitive Behavior. *The Journal of Genetic Psychology, 105*(1964), 13-37.

Talamini, J. School Athletics: Public Policy Versus Practice. In *Sport and Society.* Edited by J. Talamini and C. Page. 1973.

Tutko, T., and Bruns, W. *Winning Is Everything and Other American Myths.* New York: Macmillan, 1976.

Vornberg, J. Student Activities: What Are the Problems Now? *The Clearinghouse, 56*, no.6(1983), 269-270.

Webb, H. Professionalization of Attitudes Toward Play Among Adolescents. In *Aspects of Contemporary Sport Sociology.* Edited by G. Kenyon. Chicago: The Athletic Institute, 1969.

Winer, F. The Elderly Jock and How He Got That Way. In *Sports, Games, and Play: Social Psychological Viewpoints.* Edited by J. Goldstein. New York: Wiley, 1979.

PLAY IN SPECIAL EDUCATION SETTINGS

Mayer Shevin

This chapter will address the ways in which play is conceptualized and used in special education settings. The chapter will also examine the impact which common curriculum models and classroom practices have on the productive exercise of play by special education students. For the purposes of this chapter, the term *special education* will be used to describe those classes or school activities in which the majority of student participants are tagged with one or more disability labels, such as "mentally retarded," "orthopedically handicapped," "hearing impaired," "emotionally disturbed," "behavior disordered," and so forth.

Students in these categories traditionally have been dealt with separately from the school population as a whole because of their perceived deficits. Here, however, these students will be considered as members of a separate class, *not* because of their defects or weaknesses, but because their experiences in school differ substantially from the experiences of other students.

Special education students, even in many supposedly "mainstreamed" school settings, are usually physically separated from the student body as a whole. For example, many special education students are taught in separate classes in the "special education wing" of a school building, isolated from the daily activities of that school. Others attend separate, special schools serving only children with disabilities from a given district, or, as in Missouri or Ohio, may attend special county schools serving retarded or multiply handicapped students from a number of school districts.

Administratively, special education students are separated, too. For example, planning for their education is addressed by the specific federal administrative guidelines set forth in relation to PL 94-142, The Education for All Handicapped Children Act.

Socially, special education students are separated in two more ways from the daily life of their schools. First, special education students are taught both those skills which society assumes that children in general will merely "pick up somewhere," (e.g., speech and "body language") and those skills which, according to social consensus, should be taught in the home (e.g., self-feeding and "table manners"). Second, implicit within much that special education students are taught are low expectations for achievement and high expectations for behavioral control. Both of these expectations are related to the tendency of special education to focus attention on student deficits and weaknesses (Certo, 1983). Special educators are frequently concerned that their more "excitable" students are at constant risk of "getting totally out of control" and will take positive behavior management steps to prevent this from happening (Beveridge and Hurrell, 1980). These steps often focus on the students' development of "passive skills" (Shevin, 1982)--that is, those skills related to not doing things such as interrupting, moving about inappropriately, and "playing with things you're not supposed to."

Given the physical and administrative separation and the social "otherness" experienced by special education students, why should regular education professionals be concerned about how "the other half" lives and plays? Three major reasons come to mind. First, some students do change status, moving into and out of the category of "special education student" at various times during their school careers. An understanding of typical work and play practices in the settings from which a given child comes or for which that child is being prepared will help both regular education and special education teachers to manage students' transitions effectively (Vincent, Salisbury, Walter, Brown, Gruenwald, and Powers, 1980). Second, both regular education and special education teachers possess areas of theoretical knowledge and day-to-day fluency which are potential sources of strength for their "opposite numbers." The special educator's skills in individualization and multi-level teaching, and the regular educator's skills in large-group management and curricular continuity, are ones that represent desirable innovations in each other's settings. Third, knowledge of the commonalities of the two fields will help decrease the perceived barrier between the two disciplines; if special educators and regular educators had a clear picture of what it is that each other does, the barriers to student movement and student integration would probably seem a good deal less insurmountable.

For both regular and special educators, it is relatively easy to find out the publicly announced principles and practices of each others disciplines. However, it is both more difficult and more important to learn the underlying assumptions of each others' fields; in other words, those basic principles which go undiscussed precisely because they are most taken for granted. It would probably be overstating the case to say that looking at the play of special education students is a way of studying that which is most basic to special education. Nevertheless, such a focus does permit us to look at an area in which the public pronouncements are few, but in which there are a variety of recurring patterns of common practice for both regular and special educators. By studying the play of special education students, we are looking at an area of potentially major importance for all educators in terms of both academic achievement and social integration (Wuerch and Voeltz, 1982).

WHAT DOES "PLAY" MEAN IN SPECIAL EDUCATION?

Many of the past discussions of the role of play in regular education programs and especially in early childhood education programs have had relatively little impact on the theoretical bases and the daily practices of most special education programs. Special educators frequently appear to regard the concept of play and its role in the lives of their students somewhat disingenuously.

Most authors who design curriculum and describe pedagogical approaches in special education do not attempt to define play, even though they speak of its importance in the overall curriculum (e.g., Wehman, 1977; Voeltz, Wuerch, and Wilcox, 1982). Wehman (1977), for example, after briefly reviewing efforts of Ellis (1973) and others to define play, concludes that theoretical and definitional issues are secondary to the primary task of identifying the most efficacious approaches for increasing student "play skills." Other authors also find that the lack of a definition for play does not serve as a barrier to the development of either individual "play skills" (e.g., Donder and Nietupski, 1981; Peck, Apolloni, Cooke, and Raver, 1978; or of broad ranges of techniques and curricula for play skill development (e.g., 1982; Odom and Strain, 1984; Wuerch and Voeltz, 1982).

Given the existence of a body of professional special education literature and a body of common special education practice which assume "play," however it is defined, to be a more or less typical part of the daily activities of the special education student, it will be useful to search for *implicit* meanings of play in research literature, curriculum designs, and common classroom practice. It will also be useful to discuss those implicit definitions of play in regular education settings which do not carry over into the world of special education.

Play: What you do with toys or games, or what you do on the playground.

One possible approach to defining play in the classroom concerns the materials with which a child is engaged at a particular point in time and the special play areas in which such engagements take place, such as play-corners or playgrounds (Crawley and Chan, 1982; Donder and Nietupski, 1981). Outside of school, play is often defined in this way. To the casual observer of children in non-school settings, if children are seen to be engaging in an activity which involves blocks, trucks, dolls, or paints, then it will probably be classified as play. If the activity involves making beds or washing dishes at home, then it probably will not be considered play; if it involves engaging in these activities in a simulation setting, such as with a tea set or a doll's bed, then it probably will be considered play.

Concerning the dimension of materials, we may begin to distinguish between the concepts of play and play skills on one hand, and the growing concerns in the field of special education with leisure activities and leisure skills on the other (Collard, 1981; Dixon, 1979; Wehman and Schlein, 1981; Wuerch and Voeltz, 1982). In comparing these two areas, we can see that discussions of play seem to assume that "play is with toys and games." Discussions of leisure activities, on the other hand, while including engagement with toys and games, also include activities such as hobbies, which may involve objects and materials with intrinsic value outside of the leisure setting (Wehman and Schlein, 1981), e.g., vegetables grown as a hobby, crocheted clothes, and so forth.

It would be a mistake to assume that the use of toys alone can define play. Were one to walk into many elementary-level special education classrooms after the children had gone home, especially classrooms for younger and for more severely disabled children, the general impression one might receive is of an environment "made for play." However, the pegs, blocks, jigsaw puzzles, colored rods, and other objects, although they share with toys their bright colors and the materials from which they are made, are not likely to be regarded as toys by either teachers or students due to the narrowly-defined, highly task-oriented uses of these objects. Teachers and students are unlikely to have a generic term such as "play" which can be used to describe all such materials; children being told to clean up their pegs or blocks are likely to be told to "put your work away."

Play: Doing what you want to do during free-time.

Another way of defining the parameters of play in school settings might be in terms of who initiates the activity--i.e., play involves any activity which a child, rather than the teacher, has initiated. This type of definition of play has been found to exist among children in a regular education setting who have been socialized to kindergarten norms (King, 1979). However, defining play as child-initiated activity is not necessarily inevitable in settings for young children; for example, such a definition may *not* exist in many day-care and other pre-kindergarten settings, where most activities are likely to be classified as "play" regardless of who initiates them. Once children are socialized to the world of school, though, the concept of "play" is likely to be closely connected to the concept of "free time," "play corner time," or "recess," times over which the teacher may exercise little apparent control unless a student has, through the violation of rules, forfeited his or her "rights" to this time of student-initiated, free- choice activity.

Special education settings are far less likely than regular education settings to provide either unambiguous free times or the orientation that leads students to consider those free-play times as "belonging to them." This lack of unambiguous times which belong to the students can be partially attributed to the comparatively high rate of interruption existing in most special education settings other than those connected with university-based experimental programs (Townsend, 1980). It is a common practice for special education students to be pulled unceremoniously out of planned classroom activities by therapists, special teachers, and others working with heavy caseloads and inflexible schedules. When a time *is* available for student play, it is unlikely, in special education settings, to be as *freely* available as a similar "playtime" might be in a regular education setting. The teacher's commitment to behavior management and to ongoing work on social interaction goals may lead that teacher to view playtime as one more opportunity to have students emit, maintain, and generalize target behaviors (Orlansky, 1979). Also, the discomfort of special education teachers with student-initiated behavior by many of their students (Beveridge and Hurrell, 1980) may lead many teachers to see free time as a potentially dangerous period in which "excitable" children are likely to "go out of control." For teachers of such students, arranging the environment to decrease the likelihood of the students' display of inappropriate "excess behaviors" is likely to be seen as a paramount educational priority (Voeltz, Evans, Freedland, and Donellon, 1982).

Play: What you do when there's no work to do.

This definition does not overtly appear in the literature of special education but it represents an attitude which is occasionally seen in special education classes for severely-and multiply-handicapped students, and is more frequently seen in sheltered workshop settings for disabled adults, adult day treatment centers, and so forth. Many of the *laissez-faire* attitudes toward play seen in regular educators at recess time (King, 1982) are also seen in the behavior of supervisory staff members in adult settings. Because of the limited responsibility of staff members in adult settings for the establishment of new behaviors in their clients and the generally low societal expectations of change in those clients, the contingencies for workers at sheltered workshops during "down-time" (i.e., time when work is not available) probably most closely resemble contingencies for students in regular education at recess time--that is, "do what you want as long as you stay out of trouble."

Play: Developmentally normative behavior informally demarcated play settings.

This implicit definition of play appears to be much more prevalent in the literature which discusses children with disabilities than in the regular education literature. In the former literature, the term "play" carries an implication of socially normative, chronological-age-appropriate behavior. In Whittaker (1980), for example, the term "play" is used to characterize "doll-related," but never "self-related," behavior. Other studies refer to socially non-normative behavior with qualified play terms or with terms which discriminate totally between the action being engaged in and real play. Watters and Wood (1983), for example, contrast "disruptive play" and "self-stimulatory behavior" with "play," while Wing, Gould, Yeates, and Brierly (1977) contrast "symbolic play" with "stereotyped play" and with no "symbolic play", a category used to describe repetitive manipulation. The message of this coding is that children who behave atypically--who wave their fingers in front of their faces or spin the wheels repeatedly on toy trucks--even if it's during recess time, even if they are engaged with toys, and even if the teacher has not specifically assigned them other duties, are somehow *not* engaged in play but are, rather, involved in "something else."

Play: Instructional games.

Instructional games seem to occupy a shadowy territory somewhere between "play" and "work." Although the teacher's labeling of an activity as play may lead the students to call the activity play, the students may behave as though it is one more classroom task. Both the language used by teachers and students to describe the activity, and their behavior related to the activity are likely to reflect this ambiguity. This author, for example, conducted an observational study (Shevin and Miller, 1983) in two classes for students labeled as "educable mentally retarded." During that study, one teacher summoned the students to a game activity by saying, "OK, everybody, let's get to work. We're going to play 'Simon Says.'" She criticized one of the students after the game by telling her, "I can't give you a sticker for good work--you weren't using your thinking cap." In the other class, however, the teacher treated classroom games such as spelling bees and "seven-up" in much the same way that other teachers often treat free play time--that is, as a reinforcer for good behavior to be delivered at the end of the day or just before lunch. She encouraged them to finish their worksheets before lunch: "If you finish up quickly, we'll all get to play." Although play was supposed to function as a reward in that setting, the students seemed to work no faster when told they would have a chance to play a game before lunch, and when they did begin the game, several students chose to stay at their desks without participating.

Play: Other possibilities.

There are a number of different types of behavior which are currently not typically regarded as play behavior in special education settings and which may be revealing in terms of what they tell us about the field's preconceptions concerning the nature and role of play in school life for students with disabilities. Among these behaviors are (1) onlooker behavior, in which the play of other children is observed; (2) non-standard toy use or non-standard use of utilitarian objects (other than use which is identifiable as "symbolic" by the observer); (3) use of instructional materials in ways other than those specified by the teacher; and (4) what King (1982) refers to as "illicit play," that is, clandestine activity centered on unsanctioned social contact among students. Although such behaviors might be regarded as "playful" by outsiders, they tend to be lumped together as "off-task" behaviors, devalued, and systematically reduced by special educators, often by the same teachers who are highly committed to the establishment of appropriate recreation and leisure skills in their students. The term "play" is often used pejoratively to refer to off-task behavior, as in "Stop playing around and get back to work!" Thus, for students, "play" may have an additional meaning of "anything other than what I'm supposed to be doing."

RESEARCH ON HANDICAPPED CHILDREN'S PLAY

There are two general types of research into the play of children with handicaps: (1) comparative studies, that is, those studies directed at a labeled population which attempt to identify "characteristics of the blind" or "characteristics of the retarded" by contrasting aspects of their play with the play of "normal" or "non-handicapped" children; and (2) intervention studies, that is, studies which attempt to demonstrate the efficacy of a specific treatment in changing the play behavior of a narrowly defined population of disabled children. Reviews of the research in this area characterize the literature as "limited," "meagre," and "sporadic" (Li, 1981; Mogford, 1977; Quinn and Rubin, 1984; Wehman, 1977). Nevertheless, the section below summarizes the findings of this research.

Comparative studies

Direct comparisons of handicapped and non-handicapped children's play.

Some authors have characterized the "abnormal" or "deficient" aspects of the play of children in a labeled disability category by comparing their play with that of "normal" children matched either by mental age (Horne and Philleo, 1942), or by both mental and chronological age (Tait, 1972; Weiner and Weiner, 1974). In such studies, groups of children are compared in terms of rates or percentages of various coded classes of play and non-play behavior, rank-ordered according to the ages at which different types of play appear in the population at large. In this type of study, children are observed in "free-play settings." In earlier studies, handicapped and non-handicapped children were studied separately. More recently, the existence of mainstreamed early childhood programs have provided the opportunity for observing the play behavior of handicapped and non-handicapped children with each other (Faught, Balleweg, Crow, and Van den Pol, 1983; Fitzgerald, 1985). Findings in these studies have included the retarded child's preference for more structured, less "open-ended" materials as compared to non-retarded children (Horne and Philleo, 1942); the decreased likelihood of retarded children playing with combinations of toys (Weiner and Weiner, 1974); and the increased likelihood of blind children, as compared to sighted children, engaging in play involving direct object manipulation (Tait, 1972).

Descriptions of developmental progressions in the play of handicapped children.

Another type of comparative study examines longitudinal differences in play behavior among children of various ages in a given disability category (Crawley and Chan, 1982; Odom, 1981; Whittaker, 1980). In such studies, the most common basis of comparison is in terms of progression through Piagetian stages of behavior; the data collected concerns the presence, absence, or relative frequencies of various coded classes of play behavior. Studies may either be in free-play (Odom, 1981) or in highly structured settings (Whittaker, 1980). Odom (1981), for example, observed moderately and severely retarded children during free-play time in a nursery school setting, and coded their behavior at 15-second intervals using a combination of one scale for coding the social dimensions of play (Parten, 1932) and one scale for coding the cognitive dimensions of play (Smilansky, 1968). Scores on these scales were then correlated with scores on a general developmental screening test. Whittaker (1980), in contrast, presented profoundly retarded children with sets of miniature dolls and domestic objects and observed the presence or absence of various categories of symbolic and non-symbolic play with those materials.

Longitudinal researchers, although often focusing only on the play of disabled children, typically have as their purpose the comparison of disabled and non-disabled children. Researchers attempt to discover the extent to which patterns of developmental progression in the play of disabled children parallels patterns documented by other researchers in the play of non-handicapped children. Some researchers have found typical developmental progressions in the play of handicapped children (Odom, 1981; Whittaker, 1980), while others have found significant differences between the two (Crawley and Chan, 1982).

Intervention studies

The intervention literature can be divided into (1) those studies in which changes in play behavior are the goal toward which the study is directed (Devoney, Guralnick, and Rubin, 1974; Knapczyk and Yoppi, 1975; McConkey and Jeffree, 1979; Wambold and Bailey, 1979; Wehman, 1977; Watters and Wood, 1983; Wuerch and Voeltz, 1982), (2) those in which play is not taught, but in which it is the means by which other objectives are reached (Kissel and Whitman, 1977; Morrison and Newcomer, 1975; Odom and Strain, 1984; Santomier and Kopczuk, 1981; and (3) those in which play is used as reinforcement for classroom behavior (Ayllon and Roberts, 1974; Jones and Kazdin, 1975). In some studies (e.g., Donder and Nietupski, 1981; Peck, Appoloni, Cooke, and Raver, 1978), play is both the goal and the means toward another objective, such as social integration.

This section of the chapter will be concerned only with those interventions in which changes in play and play skills are one of the primary objectives of the intervention. Studies in which play is a reinforcer will not be addressed here because, by and large, those studies provide little information on either the nature of the play, the settings in which it is displayed, or the changes in the students' play behavior over time. In other words, play is a given--it is not typically a topic of discussion in such studies, any more than would be the nutritional content or the reinforcing characteristics of the pellets furnished to rats in a maze-running experiment.

Authors dealing with interventions related to children's play do not usually describe their task as that of "teaching children to play"; the objective, instead, is conceptualized by some as "teaching children play skills," and by others as "fostering the development of play." When the focus is on teaching play skills, play is equated with the array of social, cognitive, fine motor, gross motor, and language skills which the child brings to the setting in which play is permitted or encouraged. When the emphasis is on fostering play development, changes in children's play are seen as following an unvarying developmental sequence; the teacher or therapist's role is that of one who manages an environment which encourages the child's movement through this progression.

Most of the literature on teaching play skills to children identified as handicapped focuses on the younger and on the more severely handicapped students (see Wehman, 1977, for a notable exception). Typically, the play skills worked on are those corresponding to the child's deficiencies relative to an accepted developmental progression. None of the studies suggest the possibility of working on skills "out of sequence." Thus, for example, for a child who is considered profoundly retarded and who spends much of his time in a free-play setting waving a toy in front of his face, efforts to develop his or her play skills are likely to focus on increasing appropriate isolated toy play (Wambold and Bailey, 1979), rather than on some alternative goal, such as group play, playroom exploration, or peer observation. This adherence to normative developmental progressions is typically followed, whether the teacher is seen primarily as a systematic programmer, cuing and reinforcing specific bits of appropriate behavior (e.g., Wambold and Bailey, 1979; Wehman, 1977) or as a facilitative, "suggestive" arranger of the environment (e.g., McConkey and Jeffree, 1979).

The teaching procedures used in the establishment of play skills are, by and large, the same teaching procedures used by special educators in other curricular domains. These include reinforcing successive approximations to appropriate behavior with social praise (Santomier and Kopczuk, 1981; Wambold and Bailey, 1979; Wehman, 1977); redirection of students through verbal, visual, and physical prompts when "inappropriate" toy play is displayed (Wambold and Bailey, 1979); fading of prompts (Wambold and Bailey, 1979; Wehman, 1977; Wuerch and Voeltz, 1982); sequencing the task through task analysis (Wehman, 1977; Wuerch and Voeltz, 1982) reinforcer sampling (Wehman, 1977; Wuerch and Voeltz, 1982); and modeling of appropriate behavior by non-handicapped peers (Devoney, Guralnick, and Rubin, 1974; Donder and Nietupski, 1981; Morris and Dolker, 1974; Snyder, Appoloni, and Cooke, 1977) Some authors, recognizing that focusing the student's attention both on the teacher and on the play materials is impossible, identify typical teaching practices which they consider inappropriate for teaching play skills, including teaching attending behaviors as an isolated skill (Wuerch and Voeltz, 1982), and providing extensive tangible or social reinforcers during toy play (Wambold and Bailey, 1979; Wehman, 1977; Wuerch and Voeltz, 1982). Occasionally, teaching techniques are recommended in which the common early childhood education approach of environmental programming (arranging an environment which invites play) is used more prominently than direct teacher control of student behavior (McConkey and Jeffree, 1979, 1980); however, such an approach is an exception in the special education intervention literature.

Methodological problems in research into the play of disabled children

Several of the reviews of the sparse research literature related to the play of handicapped children (Mogford, 1977; Rubin, Fein, and Vandenberg, 1983; Quinn and Rubin, 1984) have identified common methodological flaws in that literature. Some of the methodological difficulties are those related to faulty use of experimental research design (i.e., poor experimental control and failure to account for artifacts of the experimental setting). Other more fundamental critiques call into question the validity of research into play which lacks a phenomenological, naturalistic perspective.

Unsupported assumptions concerning experimental settings.

Research into the play of children with disabilities usually takes place in prototypical play research settings. Rubin, Fein, and Vandenberg (1983) describe play research in general as taking place in contexts which "...reflect the belief that a describable and reproducible set of environmental arrangements will evoke in children a set or inclination to play" (p.700). They describe the properties of those settings in which most research on children's play takes place:

> (1) an array of familiar peers, toys, or other mate-
> rials likely to engage children's interest; (2) an agreement
> between adults and children... that the children are free to
> choose from the array whatever they wish to do... (3) adult
> behavior that is minimally intrusive or directive; (4) a friendly
> atmosphere designed to make children feel comfortable and
> safe; and (5) scheduling that reduces the likelihood of the
> children being tired, hungry, ill, or experiencing other types of
> bodily stress (p.701).

Although there is limited information on the precise nature of the play settings in the studies of disabled children cited above, (Crawley and Chan, 1982; Faught, Balleweg, Crow, and Van den Pol, 1983; Horne and Philleo, 1942; Odom, 1981; Tait, 1972; Weiner and Weiner, 1974), it appears that by and large the attempt has been made to establish "optimum play-fostering settings." Researchers have found such arrangements to be generally appropriate; nevertheless, those properties of the environment which actually serve to foster play for a particular individual are highly variable and tend to be culturally and experientially determined (Rubin, Fein, and Vandenberg, 1983). This issue has gone unaddressed in the special education research literature. The field is left with unanswered questions: How do disabled children play in more typical special education settings which have not been consciously designed for play? Might disabled children play even more productively and enthusiastically in as-yet-unidentified settings?

Unsupported assumptions concerning play materials.

The play of handicapped children is generally studied using materials which have been identified over the years as those which optimize the likelihood of play by typical children. However, some of the differences seen between the performance of handicapped and non-handicapped children in research settings may be artifacts of those experimental settings rather than true representations of disability-related behavioral variation. For example, it is commonly accepted in the general play research literature that variations in the novelty/familiarity of materials, settings, play partners, and adult authorities affect the types of behavior displayed in play settings (Hutt, 1970; Rubin, Fein, and Vandenberg, 1983). However, the specific materials and settings with which play is expected to take place vary along dimensions other than those of novelty and familiarity. Familiar objects may have their familiarity established in contexts that tell the child, "This is not something to play with." King (1976), observing longitudinally in a regular kindergarten setting, noted that objects used as part of teacher-directed, task-oriented activities in the classroom were never classified as "toys" and were unlikely to be chosen for use during free-play activities. Similarly, in the special education classroom, materials which are considered to be "toys" in the mainstream culture may acquire additional significance as instructional materials at a cost to their potential function as toys. By way of illustration, consider this hypothetical example:

> A teacher is working with a severely physically handicapped 4-year-old in order to get her to use both hands in manipulating objects. In order to do this, the teacher places a weighted "carousel ball" in front of the child and says, "Look, Bianca, play with the ball." The teacher rocks the ball as a demonstration and says, "Bianca, you do it." (When the ball moves, the little horses rock back and forth, and the chimes inside ring.) After three or four requests, Bianca rocks the ball. The teacher says, "Good work, Bianca! You rocked the ball! Do it again!" Bianca puts her right hand in her mouth (an extremely frequent habit of hers), and the teacher takes Bianca's hand out of her mouth and says, "No, Bianca, rock the ball." Bianca rocks the ball, the teacher says, "Good girl! You did it!" and goes to help another child. Bianca puts her hand in her mouth. This activity is repeated, using the carousel ball, a "musical apple," and a "busy box," at various times over the next three weeks.

In the above example, we can ask: "From Bianca's perspective, is the carousel ball a 'toy'?" Having been used repeatedly as part of an activity in which specific movements were solicited and reinforced by the teacher, it is likely that the potential of the ball as an object of intrinsically motivated behavior, in which the goals of the play activity are self-imposed by the child, will be diminished. In practical terms, when the teacher leaves, Bianca is likely to go back to sucking her hand, and an observer doing a coded time-sample study of play behavior in Bianca's classroom will classify her as "not yet having developed exploratory play."

Lack of a phenomenological perspective--limitations of "the experimental method."

The comparative studies of the play of handicapped children are limited by what Goode (1984) has described as the "fault-finding" perspective present in clinical diagnosis. That is, working with a population of children already diagnosed and labeled with a disability, the clinician or researcher's perceived task:

> is one in which some standard of normal structure ...is employed to locate deviations or pathologies whose identification, in turn, forms the rationale of a plan for treatment or remediation (p.233).

Goode criticizes this approach as failing to consider the child's perspective, failing to utilize "emic," phenomenological perspectives to determine what is taking place in that setting from the child's point of view. The danger posed by these deficiencies is that although reliable, verifiable data about school and children may be collected, that information may turn out to be totally irrelevant to the central, vital concerns in the lives of the children being studied. According to Goode, these limitations in the way in which the profession approaches assessment and program design for children identified as handicapped can be overcome through the utilization of longitudinal, participant-observer data collection. However, such a perspective is almost totally lacking in the studies reviewed here.

The intervention studies share both the methodological strengths and weaknesses of special education research in general. The strengths are those of attention to detail in experimental design, and the use of refined practices of single-subject and "small-n" research designs. The weaknesses of such studies is summarized in technical terms by Rubin, Fein, and Vandenberg (1983) and in practical terms by Blatt and Garfunkel (1981).

Rubin and his colleagues criticize play research with disabled subjects, for the use of small sample sizes with heterogeneous mixes of exceptional children, for the failure to control for related handicapping conditions or for sex differences, and for a level of conceptual confusion in which training in play behavior is actually training in "...peer interactive social behavior, which may incidentally include such indexes of play as pretense. However, since play is but an incidental feature of the outcome measures, the results of the studies are difficult to interpret" (p.744). They recommend a shift in focus of research to the collection of developmentally relevant information concerning the effects of training on the complexity of play.

Blatt and Garfunkel (1981) find that most intervention research in special education focuses on narrowly defined studies of the relation between input (i.e., a specific intervention) and output (i.e., changes in student performance on some scale or measure) with little or no attention to the process or the human interactions of the context in which these interventions and behavioral changes take place. They write:

> Our goal as educational researchers is to examine the components of the teaching-learning interaction. We conclude that, to accomplish this goal, individual components cannot be amputated; that is, as we amputate, we both change the natural setting and destroy much of any understanding we might have gained from a more holistic view (p.84).

The alternative, Blatt and Garfunkel suggest, is an approach that focuses less on specific techniques and interventions and more on the overall nature of the social environment and the relationships which develop between teachers and learners. Such an approach directed toward the play of children in special education settings would lead away from the consideration of the assessment and establishment of specific "play skills" toward the creation of environments which tell the child that this is the place where one may play.

THE USES OF PLAY IN THE SPECIAL EDUCATION CLASSROOM

The research literature discussed above includes many theoretically and methodologically sound studies in which the effectiveness of interventions is demonstrated according to the rigorous professional consensus represented by journal publication standards. However, as Townsend (1980) has described, there is a great deal of slippage between the neatly conceptualized and executed programming in university-based demonstration programs and the daily world of most special education classrooms. Townsend identified built-in properties of schools that *prevent* exemplary practices from actually taking place.

In this section, the general role of play in special education classrooms will be described. This section is based both on special education literature, which deals with general issues of classroom environment and program priorities, as well as on structured and informal classroom observations by the author over the past several years.

Play has not been a planned part of the curriculum in most special education programs except in those for preschool-aged children. This is not to say that no play takes place; however, its role in most classrooms is not a central one. In most special education settings, play is used as one of several possible means toward various ends rather than as a valued activity in its own right. The three major uses of play in the special education classroom are (1) play used as a reinforcer; (2) play used as a down-time activity; and (3) instructional games used for skill practice and development.

Play as a reinforcer.

Teachers trained in behavior management always learn that access to free play is a particularly effective "activity reinforcer" (e.g., Alberto and Troutman, 1982; Sulzer-Azaroff and Mayer, 1977) The behavioral research literature abounds with examples of interventions in which access to free play is contingent on the extended display of target academic or "non-disruptive" behaviors in the classroom (e.g., Campbell and Sulzer 1971; Jones and Kazdin, 1975).

Many special education teachers use access to free play time as a reinforcer with students earning the time in several ways. Students may, within a highly structured system, receive points or tokens, which either must reach a certain threshold in order to "buy" access to the free play area during play time or which may be used to "buy" specific toys or activities for use during that play time. Students may start out the day "at zero" with the right to go to the play area during free play, a right which can be lost by "losing points" during the day through behavior considered inappropriate by the teacher. Finally, students may earn access to the play area during play time with a very informal set of contingencies; there may have been little feedback during the day, but late in the school day the teacher may tell the student, "Charlie, you were good today, so you get to play."

Teacher training programs typically stress the desirability of following through with promised reinforcers. However, in practice, teachers are often highly inconsistent in providing regular access to contingent free play time (Shevin and Miller, 1983). This inconsistency comes from several factors.

One factor is the timing of the free play activity, usually sandwiched in after the last academic activity and before lunch, or after the last "special" (art, music, or gym) class and before the bus comes. Thus, free play is particularly susceptible to interruption, truncation, and postponement. Another factor is the teacher's attitude toward the free play time--even if the students have "earned" their free play, the teacher may perceive it as being less importance than a "real" class activity. Teachers frequently run over into play time rather than terminate an academic lesson. A third factor is the way in which free play is earned--a student will frequently earn points or tokens exchangeable for free time at the end of the day but may get into trouble shortly before the free time period. Many teachers feel it is more important to avoid inadvertently reinforcing the inappropriate behavior than it is to provide the free time: "You've all been so noisy out in the hall coming back from gym, you don't get your free time today." A fourth factor, very common in those settings in which students are worked with by an interdisciplinary team or in those settings in which a good deal of mainstreaming is taking place is that students are frequently out of the classroom at another activity during time officially allocated to free play.

Play as a "down-time" activity.

"Down-time" is a phrase used in sheltered workshop settings to refer to time during which no jobs are available, leaving workers without assigned jobs to do. The typical school day in special education settings presents many periods of down time which could be available for non-contingent student play. Examples include time after a student has completed his or her assigned work, time in which students are supposed to wait for an upcoming activity, time in which students are waiting for all the participants in an upcoming group activity to be assembled, and so forth. In practice, such use of down-time is extremely rare outside of adult settings. In several years of supervising practicum and student teachers in classes for mildly, moderately, and severely handicapped students, only twice has this author seen a student permitted to go and play after his work was done during a time which had not specifically been set aside for play.

The reluctance on the part of teachers to relinquish control over a student's activity for even a brief period of the day is not unique to special education; however, its near-universality in special education is striking. What might be some of the reasons for this tight grip on the reins by special educators?

One approach in exploring this issue is to look at the students themselves. Many children in special education classes are easily distractable; the teachers might worry that control over those students who were still working would diminish if students who were finished could play. Also, many teachers whose daily activities are focused on the "destigmatization" of their students are extremely reluctant to provide the student with a setting in which non-normative behavior might be displayed. Levitt (1975) has shown, for example, that the behavior of children with cerebral palsy can shift into more primitive, less well-developed movement patterns during the excitement of playground play. Similarly, children who move their hands around when excited or who talk strangely and loudly may be more likely to do so during a play activity. Such behavior may be intolerable for many special education teachers. Nothing in teacher training, in the philosophical orientation of the field of special education, or in the overt and covert messages special education teachers receive from the regular school students and staff tells those teachers that it's permissible to allow a certain amount of behavior to "get by" the school's most exacting standards.

Finally, many special education teachers are oriented toward using a curriculum which, through the positive practices of systematic use of shaping, backward chaining, fading and prompting, and through the possibly negative practices of massed practice and frequent repetition, are geared toward learning in which trial and error are minimized. For the teacher with an orientation toward "errorless" learning, many of the most typical play behaviors (which include experimentation, nonstandard and nonfunctional usage of materials, and inefficient movement patterns (Rubin, Fein, and Vandenberg, 1983) may be perceived merely as errors or as incompletely developed skills, that call for direct teacher intervention.

Instructional games.

Instructional games are widely used in special education classrooms as motivators of academic performance. Teachers frequently incorporate instructional games into large-group and small-group academic activities. Games as formal as spelling bees or Math Baseball or as informal as scoring points competitively for two teams during flash card drill are common. Instructional games typically combine some standardized presentation of a question-and-answer component with a moving or scoring procedure drawn from either sports or board games. Frequently, these classroom games are participated in more enthusiastically by the students than any academic activities. Although the teacher-directed, mandatory nature of instructional games (Shevin and Miller, 1983) makes their characterization as "play" problematical, instructional games can expose special education students to game- playing situations that may have some carry-over to independent, normalized, integrated playground and after-school settings.

EFFECTS OF CLASSROOM PLAY ON PLAYFULNESS

What effects do these typical uses of play in special education settings have on either the fostering or the suppression of play and playfulness in those settings? It is the contention of this author that, without explicitly setting it as a goal, without either an ideology or a cultural consensus, these common special education practices are extremely effective in turning special education classrooms into places where play is infrequent and unrelaxed. Moreover, common special education practice muddies the waters by adopting the language of play to refer to a range of events similar only in their lack of playfulness.

As discussed above, play is frequently used as an activity reinforcer in special education settings. Further, play as an activity reinforcer was described as being frequently administered inconsistently. What is the effect of free play time being something which the student has earned but which may or may not be delivered depending on factors outside of the students' control? In that context, the play of special education students is much the same as the play of regular education students--it is time in the Giant's Garden, in which one sometimes has the opportunity to frolic cautiously without ever forgetting who owns the garden. Access to play time is in the hands of the teacher, and the rules for access or denial of access are administered with varying levels of consistency.

In those settings in which rules for earning free time are administered consistently within a shared, commonly understood rule system, students come to appear "at home" in following the rules. In those settings, the rules come to be internalized and reified in ways resembling very closely those identified by King (1976) in her observation of a typical kindergarten setting. More typical is the slightly chaotic, frequently interrupted special education class (Townsend, 1980). In these settings, the consequences for obeying established rules are followed through by the teacher inconsistently; a student is unlikely to be able to predict on the basis of self-evaluation of his or her own performance whether he or she will be able to have access to play time. Such inconsistency on the part of a teacher breeds student dependence on that teacher; if I am a student who can't predict on the basis of my own behavior what will be the outcome for me during free time this afternoon, then I must attend in great detail to the teacher's behavior--to her moods, evaluations, definitions of reality, priorities, and so forth--so as to be able to make predictions about the world around me.

What effect does the lack of noncontingent "down-time" play have on the overall school experience of special education students? One likely effect is a chronic problem described by staff and administrators in adult-sheltered workshop settings--the lack of leisure skills and "breaktime skills" displayed by the disabled workers during down time. The workers in sheltered workshops are frequently described as lacking ability to initiate leisure-time activities at moments in which it would be appropriate. Such an outcome is not surprising, considering the extremely limited opportunities available for noncontingent play in special education classroom settings. The lack of opportunity is unfortunate, considering the particular importance of such play for special education students, even beyond its importance in regular education.

Regular education schools are unabashed workplaces in a society which, at least in theory, values children's play. This apparent contra-diction causes little public disturbance because it is well understood that most kids will, to a greater or lesser extent, "learn how to play" without training, official sanction, or opportunity for play being presented in elementary school settings. Typical children have a host of resources to draw upon--siblings, neighbors, "the kids down the block"--who will provide the opportunity for practice of the cognitive and affective skills required to be an "active player."

The disabled child, however, is often ignored or avoided by others in the neighborhood, protected from potentially unpleasant experiences (and thus functionally isolated) by his or her parents, and denied access to environments which, although they present some potential danger to the child, are more importantly recognizable as settings in which information about the world can be acquired and in which skills and self-confidence can be developed (Porter, Ramsey, Tremblay, Iaccobo, and Crawley, 1978). Thus, the number of environments in which disabled young children can "pick up" play skills are seriously limited, and the need of disabled children for systematic assistance in the acquisition of those cognitive, behavioral, and affective skills is correspondingly increased. Leaving the development of play skills to chance in the light of strong evidence that such development will not spontaneously take place (Wuerch and Voeltz, 1982) is a way of both reifying and perpetuating the social placement of disabled children on the nonparticipatory fringes of society.

Could the gap between the play practice experienced informally in nonschool settings by nonhandicapped children and the lack of such opportunity for handicapped children be bridged by the use of instructional games in the special education classroom? Unfortunately, the formal nature of classroom games probably provides very little generalization to playful behavior in settings which are not carefully structured and teacher managed. Playing "Simon Says" or "Spelling Baseball" in the classroom does little to prepare any child, in regular or special education, for life on the playground. Moreover, in many instructional game settings very little takes place that serves to prepare students to take part independently in "games with rules." In fact, several typical teacher practices may be linked to a decrease in the student's ability to play games. This effect does not necessarily indicate teacher mismanagement; rather, it reflects conflicts which may arise when the teacher is simultaneously playing the conflicting roles of "pedagogue" and "gamesmaster."

A teacher playing an instructional game with a small group of special education students may be faced with students with greatly varying skill levels, and with low likelihood of persisting in frustrating activities. In addressing this situation, the teacher will frequently: (1) give additional help or assistance to a student to increase the likelihood of getting the answer right (modeling, cuing, or prompting); (2) provide the student with easy bonus points (i.e., an enriched schedule of reinforcement); (3) accept an answer from one student which would be unacceptable from another more skilled student (shaping); and (4) change the rules mid-game so that partial completion of the activity is declared to be "winning" (terminating the session while the probability of appropriate behavior is still high).

As can be seen from the preceding examples, the teacher may have followed some of the principles designed to promote error-free learning in structuring the game, and the teacher may be reinforced for this by the continued active participation of unskilled, easily frustrated students. However, the student may have learned some game-playing "rules" in the process that ultimately close him or her off from successful initiation of, and participation in, games outside of the teacher- controlled setting. Some of these "rules" are:

(1) "Rules can be changed mid-game--by somebody else";

(2) "Somebody else will tell me whether I got it right or not";

(3) "If I mess up, somebody else might change the rules so I can keep winning";

(4) "If I mess up, I can still stay in the game";

(5) "I'm still winning, but it's not because of how I have been playing. Maybe the teacher likes me."

A teacher who is cognizant of the need of students to learn to "play by the rules" may alternatively manage games impartially with an emphasis on rigidly defined fairness, objective standards of success or failure, and complete disclosure of all rules and standards at the outset of the game. Such an approach will potentially avoid some of the nonnormalizing messages concerning game-playing which are described above. Unfortunately, the less skilled students may come away from such a game-playing situation with another set of negative messages that may stand in the way of their independent participation in voluntary game situations with other children: "I'm no good at games"; "I always lose"; "Why bother playing?"

There are two potentially useful approaches in avoiding this dilemma. One straightforward approach is to render the issue moot by shifting the emphasis from competitive instructional games to cooperative ones. The latter games have been shown to be particularly effective in fostering positive attitudes toward student diversity (Johnson and Johnson, 1978; Sapon-Shevin, 1978; 1980; Slavin, 1983). A second approach would be to limit individualization to special instruction outside of the actual game setting--the teacher thus moving from the role of "crooked referee" to the role of "coach." Such coaching might even become student initiated, with students contracting to trade completion of academic tasks for additional assistance ("If you finish all of your work, I'll help you practice your facts for Geography Trivia.")

To summarize, then, play in typical special education classrooms falls, in an unexamined, *ad hoc* way, into a little-valued spot in the daily or weekly routine. The overall sum of typical attitudes toward, and practices of, play in special education classrooms combine to produce an environment in which play is infrequent, nonnormalizing, unconnected with the development of skills of autonomy and self-direction, and unconnected with the types of play typically available to nonhandicapped children in nonschool environments.

THEORY-BASED BARRIERS TO PLAYFULNESS IN THE CLASSROOM AND SOME ALTERNATIVES

In the preceding section, several typical play practices in special education classes were identified. By and large, these practices represent a pragmatic response to the everyday reality of coping in a challenging environment, and do not have strong philosophical underpinnings. There are, however, some theory-based practices which affect the play environments of special education classrooms. These practices fall into the areas of (1) *tightly defined sequencing of objectives* based on normative developmental guidelines; and (2) *tightly defined instructional approaches* based on applied behavior analysis, task analysis, and precision teaching.

Developmental sequencing: playing step by step.

The power of a developmental sequence of play skills is that it draws both on a coherent theoretical base (e.g., Piaget, 1962; Smilansky, 1968) and on a body of observational data demonstrating that a sequence of a nearly universal set of behaviors neatly characterizes the longitudinal development of non-handicapped children. This theoretical base and these observational data naturally lead special educators to approaches that focus on providing their handicapped students the appropriate next developmental step. It is assumed that such approaches will take advantage of the skills which their students have already mastered, and will avoid the frustration of attempting to force a handicapped child to acquire and display new skills which are beyond his or her capability. Why frustrate the child with attempts to establish social play when his or her exploratory toy play skills are so limited? Why even talk about initiating pretend play with a child who avoids eye contact and sucks his fingers?

However, as some authors have pointed out in relation to severely handicapped students (Brinker, 1984; Certo, 1983), there are some risks associated with curricular selections based on a strict adherence to normative sequences of development. Specifically, such selections lead to a widening gap between the behavior of disabled and non-disabled students over time.

Such selections make playful responses to *all* the daily activities of the special education classroom less likely. If a student works on a single skill until mastery, at which time he is led on to the next one in sequence, then two things will happen: (1) the point of mastery is also likely to be a point of intense boredom; and (2) when the student is ready to go back and use the skill in a playful way, the teacher has moved the student on to something else, and the student's playing with the previously mastered skill is seen as "regression." In a very real sense, a student who is constantly protected from "regressing" may, in the process, be protected from play.

Finally, focusing on replicating the behavior of infants and toddlers does not provide the incentive to develop methods to teach students to participate at least partially

(Brown, Branston, Baumgart, Vincent, Falvey, and Schroeder, 1979) in performing age- appropriate and functional skills in natural environments. Rather, it justifies 21 years of extensive training focusing exclusively on presumed prerequisite skills, regardless of their functional use (Certo, 1983, p.12).

An approach which does focus on functional skills bases curricular development on an ecological analysis of the optimum environments to which the student might have access. Rather than focusing on "the next developmental step," this approach focuses on "the next educational environment" (Vincent, Salisbury, Walter, Brown, Gruenwald, and Powers, 1980). Curricula are based on those skills which are justifiable because the student mastering them will, from early stages of his or her acquisition of those skills, be partially or fully participating in increasingly integrated, normalized, diverse, and age-appropriate experiences.

This ecological approach has gained a wide following among educators working with severely handicapped children; increasingly, it is being applied in other areas of special education as well. It is particularly useful in setting specific play skill objectives for students with wide disparities between their chronological ages and "developmental ages." Such an approach leads professionals to the identification of play objectives which will be quickly functional in diverse environments, non-stigmatizing, age-appropriate to the extent that the activities are within the range of chronological age-normative behavior, and of potentially independent or at least self-initiated activities.

An excellent example of the utilization of the ecological approach in the development of a play curriculum is the guide by Wuerch and Voeltz (1982). The activities on which this guide focuses are ones that can be engaged in by people of a wide variety of ages (e.g., bowling, hand-held pinball games, target games, construction toys). They are also open-ended activities which can be engaged in at any skill level. Moreover, they are activities which lend themselves to both individual and group play, including group play by individuals with varying skill levels. Finally, they are activities which can be transferred easily from school, to home, to independent living environments. Wuerch and Voeltz (1982) have sequenced the instructional steps related to each activity in developmental sequences; however, their emphasis is on incorporating developmental concerns into an ecological analysis.

Can behavior analysis and playfulness coexist?

This question sums up one of the key paradoxes related to play in the special education classroom and identifies a major point of tension in other areas of special education as well. Applied behavior analysis has become extremely influential in special education settings over the past 20 years, especially in its successful applications with those severely handicapped students most easily written off as hopeless by the educational mainstream. However, within the last several years, a number of authors have begun to focus their attention on some of the costs of the behavioral quest for increasingly precise methodologies of control. The discussion has led some authors to criticize this tight control as self-perpetuating, and as further handicapping of already handicapped students. Guess and Siegel-Causey (1984), in particular, have suggested that teacher efforts be less directed at controlling students and more directed at learning from and following student-initiated behavior.

Shevin (1984) has also focused on the gap between this applied behavioral analysis and traditional teaching practices in special education, speaking of:

> ...the lack of coherence between the traditional conception of a teacher as one who *analyzes, fragments, pinpoints, refines, manages,* and *evaluates,* ...and a new conception of a teacher as one who *empowers, facilitates, validates, negotiates,* and *advocates.* There is a common societal consensus surrounding the first set of roles described for the special educator, and a lack of consensus for the second set of roles (p.7).

In terms of play in the classroom, this second set of teacher roles characterizes a setting in which students (and probably the teacher as well) will be more likely to incorporate student initiative, play, and discovery into the everyday tasks of being in school.

However, applied behavior analysis methodology need not be rejected by those with an interest in student autonomy and self-fulfillment. If that technology is used selectively, focusing on its strength at providing a decision-making data base rather than on its powers of control, it can assist the teacher in learning about the preferences and skills of students, within a context of expanding student autonomy (Shevin, 1984). We know, for example, that teaching techniques derived from applied behavior analysis can be used in shaping play skills (e.g., Wambold and Bailey, 1979; Wehman, 1977; Wuerch and Voeltz, 1982). The basic challenge for special educators is to prevent the tight structure imposed by applied behavior analysis, task analysis, and precision teaching from creating a classroom climate in which the general message that the student assimilates is, "This is neither the right time, the right place, nor the right company for play."

MAKING PLAY WELCOME IN THE SPECIAL EDUCATION CLASSROOM

If a special education teacher is serious about making his or her classroom an environment that invites playfulness and exploration, how might he or she proceed? Certainly, specific instruction related to individual "play skills" has its place, as described in some of the intervention literature. However, this attention to fragmentary skills will, by itself, probably do little to increase the likelihood of a disabled child being playful in school; it will probably do even less to help the student become an active player in settings outside of school. What is needed are approaches in which an orientation which values playfulness and exploration is integrated throughout the daily activities of school.

The manipulation of aspects of the physical environment to create a setting that invites play is an area in which special educators can learn much by observing current practice in regular early childhood settings. Christie and Johnsen (in this volume) have reviewed extensively the research findings which apply to preschool play. Although concerns for chronological age-appropriateness require us to reject a wholesale adoption of the environmental manipulation practices of early childhood education, the general orientation toward environmental manipulation, rather than behavior modification, is a useful one to consider for special education students of all ages.

Much more work needs to be done to apply these findings to disabled children and special education settings. As Baker (1980) points out, most special education takes place in settings which were not designed for special education, and activities proceed "in spite of" rather than "in response to" the environment. In such jury-rigged settings, dependence upon the teacher as arbiter of "the right things to do" is increased, and the students' opportunities for autonomy and exploration are correspondingly limited.

Much can be done to expand the likelihood of play in special education classrooms through careful planning of physical arrangements, toys, and play materials. However, environmental manipulation, by itself, can only be part of the answer. The most inviting play area and the most stimulating toys will not promote playfulness in a setting in which the child has received explicit or tacit messages of "thou shalt not play," or "play at your own risk." There are aspects of the social environment, as well as the physical environment, which deserve to be investigated further as potential contributors to exploration, playfulness, and self-sufficiency in special education students. Precise definitions of such social environments as well as the identification of what constitutes success for purposes of program evaluation represent real challenges in research design. However, these difficulties for the researcher should not deter adventurous and playful teachers from finding out "what works for them." Suggested below are five areas in which such exploration might fruitfully be pursued.

Fostering play in relaxed environments.

Active play is unlikely to take place in settings in which the student fears pain, ridicule, or punishment. Unfortunately, such fears are neither rare nor unfounded in special education settings. For example, a partially blind, severely retarded student in a class with several other multiply handicapped children may frequently, despite the best efforts of the teacher, be accidentally bumped into or knocked over or purposely pinched or shoved by classmates. That student's lack of vision may keep him or her from "seeing what's coming"; such a student will frequently adopt a defensive physical posture which makes exploration and play difficult, if not impossible.

In a related fashion, a student who has difficulty in understanding a teacher's unclear or inconsistent expectations may unexpectedly find him or herself a frequent target of verbal punishment from the teacher and ridicule from classmates; *that* student may well adopt a "defensive behavioral posture." Passive, reactive, minimalist behaviors may indeed decrease the likelihood of that student's getting hurt; however, they do so at the expense of spontaneity, exploration, playfulness, and environmental control.

Teachers who are concerned about the risk of such passivity in their students focus their classroom management on the reinforcement of positive behaviors, rather than the suppression of inappropriate ones. They adopt a proactive, problem-solving approach, rather than a *laissez-faire* one, to the resolution of interstudent conflicts. This is a delicate balance to strike, in which teachers provide enough management of student interaction to make students feel safe, while not providing so much structure that students interact only with the teacher's seal of approval. They provide students with ample time to try alternative approaches and do not take one mistake on the part of a student as a signal to step in and do the activity for him. In short, they create environments in which trying things and doing things are reinforced. They do not create environments in which waiting and not doing things are reinforced, and unauthorized activity is punished.

Celebrating play in choice-making environments.

As pointed out by several authors in recent years (Guess and Siegel-Causey 1984; Guess, Benson, and Siegel-Causey, 1985; Shevin, 1984; Shevin and Klein, 1984), the opportunity for engaging in choosing activities is conspicuous in its absence from the daily activities of typical special education classrooms. Care must be taken to avoid locking special education students into activities characterized primarily by passive skills (e.g., compliance and instruction-following) rather than active ones (e.g., exploration, discovery, problem-solving, playing, and making friends). To foster such active skills, teachers must provide special education students with the opportunity to acquire both cognitive skills related to choice-making and the perception of oneself as a *powerful* person, with the potential for affecting and controlling at least some aspects of one's environment.

One of the most important tools teachers have for establishing the classroom as a choice-making environment is the integration of choice-making opportunities into the daily routine. As Shevin and Klein (1984) point out, the potential exists for students to have daily opportunities to choose among activities, whether or not to engage in an activity, when to terminate an activity, alternative means of accomplishing an objective, and who will be one's partner in an activity. Students who have learned and who expect to be able to apply these skills throughout the school day are able to use these skills in settings in which play is permitted.

Welcoming play in familiar environments.

If much of play revolves around repetition and variation of familiar activities in familiar settings (Rubin, Fein, and Vandenberg 1983), then play can be fostered in special education by providing students with access to the familiar. Part of that access is achieved through providing students with multiple opportunities for free choice as mentioned above. A second aspect of providing familiar environment is achieved through the practice of what Brown, Nietupski, and Hamre-Nietupski (1976) refer to as "systematic variation"--that is, the structuring of the classroom in such a way that partial variation takes place in the provision of familiar tasks, materials and activities. A balance must be struck between continuity and change in the classroom environment, with students neither constantly disoriented by a continuous barrage of novel stimuli nor locked into an unchanging environment in which any slight variation, such as an absent teacher or a broken toy, is perceived as a major disruption.

Another way for teachers to provide activities that welcome play is to give students access to academic tasks and activities that they have already mastered in the past. In typical special education practice, once a skill or skill cluster has been displayed a specified number of times at a specified level of mastery, the skill is classified as "mastered," and its performance is rarely solicited by the teacher. What is needed are new definitions of mastery, going beyond the fluency of display of a skill in a carefully managed setting. A new definition of mastery might have students continue to have the opportunity to practice a skill until they not only do it accurately but also have learned the shortcuts, "tricks," and games associated with the skill. As an example, Student A may have learned to brush his teeth in perfect sequence and may have displayed the sequence on five consecutive school days; but it may be Student B, who has learned to play "The William Tell Overture" on his molars with the brush bristles, who becomes the life-long independent tooth-brusher.

Engendering play with real playmates.

If I am a student in a special education class with limited verbal and social skills and my classmates are likewise limited, then not only am I not very good at playing but my classmates are not much fun to play with either. In order to reach a level of fluency or "flow" in a game or play activity involving several similarly limited children, the teacher may need to become involved in a structured, highly directive way. Although this makes the specific activity work well, the long-term effects may be those of decreased student autonomy. The typical segregated, disability-homogeneous special education classroom may present a no-win situation in addressing this problem. Classmates may be of limited potential as playmates; teachers following the usual structured routines of classroom management and carefully paced curriculum delivery may be "good teachers" only at the cost of being "bad playmates."

Two potentially useful directions present themselves as ways of addressing this dilemma: changing the makeup of the cast of peer playmates and providing teachers or other adults who fill roles more conducive to play than the traditional teacher role. Various forms of mainstreaming represent the most likely possibilities for in-school provision of competent, socially adept playmates for disabled children. As several authors have pointed out (Guralnick, 1976; Peck, Appoloni, Cooke, and Raver, 1978; Wynne, Ulfelder, and Dakoff, 1975), merely placing handicapped and non-handicapped children in the same classroom environments does not lead to frequent positive social interactions. However, such placement is necessary (though not sufficient) for disabled students to learn the subtle minutiae of the play of typical children. In some settings, integration of disabled and non-disabled children for substantial parts of the school day, although desirable, does not represent a currently utilized option; for those classes, adults need to function as models of the role of the skilled, socially adept player.

The role of model is a nearly impossible one for the teacher whose other roles are those of behavioral enforcer and playtime arbitrator. However, many special education classes have other adults as part of the scene: education aides, volunteers, ancillary professionals such as language therapists, and so forth. With a number of adults actively involved in a special education classroom, responsibilities in play situations can be divided. One adult (the "teacher") can be responsible for keeping the peace, managing behavior, determining who is authorized to be playing at a given moment, and so forth. At the same time, a second adult (the "player") can be responsible for playing nicely and cooperatively, for sharing, for asking children to play with him or her, and for responding appropriately when children ask him or her to play. Although this represents a highly contrived, less-than-optimum situation for showing disabled children how to play, in some settings, it may be the best option currently available.

Encouraging play in validating environments.

Students need to receive the message that there are values in life other than "doing what you're told." Teachers can increase the spontaneity and the exploratory nature of students' approach to tasks in a number of ways. Focusing comments on the parts of an activity which a student has done right, rather than on the student's mistakes, is one way. Allowing the student who has made a mistake the opportunity to check and correct what he or she has done, rather than making the teacher the sole source of validation, is another strategy. A third approach is to resist students' requests for evaluative comments--turning the question back to the student, asking her what she thinks about what she has just done, and then reinforcing the notion that that is what counts. Over time, students can come to evaluate their work on the basis of their own reactions. The message to be communicated here is, "What you are doing is OK because you think it is OK." Certainly this is not the only message we wish to communicate to special education students, but it is a message which they typically have heard rarely in the past; there is little risk of over-repetition.

For some special educators, turning their classes into settings in which play is valued, fostered, and threaded through the fabric of daily classroom activity would represent a total reorientation of approaches and priorities, to the extent that they do not even possess a framework within which to consider such changes. Happily, for many other special educators, it may represent a key to solving some of the puzzles with which they have long been struggling. For those teachers, small, tentative changes in the direction of increasing student playfulness and autonomy may lead quickly to more profound transformations. In the revitalized atmosphere of their classrooms, happier and more independent students may suddenly remind them why they became teachers in the first place.

REFERENCES

Alberto, P., and Troutman, A. *Applied Behavior Analysis for Teachers: Influencing Student Performance.* Columbus, Ohio: Merrill, 1982.

Ayllon, T., and Roberts, M. Eliminating Discipline Problems by Strengthening Academic Performance. *Journal of Applied Behavior Analysis,* 7(1974), 73-81.

Baker, D. Applications of Environmental Psychology in Programming for Severely Handicapped Persons. *Journal of the Association for the Severely Handicapped, 6*(1980), 234-249.

Beveridge, M., and Hurrell, P. Teachers' Responses to Severely Mentally Handicapped Children's Initiations in the Classroom. *Journal of Child Psychology and Psychiatry, 21*(1980), 175-181.

Blatt, B., and Garfunkel, F. Teaching the Mentally Retarded. In *In and Out of Mental Retardation: Essays on Educability, Disability and Human Policy.* Edited by B. Blatt. Baltimore: University Park Press, 1981.

Brinker, R. Curricula without Recipes: A Challenge to Teachers and a Promise to Severely Mentally Retarded Students. In *Severe Mental Retardation: From Theory to Practice.* Edited by D. Bricker and J. Filler. Reston, Virginia: Division on Mental Retardation of the Council for Exceptional Children, 1984.

Brown, L., Branston, M., Baumgart, D., Vincent, L., Falvey, M., and Schroeder, J. Utilizing the Characteristics of a Variety of Current and Subsequent Least Restrictive Environments as Factors in the Development of Curricular Content for Severely Handicapped Students. *AAESPH Review, 4*(1979), 407-424.

Brown, L., Nietupski, J., and Hamre-Nietupski, S. Criterion of Ultimate Functioning. In *Hey, Don't Forget About Me: Education's Investment in the Severely, Profoundly and Multiply Handicapped.* Edited by M. Thomas. Reston, Virginia: Council for Exceptional Children, 1976.

Campbell, A., and Sulzer, B. Naturally Available Reinforcers as Motivators towards Reading and Spelling Achievement by Mentally Handicapped Students. Paper presented at the Annual Meeting of the American Educational Research Association, New York, February, 1971.

Certo, N. Characteristics of Educational Services. In *Systematic Instruction of the Moderately and Severely Handicapped.* Edited by M. Snell. Columbus, Ohio: Merrill, 1983.

Collard, K. Leisure, Education, and the Schools: Why, Who, and the Need for Advocacy. *Therapeutic Recreation Journal, 15*(1981), 8-16.

Crawley, S., and Chan, K. Developmental Changes in Free-Play Behavior of Mildly and Moderately Retarded Preschool-Aged Children. *Education and Training of the Mentally Retarded, 17*(1982), 234-239.

Devoney, C., Guralnick, M., and Rubin, H. Integrating Handicapped and Nonhandicapped Pre-School Children: Effects on Social Play. *Childhood Education, 50*(1974), 360-364.

Dixon, J. The Implications of Attribution Theory for Therapeutic Recreation Service. *Therapeutic Recreation Journal, 13*(1979), 3-11.

Donder, D., and Nietupski, J. Non-handicapped Adolescents Teaching Playground Skills to Their Mentally Retarded Peers: Toward a Less Restrictive Middle School Environment. *Education and Training of the Mentally Retarded, 16*(1981), 270-276.

Ellis, M. *Why People Play.* Englewood Cliffs, New Jersey: Prentice-Hall, 1973.

Faught, K., Balleweg, B., Crow, R., and Van Den Pol, R. An Analysis of Social Behaviors Among Handicapped and Non-handicapped Preschool Children. *Education and Training of the Mentally Retarded, 18*(1983), 210-214.

Fitzgerald, N. Competencies and Contexts of Friendship Development in a Reverse Mainstreamed Preschool. Paper presented at the Annual Meeting of the American Educational Research Association, Chicago, May, 1985.

Goode, D. Socially Produced Identities, Intimacy, and the Problem of Competence Among the Retarded. In *Special Education and Social Interests.* Edited by L. Barton and S. Tomlinson. London: Croom Helm, 1984.

Guess, D., Benson, H., and Siegel-Causey, E. Concepts and Issues Related to Choice-Making and Autonomy Among Persons with Severe Disabilities. *Journal of the Association for Persons with Severe Handicaps, 10*(1985), 79-86.

Guess, D., and Siegel-Causey, E. Behavioral Control and Education of Severely Handicapped Students: Who's Doing What to Whom? And Why? In *Severe Mental Retardation: From Theory to Practice.* Edited by D. Bricker and J. Filler. Lancaster, Pennsylvania: The Division on Mental Retardation of the Council for Exceptional Children, 1984.

Guralnick, M. The Value of Integrating Handicapped and Nonhandicapped Preschool Children. *American Journal of Orthopsychiatry, 42*(1976), 236-245.

Horne, B., and Philleo, C. A Comparative Study of the Spontaneous Play Activities of Normal and Mentally Defective Children. *Journal of Genetic Psychology, 61*(1942), 33.

Hutt, C. Specific and Diverse Exploration. In *Advances in Child Development and Behavior.* Edited by H. Reese and L. Lipsett. New York: Academic Press, 1970.

Johnson, D., and Johnson, R. Cooperative, Competitive, and Individualistic Learning. *Journal of Research and Development in Education, 12*(1978), 3-15.

Jones, R., and Kazdin, A. Programming Response Maintenance After Withdrawing Token Reinforcement. *Behavior Therapy, 6*(1975), 153-164.

King, N. The Hidden Curriculum and the Socialization of Kindergarten Children. Unpublished Ph.D. dissertation, University of Wisconsin, 1976.

King, N. Play: The Kindergartener's Perspective. *Elementary School Journal, 80*(1979), 81-87.

King, N. Children's Play as a Form of Resistance in the Classroom. *Boston University Journal of Education, 164*(1982), 320-329.

Kissel, R., and Whitman, T. An Examination of the Direct and Generalized Effects of a Play-Training and Overcorrection Procedure Upon the Self-Stimulatory Behavior of a Profoundly Retarded Boy. *AAESPH Review, 2*(1977), 131-146.

Knapczyk, D., and Yoppi, J. Development of Cooperative and Competitive Play Responses in Developmentally Disabled Children. *American Journal of Mental Deficiency, 80*(1975), 245-255.

Levitt, S. A Study of the Cross-Motor Skills of Cerebral Palsied Children in an Adventure Playground for Handicapped Children. *Child Care, Health, and Development, 1*(1975), p. 29.

Li, A. Play and the Mentally Retarded Child. *Mental Retardation, 19*(1981), 121-126.

McConkey, R., and Jeffree, D. First Steps in Learning to Pretend. *Special Education: Forward Trends, 6*(1979), 13-17.

McConkey, R., and Jeffree, D. Developing Children's Play. *Special Education: Forward Trends, 7*(1980), 21-23.

Mogford, K. The Play of Handicapped Children. In *Biology of Play.* Edited by B. Tizard and D. Harvey. London: Spastics International Medical Publications, 1977.

Morris, R., and Dolker, M. Developing Cooperative Play in Socially Withdrawn Retarded Children. *Mental Retardation, 12*(1974), 24-27.

Morrison, T., and Newcomer, B. Effects of Directive vs. Nondirective Play Therapy with Institutionalized Mentally Retarded Children. *American Journal of Mental Deficiency, 79*(1975), 666-669.

Odom, S. The Relationship of Play to Developmental Level in Mentally Retarded, Preschool Children. *Education and Training of the Mentally Retarded, 16*(1981), 136-141.

Odom, S., and Strain, P. Classroom-based Social Skills Instruction for Severely Handicapped Preschool Children. *Topics in Early Childhood Special Education, 4*(1984), 97-116.

Orlansky, M. Sam's Day: A Simulated Observation of a Severely Handicapped Child's Educational Program. *AAESPH Review, 4*(1979), 251- 258.

Parten, M. Social Participation Among Pre-School Children. *Journal of Abnormal and Social Psychology, 27*(1932), 243-269.

Peck, C., Apolloni, T., Cooke, T., and Raver, S. Teaching Retarded Preschoolers to Imitate the Free-Play Behavior of Nonretarded Classmates: Trained and Generalized Effects. *Journal of Special Education, 12*(1978), 195-207.

Piaget, J. *Play, Dreams, and Imitation in Childhood.* London: Heinemann, 1962.

Porter, R., Ramsey, B., Tremblay, A., Iaccobo, M., and Crawley, S. Social Interactions in Hetero-geneous Groups of Retarded and Normally Developing Children: An Observational Study. In *Observing Behavior.* Volume 1. Edited by G. Sackett. Baltimore: University Park Press, 1978.

Quinn, J., and Rubin, K. The Play of Handicapped Children. In *Child's Play: Developmental and Applied.* Edited by T. Yawkey and A. Pellegrini. Hillsdale, New Jersey: Lawrence Erlbaum, 1984.

Rubin, K., Fein, G., and Vandenberg, B. Play. In *Handbook of Child Psychology.* Fourth edition. Edited by P. Mussen. New York: Wiley, 1983.

Santomier, J., and Kopczuk, W. Facilitation of Interactions Between Retarded and Nonretarded Students in a Physical Education Setting. *Education and Training of the Mentally Retarded, 16*(1981), 20-23.

Sapon-Shevin, M. Cooperative Instructional Games: Alternatives to the Spelling Bee. *Elementary School Journal, 79*(1978), 81-87.

Sapon-Shevin, M. Who Says Somebody's Gotta Lose? Competition as an Obstacle to Mainstreaming. *Education Unlimited, 2*(1980), 48-50.

Shevin, M. Must Normalization Mean Settling for the Norm? Socialization of Young Retarded Students to the World of Work. Paper presented at the Annual Meeting of the American Educational Research Association, New York, May, 1982.

Shevin, M. Choicemaking in the Classroom. Paper presented at the Annual Meeting of the Association for Persons with Severe Handicaps, Chicago, November, 1984.

Shevin, M., and Klein, N. The Importance of Choice-Making Skills for Students with Severe Disabilities. *Journal of the Association for Persons with Severe Handicaps, 9*(1984), 159-166.

Shevin, M., and Miller, C. 'Did I Say You Could Do That?' How Retarded Children Learn About Work in the Classroom. Paper presented at the Annual Meeting of the American Educational Research Association, Montreal, Quebec, April, 1983.

Slavin, R. *Cooperative Learning.* New York: Longman, 1983.

Smilansky, S. *The Effects of Sociodramatic Play on Disadvantaged Preschool Children.* New York: John Wiley and Sons, 1968.

Snyder, L., Apolloni, T., and Cooke, T. Integrated Settings at the Early Childhood Level: The Role of Nonretarded Peers. *Exceptional Children, 43*(1977), 262-266.

Sulzer-Azaroff, B., and Mayer, G. *Applying Behavior Analysis Procedures with Children and Youth.* New York: Holt, Rinehart, and Winston, 1977.

Tait, P. Behavior of Young Blind Children in a Controlled Play Session. *Perceptual and Motor Skills, 34*(1972), 963-969.

Townsend, C. An Ecological Analysis of the Transition from Research in Model Demonstration Projects to Practice in Service Programs. Paper presented at the Annual Meeting of The Association for the Severely Handicapped, Los Angeles, November, 1980.

Vincent, L., Salisbury, C., Walter, J., Brown, P., Gruenwald, L., and Powers, M. Program Evaluation and Curriculum Development in Early Childhood Special Education: Criteria of the Next Environment. In *Methods of Instruction for Severely Handicapped Students.* Edited by W. Sailor. Baltimore: Brookes, 1980.

Voeltz, L., Evans, I., Freedland, K., and Donellon, S. Teacher Decision Making in the Selection of Educational Programming Priorities for Severely Handicapped Children. *Journal of Special Education, 16*(1982), 179-198.

Voeltz, L., Wuerch, B., and Wilcox, B. Leisure and Recreation: Preparation for Independence, Integration, and Self-Fulfillment. In *Design of High School Programs for Severely Handicapped Students.* Edited by B. Wilcox and G. Bellamy. Baltimore: Brookes, 1982.

Wambold, C., and Bailey, R. Improving the Leisure-Time Behaviors of Severely/Profoundly Mentally Retarded Children Through Toy Play. *AAESPH Review, 4*(1979), 237-250.

Watters, R., and Wood, D. Play and Self-Stimulatory Behaviors of Autistic and Other Severely Dysfunctional Children with Different Classes of Toys. *Journal of Special Education, 17*(1983), 27-35.

Wehman, P. *Helping the Mentally Retarded Acquire Play Skills.* Springfield, Illinois: Charles C. Thomas, 1977.

Wehman, P., and Schlein, S. *Leisure Programs for Handicapped Persons.* Baltimore: University Park Press, 1981.

Weiner, E., and Weiner, B. Differentiation of Normal and Retarded Children Through Toy-Play Analysis. *Multivariate Behavioral Research, 2*(1974), 245-252.

Whittaker, C. A Note on Developmental Trends in the Symbolic Play of Hospitalized Profoundly Retarded Children. *Journal of Child Psychology and Psychiatry, 2*(1980), 253-261.

Wing, L., Gould, J., Yeates, S., and Brierley, L. Symbolic Play in Severely Mentally Retarded and in Autistic Children. *Journal of Child Psychology and Psychiatry, 18*(1977), 167-178.

Wuerch, B., and Voeltz, L. *Longitudinal Leisure Skills for Severely Handicapped Learners: The Ho'onanea Curriculum Component.* Baltimore: Brookes, 1982.

Wynne, S., Ulfelder, L., and Dakoff, G. *Main-streaming and Early Childhood Education for Handicapped Children: Review and Implications of Research.*

Washington, D.C.: Division of Innovation and Development, BEH-USOE, 1975.

PART III: REVIEW AND COMMENTARY

SCHOOL PLAY: A REVIEW

James H. Block

Five days a week from September to June, millions of humans migrate from their homes to school. Here they will spend over ten thousand hours moving from childhood, through adolescence, to youth, and, perhaps, to young-adulthood (Bloom, 1976; Rutter, Maughan, Mortimer, and Ouston, 1979). These persons, of course, are commonly called students; their transit is called the student career (Lancy, 1978).

Despite its size, duration, and developmental significance, educators know relatively little about the student career (Doyle, 1982). To be sure, we do know something about certain career by-products such as student learning and behavior. And, based on these by-products, some of us have even proposed fledgling theories about the student career and its place in the entire human life span (e.g., Super, 1980). We still know little, however, about the personal or social processes by which these by-products are produced (Mehan, 1978, 1980).

This volume has focused on one of these processes--school play. That students play at school seems obvious; indeed, playing, especially with friends, may be the primary reason that many students attend school at all (Cusick, 1973). But the various forms that school play takes and their mediating impact on student learning and behavior have rarely been studied systematically. This volume begins that study. It is time to review its story.

Since this story is multifaceted, I will not attempt to repeat the particular findings and arguments of each preceding chapter. Rather, I will attempt to draw out and comment upon some of the interesting cross-chapter themes. To this end, the chapter is arranged into two parts.

The first part, written primarily for educational researchers, outlines some of the theoretically and methodologically significant school play findings. These findings are sketched according to a template suggested by Weinstein (1983) for integrating multi-disciplinary/multi-methodological developmental research on student perceptions of the schooling process.

The use of the this template allows me to do three things. First, I can focus on "student perspectives" on school play, thereby recognizing, as does King, that school play is ultimately an insider phenomena (Smetherham, 1978). Even if outsiders--teachers, parents, or other adult observers--can agree on calling students' actions "school play," only the students know and feel for sure whether they are playing. Second, since a student perspective on school play is jointly concerned with students' actions, feelings, and thoughts (Becker, Geer, and Hughes, 1968), I can readily combine lines of research where school play is variously defined in terms of students' activities (e.g., Pepler), experiences (e.g., Klieber and Roberts), verbal self-reports (e.g., King), or some combination of these (e.g., Everhart). Moreover, in combining these lines, I can begin to distinguish conceptually, if not phenomenally, research on school play from research on the play of humans at school. A student perspective focuses attention on only those play thoughts, feelings,

253

and actions that students develop in response to issues they really face at
school, not on ones they develop in response to issues outside of school but
manifest inside it. Third, since this template is explicitly concerned with
human development research issues, and especially issues across the student
career span, I can link the school play research with life-span developmental
research. Central to such research, of course, has been an enduring concern
with how educational research can help optimize individual and social
development, especially through the design of appropriate preventive
instructional interventions (Reinert, 1980; Schaie and Willis, 1978).

The second part of the chapter, written primarily for educational
practitioners, explores the practical significance of these findings. Specifically, it suggests how the nascent knowledge about school play might be used
to redesign ordinary instructional activities along more playlike lines.

The use of the play-like gambit allows me to do two more things.
First, I can nudge practitioners to think more about the import of the school
play research for students' motivation to learn. After two decades of research
on school learning, I have come to the conclusion that the chief problems in
our schools are no longer that virtually all students cannot learn excellently,
swiftly, and self-confidently, but that most do not want to (Block, Efthim,
Burns, and Anderson, 1987). Second, following the lead of Goodlad (1984),
Sarason (1983), and Sizer (1984), I can press the bounds of existing school
play practice. In particular, I can indicate how practitioners might use the best
of contemporary school play research not only in a technical fashion to
assemble particular instructional techniques but also, and perhaps more
importantly, in a conceptual fashion to challenge old preconceptions of
teaching with fresh ones.

SCHOOL PLAY RESEARCH

Terrain

Weinstein's first concern regarding student perspectives on schooling
was that much of the terrain has not yet been mapped. She called, therefore,
for more systematic charting of this terrain, paying special attention to its
various forms.

The chapters in this volume begin to map that portion of the schooling
terrain that students devote to play. Judging from the quantity of research
reported, the preschool play terrain has already been mapped in some depth.
Its central play forms seem to be cognitive play--functional, constructive,
dramatic, and rule-bound--and social play--solitary, parallel, and group. The
terrain of elementary, junior-high, senior-high, and special school play,
however, has barely been mapped at all. Its major play forms seem to be
instrumental, illicit, recreational, and sanctioned-recreational play.

Clearly, the school play terrain requires more even mapping, and all of
these potential school play forms require further study. It is especially
interesting that the mapping of school play terrain past the preschool level
may require more study of areas such as instrumental, illicit, recreational, and

sanctioned-recreational play. Instrumental play, or what some educators refer to as "educational" (Moore, Evertson, and Brophy, 1974), or "instructional" (Gehlbach, 1980) play, is currently an area of growing interest to researchers since it commonly occurs when students are considered "on task," that is, actively engaged in learning from instructional events. Consequently, further research on instrumental play can only fuel this interest and draw school play research more squarely into the mainstream of educational thought. Illicit, recreational, and sanctioned-recreational play, however, tend to occur at times in the schooling process when students are considered to be "off-task," that is, not actively engaged in instructional events or actively engaged in non-instructional ones. Consequently, these forms of play have tended to be of little interest to many educational researchers. Additional study of illicit, recreational, and sanctioned-recreational play might, therefore, rekindle mainstream theoretical interest in students' "off-task" play activities.

I have a hunch, for example, that their study may provide a meta-social commentary (see Schwartzman, 1978a) on students' "on-task" school work activities (Block, 1981). Through such play activities, students may be telling their teachers (and other adults) precisely what is wrong with their school work activities; indeed, both King and Everhart suggest that illicit play, in particular, is a calculated form of student resistance to school work. And through such play activities, students may also be suggesting how educators can make wrong school work activities right. That is, they may be suggesting precisely how these activities can be reformed. By studying how students *resist* existing school work activities through their illicit, recreational, and sanctioned-recreational play, therefore, educational researchers may find the seeds for the *reformation* of these activities. The time is ripe, as Finkelstein notes, for more study of the dialectical relationship between school play's resistive and reformative properties.

Developmental Milestones

Besides calling for more general charting of the schooling terrain, Weinstein also called for specific mapping of the terrain's major socio-cognitive developmental milestones. She was concerned that researchers discover how particular terrain forms might change as students develop.

The chapters in this volume do begin to suggest several potential developmental milestones in school play. Some of these milestones are, by now, very familiar to play researchers--shifts in preschoolers' cognitive play from functional to rule governed and in social play from solitary to group. Accordingly, I will not comment more on them here except to say that, like Pepler and Christie and Johnson, I believe the failure of past research to document these shifts stems partially from researchers' tendencies to treat cognitive developments separately from social ones. Research on the interaction of cognitive and social development in all students' play is sorely needed.

I do wish to comment, however, on two less familiar milestones. One seems to be cognitive/emotional shifts in the perceptual criteria elementary school students use to classify their various school activities. King's chapter, in particular, suggests that older elementary students increasingly use the criterion of "fun" to distinguish their school activities as being "play" or "work." They are "play" when "fun" is perceptually present and "work" when it is not. The other milestone seems to be social shifts in the primary forms of post-preschoolers' play. King's chapter indicates that most elementary school students play in instrumental, illicit, and recreational ways. Everhart's and Klieber and Robert's chapters indicate, though, that most secondary school students play in only illicit, recreational, and sanctioned-recreational ones. Apparently, instrumental play becomes less available or appealing to secondary than elementary school students.

I believe that these two post-preschool developmental milestones may be intimately related. Opportunities for instrumental play or play-in-instruction seem to peak in the very early elementary school years and decline thereafter (Cusick, 1973; Everhart, 1983; Jackson, 1970). Consequently, older elementary and secondary school students have fewer and fewer opportunities to find "fun" in their school work and, if Dewey is correct (see Dennis, 1970), more and more to find drudgery. If older students cannot find "fun" in instruction and if "fun" is central to their play, then they will find "fun" outside of instruction or even despite it. As Everhart and Klieber and Roberts note, illicit, recreational, and sanctioned-recreational school play could provide such opportunities.

Some preliminary evidence for a developmental interaction between school work and school play comes from a series of studies on the student role (Allen, 1982; Block, 1981; DeVoss, 1978; Elmore and Thompson, 1980; Hartwig, 1983; Mouncer, 1986). In these studies, my students and I have naturalistically mapped local elementary, junior high and senior high school student perspectives on learning, studying, and classroom behavior (see, Block, 1980; Elmore and Thompson, 1980; and Hartwig, 1983 for technical details).

Our findings indicate that students mapped their school day in terms of accomplishing certain routine activities (cf. Everhart, 1983; Lancy, 1978). But school learning activities were only part of these maps and a relatively insignificant part at that for older students. Moreover, most common school learning activities--especially assignments, homework, and tests--were classified to be "work" not "play." That is, they were perceived by students as being activities they had to do, whether or not they wanted to do them, because they were evaluated rather than ones they did not have to do, indeed might get into trouble for doing, but they wanted to do because they were "fun." And because they were so perceived, students approached them as occasions for less-than-whole-hearted studying and learning and for mild to severe classroom "fight or flight" behavior. Specifically, our students attempted to dilute or eliminate these activities' unnecessary intellectual, emotional, and behavioral demands, to mock studying in class or at home, to goof-off, and to escape from the activities as soon as possible. In short, they learned, studied, and behaved much like other students have been described to do in response to their school work (cf. Batcher, 1981; Csikszentmihalyi and Larson, 1978; Cusick, 1973; Doyle, 1983; Everhart, 1983; Jackson, 1970; Licata, 1979; Metz, 1978; Ogbu, 1974; Smith and Geoffrey, 1968). They knowingly settled for far less excellent, swift, and self-confident learning than that of which they were self-acknowledged to be capable.

We are currently examining why learning, studying, and behavior problems seem to be more prevalent in school situations students classify as "work" rather than "play." Earlier, I had speculated, following Bateson (1972) and Deci (1980), that worklike, as opposed to playlike school, learning activities send meta-communications to students about their growing lack of self-determination in matters of learning, studying, and acting. Hartwig (1986), refining this speculation, has hypothesized and found that perceived worklike school learning situations do indeed send messages that suppress rather than stimulate students' intrinsic motivation to learn, study, and behave. Playlike situations seem to do just the reverse.

Classroom Context

A third concern of Weinstein was that educational researchers pay more attention to the social context of students' perceptions of schooling. She was concerned with understanding why students perceive schooling as they do, not just how they perceive it.

The papers in this volume build on such seminal works as Cheska (1981), Salter (1978), and Schwartzman (1978a, 1978b) in examining the social context of school play. Once again, some of the contextual factors highlighted should be familiar to play researchers. Personal variables such as age, sex, and social class and social variables such as history, society, and culture have long been staples in the study of human context effects (Bronfenbrenner, 1979; Moos, 1976).

One context factor that should be relatively new to many play researchers, however, is the school. As with other human contexts (Moos, 1976), schools apparently contextualize student play by confining it within certain physical, demographic, social, behavioral, and perceptual boundaries. At school, for example, students must play at certain times and places and with certain classmates and props. Moreover, they must do so within particular curricular structures and under increasing adult supervision. These constraints apparently conspire to create certain formal--e.g., instrumental, recreational, and sanctioned-recreational--and informal--e.g., illicit--forms of playful behavior. They even create specific thoughts and feelings about what is play and about with whom, when, where, and how one can play.

Nowhere in this volume, of course, is the case for school context effects on students' play more clear than in Shevin's chapter. Here the tangle of certain physical, demographic, and social factors seems to have created a school setting where student play behavior and perceptions that school is a place to play are rare.

However, this bleak picture of the schooling of play (to borrow Pepler's notion) is, in many respects, also analogous to the pictures drawn in several chapters of this volume. And it is certainly similar to the picture of the schooling of "work" rather than "play" painted by numerous other educational researchers (e.g., Anyon, 1980, 1981; Behn, Carnoy, Carter, Crain, and Levin, 1974; Bowles and Gintis, 1976; Carroll, 1975; Grannis, 1967; LeCompte, 1979; Wilcox, 1982).

I do not want to overstate the case for school context effects on students' play until more systematic school effects research designs are executed, designs which are receiving greater attention in both the educational (Rowan, Bossert, and Dwyer, 1983) and human development literature (Bronfenbrenner, 1979). I do want to note, however, that most studies of context in play research have tended to ignore the school or to treat it as a black-box variable influencing students' play in unknown ways. The recent Yawkey and Pellegrini (1984) volume on child's play, for example, devotes only two of nineteen chapters to play in school settings, one of which considers play in only preschool settings (Curry and Arnaud, 1984), while the other (Glickman, 1984) questions play's place in public school at all.

I also want to raise the possibility of using school effects thinking to elaborate a classical line of inquiry in play research--namely, that line concerned with play acculturation and socialization. Even with the recent reinvigoration of this line (see Cheska, 1981; Salter, 1978; Schwartzman, 1978a, 1978b), play context researchers still seem to focus on large-scale or macro-context variables such as "society" or "culture." More intermediate scale or molar-context variables such as the "family" or the "school" or more small scale or micro-context variables such as the "classroom" have hardly been touched. Hence, play context research has not yet yielded the important macro-molar-micro linkages which contemporary anthropologists (e.g., Spindler, 1982), sociologists (e.g., Kerckhoff, 1980), and human developmentalists (e.g., Bronfenbrenner, 1979; Darvill, 1982) see as being essential for fully understanding and optimizing human development. In so far as schools help mediate between humans and their culture/society, research on the schooling of play could begin to provide some of these linkages.

Consider, for example, the links that might exist between school play and adult work. Several researchers (e.g., Anyon, 1980, 1981; Spring, 1976) have suggested that certain types of schools differentially prepare specific types of students for particular types of adult work. Other researchers such as Goldstein and Oldham (1979) and Smith and Proshansky (1967) have suggested that the seeds of adult work orientations are sown in students' play. Might not, therefore, schools somehow use school play to socialize certain kinds of students for different kinds of adult work?

Suppose that they provided certain types of students particular types of opportunities to play (cf. Cohen and Lazerson, 1977). Students who are being socialized for managerial and executive adult work might receive unusually liberal opportunities to engage in instrumental school play activities (see Anyon, 1981). Such activities would not only reinforce their academic training but would also prepare them to find "fun" in their future work. Speculation is currently rampant, for example, that these students have unusual access to one of the major instrumental play devices of recent times, the computer.

Similarly, students who are being socialized to do service work might be given liberal opportunities for recreational or sanctioned-recreational play activities. Such activities would help train them to tolerate future office or field work by periodically escaping to their outside of work recreations (King, 1982). As Levin and Rumberger (1983) suggest, most service work, especially in the most rapidly growing occupations, demands not high-tech but low-tech and often no-tech skills. The basic work issue most future service persons may face, therefore, may be more motivational than technical, namely, how to get through the boring day or week.

Lastly, students who are being trained for labor or unskilled work might receive more than their share of opportunities for illicit school play activities. There is evidence that such horseplay is basic to preparation for adult life in laboring cultures (e.g., Willis, 1979; Woods, 1979). There is also evidence that such horseplay can interfere with the academic preparation of future laborers (Schwartz, 1981), perhaps forcing them to expect low paying and unrewarding adult jobs. In high school, for example, it can lead to the bad grades and misbehavior that contribute to placement in functional track classrooms such as those of the continuation school (cf. Cicourel and Kitsuse, 1963). In the elementary school, it can even land perfectly normal students in special education classes (Christiansen, Gerber, and Everhart, 1986).

Methodology

A fourth concern of Weinstein was that of research methodology. Since the student perspective on schooling can be studied from a variety of methodological as well as theoretical stances, she was concerned about the interpretive problems posed by methodological differences among various studies. The differences in findings from one study to another might simply be an artifact of different research methods.

The papers in this volume illustrate Weinstein's concern. So far in this review, I have suggested that different researchers have tended to map different parts of the school play terrain, have offered different developmental milestones in this terrain, and have proposed different contextual explanations for these milestones. While some of these differences are, no doubt, attributable to our authors' various theoretical interests, some must also be attributed to their various methodological biases. By use of the term "bias," I do not mean to imply that these scholars have rigged their research to unduly or unfairly affect its results. But I do mean they have shown a tendency to focus on some play subjects, objects, and predicates (to use Miracle's terms) to the exclusion of others. In short, they have shown a predilection rather than a prejudice in studying and analyzing the school play phenomena.

One striking bias that runs through the volume is personal in nature. Much of the school play research has been executed using the methods of psychologists to discover ontogenetically generated individual differences and commonalities in students' play thoughts, feelings, and behavior. The other bias is more social in nature. A growing amount of school play research is being executed using the methods of sociologists, anthropologists, and historians to discover socially generated group differences and similarities in students' play thoughts, feelings, and behavior.

To suggest that this volume illustrates, to use Getzels (1969) terms, the "idiographic" versus "nomothetic" methodological bias in the study of school play may at first seem obvious. My intent in making the obvious obvious, however, is to drop the school play research into a growing and far reaching methodological debate within the field of human development. At the heart of this debate are strong (and hotly contested) charges that the field of human development, especially life-span development, has long had an unrecognized methodological bias. Critics contend that this bias tends "...to treat the individual as a self-contained entity and fails to recognize the profoundly interactive nature of self-society relations and the complexity and variability of social environments" (Dannefer, 1984, p.100). In short, it creates an "ontogenetic fallacy" where socially-produced, age-related patterns of human thinking, feeling, action, and interaction are all treated as being "naturally produced." This fallacy, in turn, occasions life span researchers to treat these patterns as normal aspects of individual development and to ignore their social determinants and social construction.

In reviewing the various chapters of this volume, I am convinced that the bulk of school play research, especially at the preschool level, is open to the "ontogenetic fallacy" interpretation. I am struck, in particular, by the surfeit of largely psychological studies reviewed and the paucity of more historical/ anthropological/ sociological studies. And I am not alone. Even scholars of areas where psychologically-based research methodologies are rampant have raised the same issue. Both Rubin, Fein, and Vandenberg (1983) and Christie and Johnsen (1983), in major reviews of children's' play, allude to the psychological bias and explicitly call for more conceptualizations of play drawn from more sociogenically-based research methodologies.

Clearly, school play research could profit from increased use of such methodologies: ethnography, qualitative research, participant observation, case study, symbolic interaction, phenomenology, constructivism, or inter-pretive studies (Ericksen, 1986). These methodologies adequately recognize "(1) the malleability of the human organism in relation to environments; (2) the structural complexity and diversity of the social environment; (3) the role of the symbolic--of social knowledge and human intentionality--as factors mediating development" (Dannefer, 1984, pp. 106-107). In short, they recognize the strong interaction between individual and the social envi-ronment and pay more than lip service to the latter.

Sufficiently rigorous sociogenically-based methodological tools are now widely available in education (see, e.g., Ericksen, 1986). And they have been used with some success not only by various authors in this volume but by other school play scholars as well (e.g., Borman, 1981; Carroll, 1975; Finnan, 1982; Glickman, 1981; Henderson, 1980; Iverson, 1981). Even these researchers, however, have only touched the tip of the social aspects of school play iceberg. Block's, Everhart's, and King's work, for example, deals only with what Ogbu (1974) refers to as the "techno-economic" aspects of school play, i.e., school play's relationship to the adult world of work. As Yawkey (1980) and Finkelstein suggest, researchers may never really fully understand school play unless we move beyond its economic aspects to its political, social, cultural, and historical aspects as well.

Weinstein's final concern was that educational researchers begin to relate student perspectives on schooling to the perspectives of teachers and other adult observers. Among other things, she was concerned that students might perceive schooling differently than teachers or adults. Hence, she encouraged researchers to pay attention to the incongruities as well as the congruities in students', teachers', and outside experts' schooling perceptions.

Once again, the papers in this volume illustrate Weinstein's concern. Though all of this volume's school play experts have been very concerned with defining school play, apparently they agree on only designated pieces of the school play beast and not the beast itself. These expert disagreements were to be expected. After all, the school play field is still very young, and such disagreements are still common even in the mature field of general play research (Miller, 1973). Moreover, as Miracle suggests, they are probably healthy, for they herald the remarkable conceptual and methodological problems which must be recognized and addressed if programmatic, interfield school play research is to proceed.

But if experts cannot agree on the nature of the school play beast, apparently at least Westernized students can. Indeed, American elementary and secondary school students perceive school play in ways remarkably similar to students in Canada (Day, 1981) and England (Woods, 1979). For students, school play is apparently a state of mind or attitude characterized by certain parameters which are recognized by all students, but as King notes, differentially valued by each. If students subjectively perceive a given school activity, regardless of its objective form, as being voluntary, desirable, and/or pleasurable, then they consider it to be "play" (Block, 1981; Hartwig, 1983; King, 1980, 1982). School play activities, in particular, would appear to give students perceptual choices as to what is taught and/or how it is taught; to minimize what students perceive as being unnecessary physical, emotional, intellectual, and/or social discomforts; and to give students perceptual opportunities for "fun" (Block, 1980; Day, 1981; Hartwig, 1983; King, 1980, 1982).

Lever (1981) has suggested, as Miracle notes, that play may be a multi-reality notion in which, with appropriate multiple methodologies, one would find that players have one reality and observers another. Moreover, she has suggested that each reality has its particular truth. If there is indeed more agreement among students about how to define school play than among experts, then cannot the "truth" of the students' definitions serve as one starting point for future expert research on school play? After all, electivity, desirability, and pleasure are common elements of many popular and scholarly definitions of play.

I do not doubt for a minute that students' views of school play are overly simple and that experts need to dig into them in greater detail. But, as Weinstein (1983) points out, insofar as such perceptions simplify complex social environments like schools, educational researchers could respect and build from these simplified understandings. School play perceptions might be an excellent starting place.

SCHOOL PLAY: PRACTICE

Now let me turn to the practical significance of the school play research. As Glickman (1984) notes:

> The times in which we sit are characterized as essentialist. The political and social climate is one of fiscal austerity and accountability for predetermined ends. Schools have been reduced in budget, staff, and materials. Schools are being asked to limit their purpose and to focus on reversing declining achievement scores. Unless research can show the benefits of play to such goals, it will not find a place in today's schools. (p. 268)

While one may quibble with Glickman's view of contemporary education, he does raise, nevertheless, the central practical dilemma. How can the school play literature serve educative goals? After all, many practitioners still remember the legacy of the progressive education movement in which school play became a fad and "... elicited not only first rate art, but every manner of shoddiness and self-deception as well. In too many classrooms license began to pass for liberty, planlessness for spontaneity, recalcitrance for individuality, obfuscation for art, and chaos for education" (Cremin, 1964, p. 207).

Perhaps the major way that school play research can serve educative goals is by helping to improve the quality of contemporary public school instruction. Parents, press, and public alike seem to share a perception that current instructional practices stifle students' intrinsic motivation to learn excellently, swiftly, and self-confidently. The school play research offers avenues for redesigning these practices so that they stifle this motivation no more.

This literature suggests a useful starting point for making ordinary school learning activities more inviting to students, namely, the concept of playfulness (cf. Hutt, 1981; Lieberman, 1977). As Csikszentmihalyi (1981) has noted, playfulness involves not the reality of what one is doing, but one's attitude toward that reality . I believe, along with Day (1984) and Condry and Koslowski (1979), that the school play literature can be used to redesign all school learning activities so that students approach them with a more playful attitude. As I have already indicated, Western elementary and secondary school students seem to perceive their school learning activities as "work" or "play" depending upon whether they possess certain perceptual features, namely, electivity, desirability, and pleasure. The key to this redesign, therefore, will be to build all or some of these features into our school learning activities. Building objective elements of electivity, desirability, and pleasure into our school learning activities does not necessarily mean that all students will subjectively perceive them as opportunities for "play." But preliminary research (Lepper and Malone, 1986; Malone and Lepper, 1986) and experience (Block, 1985a) suggest that it is a start.

The school play literature also suggests at least five potential approaches that practitioners can use to make their current school learning activities more playlike. All of these approaches are practicable, but none has been honed to a state of "nuts and bolts." So each will require some background reading and some technical and conceptual tinkering. Much of this reading can be found in Wagner's bibliography at the end of this book. The tinkering must be your own.

One approach is suggested by such writings as Pepler's, Christie, and Johnson's, and Vandenberg's (1979). This is the **play training** strategy. Here the practitioner would examine the school play literature and select one or more play training *procedures*. The practitioner might, for example, be interested in "socio-dramatic" or "symbolic" play techniques (see Christie, 1982, 1985). The practitioner would then start the quarter, semester, or school year by training students with these procedures and hoping that this training transfers to their subsequent school work.

A second approach is suggested by writings such as King's. This is the **practical** strategy. Here the practitioner would search the school play literature not for general procedures for making school learning activities more playlike but for subject matter specific *techniques*. King's chapter, for example, highlights some strategies for teaching: logical reasoning and social concepts; language arts; and math and science. The practitioner would then select, adapt, and implement selected techniques for the particular subject or subjects of interest.

A third approach is suggested by writings such as Csikszentmihalyi (1975) and Gehlbach (1982). This might be called the **pragmatic** strategy. Whereas in the practical strategy the practitioner would review the school play literature for particular techniques for making a given subject or subjects more playlike, in the pragmatic one she or he would search for certain *concepts*. Csikszentmihalyi (1975) and other schooling scholars (e.g., Block, 1985a; Brophy, 1983; deCharms, 1983), for example, have repeatedly advanced the notion of "flow" as a stepping stone for making ordinary school learning activities more playlike. The practitioner would then need to translate the selected concept or concepts into practice.

A fourth approach is found in writings such as Montessori (1964) and, more recently, Block (1985a) and deCharms (1976). This is the **programmatic** strategy. Here the practitioner would search the school play literature not for particular techniques or concepts for making school learning activities more playlike but for entire *programs* of related concepts and techniques. Block's "mastery learning" program, for example, purports to promote greater "flow" in school learning activities while deCharms' "personal causation" program provides greater "personal control." The practitioner would then adopt selected programs for application in a particular subject, several subjects, or the entire curriculum.

A fifth approach is suggested by the writings of Malone and Lepper (1986). This is the **protean** strategy. Whereas the practical, pragmatic, and programmatic strategies are all ultimately concerned with finding and applying specific school play techniques, concepts, and programs respectively, the protean strategy is concerned with organizing these specifics into some *meaningful whole.* The proteanist recognizes that certain concepts have to be designed into any instructional activity to make it more playlike. But he or she also recognizes that there are functionally a multitude of ways by which this can be accomplished. Accordingly, the proteanist attempts to inventory each important playlike concept, to pair it with appropriate techniques and programs, and to organize the resultant concept-techniques-programs pairings. The result is a taxonomy of concepts, related programs, and techniques for making school learning activities more playlike. From this taxonomy any number of particular concepts, programs, and techniques can be chosen and developed for classroom use.

Malone and Lepper (1986) provide an instructive example of the protean approach. Generalizing from their work on computer games, they have developed a taxonomy of ways in which ordinary school learning activities might be made made more fun and, hence, more playlike. This taxonomy suggests a whole variety of individual and interpersonal intrinsic motivational concepts that might be systematically built into any instructional activity, a number of technical and programmatic possibilities for using each concept to embellish instruction, and even criteria by which the impact of each embellishment might be evaluated. The individual intrinsic motivational concepts are challenge, control, self-esteem, and fantasy; the interpersonal ones are competition, cooperation, and public recognition. Each of these personal intrinsic motivators, of course, already has champions in the school play literature. The concept of challenge is central, for example, to the writings of Csikszentmihalyi (1975) and myself (1985a), curiosity to the writings of Berlyne (1968) and Gehlbach (1980), control to the writings of deCharms (1968) and Deci (1981), and fantasy to the writings of Singer (1973) and Sutton-Smith (see Sutton-Smith and Kelly-Byrne, 1984). Moreover, many of the interpersonal intrinsic motivators, especially competition and cooperation, will have champions as various modern theories of school motivation (see, e.g., Ames and Ames, 1984) seep into play theory and practice

These five approaches to making school learning activities more playlike have several general advantages. Some apply to any school subject (play training, pragmatic, programmatic, and protean), while others apply to particular ones (practical). Some can be readily adopted for classroom use (practical and programmatic), while others can be adapted (pragmatic and protean). And some can be used in connection with existing school curricula (practical, pragmatic, programmatic, and protean), while others can be employed separately (play training).

Each approach has specific advantages, too. Programmatic approaches, for example, provide proven teaching techniques that can help make students' learning not only more motivating but also more excellent and swift. Mastery learning programs, in particular, have consistently helped 50th percentile students to learn various school subjects like 80-85th percentile ones (Burns, 1986; Guskey and Gates, 1986). And protean approaches,to take another example, offer a conceptual smorgasbord not only of existing concepts, techniques, and programs for making school learning activities more playlike but of new possibilities as well. Consider, for example, the possibility of building more "cooperation" into school work. Malone and Lepper's scheme suggests that practitioners might turn to either new research in "cooperative learning" (Slavin, 1983), "goal" structures (Ames and Ames, 1984), or "activity structures" (Bossert, 1979) for a host of general and specific classroom concepts and techniques.

Conversely, these five approaches have some general disadvantages. Adopted approaches (practical and programmatic) may simply not work under teaching-learning conditions too different from those under which they were originally developed. Mastery learning programs, for example, seem to fail when they are implemented overnight (Block, 1985b). Adapted approaches (pragmatic and protean) may stumble, too, on particular school play concepts that prove to be difficult, if not impossible, to translate into practice. Fantasy, in particular, may be an attractive playlike concept on paper, but it can be a tough concept to implement even in simple instructional games (Malone and Lepper, 1986). And approaches that are typically taught separately from (play training), rather than in connection with, the regular school curriculum (practical, pragmatic, programmatic, and protean) may simply be instructionally outmoded. Indeed, the trend in instruction is toward curriculum embedded, rather than disembedded, approaches (see, e.g., Jones, 1985).

Certain of these approaches have specific disadvantages as well. Play training, in particular, has a checkered and controversial past (see Pepler, this volume; Christie and Johnsen, this volume). Suppose, too, that the training does not generalize to the students' subsequent school work. Programmatic approaches may force school play practitioners to adopt more concepts and techniques than they need. Mastery learning programs, in particular, have periodic learner feedback and correction features that some research suggests may be superfluous for challenging students to learn (Slavin and Karweit, 1984). Finally, protean approaches may prove to be practically interesting but theoretically thin. At the heart of such approaches is an effort to broaden practitioners thinking about school play by defining and organizing not only old concepts but also new ones. Play scholars such as Berlyne (1968) and school play scholars such as Gehlbach (1980) have wondered whether the play field is not too broadly defined and organized already.

Clearly, the general and specific advantages and disadvantages of each of these approaches will require systematic evaluation in the crucible of practice. As the comments of Baker, Herman, and Yeh (1981), Malone and Lepper (1986), and many of this volume's authors suggest, there are already enough "fun and games" concepts, techniques, and programs in schools that have negative or no effects on students' motivation to learn. I certainly do not want to fill the classroom with more.

SUMMARY

In the first portion of the chapter, I reviewed the school play research. This past research has both substantive and methodological implications for future research.

Substantively speaking, students engage in various kinds of play over their school career. Preschool students, in particular, engage in various forms of cognitive and social play, while post preschool students engage in instrumental, illicit, recreational, and sanctioned-recreational play. The kinds of school play in which students engage also change as they develop. Preschoolers shift from simple to more complex forms of cognitive and social play and post preschoolers from instrumental, illicit, and recreational to illicit, recreational, and sanctioned-recreational play. Some of these developmental changes may be psychologically or ontogenetically based, others may be socially or contextually caused. Some, in fact, may be traced directly to the nature of the school. Apparently, schools confine students play within certain contextual parameters that influence not only student definitions of what is play but also the details of the play itself. School "play" becomes a state of mind influenced by factors of electivity, desirability, and pleasure. Students perceive they are playing only when the "who, what, when, where, and why" of a given school activity lead them to perceive it as being one they do not have to do, but they want to do, because it is "fun."

Methodologically speaking, the terrain and developmental milestones of school play still require substantial mapping, especially past the preschool level. The mapping of post-preschoolers illicit, recreational, and sanctioned-recreational play seems especially important. This mapping should be more sensitive to past conceptual slights and methodological biases. Future research might, in particular, strive conceptually to explore possible "school effects" on students' play and methodologically to use more sociogenically-based research techniques. Student, rather than expert, perspectives on school play might serve as initial foci for this research.

In the second part of the chapter, I considered school play practice. I raised the central practical issue of how the school play research literature might serve educational goals and proposed that it be used to redesign contemporary instructional practices. The key to this redesign is to make them more playlike from the student perspective, that is, perceptually more voluntary, desirable, and pleasurable.

Five approaches were then proposed for using the school play literature to develop more playlike school learning activities. One strategy utilizes the literature to find play training procedures; the second to discover subject matter specific techniques; the third to apply general concepts; the fourth to reveal general programs; and the fifth to organize particular techniques and programs around particular concepts. These strategies were labelled play training, practical, pragmatic, programmatic, and protean respectively and some of their general and specific advantages and disadvantages were indicated.

Some school play researchers and practitioners, of course, will find controversial the use of school play research to propose any strategy, let alone five, to promote play in instruction. These researchers will pessimistically contend that the current fledgling state of the research makes application impossible. And their practitioner colleagues will argue instrumental play is undesirable and that play despite instruction (illicit play) or especially outside of instruction (recreational and sanctioned-recreational play) will suffice to meet students' school play needs.

Frankly, I welcome the controversy because I believe that instrumental play is possible. Past attempts to provide it have failed not because most teachers and other playmasters were insensitive, incompetent, or lazy but because they lacked the necessary human technology. That is, they lacked the human know-how and can-do to translate critical play beliefs and concepts into effective and practicable techniques. The research in this volume, though sometimes sketchy, provides school play practitioners with some of the rudiments of this technology. We possess not only some central concepts but also some fledgling techniques for making ordinary school learning activities more playlike. Moreover, many of these techniques might build on, rather than replace, the teachers' customary ones. It is time, therefore, that we begin to use this high human technology.

I also welcome the controversy because I believe that instrumental play is desirable. While I accept that illicit activities offer many opportunities for students to play at school, I am not persuaded that they sometimes offer the right ones. After all, while some of these activities are relatively harmless (Licata, 1979), others may set the stage for "delinquency" (Csikszentmihalyi and Larson, 1978), even in the best of schools (Larkin, 1979). Nor am I persuaded that school-sponsored recreational or sanctioned-recreational activities offer enough opportunities for school play. Opportunities to participate in such activities are already economically and academically constrained, and these constraints, especially in trend setting states like Texas and California, are growing steadily tighter. Moreover, some of those opportunities that do exist may not be developmentally un-problematic (see, e.g., Klieber and Robert's discussion of sports).

Marcuse (quoted in Csikszentmihalyi, 1975, p. 12), has written that "...the qualitative difference between a free and unfree society lies precisely in our ability to discover the realm of freedom in labor and not merely beyond it." Research-based and well-designed instrumental play activities can provide both appropriate and sufficient opportunities for virtually all students to play in school and to begin to find freedom in one of their earliest work experiences. Making school learning activities more playlike may not necessarily make them "play," but it is one essential step. Just as past play concepts such as "flow" have moved play researchers and practitioners toward the notion of "playfulness," so does the notion of playfulness now move school play researchers and practitioners toward the notion of "play." I look forward to the day when students, regardless of their grade level, when asked what they did at school perceived they really "played." That their teachers think and feel that students actually "worked" will simply be frosting on the cake.

REFERENCES

Allen, J. Classroom Management: A Field Study of Students' Perspectives, Goals, and Strategies. Unpublished Ph.D. dissertation, University of California, Santa Barbara, July, 1982.

Ames, C., and Ames, R. Systems of Student and Teacher Motivation: Toward a Qualitative Definition. *Journal of Educational Psychology, 76*(1984), 535-556

Ames, R., and Ames, C. *Research on Motivation in Education: Volume 1: Student Motivation.* Orlando, Florida: Academic Press, Inc., 1984.

Anyon, J. Social class and the hidden curriculum of work. *Journal of Education, 162*(1980), 67-92.

Anyon, J. Elementary Schooling and Distinctions of Social Class. *Interchange, 12*(1981), 118-132.

Baker, E., Herman, J., and Yeh, J. Fun and Games: Their Contribution to Basic Skills Instruction in Elementary School. *American Educational Research Journal, 18*(1981), 83-92.

Batcher, E. *Emotion in the Classroom: A Study of Children's Experience.* New York: Praeger Publishers, 1981.

Bateson, G. *Steps to an Ecology of Mind.* New York: Ballantine Books, 1972.

Becker, H., Geer, B., and Hughes, E. *Making the Grade.* New York: Wiley, 1968.

Behn, W., Carnoy, M., Carter, M., Crain, J., and Levin, H. School is Bad; Work is Worse. *School Review, 83*(1974), 49-68.

Berlyne, D. Laughter, Humor, and Play. In *The Handbook of Social Psychology.* Edited by G. Lindzey and E. Aronson. Second edition. Volume 3. Boston: Addison-Wesley, 1968.

Block, J. Some Neglected Parameters of the Student Role in Teaching: Play and the Play/Work Dialectic. Final Report, NIE G-80-0070, Washington, D.C., 1981.

Block, J. Making School Learning Activities More Playlike: Flow and Mastery Learning. *Elementary School Journal, 85*(1985a), 65-75.

Block, J. Belief Systems and Mastery Learning. *Outcomes, 4*, no. 2(1985b), 1, 4-14.

Block, J., Efthim, H., Burns, R., and Anderson, L. *Excellence, Equity, and Mastery Learning*. White Plains, New York: Longman, 1987.

Bloom, B. *Human Characteristics and School Learning*. New York: McGraw-Hill, 1976.

Borman, K. Children's Interpersonal Relationships: Playground Games and Social Cognitive Skills. Final Report. Washington, D.C.: National Institute of Education, 1981.

Bossert, S. *Tasks and Social Relationships in Classrooms*. New York: Cambridge University, 1979.

Bowles, S., and Gintis, H. *Schooling in Capitalist America*. London: Routledge and Kegan Paul, 1976.

Bronfenbrenner, U. *The Ecology of Human Development: Experiments by Nature and Design*. Cambridge, Massachusetts: Harvard University Press, 1979.

Brophy, J. Conceptualizing Student Motivation. Occasional paper no. 70, Institute for Research on Teaching, Michigan State University, East Lansing, Michigan, November, 1983.

Burns, R. Accumulating the Accumulating Evidence on Mastery Learning. *Outcomes, 5*, no. 2(Winter, 1986), 4-10.

Carroll, T. Transactions of Cognitive Equivalence in the Domain of 'Work' and 'Play'. *Council on Anthropology and Education Quarterly, 6*, no. 2(May, 1975), 17-22

Cheska, A. *Play as Context: 1979 Proceedings of the Association for the Anthropological Study of Play*. Edited by A. Cheska. West Point, New York: Leisure Press. 1981.

Christiansen, C., Gerber, M., and Everhart, R. Towards a Sociological Perspective on Learning Disabilities. Unpublished paper, Department of Education, University of California, Santa Barbara, April, 1986.

Christie, J. Sociodramatic Play Training. *Young Children, 37*(1982), 25-32.

Christie, J. Training of Symbolic Play. *Early Child Development and Care, 19*(1985), 43-52.

Christie, J., and Johnsen, E. The Role of Play in Social-Intellectual Development. *Review of Educational Research, 53*(1983), 93-115.

Cicourel, A., and Kitsuse, J. *The Educational Decision-Makers*. New York: Bobbs-Merrill, 1963.

Cohen, D., and Lazerson, M. Education and the Corporate Order. In *Power and Ideology in Education.* Edited by J. Karabel and A. Halsey. New York: Oxford University Press, 1977.

Condry, J., and Koslowski, B. Can Education be Made 'Intrinsically Interesting' to Children. In *Current Topics in Early Childhood Education, Volume 2.* Edited by L. Katz. Norwood, New Jersey: Ablex Publishing Co., 1979..

Cremin, L. *The Transformation of the School: Progressivism in American Education.* New York: Vintage Books, 1964.

Csikszentmihalyi, M. *Beyond Boredom and Anxiety.* San Francisco: Jossey-Bass, 1975.

Csikszentmihalyi, M. Some Paradoxes in the Definition of Play. In *Play as Context.* Edited by A. Cheska. West Point, New York: Leisure Press, 1981.

Csikszentmihalyi, M., and Larson, R. Intrinsic Rewards in School Crime. *Crime and Delinquency, 24*(1978), 322-338.

Csikszentmihalyi, M., Larson, R., and Prescott, S. The Ecology of Adolescent Activity and Experience. *Journal of Youth and Adolescence, 6*(1977), 281-294

Curry, N., and Arnaud, S. Play in Developmental Preschool Settings. In *Child's Play: Developmental and Applied.* Edited by T. Yawkey and A. Pellegrini. Hillsdale, New Jersey: Lawrence Erlbaum Associates, Inc., 1984.

Cusick, P. *Inside High School: The Students' World.* New York: Holt, Rinehart and Winston, 1973.

Dannefer, D. Adult Development and Social Theory: A Paradigmatic Reappraisal. *American Sociological Review, 49*(1984), 100-116.

Darvill, D. Ecological Influences on Children's Play: Issues and Approaches. In *The Play of Children: Current Theory and Research.* Edited by K. Rubin and D. Pepler. Basel, Switzerland: Karger AG, 1982.

Day, H. Play: A Ludic Behavior. In *Advances in Intrinsic Motivation and Aesthetics.* Edited by H. Day. New York: Plenum, 1981.

Day, H. Work and Play in the 21st Century: Workfulness at Play and Playfulness at Work. Paper presented at the Annual Meeting of the Ontario Psychological Association, Toronto, Ontario, February, 1984.

deCharms, R. *Personal Causation.* New York: Academic Press, 1968.

deCharms, R. Intrinsic Motivation, Peer Tutoring, and Cooperative Learning: Practical Maxims. In *Teacher and Student Perceptions: Implications for Learning.* Edited by J. Levine and M. Wang. Hillsdale, New Jersey: Lawrence Erlbaum Associates, Inc., 1983.

Deci, E. *The Psychology of Self-Determination.* Lexington, Massachusetts: D. C. Heath and Company, 1980.

DeVoss, G. A. Field Study: Elementary Student Activity and Attitude From Observer and Student Perspectives. Unpublished Ph.D. dissertation, University of California, Santa Barbara, 1978.

Dennis, L. Play in Dewey's Theory of Education. *Young Children, 25*(1970), 230-235.

Doyle, W. Stalking the Mythical Student. *Elementary School Journal, 82*(1982), 529-533.

Doyle, W. Academic Work. *Review of Educational Research, 53*(1983), 159-199.

Elmore, R., and Thompson, A. Researching the Student's Perspective: The Development of an Instrument and Methodology for Interviewing Seventh Grade Students. Unpublished paper, Far West Laboratory for Educational Research and Development, 1980.

Ericksen, F. Qualitative Methods in Research on Teaching. In *Handbook of Research on Teaching.* Edited by M. Wittrock. Third edition. New York: Macmillan Publishing Company, 1986.

Everhart, R. *Reading, Writing, and Resistance: Adolescence and Labor in a Junior High School.* London: Routledge and Kegan Paul, 1983.

Finnan, C. The Ethnography of Children's Spontaneous Play. In *Doing the Ethnography of Schooling: Educational Anthropology in Action.* Edited by G. Spindler. New York: Holt, Rinehart, and Winston, 1982.

Gehlbach, R. D. Instructional Play: Some Theoretical Prerequisites to Systemic Research and Development. *Educational Psychology, 15*(1980), 112-124.

Getzels, J. A Social Psychology of Education. In The *Handbook of Social Psychology.* Edited by G. Lindzey and E. Aronson. Second edition. Volume 5. Reading, Massachusetts: Addison-Wesley, 1969.

Glickman, C. Play and the School Curriculum: The Historical Context. *Journal of Research and Development in Education, 14*(1981), 1-10.

Glickman, C. Play in Public School Settings: A Philosophical Question. In *Child's Play: Developmental and Applied.* Edited by T. Yawkey and A. Pellegrini. Hillsdale, New Jersey: Lawrence Erlbaum Associates, Inc., 1984.

Goldstein, B., and Oldham, J. *Children and Work: A Study of Socialization.* New Brunswick, New Jersey: Transaction Books, 1979.

Goodlad, J. *A Place called School: Prospects for the Future.* New York: McGraw-Hill Book Company, 1984.

Grannis, J. The School as a Model of Society. *Harvard Graduate School of Education Bulletin, 21*(1967), 15-27.

Guskey, T., and Gates, S. A Synthesis of Research on Group-Based Mastery Learning Programs. Paper presented at the Annual Meeting of the American Educational Research Association, Chicago, Illinois, April, 1985.

Hartwig, M. School Work and School Play: Some Implications for Student Motivation. Paper presented at the Annual Meeting of the American Educational Research Association, Montreal, Canada, April, 1983.

Hartwig, M. The Development and Validation of an Ethnographically-Based Instrument to Elicit Students' Perceptions of Their Classroom. Unpublished Ph.D. dissertation, University of California, Santa Barbara, June, 1986.

Henderson, J. The Foreshadowing of Work and Play Elements in School Settings. Unpublished Ph.D. dissertation, Stanford University, Stanford, CA, 1980.

Hutt, C. Toward a Taxonomy and Conceptual-Model of Play. In *Advances in Intrinsic Motivation and Aesthetics.* Edited by H. Day. New York: Plenum, 1981.

Iverson, B. Haha, Aha, Ah: A Model for Playful Curricular Inquiry and Evaluation. Paper presented at the Annual Meeting of the American Educational Research Association, Los Angeles, April, 1981.

Jackson, P. *Life in Classrooms.* New York: Holt, Rinehart, and Winston, 1970.

Jones, B. Guidelines for Instruction-Enriched Mastery Learning to Improve Comprehension. In *Improving Student Achievement Through Mastery Learning Programs.* Edited by D. Levine. San Francisco: Jossey-Bass, 1985.

Kerckhoff, A. Looking Back and Looking Ahead. In *Research in Sociology of Education and Socialization: Longitudinal Perspectives on Educational Attainment.* Edited by A. Kerckhoff. Greenwich, Connecticut: JAI Press, 1980.

King, N. Play: The Kindergartner's Perspective. *The Elementary School Journal, 80*(1980), 81-87.

King, N. Work and Play in the Classroom. *Sociology of Education, 46*(1982), 110-113.

Lancy, D. The Classroom as Phenomenon. In *Social Psychology of Education.* Edited by D. Bar-Tal and L. Saxe. Washington, D.C.: Hemisphere Publishing Corporation, 1978.

Larkin, R. *Suburban Youth in Cultural Crisis.* New York: Oxford University Press, 1979.

LeCompte, M. Learning to Work: The Hidden Curriculum of the Classroom. *Anthropology and Education Quarterly, 9*(1979), 22-37.

Lepper, M., and Malone, T. Intrinsic Motivation and Instructional Effectiveness in Computer-Based Education. In *Aptitude, Learning, and Instruction: III. Conative and Affective Process Analysis.* Edited by R. Snow and M. Farr. Hillsdale, New Jersey: Lawrence Erlbaum Associates, Inc., 1986.

Lever, J. Multiple Methods of Data Collection: A Note on Divergence. *Urban Life, 10*(1981), 199-213.

Levin, H., and Rumberger, R. The Educational Implications of High Technology. Project Report no. 83-A4, Institute for Research on Educational Finance and Governance, Stanford University, February, 1983.

Licata, J. Student Brinkmanship: Some Field Observations, Findings, and Questions. Paper presented at the Annual Meeting of the American Educational Research Association, San Francisco, April, 1979.

Lieberman, J. *Playfulness: Its Relationship to Imagination and Creativity.* New York: Academic Press, 1977.

Malone, T., and Lepper, M. Making Learning Fun: A Taxonomy of Intrinsic Motivations for Learning. In *Aptitude, Learning, and Instruction: III. Conative and Affective Process Analysis.* Edited by R. Snow and M. Farr. Hillsdale, New Jersey: Lawrence Erlbaum Associates, Inc., 1986

Mehan, H. Structuring School Structures. *Harvard Educational Review, 48*(1978), 32-64.

274   *Block*

Mehan, H. The Competent Student. *Anthropology and Education Quarterly,*
    9(1980), 131-152.

Metz, M. *Classrooms and Corridors.* Berkeley, California: University of
    California Press, 1978.

Miller, S. Ends, Means, and Galumphing: Some Leitmotifs of Play. *American*
    Anthropologist, 75(1973), 87-98.

Montessori, M. *The Montessori Method.* Cambridge, Massachusetts: Bentley,
    Inc., 1973.

Moore, N., Evertson, C., and Brophy, J. Solitary Play: Some Functional
    Reconsiderations. *Developmental Psychology, 10*(1974), 830-834.

Moos, R. *The Human Context.* New York: John Wiley and Sons, 1976.

Mouncer, F. The Work and Play of Learning and Studying in the Elementary
    School. Manuscript in progress, Department of Education, University of
    California, Santa Barbara, 1986.

Ogbu, J. *The Next Generation: An Ethnography of Education in an Urban Neighborhood.*
    New York: Academic Press, 1974.

Reinert, G. Educational Psychology in the Context of the Human Life Span.
    In *Life-Span Development and Behavior.* Edited by P. Baltes and O. Brim, Jr.
    Volume 3. New York: Academic Press, 1980.

Rowan, B., Bossert, S., and Dwyer, D. Research on Effective Schools: A
    Cautionary Note. *Educational Researcher, 12,* no. 4(1983), 24-31.

Rubin, K., Fein, G., and Vandenberg, B. Play. In *Handbook of Child Psychology.*
    Volume 4. Edited by E. Heatherington. New York: Wiley, 1983.

Rutter, M., Maughan, B., Mortimer, P., and Ouston, J. *Fifteen Thousand Hours:*
    Secondary Schools and Their Effects on Children. London: Open Books Pub-
    lishing Limited, 1979.

Salter, M. *Play: Anthropological Perspectives, 1977 Proceedings of the Association for*
    the Anthropological Study of Play. West Point, New York: 1978.

Sarason, S. *Schooling in America: Scapegoat and Salvation.* New York: The Free
    Press, 1983.

Schaie, K., and Willis, S. Life-Span Development: Implications for Edu-
    cation. In *Review of Research in Education.* Volume 6. Edited by L.
    Shulman. Itasca, Illinois: F.E. Peacock, 1978.

Schwartz, F. Supporting and Subverting Learning: Peer Group Patterns in Four Tracked Schools. *Anthropology and Education Quarterly, 12*(1981), 99-120.

Schwartzman, H. *Transformations: The anthropology of Children's Play.* New York: Plenum, 1978a.

Schwartzman, H. *Play and Culture.* Edited by H. Schwartzman. West Point, New York: Leisure Press, 1978b.

Singer, J. *The Child's World of Make Believe.* New York: Academic Press, 1973.

Sizer, T. *Horace's Compromise: The Dilemma of the American High School.* Boston: Houghton Mifflin Company, 1984.

Slavin, R. *Cooperative Learning.* White Plains, New York: Longman, 1983.

Slavin, R., and Karweit, N. Mastery Learning and Student Teams: A Factorial Experiment in Urban General Mathematics Classes. *American Educational Research Journal, 21*(1984), 725-736.

Smetherham, D. Insider Research. *British Educational Research Journal, 4*(1978), 97-102.

Smith, L., and Geoffrey, W. *The Complexities of an Urban Classroom.* New York: Holt, Rinehart, and Winston, 1968.

Smith, R., and Proshansky, H. Conceptions of Work, Play, Competence, and Occupation in Junior and Senior High School Students. Final report, Project No. 1866, Office of Education, Bureau of Research, Washington, D.C., September, 1967.

Spindler, G. *Doing the Ethnography of Schooling: Educational Anthropology in Action.* New York: Holt, Rinehart, and Winston, 1982.

Spring, J. *The Sorting Machine: National Educational Policy Since 1945.* New York: David McKay Company, Inc., 1976.

Super, D. A. Life-Span, Life-Space Approach to Career Development. *Journal of Vocational Behavior, 16*(1980), 282-298.

Sutton-Smith, B., and Kelly-Byrne, D. *The Masks of Play.* West Point, New York: Leisure Press, 1984.

Sutton-Smith, B., and Roberts, J. Play, Games, and Sports. In *Handbook of Cross-Cultural Psychology.* Volume 4. Edited by A. Triandis and A. Heron. Boston, Massachusetts: Allyn and Bacon, Inc., 1981.

Vandenberg, B. Play as Curriculum. *Journal of Curriculum Theorizing, 1-2*(1979), 229-237.

Weinstein, R. Student Perceptions of Schooling. *Elementary School Journal, 83*(1983), 286-312.

Wilcox, K. Differential Socialization in the Classroom: Implications for Equal Opportunity. In *Doing the Ethnography of Education.* Edited by G. Spindler. New York: Holt, Rinehart, and Winston, 1982.

Willis, P. *Learning to Labour: How Working Class Kids Get Working Class Jobs.* Westmead, England: Saxon House, 1979.

Woods, P. *The Divided School.* London: Routledge and Kegan Paul, 1979.

Yawkey, T. Why Play? *Educational Research Quarterly, 5*(1980), 74-77.

Yawkey, T., and Pellegrini, A. *Child's Play: Developmental and Applied.* Edited by T. Yawkey and A. Pellegrini. Hillsdale, New Jersey: Lawrence Erlbaum Associates, Inc., 1984.

SCHOOL PLAY: A COMMENTARY

Brian Sutton-Smith

To my knowledge, this is the first systematic book length compilation of research studies on play in school. There have been such studies of: animal play, children's folk games, play in different cultures, play in experimental settings, games in culture, sport psychology and sport sociology, play in therapy, and children's play in playgrounds, but none of these has addressed specifically the issue of the difference it makes for play to take place in schools or the difference it makes for schools to have play going on there.

Are schools good for play, and is play good for schools? Unfortunately, the reading I take from the bulk of the present work is that schools are not particularly good for play, and play is not particularly acceptable in schools. Still, the authors deserve considerable commendation for being the first to bring these matters to our attention while using systematic social science research in so doing. As children spend increasing amount of their time in educational contexts (including preschool ones) and have less time left over to themselves, the relationships between schooling and their play become increasingly important to understand.

Although the authors seem to be generally optimistic about play and its benefits for the human spirit and mind, the evidence that they lay before us is largely pessimistic. We are given a picture of teachers using play for their own instrumental or regulative purposes and of children evading, contesting, or escaping these influences either in recess, in illicit play, or in simply goofing off. Despite some of the theoretical contentions that play is connected to creativity, we see little evidence of such creative play in these accounts. Play is presented most often as a fulcrum of contest between the irrevocably opposed forces of socializing adults and pleasure bound children. At least that is how the issue comes through most strongly in the striking descriptions of elementary school play by Nancy King, of junior high school play by Robert Everhart, and of special education play by Mayer Shevin.

In part, this pessimistic picture of the relationship between play and schooling occurs because King, Everhart and Shevin describe those relatively total school environments where the children have little escape from the regulations of their caretakers. In part, it also occurs because most of the volume's authors are dealing with children in school rather than on the playground. It seems that we might draw a different conclusion about the relationship of play and schooling if this book gave as much space to children's free playground play as it does to the other kinds of play perpetrated in the classroom. Only Andrew Miracle and Nancy King demonstrate some of the vitality and authentic peer development that appears to occur in the playground. In those schools where the playground is more freely available and recess is still a reality, many children will still tell you recess is their favorite school subject, but what that means to children's perception of going to school has not yet been fully explored.

I remember that my own life in school was made tolerable largely because it was the place in which I had access either to peer-organized games or teacher-organized sports. This was true of elementary school but even more true of high school. When I became a schoolteacher myself, what made school good for me, as well as for the children, was not that we mixed work and play but that we alternated between them. I was involved with the concepts of psychodrama in those days. Whenever there was an interlude between work sessions, I would precipitate role-playing sessions that we would play through to some kind of finish and then return to our studies with renewed vigor. In short, I found it necessary to make the boundaries fairly clear between play and work and to use one to reinvigorate the other. Without such clear boundaries, the seven-and-eight year-olds that I taught seemed to have great difficulty in knowing where they were. Mind you, in their schoolwork I gave them a great deal of autonomy; they did a great deal of exploration, they spent much time on mastering things they enjoyed, and they applied their imaginations to many of their projects, but I did not then, nor would I now, confuse those often voluntary activities of intelligence and learning with play.

In my recent book *Toys and Culture*, (Sutton-Smith, 1986) I have endeavored to understand why we seem to assume that everything children do voluntarily is playing. In all fairness to children, we should be clear about the distinctions between illicit play or illicit behavior. Mastering most of the "games" presented by teachers to children often has very little to do with play. They are "instrumental" to the teacher's goals and the child's mastery but are not instrumental "play".

Returning, again, to my personal preference for a dialectic rather than a fusion between work and play, I am intrigued with James Block's speculation on a parallel between the economy and the work/play relationship, with descending economic status levels (executive, service, and factory) relating to play types (playful, disjunctive (recess), and illicit). What one makes of all this, in a practical sense, because Block himself advocates playfulness for all and implies that everyone can become an executive, I find hard to determine. But I do believe that it is a powerful idea and that my own preference for a disjunctive relationship between play and work (role playing, then back to arithmetic), may well betoken the kind of separate class and role relationships of which I was a part in my British days. It might also help explain the relativity of some of my forthcoming comments.

PLAY DISCOURSES

Although many of the authors in this book seem to wish that teachers would pay more attention to children's play in the classroom, because the teachers in this book often seem so frightening as human beings, I could be led to quite the opposite conclusion--that the less these teachers know about children's play the better, and the more that children can be given their legitimate periods for their own recess or recreation the better. What is immediately apparent from the various chapters is that this volume's authors are often talking about very different kinds of play in very different contexts, and even more important, that they use different ways of talking about play. There is no unanimity either in this book or in the field of play studies in general about the empirical or philosophical meanings of play. It seems of some value, therefore, to engage here in a discussion of play discourses; that is, a discussion of the ways that have been developed in recent years for talking about play. This is the opposite approach to what most of the volume's authors have been doing. All assume that their subject matter is the empirics of play in schools and that their way of talking about these empirics is a transparent effect of their methodology. I believe, however, that the approaches they adopt are just as remarkable for what they reveal about their own presuppositions as for what is discovered empirically about play. Some clarity might perhaps be introduced, by my trying to focus on these presuppositions or, to put it more humbly, on the authors' particular ways of talking about play --their play discourses. It seems more appropriate to call their approaches "discourses," because they are not really theories or even paradigms in any implicit sense but are, rather, the blend of common-sense, cultural heritage, theory, and evidence that has become a form of parlance amongst the community of scholars involved.

Idealistic Play Discourse.

I have elsewhere outlined at some length the gradual idealization of play that has occurred in our century and have suggested that it has its origins in such phenomena as the separation of child play from adult play, in the class based origin of "amateur" sports, in the usefulness of sports and recreations for the domestication of childhood, in evolutionary theory and, in more recent years, in the feminist movement (Sutton-Smith and Kelly-Byrne, 1984(b). All of these are, in part, reverberations of the development during the late eighteenth and early nineteenth century of fundamentally romantic attitudes toward the imagination, toward play and toward aesthetics. In many respects, these three concepts replaced the soul as the ultimate guarantor first of man's spiritual self and, later, in more secular times, of his or her creative self (Engell, 1981).

For example, to take our own focus on play, every modern theory of play says that play is of benefit to the player in some way, whether the emphasis be on growth, mastery, knowledge, or metacommunication. Major play theorists Groos, Freud, Piaget, Berlyne, and Bateson are as one in this respect. Yet, as we know from animal and human accidents, play is often dysfunctional; and as we know from anthropological examples, it is often associated with injury and death. Further, as we know from the examples in this book, particularly of illicit play, much play would not be regarded as salutary by the citizenry. It is a profound paradox that, in this work, the most novel revelations are about illicit play, which is hardly of a socially redeeming character, and yet all the authors cling to the advocacy of "play" as something fundamentally good for children. Let me take each author in turn and point to his or her idealistic assumptions about the virtues of play for schools.

Finkelstein explicitly identifies a historical trend that views play as creative and emancipatory and correctly points to Huizinga as the most influential modern historian of play. We should add, however, that his impact has been greater on sports theorists than play theorists. She also identifies other theorists who are, in contrast, concerned with play as a form of regulation and indoctrination or with play as a contested terrain where different power groups struggle to use it in stabilizing or revolutionary ways. There is a useful parallel between her historical extensions and the instrumental and illicit play categories developed by Nancy King. The distinction between good and bad play (or between the imagination and mere fancy), which began with the German idealists, Kant, Schiller, etc., reverberates throughout her article as subsequent historians argue either that schools kill play or that children transform their schools through their own play vitality. While her chapter is a powerful demonstration of the durability and extensiveness of this dualism, she nevertheless ends her description with the admonition that some unity about the nature of play can be brought about by some unifying historical thought about the nature of play. But on closer examination, what seems involved here perhaps is more romanticism about history than about the empirical unity of play. "Above all," she concludes, the historical study of children's play in school provides opportunities to address many of the important dilemmas associated with modern life and to assess its impact on the human capacity for meaningful fun and play. It is a history just waiting to be written." This is at least a romanticism about the diagnostic usefulness of play-history if not about play's existence for children, a romanticism with which we first become familiar in the notion of play diagnosis in Freudian theory and practice.

Although Miracle, as an anthropologist/ sociologist, makes the necessary genuflections toward the need for more tolerance in schools for informal play. The general tenor of his very solid review is profoundly pessimistic as he reflects, for example, "...that the teacher's role is so authoritarian and control oriented, that it may be difficult for teachers to stay uninvolved and to allow children to develop their own patterns of social interaction." The trend of the century, he says, has been from child control to adult control of play.

We might expect optimism about play to be greatest amongst psychologists who have carried out the bulk of studies over the past twenty years. In Pepler's chapter and in the one by Christie and Johnsen, enthusiasm is derived from the animal and psychological studies of the 1960's (Fagen, 1982). Yet one can also read their chapters and come away believing that they are but a colligation of truisms and contradictory findings, very little of which gives a skeptic confidence in their empirical or practical relevance. Even the most careful Pepler, having demonstrated at length that researchers have not been able to prove that "...play is the best way to learn problem-solving skills, perspective taking, or other competencies" nor shown "...any clear directions for the incorporation of play in educational programs" still goes on to conclude that: "The role of educators will be to continue to provide children with a variety of play experiences to facilitate learning and prepare children to face the diverse problems of everyday life." Likewise,

Christie and Johnsen who are, in general, more sanguine about these psychological research findings (like Pepler, I am not), contend that, "...more research is needed before any firm recommendations for practice" can be made, but also state: "Play is also inherently satisfying and pleasurable. Schools...might reconsider the importance of social fun and its role in guaranteeing children's rights to childhood." Indeed schools might so do, but that is in no way a research conclusion, not, at least, as psychological research is reviewed in these two chapters.

So, despite the evidence in their own hands, Pepler, Christie, and Johnsen are clinging to a positive attitude towards play like most other play theorists of this century, and like Wordsworth, Coleridge, and the other romantics in the past century. This romanticism has nothing much to do with research but much to do with widespread cultural preconceptions about play these past two hundred years. It is crystallized in their psychological definitions of play which clearly presuppose what it is their duty to prove. They define play to include, flexibility, positive affect, non-literality, intrinsic motivation, attention to instrumental behaviors, active engagement, self-generation, and freedom from extremes of anxiety and pressure. The fact that children arrive at some consensus on some of these descriptors (as in King's chapter) or that adults can use them reliably as descriptors of play (in the Pepler chapter) only shows the widespread nature of these historically based contemporary cultural agreements, at least, as far as research on preschools and in laboratories are concerned. In these settings the "players" are kept free from other pressures, are given "free time" to play with materials carefully selected for them beforehand, and are not permitted to interfere with and aggress against each other in any very stressful manner.

If one should doubt the contextually contingent nature of these play definitions, then Mayer Shevin's chapter may cause something of a shock. The teachers he reviews in special education adopt play as something they use and abuse quite cynically for the control of their children. If the consensus about play has "reliability" in these special education circles, we might come to consider play as some kind of addiction which children are so disposed to that it can be used for their control. The children are, thus, victims of their own need for play. They are clearly not free of it and might be supposed to be put under stress by any lack of play. Play researchers who adopt the earlier definitions might do well to consider much more carefully the character of agency in play, the character of pleasure, the degrees of flexibility as well as the role of anxiety, of risk, of compulsion, and of conformity.

When one moves out of the context which these researchers so take for granted in their supposedly universal and supposedly empirical definitions, many other connotations come to mind. In folklore, playground play has been called traditional because of its conformist and routine nature. One gets to play by submitting to the playground bosses, and then one becomes engaged in an endless cycle. There is nothing notably flexible in most of this play and a great deal is very stressful, as Andrew Sluckin's (1981) recent British study, *Growing Up in the Playground*, has shown once again. One wonders, incidentally, why the British playgrounds always seem to be so much more savage than the American ones (contrast Knapp and Knapp, 1976). It is hard to know whether the British have a monopoly on the "Lord of the Flies" phenomenon or whether the Americans have a monopoly on rosy-tinted children. Seeing we have so few studies of any playgrounds, the issue is moot. But reference to King's material on "Illicit Play" and Everhart's on "Goofing Off," once again, shows that playing under stress and playing with stress are not to be so lightly defined. Their examples are more striking for their rebellious character under fire and for their Bakhtin-like protestive laughter against circumscribing fate than for freedom (they are conspiratorial), intrinsic motivation (they are provoked by authoritarianism), or their flexibility (they are more in the nature of an addictive-repetition compulsion). Given that Victor Turner has argued that most play in preliterate societies was obligatory not optional and sacred rather than profane (Babcock, 1978), one has to wonder about the cultural relativity and romanticism of definitions of play offered by psychologists such as Pepler, Christie, and Johnsen.

There is little implicit romanticism in King's chapter on elementary school play because she is so aware of the different kinds of play and is, in particular, a specialist in illicit play. In fact, she notes that if teachers knew more about these other kinds of play they might be less inclined to illicit play's idealization since it is easier for them to idealize that which they control themselves. They should know illicit play's unsavory, uncouth, and excessive aspects to keep their understanding in balance.

While there has to be some truth to what King says, I have to record that in my own school teaching experience I never met a teacher who had any misconceptions about unsavory play. I suspect, therefore, that these misconceptions are more likely to arise in the minds of those who do not deal regularly with everyday childhood--researchers, librarians, and academics. More importantly, I think they arise more from our humanistic and romantic cultural legacy than from perceptions of actual children. If you deal only with preschoolers or in laboratories with children, there is relatively little rebuttal to your preconceptions. Still, if King is not a romanticist about play, there is, at least, optimism in her expectation that if teachers know illicit play, they will be more aware of what is going on in childhood and in their own school.

Everhart's chapter, after its most enlightening if sobering and fairly depressing account of life in the totalitarian junior high school, also finishes with a romantic filip. The students need "goofing off" if they are to survive in that atmosphere and maintain their own mental health, he says. And teachers, who understand this, need to play, too, if they are to realize the poor situation in which they find themselves. Everhart claims that these "goofing off" phenomena are "normal" only to the extent we have accepted them as a natural dimension of school life. "To the extent that these premises are challenged, then illicit play can be useful in assisting educators to be actively involved in personal, organizational, and cultural renewal." In short, diagnosing what is going on and changing the circumstances of life will make goofing off no longer necessary. It will have served its purpose in cultural change. But once again I see this argument giving great credence to play as diagnosis but very little to play as it exists except as justified by the oppressive character of the school. If all was well, according to this theory, there need be no illicit play. The idealization here is paradoxically of the sensitive teacher rather than of play.

Kleiber and Roberts' chapter finds sports a beneficial contribution to school life and the lives of those who play them. They even see as exemplary the discipline sports require; but, on the other hand, they abhor the domination of leisure time by sports to the exclusion of other leisure pursuits or to the exclusion of academic seriousness. What they ask for is more playfulness in sports, and by that they mean more time for spontaneity and self-determination. But we have already noted there is limited scope for spontaneity and self-determination even in regular playground play. Concentrating on these particular cultural connotations of play is mindful of the protest against mechanization, technology, industrialism, conformity, and institutionalization which has been so much a part of the romantic movement. The spontaneous and self-generating play of which they speak is more characteristic of solitary children in their own playrooms than it is of any other well established historical period (Sutton-Smith, 1986).

No one could accuse Mayer Shevin's account of special education settings of being idealistic. This is a remarkably sobering account of the treatment of these children and the manipulation of their play by teachers. The chapter is in many ways a criticism of the material in the earlier chapters. It demonstrates so clearly how contextually dependent are play's definitions (as King also shows) and how relatively useless is the knowledge of developmental stages as a way of guiding these special children to play behavior and how irrelevant to understanding children's vital concerns, including play, are most of the variable- oriented studies that have been conducted under the name of psychological research. Indeed, one can hardly read through Shevin's final recommendations on how to make play welcome in the special education classroom without fear and trembling. So that when he finally says, "...small, tentative changes in the direction of increasing student playfulness and autonomy may lead to more profound transformations," one knows that there is little chance of Shevin's becoming bloated with optimism should these arrive. Play in his context is a tough minded and begrudging reality rather than a tender minded deception.

In James Block's review chapter, the book takes up its more positive character once again. His suggestions for infusing the schools with playfulness through sociodrama, pragmatics, etc., are most enthusiastic. And yet if you believe that play is a fundamentally irrational phenomenon (as I do) or at least a synthesis of both primary and secondary processes (as Bateson puts it), then such enthusiasm has to be suspect (1972). One has to ask whether play can be truly subordinated to such rational schemes or whether these idealistic "play-work" programs will cease to be real play and become themselves the target for playful parody. Still, having raised this caution, I have to admit that I would not be writing here if I were not also a romantic along with Dr. Block. One part of me would love to see his recommendations fulfilled, but the rational part of my mind suspects that his wish is sheer fantasy.

Maledictive Games Discourse

To this point I have been discussing what the authors have said about play. There has been little reference to games. It is also important to take games into account, for if the twentieth century discourse on play has been quite positive, that on games has been quite maledictive. Games do figure here in the instrumental play controlled by teachers, in some of the goings on within illicit play, and in sports. In my lifetime, game discourse has changed from an idealized to a cynical form. I was brought up within sound of such Kiplingesque metaphors as "Play up, and play the game"; "The game's the thing"; "It's not whether you won or lost, it's how you played the game."

Most of these statements were supposedly derived from physical skill games of ball and bat or football--in my case from cricket and rugby, but they were also a part of the myth of amateurism which pervaded the early Olympics of this century and which now appears to have been more of a Western upper-status, self-serving ideology than any truthful application within ancient Greece (Young, 1984). More recent uses of the game metaphor, however, appear to be derived from strategy games, and that very switch is itself representative of the shift from the physical to the symbolic in much modern play (and from the manual to the nonmanual in economic life). As a consequence of this switch, information games (e.g. Trivial Pursuits) and fantasy games (e.g. Dungeons and Dragons) have come to have a greater role than ever before in human history. We live in a world, after all, in which the two greatest military powers practice constantly for the final holocaust in terms of non-zero sum game theory.

To say that someone is playing "games" today is to suggest that they are engaged in a deception of some kind. The best selling clinical work by Eric Berne (1964), *The Games People Play*, was based on the assumption that people who are not honest with each other end up by playing "games" with each other. In Berne's world this means the parties end up acting as if they intend one thing, whereas, in fact, both parties intend something else. Here the game metaphor which Berne used to describe these dyadic interaction systems is a reference to their distorted psychology, and no truly healthy person would engage in such games at all. As we have seen there are overtones of this attitude in the above notion that we can use our understanding of illicit play to so improve our schools that we "cure" the children of any need for it.

In another best seller, *The Gamesman* by Michael Maccoby (1976), likewise the executive, who treats his business as if it were a game, is much more successful than others who are contaminated by humanistic interests and not totally disciplined by the need for straightforward winning (meaning making profits). Maccoby does not particularly approve of this person but suggests that in the present economic conditions he is more likely to be the winner. A couple of outstanding films, "Sleuth" with Laurence Olivier and "Games" with Simone Signoret, also use the term "game" as a metaphor for deception.

Within more systematic social science, the game metaphor for human events has also played an important role in the writings of anthropologist

Clifford Geertz and sociologist Erving Goffman. Geertz, writing somewhat one-sidedly about Goffman, says: "The image of society that emerges from Goffman and from the swarm of scholars who, in one way or another, follow or depend upon him, is of an unbroken stream of gambits, plays, artifices, bluffs, disguises, conspiracies and outright impostures as individuals and coalitions of individuals struggle, sometimes cleverly, more often comically, to play enigmatical games whose structure is clear but whose point is not" (1980, p. 170).

In our present examples of play as being maledictive from King's and Everhart's chapters, the children are quite often pictured playing "games" against their teachers. On one level the teacher is endeavoring to establish a relationship of authority over dependents, and on a barely covert level the children are establishing a relationship amongst themselves as cohorts in resistance to the teacher. The teacher is attempting to be Mother in "Mother May I," and the children are attempting to make the teacher the scapegoat in "Blind Man's Bluff." Much of the time, of course, they are not directly involved with the teacher but are engaged in their own endless "playfighting," in which the agonistic elements are used constantly in balance with the affiliative elements so that the partners come to learn both to limit the former and to disguise the latter. They will not fight to the death, but their competiveness will continue to be haloed; they will not display any open need for affiliation except through mock competitive gestures and considerable body contact.

At any moment, of course, this internal "game" can be used to annoy and "bug" the teacher, and then as Everhart says it becomes an external game of brinkmanship, risking reprimand and punishment. Such an element of risk is an important part of most of the world's games throughout history and across cultures whether games of gambling, physical skill, or strategy, though the kind of risk differs in each case. Clearly "risk" is an important part of much of the world's play even though that seems to have been omitted in the definitions offered within this book. But little sense can be made of much of the "illicit play" discussed here without introducing risk as an important part of the players' motivation.

In their relationships with adults there are many times when children like to take risks with those adults. It is easier for them if the risks are taken in a play form in which one can use the mask of not being serious in order to avoid detection or punishment (Sutton-Smith and Kelly-Byrne, 1984c). If I am then asked to tell you whether not being serious is play or not play, I must answer that it is one of characteristics of informal play to switch in and out of everyday life in just such a labile and difficult to define manner. As academics we prefer tighter logical boundaries. And cultures also prefer tighter boundaries for play, games, and sports for these are, as Finkelstein points out, always a fulcrum of potential social conflict.

Cultures institutionalize their games and sports, and they confine their children to playgrounds and playrooms; but the basic play itself is not so easily boundaried. There are anthropological examples of games in which the losers were beheaded. Tribal wars have sometimes been so bound by rules that they resembled games more than wars and usually ceased after a certain number of protagonists had been killed. We should not see these forms of games as anomalies but rather as fortunate surviving examples of the protean character of life forms. The children's playground is rife with such ambiguity as Sluckin's (1981) work so abundantly demonstrates.

Whatever may be play's internal motivation, it is also a most valuable social technique for adaptation to other people. Social play requires incredible practice and skill in negotiation merely to survive within the play. It is truly the most important political context of childhood and, once acquired, it becomes a skill to be used in the midst of all the other life forms. The child who first defends herself from parental prying by saying "I am only pretending" is on the way to using playfulness throughout life as a barrier to the interference of intrusive others and as a bridge to the companionship of others of like mind and impulse.

In sum, I am arguing that the modern maledictive use of the metaphor "game" can also be seen to tell us something about children's play. The examples from King and Everhart are not a mistake. Only if play is thought of in a solitary way, can we confine ourselves to the kind of definitions offered earlier in which its spontaneity, intrinsic motivation, and freedom are stressed. But solitary play is a modern "sport" or mutant in a cultural evolutionary sense and hardly a basis for any universal definitions. Contrary to some play theorists (Schwartzman, 1978), I would argue that we need the game metaphor for understanding informal play just as much as we need the play metaphor when understanding games. Play and Games are primarily a communication with others and as such involve innumerable strategies, many of which are deceptive or at least paradoxical. Therefore, the kind of parlance or discourse that I am discussing in this section has relevance also to schools. As we shall see, this side of play often makes romanticists of play quite uncomfortable.

DISCOURSE ON METAPHORS

In addition to showing that there are at least two major ways of talking about play that have relevance to this book, there is also the issue of metadiscourse. What kind of discourse talks about these ways of talking in this manner? For example, can one even use the modern maledictive metaphoric term "game" to describe what is going on in this book as an implicit contest between researchers and teachers? The authors of these chapters are to a person dissatisfied with what they see of play in schools. All of them think they want more play and are using their scholarly skills to convince teacher to use more of it or to perceive more of it rightfully. The sharpest and most agonistic attack on teachers in these terms is that by Mayer Shevin.

Teachers, who in general have not the time to read these kinds of books, may defend against the "game" by not even turning up at the playing field. But you never can tell. Academics live a life of "adaptive potentiation," (Sutton-Smith, 1969) spawning their works into a sea of anomia and serendipity. Some teachers may become engaged with such works, and then the "game" metaphor is on.

But perhaps it is no contest, and the teachers co-operate in which case we have a co-operative game or no game at all but might still want to use the game metaphor for the researcher's self-deceptions. For example, perhaps these authors are claiming for children what they are really claiming for themselves. Perhaps their romanticism about play is a projection of their own nostalgia, and in this case we have an Eric Berne "game" going on in which both parties appear to be talking about play (researcher and teacher) and its value for children when they are actually talking about their own personal desire for, or loathing of, it.

Of course, some of the authors will fairly resist my using play metaphors to describe their research activities. Some might be likely to protest that what they are doing is reviewing objective studies of an empirical character. To that I might reply that they are using, therefore, a basically narrative metaphor, their studies being readings from the "book of nature." To which they would have the right to protest that, on the contrary, they live in a Cartesian dualistic world and feel it more productive not to mix "objective" and "subjective" phenomena in their analyses. They prefer to keep their data separate from their interpretations and look, rather, for causes or correlations which are a part of the lawful character of the human universe. They might argue that the physical sciences have transformed the world by such assumptions, and that we do better in the social sciences, therefore, by following the same formula.

In that case, of course, these authors would differ from others in this book who seem to be using a medley of their own observations and their informants' opinions in order to grasp play in a more holistic way. These latter authors might argue that play is such a complex and nuanced combination of "objective" and "subjective" factors that any research that did not allow access to all possible types of information would be as likely to be as nugatory as that reviewed by these former authors; authors in whom the need to pursue research under the hegemonious metaphor of experimental design has led necessarily to a lust for simplistic categories that are susceptible to quantification but have yielded minimal information in the process.

By rebuttal, the "natural science"-oriented researchers might well argue that this attempt to take into account subjective and objective factors in a general or holistic way must necessarily eschew the usual "controls" over both the data and the investigator and lead to that very projection of romanticism with which this book is replete. I would then have to interject that their own quantitations do not seem to have protected the "objectivist" researchers from the same personal interpretations. Natural science theorists often do have "objective" data but usually do not have objective interpretations of that data because that is another kind of science. This situation does not mean that the interpretations of the other authors in this book are particularly objective though they may be seen by some as more interesting. But again, that is a much larger story than can be told here (Sutton-Smith, 1984a). Whether this book is a "game," a "narrative," or simply "science" has to be an initial consideration for a commentator such as myself.

Finally, it would seem only responsible to say something about play, having maligned almost every other interpretation of it in this work. First, we should remember, with Wittgenstein, that all words, including the words "play" and "games," are constituted of many overlapping connotations, and which ones happen to be relevant in a particular historical case depends upon the practical usage we make of these words. There are thus always some occasions of play and games for which the dimensions freedom-compulsion, spontaneity-conformity, pleasure-pain, intrinsic-motivation extrinsic-motivation, flexibility-inflexibility, security-risk, and many other opposites can be found to be relevant. The search for universals is difficult because we live in an era in which highly technical differentiations of world and experience are our form of commonsense. The differentiation of words psychologically is, for us, a form of myth. We believe that personal understandings are possible and are essential to our adaption in this world.

However, many events in the past and in other cultures which look like play or games to us are not so differentiated lexically by those involved. Sometimes their games seem allied to war; sometimes they seem opposed to it. Sometimes play associated with religion, sometimes it seems opposed to it. Whereas we would tend to define play and games in psychological terms, most folk throughout history would do no such thing. How, then, can we even begin to pretend to a "empirical" understanding of the laws of play? All we can do is to use the historical and anthropological materials at hand to defeat the most obviously distorted forms of our cultural ethnocentricity. And that is what I hope that I have done in this commentary.

A FINAL NOTE

As a final note, I wonder why the two major geniuses of play in the past hundred years, Freud and Bateson, are missing almost entirely from this work. I find more promise for understanding play in their fusion of the rational and the irrational than I find in any other of the theoretical sources mentioned here (Sutton-Smith and Kelly-Byrne, 1984(c); Sutton-Smith, 1986). I have stressed elsewhere that play is a primordial form of communication and expression, more primitive than language. When we play together, we "talk" to each other of our divided selves and find incredible satisfaction in so doing. Only in therapy or art can we get as near to our whole selves as we do in play. This is because play always contains within itself a potential dialectic between mimicry and mockery, between modelling and caricature, between accepting society as it is and inverting it in protest or in fantasy.

It is not surprising that such a mixture of irrationality and the rational continually disguises itself from other forms of communication and knowing with a variety of self protective masks. As Bateson (1972) would say, acknowledging Freud, it is always a mixture of primary and secondary process. Play conceived of in this way is very often quite inappropriate for classroom or other civilized discourse; and yet, as I think everyone is covertly acknowledging here, life without access to some of this play or to playful persons seems to be so much duller and lacking in vitality. Life appears to be refructified by play (Bakhtin, 1984). What we are all saying to schools and teachers is that you may do without play but only at a cost to student motivation and vitality. These are going to be very important resources for the child in the long run as far as their sense of the worthwhileness of life is concerned. Those students who go to school but never get to play in their heads or with others may still have good grades but be too depressed to do much with them.

This is, of course, a quite emotional (perhaps Dionysian) and intuitive appeal, but after 30 years of research on the matter, I offer only the same convictions with which I began. My research has simply convinced me, again and again, that play abounds with the opportunities to try on powers, risks, deceptions, and skills and to share these with others. Those who can play are fortunate to have a festive spirit in their lives. Surely this should be enough. I really distrust any endeavor to turn school play into something that is not, and I believe we betray children when we take this path. Somehow we must maintain a course between those who would do away with play altogether and make schooling dull by its total absence and those who would so domesticate it and sanctify it so that it no longer truly exists.

References

Babcock, B. (Ed.). *The Reversible World*. Ithaca, New York: Cornell University Press, 1978.

Bakhtin, M. *Rabelais and His World*. Bloomington Indiana, Indiana University Press, 1984.

Bateson, G. *Steps to an Ecology of Mind*. New York: Ballantine, 1972.

Berne, E. *Games People Play*. New York: Grove, 1964.

Engell, J. *The Creative Imagination*. Cambridge, Massachusetts: Harvard University Press, 1981.

Fagen, R. *Animal Play Behavior*. New York: Oxford University Press, 1982.

Geertz C. Blurred Genres: The Refiguration of Social Thought. *The American Scholar, Spring*(1980), 165-179.

Knapp, M., and Knapp, H. *One Potato, Two Potato*. New York: Norton, 1976.

Maccoby, M. *The Gamesman*. New York: Bantam, 1976.

Schwartzman, H. *Transformations: The Anthropology of Children's Play*. New York: Plenum, 1978.

Sluckin, A. *Growing Up in the Playground*. London: Routledge and Kegan Paul, 1981.

Sutton-Smith, B. The Role of Play in Cognitive Development. *Young Children, 6*(1967), 361-370.

Sutton-Smith, B. Text and Context in Imaginative Play. *New Directions for Child Development, 25*(1984a), 53-71.

Sutton-Smith, B., and Kelly-Byrne, D. The Idealization of Play. In *Play in Animals and Humans*. Edited by P. Smith. London: Blackwell, 1984b.

Sutton-Smith, B., and Kelly-Byrne, D. (Eds.). *The Masks of Play*. West Point, New York: Leisure Press, 1984c.

Sutton-Smith, B. *Toys as Culture*, New York: Gardner Press, 1986.

Young, D. *The Olympic Myth*. Chicago: Ares, 1984.

PART IV: SELECTED BIBLIOGRAPHY

SCHOOL PLAY: BIBLIOGRAPHY

Catherine Wagner

This bibliography was created for those interested in further study of school play. It focuses on literature from about 1970 to the present that examines the role of school play in the student's personal and interpersonal development. Relevant literature for the pre-1970 period may be found in bibliographies of such sources as Child's Play by R. Herron and B. Sutton-Smith (New York: John Wiley, 1971).

In assembling this bibliography, I have attempted to locate available North American published and unpublished literature. In cases where several references have been published, but they appear in one volume, I have referenced just the mother volume. And in cases where a reference has not been published, we have given either an ERIC (Educational Resource Information Center) or a DA (Dissertation Abstract) number to facilitate its location. ERIC numbers are preceded by the code letters ED. Dissertation Abstract numbers are preceded by the code letters DA, DAH, DEL, DEP, and DBJ.

Adcock, D., and Segal, M. *Making Friends: Ways of Encouraging Social Development in Young Children.* Englewood Cliffs, New Jersey: Prentice-Hall, 1983.

Aldis, O. *Play-Fighting.* New York: Academic Press, 1975.

Allen, J. Classroom Management: A Field Study of Student's Perspectives, Goals, and Strategies. Ph.D. Dissertation, University of California, at Santa Barbara, 1982. DEP83-10186.

Allen, P., Kluesing, C., and MacMillan, L. *An Annotated Bibliography on Play Environments: Planning, Design, and Evaluation.* Monticello, Illinois: Council of Planning Librarians, 1976.

Almy, M., Monighan, P., Scales, P., and Van Hoorn, J. Recent Research on Play: The Perspective of the Teacher. *Current Topics in Early Childhood Education, 4 .* Edited by L. Katz. Washington D.C.: National Institute of Education, 1984.

Almy, M. A Child's Right to Play. *Childhood Education, 60*(1984), 350.

Anderson, V. A Comparison of the Sociodramatic Play Ability of High Socioeconomic Status Black Kindergarten Children and High Socioeconomic Status White Kindergarten Children. Ph.D. Dissertation, The Ohio State University at Columbia, 1972. DA73-1926.

Aronowitz, S. Together and Equal: The Egalitarian Promise of Children's Games. *Social Policy, 4*(1973), 78-84.

Atkin, J. Is Play Quite the Thing? *Times Educational Supplement, 3404*(1981), 50.

Avedon, E., and Sutton-Smith, B. (Eds.) *The Study of Games.* New York: John Wiley and Sons, 1971.

Baer, N. The Dynamics of Work and Play: An Historical Analysis and Future Implications. Paper presented at Harvard Graduate School of Education, Cambridge, Massachusetts, February, 1979. ED 168 693.

Bakeman, R., and Brownlee, J. Stategic Use of Parallel Play: A Sequential Analysis. *Child Development, 51*(1980), 873-878.

Baker, E., Herman, J., and Yeh, J. Fun and Games: Their Contribution to Basic Skills Instruction in Elementary School. *American Educational Research Journal, 18*(1981), 83-92.

Barell, J. Possibilities of Play in Adolescence. Ph.D. Dissertation, Columbia University Teachers College, 1976. DA76-21,010.

Barnett, L. Play and Intrinsic Rewards: A Reply to Csikszentmihalyi. *Journal of Humanistic Psychology, 16*(1976), 83-87.

Barnett, L., and Fiscella, J. A Child by Any Other Name: A Comparison of the Playfulness of Gifted and Nongifted Children. *Gifted Child Quarterly, 2*(1985), 61-66.

Barnett, L., and Kleiber, D. Playfulness and the Early Play Environment. *Journal of Genetic Psychology, 144*(1984), 153-164.

Barnett, L., and Kleiber, D. Concomitants of Playfulness in Early Childhood: Cognitive Abilities and Gender. *Journal of Genetic Psychology, 141*(1982), 115-127.

Batcher, E. *Emotion in the Classroom: A Study of Children's Experience.* New York: Praeger Publishers, 1981.

Bates, S. (Ed.) Kindergarten Curriculum Issues: Play. Bulletin No. 8063. Wisconsin State Department of Public Instruction, Madison Division of Instructional Services, 1978. ED 172 925.

Bauman, R. Ethnography of Children's Folklore. In *Children In and Out of School.* Edited by P. Gilmore and A. Glatthorn. Washington, D.C.: Center for Applied Linguistics, 1982.

Bekoff, M. Aspects of Play as Revealed by Structural Components and Social Interaction Patterns. *Behavioral and Brain Sciences, 5*(1982), 156-157.

Belch, J. Contempory Games. A Directory and Bibliography Covering Games and Play Situations of Simulations Used for Instruction and Training by Schools, Colleges and Universities, Government, Business, and Management, 1973. ED 081 189.

Bergen, D., et al., The Influence of the Culture of an Infant/Toddler Center on Peer Play Behavior: Informant and Observational Perspectives. Paper presented at the Annual Meeting of the Midwest Association for the Education of Young Children, Des Moines, Iowa, April, 1985. ED 257 580.

Berry, P. Playing With Print. *Australian Journal of Reading, 7*(1984), 71-74.

Biber, B. *Early Education and Psychological Development*. New Haven: Yale University Press 1984.

Bishop, J. Children, Television, Play, and Our Responsibilities. *Claremont Reading Conference Yearbook, 46*(1982), 210-218.

Blanchard, K. The Mississippi Choctaws at Play: The Serious Side of Leisure. Urbana, Illinois: University of Illinois Press, 1981.

Blanchard, K. (Ed.) *The Many Faces of Play.* Champaign, Illinois: Leisure Press, 1986.

Block, J. Some Neglected Parameters of the Student Role in Teaching: Play and the Play/Work Dialectic. Final Report, NIE G-80-0070, Washington, D.C., 1981.

Block, J. Making School Learning Activities More Playlike: Flow and Mastery Learning. *Elementary School Journal, 85*(1984), 65-75.

Blohm, P., and Yawkey, T. Language and Imaginative Play Experience Approach to Reading: Fact or Fantasy?, 1976. ED 130 781

Blurton-Jones, N. (Ed.) *Ethnological Studies of Child Behavior*. Cambridge, England: Cambridge University Press, 1972.

Booth, B. Socio-Cultural Aspect of Play and Moral Development. *International Journal Sport Psychology, 13*(1982), 50-59.

Borman, K. Children's Interactions on Playgrounds. *Theory Into Practice, 18*(1979), 251-257.

Borman, K. Children's Interpersonal Relationships: Playground Games and Social Cognitive Skills. University of Cincinnati, Cincinnati, Ohio, 1981. ED 207 697.

Borman, K., and Kurdek, L. High School Play: Gender Differences in the Nature and Correlates of Motivation to Play Soccer and Soccer Knowledge. Paper presented at the Annual Meeting of the American Anthropological Association, Denver, Colorado, November, 1984. ED 253 497.

Borman, K., and Lippincott, N. Cognition and Culture: Two Perspectives on "Free Play." In *The Social Life of Children in a Changing Society.* Edited by K. Borman. Norwood, New Jersey: Ablex Publishing Corp, 1982.

Botvin, G., and Sutton-Smith, B. The Development of Structural Complexity in Children's Fantasy Narratives. *Developmental Psychology, 13*(1977), 377-388.

Bredemeier, M., and Greenblatt, C. The Educational Effectiveness of Simulation Games. *Simulation and Games, 12*(1981), 307-332.

Bright, G., Harvey, J., and Wheeler, M. Using Games to Retain Skills With Basic Multiplication Facts. *Journal for Research in Mathematics Education, 10*(1979), 103-110.

Britz-Crecelivs, H. *Children at Play: Preparation for Life .* Edinburgh: Floris Book, 1979.

Brown, C., and Gotlfried, A. (Eds.) *Play Interactions. Johnson and Johnson Baby Products Company Pediatric Round Table Series: II.* Skillman, New Jersey: Johnson and Johnson, 1985.

Brown, J. Understanding Children's Play Through Observation. Far West Laboratory for Educational Research and Development, San Francisco, 1974. ED 129 461.

Bruner, J., Jolly, A., and Sylva, K. *Play--Its Role in Development and Evolution.* New York: Basic Books, 1976.

Buchanan, H. Views from the Bridge: From Where We Are to What Play Is and Could Become. *Journal of Physical Education, Recreation, and Dance, 54*(1983), 37-41.

Bulger, M. Character Development Through Play: A Historical Perspective. *Physical Educator, 39*(1982), 156-158.

Burns, S., and Brainerd, C. Effects of Constructive and Dramatic Play on Perspective-Taking in Very Young Children. *Developmental Psychology,* *15*(1979), 512-521.

Butler, A. Children's Play Behaviors and Play Preferences: A Field Study of a Selected Subculture. Ph.D. Dissertation, University of Maine, 1979. DA8009252.

Calderia, J., Singer, J., and Singer, D. Imagining Playmates: Some Relationships to Preschoolers' Spontaneous Play, Language, and Television Viewing. Paper read at the Eastern Psychological Association, Washington, D.C., March, 1978. ED 174 303.

Campbell, S., and Frost, J. The Effects of Playground Type on the Cognitive and Social Play Behaviors of Grade Two Children. Paper read at the Seventh World Congress of the International Playground Association, Ottowa, Canada, August, 1978.

Caplan, F., and Caplan, T. *The Power of Play.* Garden City, New York: Anchor Press, 1973.

Caring about Kids: The Importance of Play. National Institute of Mental Health (DIVHS), Rockville, Maryland, Division of Scientific and Public Information, 1981. ED 208 980.

Carpenter, C. Activity Structure and Play: Implications for Socialization. In *Social and Cognitive Skills, Sex Roles, and Children's Play.* Edited by M. Liss. New York: Academic Press, 1983.

Casby, M., and Ruder, K. Symbolic Play and Early Language Development in Normal and Mentally Retarded Children. *Journal of Speech and Hearing,* *26*(1983), 404-411.

Cavallo, D. *Muscles and Morals: Organized Playgrounds and Urban Reform, 1880-1920.* Philadelphia: University of Pennsylvania Press, 1981.

Cecil, L., Ispa, J., McPhail, G., and Thornburg, K. Curiosity-Exploration-Play-Creativity: The Early Childhood Mosaic. *Early Child Development and Care, 19*(1985), 199-217.

Chaille, C. The Child's Conceptions of Play, Pretending, and Toys: A Developmental Study of the Concepts of Symbolic Play of 5- to 11-Year Old Children. Ph.D. Dissertation, University of California at Los Angeles, 1977. DA7806464.

Cherfus, J., and Lewin, R. *Not Work Alone: A Cross-Cultural View of Activities Superfluous to Survival.* Edited by J. Cherfus and R. Lewin. London: Temple Smith, 1980.

Cheska, A. (Ed.)   *Play as Context: 1979 Proceedings of the Association for the Anthropological Study of Play*.   West Point, New York: Leisure Press, 1981.

Christie, J. Cognitive Significance of Children's Play: A Review of Selected Research.   *Journal of Education, 162*(1980), 23-33.

Christie, J. Play for Cognitive Growth.   *Elementary School Journal, 81*(1980), 115-118.

Christie, J. Sociodramatic Play Training.   *Young Children, 37*(1982), 25-32.

Christie, J. The Effects of Play Tutoring on Young Children's Cognitive Performances.   *Journal of Educational Research, 76*(1983), 326-330.

Christie, J. Training of Symbolic Play.   *Early Child Development and Care, 19*, no. 1-2(1985), 43-52.

Christie, J., and Johnsen, E. Role of Play in Social-Intellectual Development. *Review of Educational Research, 53*(1983), 93-115.

Cliatt-Puckett, M. Play: The Window into a Child's Life.   *Childhood Education, 56*(1980), 218-220.

Coakley, J. Play Group versus Organized Competitive Team: A Comparison. In *Sport in Contemporary Society: An Anthology.*   Edited by D. Eitzen. New York: St. Martin's Press, 1979.

Coakley, J. Play, Games, and Sport: Developmental Implications for Young People.   *Journal of Sport Behavior, 3*(1980), 99-118.

Cole, D., and LaVoie, J. Fantasy Play and Related Cognitive Development in 2- to 6-Year Olds.   *Developmental Psychology, 21*(1985), 233-240.

Connolly J. The Relationship Between Social Pretend Play and Social Competence in Preschoolers: Correlational and Experimental Studies. Ph.D. Dissertation, Concordia University, Canada, 1980. DA42(1980), 760B.

Connolly, J., and Doyle, A. Relation of Social Fantasy Play to Social Competence in Preschoolers.   *Developmental Psychology, 20*(1984), 797-806.

Connolly, J., Doyle, A., and Ceschin, F. Forms and Functions of Social Fantasy Play in Preschoolers. In *Social and Cognitive Skills: Sex Roles and Children's Play.*   Edited by M. Liss. New York: Academic Press, 1983.

Corsaro, W. *Friendship and Peer Culture in the Early Years.* Norwood, New Jersey: Ablex Publishing Corp, 1985.

Cotton, N. Childhood Play as an Analog to Adult Capacity to Work. *Child Psychology, 14*(1984), 135-144.

Cottrell, J. *Teaching With Creative Dramatics.* Skokie, Illinois: National Textbook Co., 1975.

Cowe, E. *Free Play: Organization and Management in the Pre-School and Kindergarten.* Springfield, Illinois: Thomas, 1982.

Crawley, S., and Chan, K. Developmental Changes in Free-Play Behavior of Mildly and Moderately Retarded Preschool-Aged Children. *Education and Training of the Mentally Retarded, 17*(1982), 234-239.

Crowe, B. *Play is a Feeling.* Boston: G. Allen and Unwin, 1983.

Cruickshank, D., and Telfer, R. Classroom Games and Simulations. *Theory Into Practice, 19*(1980), 75-80.

Crum, J. An Observational Study of the Play Patterns of Elementary School Children. Ph.D. Dissertation, University of California at Berkeley. DA42(1980), 399B.

Crum, R., Thornbur, K., Benning, A., and Bridge, C. Preschool Children's Object Substitutions During Symbolic Play. *Perceptual Perception and Motor Skills, 56*(1983), 947-955.

Csikzentmihalyi, M. *Beyond Boredom and Anxiety.* San Francisco: Jossey-Bass Publishers, 1975.

Curry, N. Considerations of Current Basic Issues on Play. In *Play: The Child Strives Toward Self-Realization.* Edited by G. Engstrom. Washington, D.C.: National Association for the Education of Young Children Publications, 1971.

Cusick, P. *Inside High School.* New York: Holt, Rinehart, and Winston, 1973.

Dansky, J. Cognitive Consequences of Sociodramatic Play and Exploration Training for Economically Disadvantaged Preschoolers. *Journal of Psychology, Psychiatry, and Allied Disciplines, 21*(1980), 47-58.

Dansky, J. Make Believe: A Mediator of the Relationship Between Play and Associative Fluency. *Child Development, 51*(1980), 576-579.

Dansky, J. Questioning "A Paradigm Questioned": A Commentary on Simon and Smith. *Merrill-Palmer Quarterly, 31*(1985), 279-284.

Davis, J. Teachers, Kids, and Conflict: Ethnography of a Junior High School. In *The Cultural Experience: Ethnography in Complex Society.* Edited by J. Spradley and D. McCurdy, Chicago: Science Research Associates, 1972.

Day, H. Why People Play. *Loisir et Societe, 2*(1979), 129-147.

Day, H. Play: A Ludic Behavior. In *Advances in Intrinsic Motivation and Aesthetics.* Edited by H. Day. New York: Plenum Press, 1981.

Day, H. Work and Play in the 21st Century: Workfulness at Play and Playfulness at Work. Paper read at the Annual Meeting of the Ontario Psychological Association, Ontario, Canada, February, 1984.

Day, H., and Forteath, C. Children's Understanding of Work and Play. *Recreation Review, 5*(1976), 47-52.

Dean, D. Motor Behaviors of Kindergartners During Physical Education and Free Play. Ph.D. Dissertation, University of Texas at Austin, 1981. DA8208161.

Deci, E. *Intrinsic Motivation.* New York: Plenum Press, 1975.

Delgado-Gaitan, C. Learning How: Rules for Knowing and Doing for Mexican Children at Home, Play, and School. Ph.D. Dissertation, Stanford University, Stanford, California, 1984.

Dennis, L. Play in Dewey's Theory of Education. *Young Children, 25*(1970), 230-235.

Dennis, L. Individual and Familial Correlates of Children's Fantasy Play. Ph.D. Dissertation, University of Florida, 1976. DBJ77-01111.

Denzin, N. Play, Games, and Interaction: The Contexts of Childhood Socialization. *The Sociological Quarterly, 16*(1975), 458-478.

Dickerson, D. A Study of Use of Games to Reinforce Sight Vocabulary. *The Reading Teacher, 36*(1982), 46-49.

DiPietro, J. Rough and Tumble Play: A Function of Gender. *Developmental Psychology, 17*(1981), 50-58.

Dobbert, M. Play is Not Monkey Business! A Holistic Biocultural Perspective on the Role of Play in Learning. *Educational Horizons, 63*(1985), 158-163.

Donmoyer, R. The Politics of Play: Ideological and Organizational Constraints on the Inclusion of Play Experiences in the School Curriculum. *Journal of Research and Development in Education, 14*(1981), 11-18.

Dukes, L. Dramatic Play + Symbolic Props = Reading. *Day Care and Early Education, 9*(1982), 11-12.

Edmonds, L. Child's Play as a Library Service: The Value of Toys to the Developing Child. *Top of the News, 41*(1985), 347-353.

Eheart, B., and Leavitt, R. Supporting Toddler Play. *Young Children, 40*(1985), 18-22.

Ellis, M. *Why People Play.* Englewood Cliffs, New Jersey: Prentice-Hall, 1973.

Ellis, M., and Scholtz, G. *Activity and Play of Children.* Englewood Cliffs, New Jersey: Prentice-Hall, 1978.

Engstrom, G. (Ed.) *Play: The Child Strives Toward Self-Realization.* Washington, D.C.: National Association for the Education of Young Children Publications, 1971.

Enslein, J., and Fein, G. Temporal and Cross-Situational Stability of Children's Social and Play Behavior. *Developmental Psychology, 17*(1981), 760-761.

Erickson, R. Play Contributes to the Full Emotional Development of the Child. *Education, 105*(1985), 261-263.

Erikson, E. *Toys and Reasons: Stages in the Ritualization of Experience.* New York: Norton, 1977.

Evans, R., and Wolfgang, C. (Eds.) Play and the Preschool Child. *Early Child Development and Care, 17*(1984).

Everhart, R. The Nature of "Goofing Off" Among Junior High School Adolescents. *Adolescence, 17*(1982), 177-187.

Everhart, R. *Reading, Writing, and Resistance: Adolescence and Labor in a Junior High School.* London: Routledge and Kegan Paul, 1983.

Fagot, B. Sex Determined Consequences of Different Play Styles in Early Childhood. Paper read at the 85th Annual Meeting of the American Psychological Association, Toronto, Canada. September, 1978.

Fay, T. The Effects of Participant Decision-Making on the Play Behavior of the Preadolescent. Ph.D. Dissertation, Boston University School of Education. DEP83-00768.

Federlein, A. *Play in Preschool Mainstreamed and Handicapped Settings.* Saratoga, California: Century Twenty One Publishers, 1981.

Fein, G. Play and the Acquisition of Symbols. In *Current Topics in Early Childhood Education.* Edited by L. Katz. Norwood, New Jersey: Ablex Publishing Corporation, 1979.

Fein, G. Game of Social Criticism. *Merrill-Palmer Quarterly, 26*(1980), 429-438.

Fein, G. Pretend Play in Childhood: An Integrative Review. *Child Development, 52*(1981), 1095-1118.

Fein, G. Pretend Play: New Perspectives. In *Contemporary Readings in Child Psychology.* Edited by E. Hetherington and P. Parke. New York: McGraw-Hill, 1981.

Fein, G. Skill and Intelligence: The Functions of Play. *Behavioral and Brain Sciences, 5*(1982), 163-164.

Fein, G., et al. Pretense and Peer Behavior: An Intersectoral Analysis. *Human Development, 25*(1982), 392-406.

Fein, G., and Stork, L. Sociodramatic Play: Social Class Effects in Integrated Preschool Classrooms. *Journal of Applied Developmental Psychology, 2*(1981), 267-279.

Feitelson, D., and Ross, G. The Neglected Factor: Play. *Human Development, 16*(1973), 202-223.

Fenrick, N., et al. The Play, Attending, and Language of Young Handicapped Children in Integrated and Segregated Settings. *Journal of the Division for Early Childhood, 8*(1984), 57-67.

Fenson, L., and Schell, R. The Origins of Exploratory Play. *Early Child Development and Care, 19,* no.1-2(1985), 3-24.

Field, T. Preschool Play: Effects of Teacher/Child Ratios and Organization of Classroom Space. *Child Study Journal, 10*(1980), 191-205..

Fink, R. Role of Imaginative Play in Cognitive Development. *Psychological Reports, 39*(1976), 895-906.

Finley, G., and Layne, L., Jr. Play Behavior in Young Children: A Cross Cultural Study. *Journal of Genetic Psychology, 119*(1971), 203-210.

Finnan, C. The Ethnography of Children's Spontaneous Play. In *Doing the Ethnography of Schooling: Educational Anthropology in Action.* Edited by G. Spindler. New York: Holt, Rinehart, and Winston, 1982.

Fischman, J. Toys Across Time: The Past, Present, and Future of Child's Play. *Psychology Today, 19,* no.10(1985), 56-63.

Forman, G. *Constructive Play: Applying Piaget in the Preschool.* Menlo Park, California: Addison-Wesley, 1984.

Foster, W. Cooperation in the Game and Sport Structure of Children: One Dimension of Psychosocial Development. *Education, 105*(1984), 201-205.

Frost, J., and Campbell, S. Play and Equipment Choices of Conserving and Preconserving Children on Conventional and Creative Playgrounds. Paper presented at the Seventh World Congress of the International Playground Association, Ottawa, 1978.

Frost, J., and Klein, B. *Children's Play and Playgrounds.* Boston: Allyn and Bacon, 1979

Frost, J., and Sunderlin, S. (Eds.) *When Children Play.* Wheaton, Maryland: Association for Childhood Education International, 1985.

Galda, L. The Effect of Dramatic Play on the Story Retelling of Second Grade Children. *Journal of Instructional Psychology, 10*(1983), 200-206.

Galda, L. Playing About a Story: Its Impact On Comprehension. *Reading Teacher, 36*(1982), 52-55.

Galda, L., and Pelligrini, A. The Effects of Thematic-Fantasy Play Training on the Development of Children's Story Comprehension. *American Educational Research Journal, 19*(1982), 443-452.

Gallegos, M. Learning Academic Skills Through Play. Paper presented at the Annual Meeting of the Southwest Educational Research Association, Houston, Texas, January, 1983. ED 225 690.

Galyean, B. Guided Imagery in the Curriculum. *Educational Leadership, 40*(1983), 54-58.

Garvey, C. Communicational Controls in Social Play. In *Play and Learning.* Edited by B. Sutton-Smith. New York: Gardner Press, 1979.

Garvey, C. *Play*. Cambridge, Massachusetts: Harvard University Press, 1977.

Garvey, C., and Berndt, R. The Organization of Pretend Play. Paper presented at the 83rd Annual Meeting of the American Psychological Association, Chicago, Illinois, September, 1975. ED 114 891.

Gasparova, Y. Role of Social Experience in the Play of Preschool Children. *Questions of Psychology, 6*(1984), 38-42.

Gehlbach, R.. Natural and Educational Play: Some Preliminary Discriminations. *Interchange, 6*(1975), 1-3.

Gehlbach, R. Educational Play: A Definition for Applied Research. Paper presented at the Annual Meeting of the American Educational Research Association, San Francisco, California, April, 1976. ED 122 974.

Gehlbach, R. Instructional Play: Some Theoretical Prerequisites to Systematic Research and Development. *Educational Psychologist, 15*(1980), 112-124.

Gehlbach, R., and Partridge, M. Physical Environmental Regulation of Verbal Behavior During Play. *Instructional Science, 13*(1984), 225-262.

Gentile, L., and Hoot, J. Kindergarten Play: The Foundation of Reading. *Reading Teacher, 36*(1983), 436-439.

Ginsberg, H. Playground as Laboratory: Naturalistic Studies of Appeasement, Altruism, and the Omega Child. In *Dominance Relations: An Ethological View of Human Conflict and Social Interaction*. Edited by D. Omark, F. Strayer, and D. Freedman. New York: Garland STPM Press, 1980.

Giordano, G. Play Learning. *Day Care and Early Education, 11*(1984), 17-21.

Glassner, B. Kid Society. *Urban Education, 11*(1976), 5-21.

Glickman, C. Play and the School Curriculum: The Historical Context. *Journal of Research and Development in Education, 14*(1981), 1-10.

Goldstein, J. (Ed.) *Sports, Games, and Play*: *Social and Psychological Viewpoints.* Hillsdale, New Jersey: L. Erlbaum Associates, 1979.

Goldstein, B., and Oldham, J. *Children and Work: A Study of Socialization.* New Brunswick, New Jersey: Transaction Books, 1979.

Golomb, C., and Cornelius, C. Symbolic Play and Its Cognitive Significance. *Developmental Psychology, 13*(1977), 246-252.

Goodale, T., and Witt, P. (Eds.) *Recreation and Leisure: Issues in an Era of Change* . State College, Pennsylvania: Venture, 1980.

Gootman, M. The Relationship Between Dramatic Play and Self-concept in Middle Class Kindergarten Children. Ph.D. Dissertation, University of Georgia, 1976. DBJ76-29, 526.

Gray, P., and Chanoff, D. When Play is Learning: A School Designed for Self-directed Education. *Phi Delta Kappan, 65*(1984), 608-611.

Green, V. Teachers and the Play Curriculum: Issues and Trends. *Early Child Development and Care, 17*(1984), 13-22.

Green, V., and Schaefer, L. Preschool Teachers' Play Materials Preferences. *Early Child Development and Care, 14*(1984), 85-92.

Greenberg, P., and Epstein, B. Bridge to Reading. Section 7: Free-play Enrichment Projects (Music and Movement, Mathematics and Cognitive Skills, and Social Studies), 1973. ED 093 493.

Greenlaw, M. Facilitating Play Behavior With Children's Literature. *Childhood Education, 60*(1984), 339-344.

Griffing, P. The Relationship Between Socioeconomic Status and Sociodramatic Play Among Black Kindergarten Children. *Genetic Psychology Monographs, 101*(1980), 3-34.

Griffing, P. Encouraging Dramatic Play in Early Childhood. *Young Children, 38*(1983), 13-22.

Griffing, P., Stewart, L., McKendry, M., and Anderson, R. Sociodramatic Play--A Follow-up Study of Imagination, Self-concept, and School Achievement Among Black School-age Children Representing Two Social-class Groups. *Genetic Psychology Monographs, 107*(1983), 249-301.

Guthrie, K., and Hudson, L. Training Conversation Through Symbolic Play: A Second Look. *Child Development, 50*(1979), 1269-1271.

Halverson, C. Relation of Preschool Verbal Communication to Later Verbal Intelligence, Social Maturity, and Distribution of Play Bouts. Paper presented at the 79th Annual Meeting of the American Psychological Association, Washington, D.C., September, 1971. ED 055 673.

Hancock, R. A Comparison of Two Forms of Play Methods Which Foster Cognitive Development in Kindergarten Children. Ph.D. Dissertation, Saint Louis University, 1981. DA8207405

304 *Wagner*

Hartup, W. The Peer System. In *Carmichael's Manual of Child Psychology: Social Development*. Edited by E. Hetherington. New York: Wiley, 1982.

Hartwig, M. School Work and School Play: Some Implications for Student Motivation. Paper presented at the Annual Meeting of the American Educational Research Association, Montreal, Quebec, Canada, April, 1983.

Hartwig, M. The Development and Validation of an Ethnographically-Based Instrument to Elicit Students' Perceptions of Their Classroom. Ph.D. Dissertation, University of California, Santa Barbara, June, 1986.

Hawes, B. Law and Order on the Playground. In *Games in Education and Development*. Edited by L. Shears and E. Bowers. Springfield, Illinois: Charles C. Thomas, Publisher, 1974.

Hearn, F. Toward a Critical Theory of Play. *Telos, 30*(1976-77), 145-160.

Henderson, J. The Foreshadowing of Work and Play Elements in School Settings. Ph.D. Dissertation, Stanford University, Stanford, California, 1980. DA8103581

Henderson, J. Five Ways to Combine Work With Play. *Illinois Schools Journal, 61*(1982), 61-64.

Hendry, L. *School, Sport, and Leisure*. London: Lepus Books, 1978.

Herron, R., and Sutton-Smith, B. (Eds.) *Child's Play*. New York: Wiley, 1971.

Hetherington, E., Cox, M., and Cox, R. Play and Social Interaction in Children Following Divorce. *Journal of Social Issues, 35*(1979), 26-49.

Hipple, T., and Hipple, M. Thinking Games Teachers Can Play. *Clearing House, 57*(1983), 22.

Hobson, S., and Feldhusen, J. Freedom and Play in Creativity Instruction. Paper presented at the Annual Meeting of the American Educational Research Association, New York, New York, February, 1971. ED 131 346.

Hollis, L., and Felder, B. Recreational Mathematics for Young Children. *School Science and Mathematics, 82*(1982), 71-75.

Honig, A. Playtime Learning Games for Young Children. *Day Care and Early Education, 10*(1982), 9-11.

Hounshell, P., and Trollinger, I. Games for Teaching Science. *Science and Children, 15*(1977), 11-14.

Huges, M. Exploration and Play Revisited: A Hierarchical Analysis. *International Journal of Behavioral Development, 2*(1979), 215-224.

Huston-Stein, A., Friedrich-Cofer, L., and Susman, E. The Relation of Classroom Structure to Social Behavior, Imaginative Play, and Self-Regulation of Economically Disadvantaged Children. *Child Development, 48*(1977), 908-916.

Hyers, C. Education as Play and the Fall Into Serious Work. *Education Digest, 48*(1983), 58.

Hyland, D., and Lanham, M. *The Question of Play*. Lanham, Maryland: University Press of America, 1984.

Iverson, B. Haha, Aha, Ah: A Model for Playful Curricular--Inquiry and Evaluation. Paper presented at the Annual Meeting of the American Educational Research Association, Los Angeles, California, 1981. ED 201-552.

Iverson, B. Play, Creativity, and Schools Today. *Phi Delta Kappan, 63*(1982), 693-694.

Jackowitz, E., and Watson, M. Development of Object Transformations in Early Pretend Play. *Developmental Psychology, 16*(1980), 543-549.

Jackson, D., and Angelino, H. Play as Learning. *Theory Into Practice, 13*(1974), 317-323.

James, N., and McCain, T. Television Games Preschool-Children Play: Patterns, Themes, and Uses. *Journal of Broadcasting, 26*(1982), 783-800.

Jarvis, J. The ABCs of Educational Software: By Turning Learning into Play, the Best Programs Can Open Up a World of Knowledge for Your Child. *Money*, November(1983), 193.

Johnson, J., and Ershler, J. Developmental Changes in Imaginative Play and Cognitive Ability of Preschoolers. Paper presented at the 87th Annual Meeting of the American Psychological Association, Montreal, Quebec, Canada, September, 1980. ED 192 929.

Johnson, J., and Ershler, J. Developmental Trends in Preschool Play as a Function of Classroom Program and Child Gender. *Child Development, 52*(1981), 995-1004.

Johnson, J., Ershler, J., and Bell, C. Play Behavior in a Discovery-Based and a Formal-Education Preschool Program. *Child Development, 51*(1980), 271-279.

Kamii, C., and DeVries, R. *Group games in early education: Implications of Piaget's Theory.* Washington, D.C.: National Association for the Education of Young Children, 1980.

Kamler, B. Ponch Writes Again: A Child at Play. *Australian Journal of Reading, 7*(1984), 61-70.

Kaplan, S. Play and The gifted Child. *Education Digest, 46*(1981), 52-53.

Kauffman, C. The Inclusion of Play in the Life/Planning Process. Ph.D. Dissertation, University of Northern Colorado, 1978. DA7910299.

Kelly-Byrne, D. Dramatic Play, Childhood Drama, and the Classroom. *Australian Journal of Reading, 7*(1984), 89-97.

Kessel, F., and Goncu, A. (Eds.) *Analyzing Children's Play Dialogues. New Directions for Child Development. No. 25.* San Francisco: Jossey-Bass, 1984.

King, N. Play: The Kindergartner's Perspective. *Elementary School Journal, 80*(1979), 81-87.

King, N. School Uses of Materials Traditionally Associated With Children's Play. *Theory and Research in Social Education, 10*(1982a), 17-27.

King, N. Children's Play as a Form of Resistance in the Classroom. *Journal of Education, 164*(1982b), 320-329.

King, N. Work and Play in the Classroom. *Sociology of Education, 46*(1982c), 110-113.

King, N. Play in the Workplace. In *Ideology and Practice in Schooling.* Edited by M. Apple and L. Weis. Philadelphia: Temple University Press, 1983.

Kinsman, C., and Berk, L. Joining the Block and Housekeeping Areas: Changes in Play and Social Behavior. *Young Children, 35*(1979), 66-75.

Kleiber, D. Limitations to Play in the Context of Sport. *Journal of Physical Education and Recreation, 50*(1979), 18-20.

Kleiber, D. Of Joy, Competence, and Significant Others in Children's Sports. In *Psychology of Motor Behavior and Sport.* Edited by G. Roberts, and D. Landers. Champaign, Illinois: Human Kinetics Publishers, 1981.

Kleiber, D. Sport and Human-Development: A Dialectical Interpretation. *Journal of Human Psychology, 23*(1983), 76-95.

Kleiber, D., and Barnett, L. Leisure in Childhood. *Young Children, 35*(1980), 47-53.

Kleiber, D., and Roberts, G. The Relationship Between Game and Sport Involvement in Later Childhood: A Preliminary Investigation. *Research Quarterly for Exercise and Sport, 52*(1983), 200-203.

Klinger, E. *Structure and Functions of Fantasy.* New York: Wiley, 1971.

Knapczyk, D., and Yoppi, J. Development of Cooperative and Competitive Play Responses in Developmentally Disabled Children. *American Journal of Mental Deficiency, 80*(1975), 245-255.

Knapp, M., and Knapp, H. *One Potato, Two Potato.* New York: W. W. Norton and Company, Inc., 1976.

Kocher, S. A Study of the Relationship Between Playfulness and Two Conceptions of Creativity in Kindergarten Children. Ph.D. Dissertation, University of Kansas, 1975. DAH76-16679.

Kraus, W. Math Learning Games: Simple vs. Complex. *School Science and Mathematics, 82*(1982), 397-398.

Kraus, W. Using a Computer Game to Reinforce Skills in Addition Basic Facts in Second Grade. *Journal for Research in Mathematics Education, 12*(1981), 152-155.

Kuczaj, S. Language Play and Language Acquisition. *Advances in Child Development and Behavior, 17*(1982), 197-232.

Kuczaj, S. Language Play. *Early Child Development and Care, 19*(1985), 53-67.

Lancy, D., and Tindall, A. (Eds.) *The Study of Play: Problems and Prospects.* West Point, New York: Leisure Press, 1977.

Landers, D., Feltz, D., Obermeier, B., and Brouse, T. Socialization Via Interscholastic Athletics: Its Effect on Educational Attainment. *Research Quarterly, 49*(1978), 475-483.

Landau, G. Play for Your Life: The Stakes Are Survival. Paper presented at the Hasbro-Loyola Play Conference, New York, New York, May, 1979. ED 180 578.

Langlois, H., and Downs, A. Mothers, Fathers, and Peers As Socialization Agents of Sex-Typed Play Behaviors in Young Children. *Child Development, 51*(1980), 1237-1247.

Larkin, R. *Suburban Youth in Cultural Crisis*. New York: Oxford University Press, 1979.

Laughlin, C., Jr., and McManus, J. The Biopsychological Determinants of Play and Games. In *Social Approaches to Sport*. Edited by R. Pankin. East Brunswick, New Jersey: Associated University Press, 1982.

Le Claire, L. The Concept and Function of Play in Education. Ph.D. Dissertation, University of Oregon, 1975. DA75-18,734.

Lepper, M., and Greene, D. Turning Play Into Work: Effects of Adult Surveillance and Extrinsic Rewards on Children's Intrinsic Motivation. *Journal of Personality and Social Psychology, 31*(1975), 479-486.

Lersten, K. New Play. Paper presented at the Southwest District Convention of the American Alliance for Health, Physical Education, and Recreation, Albuquerque, New Mexico, April, 1975. ED 109 092.

Lever, J. Sex Differences in the Games Children Play. *Social Problems, 23*(1975-1976), 478-487.

Lever, J. Sex Differences in the Complexity of Children's Play. *American Sociological Review, 43*(1978), 471-483.

Lever, J. *Soccer Madness*. Chicago: University of Chicago Press, 1983.

Levinson, W. Men and Playfulness: An Investigation of the Concept and Its Implications for Education. Ph.D. Dissertation, Southern Illinois University, Carbondale, 1976. DBJ77-06233.

Levy, A. The Language of Play: The Role of Play in Language Development. A Review of Literature. *Early Child Development and Care, 17*(1984), 49-62.

Levy, J. *Play Behavior*. New York: Wiley and Sons, 1978.

Lewis, N., and Berk, L. Effects of School Environment on the Development of Young Children's Creativity. *Child Development, 52*(1981), 1153-1162.

Levy, L., and Gottlieb, J. Learning Disabled and Non-learning Disabled Children at Play. *Remedial and Special Education, 5*(1984), 43-50.

Li, A. Play and the Mentally Retarded Child. *Mental Retardation, 19*(1981), 121-126.

Li, A. Toward More Elaborate Pretend Play. *Mental Retardation, 23*(1985), 131-136.

Licata, J. Student Brinkmanship: Some Field Observations, Findings, and Questions. Paper presented at the Annual Meeting of the American Educational Research Association, San Francisco, California, April, 1979. ED 174 899.

Lieberman, J. Playfulness and Creativity: Some Developmental and Situational Aspects. Paper presented at the Annual Meeting of the American Educational Research Association, New York, New York, February, 1971. ED 050 368.

Lieberman, J. *Playfulness: Its Relationship to Imagination and Creativity.* New York: Academic Press, 1977.

Lindberg, C. Sociodramatic Play of Low Socioeconomic Black and White Kindergarten Children. Ph.D. Dissertation, The Ohio State University, 1973. DA74-03232.

Liss, M. (Ed.) *Social and Cognitive Skills: Sex Roles and Children's Play.* New York: Academic Press, 1983.

Lockette, A. Playing, Experiencing, and Growing in Language Arts. Paper presented at the 9th Annual Meeting of the National Conference on Language Arts in Elementary School, Phoenix, Arizona, April, 1977. ED 145 466.

Loy, J. (Ed.) *The Paradoxes of Play.* West Point, New York: Leisure Press, 1982.

Lynch, R. Play, Creativity, and Emotion. *The Study of Symbolic Interactions, 4*(1982), 45-62.

Makedon, A. Theories of Play. Ph.D. Dissertation, The University of Michigan, 1981. DEO 82-04706.

Makedon, A. Playful Gaming. *Simulation and Games, 15*(1984), 25-64.

Malone, T. *What Makes Things Fun to Learn? A Study of Intrinsically Motivating Computer Games.* Palo Alto, California: Xerox, 1980.

Malone, T., and Lepper, M. Making Learning Fun: A Taxonomy of Intrinsic Motivations for Learning. In *Aptitude, Learning, and instruction: III. Conative and affective process analysis.* Edited by R. Snow and M. Farr. Hillsdale, New Jersey: L. Erlbaum Associates, Inc., 1986.

Mangin, R. Please Don't Disturb. Children at Play. *Early Years, 14*(1983), 38-40.

Manning, F. (Ed.) *The World of Play*. West Point, New York: Leisure Press, 1983.

Marbach, E., and Yawkey, T. The Effect of Imaginative Play Actions on Language Development in Five-Year-Old Children. *Psychology in the Schools, 17*(1980), 257-263.

Martens, R. *Joy and Sadness in Children's Sports*. Champaign, Illinois: Human Kinetics Publishers, 1980.

Martin, L. Contributions of Play Research to Human Development. Ph.D. Dissertation, Arizona State University, 1974. DA75-10,029.

Matthews. W. Modes of Transformation in the Initiation of Fantasy Play. *Developmental Psychology, 13*(1977), 212-216.

McConkey, R. Changing Beliefs About Play and Handicapped Children. *Early Child Development and Care, 19*(1985), 79-94.

McConkey, R., and Jeffree, D. First Steps in Learning to Pretend. *Special Education: Forward Trends, 6,* no.4(1979), 13-17.

McConkey, R., and Jeffree, D. Developing Children's Play. *Special Education: Forward Trends, 7,* no.2(1980), 21-23.

McCune-Nicolich, L. Toward Symbolic Functioning: Structure of Early Pretend Games and Potential Parallels with Language. *Child Development, 52*(1981), 785-797.

McDowell, J. *Children's Riddling*. Bloomington: Indiana University Press, 1979.

McGhee, P., Ethridge, O., and Benz, N. Effect of Level of Toy Structure on Preschool Children's Pretend Play. Paper presented at the Annual Meeting of The Association for the Anthropological Study of Play, Fort Worth, Texas, April, 1981.

McGrew, W. *An ethological study of children's behavior*. New York: Academic Press, 1972.

McLoyd, V. Verbally Expressed Modes of Transformation in Fantasy Play of Black Preschool Children. *Child Development, 51*(1980), 1133-1139.

McLoyd, V. Social Class Differences in Sociodramatic Play: A Critical Review. *Developmental Review, 2*(1982), 1-30.

McLoyd, V. Class, Culture, and Pretend Play: A Reply to Sutton-Smith and Smith. *Developmental Review, 3*(1983), 11-17.

McNamee, G. The Meaning and Function of Early Childhood Play. Paper presented at the Conference of the Psychoanalytic Foundation of Minneapolis, Inc., Minneapolis, Minnesota, March, 1983. ED 227 952.

Mehan, H. The Competent Student. *Anthropology and Education Quarterly, 11*(1980), 131-152.

Mergan, B. *Play and Playthings: A Reference Guide.* Westport, Connecticut: Greenwood Press, 1982.

Metz, M. *Classrooms and Corridors. The Crisis of Authority in Desegregated Secondary Schools.* Berkeley: University of California Press, 1978.

Miller, G., and Mason, G. Dramatic Improvisation: Risk-Free Playing for Improving Reading Performance. *Reading Teacher, 37*(1983), 128-131.

Miller, S. Ends, Means, and Galumphing: Some Leitmotifs of Play. *American Anthropologist, 75*(1973), 87-98.

Mills, B. Imagination: The Connection Between Writing and Play. *Educational Leadership, 40*(1983), 50-53.

Montessori, M. *The Montessori Method.* Cambridge, Massachusetts: Bentley, Inc., 1973.

Mori, A. (Ed.) *Play and Development.* Gaithersburg, Maryland: Aspen Systems Corp., 1982.

Mouncer, F. The Work and Play of Learning and Studying in the Elementary School. Manuscript in progress, Department of Education, University of California, Santa Barbara, 1986.

Naumburg, J. A Review of Play and Its Relationship to Learning. Opinion Paper, May, 1978. ED 164 097.

Naylor, H. Outdoor Play and Play Equipment. *Early Child Development and Care, 19*(1985), 109-130.

Newmann, E. *The Elements of Play.* New York: MSS Information Corp, 1971.

Newmann, E. Observing and Planning for Play and Competence. Opinion Paper, April, 1974. ED 105 986.

Norbeck, E. (Ed.) *The Anthropological Study of Human Play.*   *Rice University Studies,* *60,* no. 3(1974), 1-8.

Norbeck, E. The Biological and Cultural Significance of Human Play: An Anthropological View.   *Journal of Physical Education and Recreation* *50*(1979), 33-36.

Noren-Bjorn, E.   *The Impossible Playground.*   West Point, New York: Leisure Press, 1982.

Noyes, M. Sandplay Imagery: An Aid to Teaching Reading.   *Academic* *Therapy, 17*(1981), 231-237.

Odom, S. The Relationship of Play to Developmental Level in Mentally Retarded, Preschool Children.   *Education and Training of the Mentally* *Retarded, 16*(1981), 136-141.

Oklahoma Child Development Associate Policy Advisory Council.   *Play is* *Everything.*   Eastern Oklahoma State College: Wilburton, Oklahoma, 1976. ED 186 134.

Olmert, M. Points of Origin: Amidst Their High-tech Toys, Children Are Still Playing Games Popular in the Middle Ages and Renaissance. *Smithsonian, 4*(1983), 40.

Olszewski, P,. and Fuson, K.   Verbally Expressed Fantasy Play of Preschoolers as a Function of Toy Structure.   *Developmental Psychology,* *18*(1982), 57-61.

Opie, I., and Opie, P.   *Childrens' Games in Streets and Playgrounds .*   Oxford: Clarendon Press, 1969.

Oppenheim, J.   *Kids and Play .*   New York: Ballantine Books, 1984.

Otto, L., and Alwin, D. Athletics, Aspirations, and Attainments.   *Sociology of* *Education, 50*(1977), 102-113.

Paley, V.   *Boys and Girls: Superheros in the Doll Corner .*   Chicago: University of Chicago Press, 1984.

Paley, V. Superheros in the Doll Corner; Play Patterns and Fantasies Help Children Define Themselves as Boys or Girls.   *Natural History,* March(1985), 20.

Parrot, S. Games Children Play: Ethnography of a Second-Grade Recess. In *The Cultural Experience: Ethnography in Complex Society.*   Edited by J. Spradley and D. McCurdy. Chicago: Science Research Associates, 1972.

Patterson, J. Sociodramatic Play as a Technique for Increasing Young Children's Generation of Potential Strategies for Solving Interpersonal Problems. Ph.D. Dissertation, The University of Wisconsin-Madison, 1979. DEM 79-28656.

Pellegrini, A. Relationship Between Kindergartner's Play and Achievement in Prereading, Language, and Writing. *Psychology in the Schools, 17*(1980), 530-535.

Pellegrini, A. The Generation of Cohesive Text by Preschoolers in Two Play Contexts. Paper presented at the Annual Meeting of the American Educational Research Association, Boston, Massachusetts, April, 1980. ED 183 291.

Pellegrini, A. Speech Play and Language Development in Young Children. *Journal of Research and Development in Education, 14*(1981), 73-80.

Pellegrini, A. The Effect of Dramatic Play on Children's Generation of Cohesive Text. Paper presented at the Annual Meeting of the American Educational Research Association, Montreal, Canada, April, 1983. ED 227 964.

Pellegrini, A. Identifying Causal Elements in the Thematic-Fantasy Play Paradigm. *American Educational Research Journal, 21*(1984), 691-701.

Pellegrini, A. The Social Cognitive Ecology of Preschool Classrooms: Contextual Relations Revisited. *International Journal of Behavioral Development, 7*(1984), 321-332.

Pellegrini, A. Training Teachers to Assess Children's Play. *Journal of Education for Teaching, 10*(1984), 233-241.

Pellegrini, A. The Narrative Organization of Children's Fantasy Play: The Effects of Age and Play Context. *Educational Psychology, 5*(1985a), 17-25.

Pellegrini, A. The Relations Between Symbolic Play and Literate Behavior: A Review and Critique of the Empirical Literature. *Review of Educational Research, 55*(1985b), 107-120.

Pellegrini, A., De Stefano, J., and Thompson, D. Saying What You Mean: Using Play to Teach Literate Language. *Language Arts, 60*(1983), 380-384.

Pepler, D., and Ross, H. Effects of Play on Convergent and Divergent Problem Solving. *Child Development, 52*(1981), 1202-1210.

Pepler, D., and Rubin, K. Current Issues in the Study of Children's Play. *Human Development, 25*(1982), 443-447.

Pepler, D., and Rubin, K. (Eds.)   *The Play of Children: Current Theory and
    Research.*   New York: S. Karger, 1982.

Phelps, P.   Creative Playgrounds for the Preschool Children.   *Early Child
    Development and Care, 17*(1984), 23-35.

Philips, J., and Schafer, W.   Consequences of Participation in Interscholastic
    Sports: A Review and Prospectus.   *Pacific Sociological Review, 14*(1971),
    328-338.

Phyfe-Perkins, E.   The Ecology of Adult and Child Behavior in the Preschool
    Setting: A Review of Research.   In   *Individuals as Producers of Their
    Development: A Life-Span Perspective.*   Edited by R. Lerner and N.
    Busch-Rossnagel. New York: Academic Press, 1981.

Piazza, C., and Riggs, S.   Writing With a Computer: An Invitation to Play.
    Early Child Development and Care, 17(1984), 63-76.

Piers, M. (Ed.)   *Play and Development: A Symposium.*   New York: Norton,
    1972.

Piers, M., and Landau, G.   *The Gift of Play: And Why Young Children Cannot Thrive
    Without It.*   New York: Walker, 1980.

Pippenger, M.   The Cognitive Learning and Attitudes of Sixth Grade Pupils
    Playing the Simulation Game, Remote Island.   Ph.D. Dissertation,
    University of Kansas, 1972. DA73-11,834

Pitcher, E., and Schultz, L.   *Boys and Girls at Play: The Development of Sex Roles.*
    New York: Praeger, 1983.

Podilchak, W.   Youth Sport Involvement: Impact on Informal Game
    Participation. In   *Studies in the Sociology of Sport.*   Edited by A. Dunleavy,
    A. Miracle, and C. Rees. Fort Worth: Texas Christian University Press,
    1982.

Polgar, S.   The Social Context of Games: Or When is Play Not Play?
    Sociology of Education, 49(1976), 256-271.

Polgar, S.   Modeling Social Relations in Cross-Color Play.   *Anthropology and
    Education Quarterly, 9*(1978), 283-289.

Powell, R.   Play as an Ideal: Toward a Biosocial Model.   *Quest III, 35*(1983),
    107-119.

Power, T., and Parke, R.   Play as a Context for Early Learning: Lab and
    Home Analyses. In   *Families as Learning Environments for Children.*   Edited
    by I. Sigel and L. Laosa. New York: Plenum, 1982.

Pratt, R. The Concept of Play in American Physical Education. Ph.D. Dissertation, The Ohio State University, 1973. DA74-03293.

Precourt, W. Basketball, Social Structure, and Cultural Transmission in an Appalachian Community. Paper read at the Annual Meeting of the American Anthropological Association, Washington, D.C., November, 1976.

Prvulovich, Z. The Nature and Criteria of Play. *Durham and Newcastle Research Review, 10*(1983), 42-49.

Pulaski, M. Play as a Function of Toy Structure and Fantasy Predisposition. *Child Development, 41*(1970), 531-537.

Purvis, B. Children Forget How to Play. *Times Educational Supplement, 3466*(1982), 14.

Quilitch, H. Bibliography of Children's Play and Toys, 1974. ED 101 749.

Rabinowitz, F., Moely, B., Finkel, N., and McClinton, S. The Effects of Toy Novelty and Social Interaction on the Exploratory Behavior of Preschool Children. *Child Development, 46*(1975), 286-289.

Ramey, C., and Piper, V. Creativity in Open and Traditional Classrooms. *Child Development, 45*(1974), 557-560.

Rees, C. Motivation-Hygiene Theory and Sport Participation--Finding Room for the "I" in "Team". In *Sport Psychology: An Analysis of Athlete Behavior.* Second edition. Edited by W. Straub. Ithaca, New York: Mouvement, 1979.

Rees, C., Hammond, R., and Woodruff, J. Participation in Sport and the Reduction of Racial Prejudice: Contact Theory, Superordinate Goals Hypothesis, or Wishful Thinking? In *Sport and the Sociological Imagination.* Edited by N. Therbege and P. Donnelly. Fort Worth: Texas Christian University Press, 1984.

Rehberg, R., and Schafer, W. Participation in Interscholastic Athletics and College Expectations. *The American Journal of Sociology, 73*(1968), 732-740.

Reid, L., and Frazer, C. Television at Play. *Journal of Communication, 30, Autumn*(1980), 66-73.

Reifel, S. Play in the Elementary School Cafeteria. Paper presented at the Annual Meeting of The Association for the Anthropological Study of Play, April, 1984.

Reinecke, M.   The Effectiveness of a Creative Free Play Program for Kindergarten Children.   Ph.D.   Dissertation, The Pennsylvania State University, 1974. DA75-09831.

Reisdorf, M.   An Investigation of Play, Playfulness, and Work and Elementary School Science.   Ph.D.   Dissertation, Marquette University, 1974. DA75-14997.

Rich, G., and Gibson, M.   Demystifying the Concept of Culture: A Teacher's Guide to the Cross-Cultural Study of Games and Play.   Monograph IV, Bilingual Education Training Series.   California State University, Sacramento, Cross-Cultural Resource Center, 1978. ED 174 739.

Richterkessing, S.   Play: A Challenge of Elementary-Grade Educators. *Lutheran Education, 117*(1981), 30-31.

Roberts, J., and Sutton-Smith, B.   Child Training and Game Involvement. *Ethnology, 1*(1962), 166-185.

Rogers, D.   Relationships Between Block Play and the Social Development of Young Children. *Early Child Development and Care, 20*(1985), 245-261.

Rogers, P., and Miller, J.   Playway Mathematics: Theory, Practice, and Some Results. *Educational Research, 26*(1084), 200-207.

Rogers, S.   Developmental Characteristics of Young Children's Play.   In *Psychological Assessment of Handicapped Infants and Young Children.*   Edited by G. Ulrey and S. Rogers.   New York: G. Thieme Verlag, 1982.

Roopnarine, J., and Johnson, J.   Kindergartners' Play With Pre-School and School-Aged Children Within a Mixed-Age Classroom. *Elementary School Journal, 83*(1983), 578-586.

Rosen, C.   The Effects of Sociodramatic Play on Problem Solving Behavior Among Culturally Disadvantaged Preschool Children. *Child Development, 45*(1974), 920-927.

Roswal, G.   The Effects of a Children's Developmental Play Program on the Self-Concept, Risk-Taking, and Motor Proficiency of Exceptional Children.   Ph.D. Dissertation, University of Maryland, 1979. DEL79 26538.

Rubin, K. (Ed.)   *Children's Play.* San Francisco: Jossey-Bass, 1980.

Rubin, K., and Dyck, L.   Preschooler's Private Speech in a Play Setting. *Merrill-Palmer Quarterly, 26*(1980), 219-230.

Rubin, K., and Hayvren, M. The Social and Cognitive Play of Preschool-Aged Children Differing With Regard to Sociometric Status. *Journal of Research and Development, 14*(1981), 116-122.

Rubin, K., and Krasnor, L. Changes in the Play Behaviors of Preschoolers: A Short-Term Longitudinal Investigation. *Canadian Journal of Behavioral Science, 12*(1980b), 278-282.

Rubin, K., and Pepler, D. The Relationship of child's Play to Social-cognitive Growth and Development. In *Friendship and Social Relations in Children.* Edited by H. Foot, A. Chapman, and J. Smith. Chichester, New York: John Wiley, 1980.

Rubin, K., and Pepler, D. Children's Play: Piaget's Views Reconsidered. *Contemporary Educational Psychology, 7*(1982), 289-299.

Rubin, K., and Ross, H. *Peer Relationships' and Social Skills in Childhood.* New York: Springer-Verlag, 1982.

Rubin, K., Fein, G., and Vandenberg, B. Play. In *Handbook of Child Psychology.* Fourth edition. Edited by P. Mussen. New York: Wiley, 1983.

Rubin, K., Maioni, T., and Hornung, M. Free Play Behaviors in Middle- and Lower-Class Preshcoolers: Parten and Piaget Revisited. *Child Development, 47*(1976), 414-419.

Rubin, K., Watson, K., and Jambor, T. Free-Play Behaviors in Preschool and Kindergarten Children. *Child Development, 49*(1978), 534-536.

Sachs, J., Goldman, J., Chaille, C., and Seewald, R. Communication in Pretend Play. Paper presented at the Annual Meeting of the American Educational Research Association, Boston, Massachusetts, 1980. ED 195 322.

Saegesser, F. The Introduction of Play in Schools: A Philosophical Analysis of the Problems. *Simulation and Games, 15*(1984), 75-96.

Sage, G. (Ed.) *Sport in American Society.* Reading, Massachusetts: Addison-Wesley, 1974.

Salter, M. (Ed.) *Play: Anthropological Perspectives.* West Point, New York: Leisure Press, 1978.

Saltz, E. Pretend Play: A Complex of Variables Influencing Development. Paper presented at the Meeting of the American Psychological Association, Montreal, Quebec, Canada, September, 1980.

Saltz, E., and Johnson, J. Training for Thematic-Fantasy Play in Culturally Disadvantaged Children: Preliminary Results. *Journal of Educational Psychology, 66*(1974), 623-630.

Sanders, K., and Harper, L. Free Play Fantasy Behavior in Preschool Children: Relations Among Gender, Age, Season, and Location. *Child Development, 47*(1976), 1182-1185.

Sanoff, H., and Sanoff, J. Learning Environments for Children. Raleigh, North Carolina: Edwards Brothers, 1981.

Sapon-Shevin, M. Cooperative Instructional Games: Alternatives to the Spelling Bee. *The Elementary School Journal, 79*(1978), 81-87.

Saracho, O. Construction and Validation of the Play Rating Scale. *Early Child Development and Care, 17*(1984), 199-230.

Saracho, O. Young Children's Play Behaviors and Cognitive Styles. *Early Child Development and Care, 22*(1985), 1-18.

Sarland, C. Piaget, Blyton, and Story: Children's Play and the Reading Process. *Children's Literature in Education, 16*(1985), 102-109.

Schilling, L. Imaginary Companions: Considerations for the Health Professional. *Early Child Development and Care, 22*(1985), 211-223.

Schleifer, M. John Doesn't Know How to Play: Play and the Grade School Child. *Exceptional Parent, 13*(1983), 33-38.

Schoedler, J. A Comparison of the Use of Active Game Learning with a Conventional Teaching Approach in the Development of Concepts in Geometry and Measurement at the Second Grade Level. *School Science and Mathematics, 81*(1981), 365-370.

Schwartzman, H. The Anthropological Study of Children's Play. *Annual Review of Anthropology, 5*(1976), 289-328.

Schwartzman, H. (Ed.) *Play and Culture.* West Point, New York: Leisure Press, 1980.

Schwartzman, H. *Transformations: The Anthropology of Children's Play.* New York: Plenum Press, 1982a.

Schwartzman, H. Play as a Mode. *Behavioral and Brain Sciences, 5*(1982b), 168-169.

Segal, M., and Adcock, D. *Just Pretending: Ways to Help Children Grow Through Imaginative Play.* Englewood Cliffs, New Jersey: Prentice-Hall, 1981.

Seidman, S. Eventful Play: Preschoolers' Scripts for Pretense. Paper presented at the Biennial Meeting of the Society for Research in Child Development, Detroit, April, 1983.

Severeide, R., and Pizzini, E. What Research Says: The Role of Play in Science. *Science and Children, 21*(1984), 58-61.

Shears, L., and Bower, M. (Eds.) *Games in Education and Development.* Springfield, Illinois: Charles C. Thomas, Publishers, 1974.

Sherrod, K. Language and Play Maturity in Preschool Children. *Early Child Development and Care, 14*(1984), 147-160.

Sieber, R. Classmates as Workmates--Informal Peer Activity in the Elementary School. *Anthropology and Education Quarterly, 10*(1979), 207-235.

Silvern, S. Play as an Avenue for Social Growth. *Journal of Research and Development in Education, 14*(1981), 106-115.

Silvern, S. Play as a Mediator of Comprehension: An Alternative to Play Training. *Educational Research Quarterly, 7*(1982), 16-21.

Simon, T. Play and Learning With Computers. *Early Child Development and Care, 19*(1985), 69-78.

Simon, T., and Smith P. Play and Problem Solving: A Paradigm Questioned. *Merrill-Palmer Quarterly, 31*(1985), 265-277.

Singer, J. *The Child's World of Make Believe: Experimental Studies of Imaginative Play.* New York: Academic Press, 1973.

Singer, J. Imagination and Make-Believe Play in Early Childhood: Some Educational Implications. *Journal of Mental Imagery, 1*(1977), 127-144.

Singer, J., Singer, D., and Sherrod, L. A Factor Analytic Study of Preschoolers' Play Behavior. *American Psychology Bulletin, 2*(1980), 143-156.

Sleet, D.. Interdisciplinary Research Index on Play: A Guide to the Literature. Toledo University, Ohio, 1971. ED 058 146.

Slesnick, T. Creative Play: An Alternative Use of the Computer in Education. *Simulation and Games, 14*(1983), 11-19.

Sluckin, A. *Growing Up in the Playground: The Social Development of Children.* London: Routledge and Kegan Paul, 1981.

Smilansky, S. *The Effects of Sociodramatic Play Upon Disadvantaged Preschool Children.* New York: Wiley, 1968.

Smith, L., and Geoffrey, W. *The Complexities of the Urban Classroom.* New York: Holt, Rinehart, and Winston, 1968.

Smith, P. *Play in Animals and Humans.* New York: Basil Blackwell, 1984.

Smith, P., and Connolly, K. *The Ecology of Preschool Behavior.* Cambridge, England: Cambridge University Press, 1980.

Smith, P., and Vollstedt, R. On Defining Play: An Empirical Study of the Relationship Between Play and Various Play Criteria. *Child Development, 56*(1985), 1042-1050.

Smith, P., Takhvar, M., and Gore, N. Play in Young Children: Problems of Definition, Categorization, and Measurement. *Early Child Development and Care, 19*(1985), 25-41.

Spady, W. Lament for the Letterman: Effects of Peer Status and Extracurricular Activities on Goals and Achievement. *American Journal of Sociology, 75*(1970), 680-702.

Spencer-Hall, D. Looking Behind the Teacher's Back. *The Elementary School Journal, 81*(1981), 281-289.

Spodek, B. The Problem of Play: Educational or Recreational? In *Play as a Learning Medium.* Edited by D. Sponseller. Washington, D.C.: National Association for the Education of Young Children, 1974.

Spring, J. Mass Culture and School Sports. *History of Education Quarterly, 14*(1974), 483-501.

Stanifold, D. Playspaces Kids Love! *Today's Education, 70*(1981), 52-53.

Steele, C. Play Variable as Related to Cognitive Constructs in Three-To-Six-Year-Olds. *Journal of Research and Development in Education, 14*(1981), 58-72.

Stephenson, J. A Rationale for the Inclusion of Play in the Elementary School Curriculum. Ph.D. Dissertation, The University of Mississippi, 1975. DA75-21, 557.

Stevens, P. (Ed.) *Studies in the Anthropology of Play.* West Point, New York: Leisure Press, 1977.

Stinchcombe, A. *Rebellion in a High School.* Chicago: Quadrangle, 1964.

Stoneman, Z. Naturalistic Observations of Children's Activities and Roles While Playing With Their Siblings and Friends. *Child Development,* 55(1984), 617-627.

Stoneman, Z., Cantrell, M., and Hoover-Dempsey, K. The Association Between Play Materials and Social Behavior in a Mainstreamed Preschool: A Naturalistic Investigation. *Journal of Applied Developmental Psychology,* 4(1983), 163-174.

Strickland, E. Free Play Behaviors and Equipment Choices of Third Grade Children in Contrasting Play Environments. Unpublished Ph.D. Dissertation, The University of Texas at Austin, 1979. DEM80-09939.

Strom, A. The Effects of Intensive Group Play Media on the Self-Concepts of Selected Second Grade Children. Ph.D. Dissertation, University of Denver, 1976. DBJ 77-00456.

Strom, R. (Ed.) *Growing Through Play Readings for Parents and Teachers.* Monterey, California: Brooks/Cole, 1981.

Sutton-Smith, B. *The Folkgames of Children.* Austin: University of Texas Press, 1972.

Sutton-Smith, B. (Ed.) *A Childrens' Games Anthology: Studies in Folklore and Anthropology.* New York: Arno Press, 1976.

Sutton-Smith, B. (Ed.) *Play and Learning.* New York: Gardner Press, 1979.

Sutton-Smith, B., *A History of Children's Play: The New Zealand Playground, 1840-1950.* Pennsylvania: University Pennsylvania Press, 1981.

Sutton-Smith, B. Growing Up in the Playground: The Social Development of Children. *Contemporary Psychology,* 27(1982), 729-730.

Sutton-Smith, B. Piaget, Play, and Cognition Revisited. In *The Relationship Between Social and Cognitive Development.* Edited by W. Overton. New York: Erlbaum, 1983a.

Sutton-Smith, B. One Hundred Years of Change in Play Research. *Newsletter of the Association for the Anthropological Study of Play, 9, no. 2*(1983b), 13-17.

Sutton-Smith, B. Ambivalence in Toyland: Playthings Can Both Isolate and Socialize. *Natural History, 3*(1985a), 6.

Sutton-Smith, B. The Child at Play: Play is Becoming Steadily Less Physical, More Computerized and, Most of All, More Isolated. *Psychology Today,* October(1985b), 64.

Sutton-Smith, B., and Kelly-Byrne, D. *The Masks of Play.* West Point, New York: Leisure Press, 1984a.

Sutton-Smith, B., and Kelly-Byrne, D. The Phenomenon of Bipolarity in Play Theories. In *Child's Play: Developmental and Applied.* Edited by T. Yawkey and A. Pellegrini. Hillsdale, New Jersey: Lawrence Erlbaum, 1984b.

Sutton-Smith, B., and Roberts, J. Play, Games, and Sports. In *Handbook of Cross-Cultural Psychology.* Volume 4. Edited by H. Triandis and A. Heron. Boston: Allyn and Bacon, 1981.

Swift, C. Symbolic Play and Rehearsal Behavior in Young Children With Learning Disability. Ph.D. Dissertation, University of Arizona, Tucson, 1978. DEL 79-09487.

Swink, D., and Buchanan, D. The Effects of Sociodramatic Goal-Oriented Role Play and Non-Goal-Oriented Role Play on Locus of Control. *Journal of Clinical Psychology, 40*(1984), 1178-1183.

Switzky, H., Haywood, H., and Isett, R. Exploration, Curiosity, and Play in Young Children: Effects of Stimulus Complexity. *Developmental Psychology, 10*(1974), 321-329.

Sylva, K. A Hard Headed Look at the Fruits of Play. *Early Child Development and Care, 15*(1984), 171-183.

Sylva, K., Roy, C., and Painter, M. *Childwatching at Playgroup and Nursery School.* Ypsilanti, Michigan: High/Scope Press, 1980.

Szekely, G. Preliminary Play in the Art Class. *Art Education, 36*(1983), 18-24.

Tamburrini, J. Play and the Role of the Teacher. *Early Child Development and Care, 8*(1982), 209-217.

Tang, T., and Baumeist, R. Effects of Personal Values, Perceived Surveillance, and Task Labels on Task Preference: The Ideology of Turning Play Into Work. *Journal of Applied Psychology, 69*(1984), 99-105.

Thelen, M. Imitation During Play as a Means of Social Influence. *Child Development, 51*(1980) 918-920.

Tipps, S. Play and the Brain: Relationships and Reciprocity. *Journal of Research and Development in Education, 14*(1981), 19-28.

Tizard, B., and Harvey, D. (Eds.) *Biology of Play.* Philadelphia, Pennsylvania: J. B. Lippincott, 1977.

Trostle, S., and Yawkey, T. Facilitating Creative Thought Through Object Play in Young Children. *Journal of Creative Behavior, 17*(1983), 181-189.

Trout, L. Drama in the Elementary Classroom: A Teacher's Discovery of Dramatic Play. Ph.D. Dissertation, Northwestern University, 1978. DEL 79-03380.

Tyler, B. Capturing the Play Spirit of the Child. *Education, 97*(1976), 98-101.

Tyson, E., and Mountain, L. A Riddle or Pun Make Learning Words Fun. *The Reading Teacher, 35*(1982), 170-173.

Udwin, O., and Shmukler, D. The Influence of Sociocultural, Economic, and Home Background Factors on Children's Ability to Engage in Imaginative Play. *Developmental Psychology, 17*(1981), 66-72.

Ungerer, J., and Sigman, M. The Relation of Play and Sensorimotor Behavior to Language in the Second Year. *Child Development, 55*(1984), 1448-1455.

Van, A. Life! Through Play. Paper presented at the Wyoming Association for Health, Physical Education, and Recreation, Laramie, Wyoming, November, 1974. ED 098 246.

Vandenberg, B. Play and Development From an Ethological Perspective. *American Psychologist, 33*(1978), 724-738.

Vandenberg, B. Play as Curriculum. *Journal of Curriculum Theorizing, 1-2*(1979), 229-237.

Vandenberg, B. Play: Dormant Issues and New Perspectives. *Human Development, 24*(1981), 357-365.

Vandenberg, B. Developmental Features of Children's Play With Objects. *Journal of Psychology, 109*(1981a), 27-29.

Vandenberg, B. Role of Play in the Development of Insightful Tool-Using Strategies. *Merrill-Palmer Quarterly, 27*(1981b), 97-109.

Vandenberg, B. Environmental and Cognitive Factors in Social Play. *Journal of Experimental Child Psychology, 31*(1982a), 169-175.

Vandenberg, B. The Essentials of Play. *Behavioral and Brain Sciences, 5*(1982b), 171-172.

Vandenberg, B., and Kielhofn, G. Play in Evolution, Culture , and Individual Adaptation: Implications for Therapy. *American Journal of Occupational Therapy, 36*(1982), 20-28.

Walsh, E. The Perils of Overprogramming Play. *Parks and Recreation, 19*(1984), 50, 53-54.

Watson, M. Competence Motivation and Children's Free-Play Preferences. Paper presented at the 86th Annual Meeting of the American Psychological Association, September, 1979. ED 192 016.

Watson, M., and Jackowitz, E. Agents and Recipient Objects in the Development of Early Symbolic Play. *Child Development, 55*(1984), 1091-1097.

Webb, H. Professionalization of Attitudes Toward Play Among Adolescents. In *Aspects of Contemporary Sport Sociology.* Edited by G. Kenyon. Chicago: The Athletic Institute, 1969.

Wehman, P. *Helping the Mentally Retarded Acquire Play Skills.* Springfield, Illinois: Charles C. Thomas, 1977.

Weingartner, T. An Analysis of the Organization and Administration of Sport in Relation to Theoretical Rationales for Play Participation. Unpublished Ph.D. Dissertation, Northwestern University, 1982. DA 82-26042.

Weininger, O. Why Play?. Opinion Paper, 1979. ED 172 939.

Weininger, O. Play, Creativity, and the Cognitive Unconscious. *Reading Improvement, 18*(1981), 98-107.

Weisle, A., and McCall, R. Exploration and Play: Resume and Redirection. *American Psychologist, 31*(1976), 492-508.

Werth, L. The Many Faces of Play. *Early Child Development and Care, 17*(1984), 3-12.

Werthman, C. Delinquents in Schools: A Test of the Legitimacy of Authority. In *School and Society.* Edited by B. Cosin, et al. London: Routledge and Kegan Paul, 1971.

Westby, C. Assessment of Cognitive and Language Abilities Through Play. *Language, Speech, and Hearing Services in School, 11*(1980), 154-168.

Wharton-Boyd, L. The Significance of Black American Children's Singing Games in an Educational Setting. *Journal of Negro Education, 52*(1983), 46-56.

Whittaker, C. A Note on Developmental Trends in the Symbolic Play of Hospitalized Profoundly Retarded Children. *Journal of Child Psychology and Psychiatry, 2*(1980), 253-261.

Wholf, F. Playground Pals. *Instructor, 93*(1984), 46-48.

Wilkinson, P. (Ed.) *In Celebration of Play: An Integrated Approach to Play and Child Development.* New York: St. Martin's Press, 1980.

Williams, R., and Beeson, B. (Eds.) *Monograph of Play Research.* Ball State University, Muncie, Indiana, 1982. ED 221 290.

Wilson, A., and Singer, J. Creative Play. *Journal of Creative Behavior, 11*(1977), 268-270.

Wing, L., Gould, J., Yeates, S., and Brierley, L. Symbolic Play in Severely Mentally Retarded and in Autistic Children. *Journal of Child Psychology and Psychiatry, 18*(1977), 167-178.

Winnicott, D. *Playing and Reality.* London: Tavistock Publications, 1971.

Wolf, D., and Gardner, H. Style and Sequence in Early Symbolic Play. In *Early Symbolization.* Edited by F. Smith. San Francisco: Jossey-Bass, 1979.

Wolf, D., and Grollman, S. Ways of Playing: Individual Differences in Imaginative Style. *Contributions to Human Development, 6*(1982), 46-63.

Wolfgang, C. An Exploration of the Relationship Between the Cognitive Area of Reading and Selected Developmental Aspects of Children's Play. *Psychology in the Schools, 11*(1974), 338-343.

Wolfgang, C. *Helping Aggressive and Passive Preschoolers Through Play.* Columbus, Ohio: Charles E. Merrill Publishing Company, 1977.

Wolfgang, C. A Study of Play as a Predictor of Socio-Emotional Development. *Early Child Development and Care, 13*(1983), 33-54.

Wolfgang, C., and Sanders, T. Defining Young Children's Play as a Ladder to Literacy. *Theory Into Practice, 20*(1981), 116-120.

Wolfgang, C., and Sanders, T. Teachers' Role a Construct for Supporting the Play of Young Children. *Early Child Development and Care, 8*(1982), 107-120.

Woodard, C. Guidelines for Facilitating Sociodramatic Play. *Childhood Education, 60*(1984), 172-177.

Woods, P. *The Divided School.* London: Routledge and Kegan Paul, 1979.

Wuerch, B., and Voeltz, L. *Longitudinal Leisure Skills for Severely Handicapped Learners: The Ho'onanea Curriculum Component.* Baltimore: Brookes, 1982.

Yawkey, T. More on Play as Intelligence in Children. *Journal of Creative Behavior, 13*(1979), 247-256.

Yawkey, T. Why Play? *Educational Research Quarterly, 5*(1980), 74-77.

Yawkey, T. Sociodramatic Play Effects on Mathematical Learning and Adult Ratings of Playfulness in Five Year Olds. *Journal of Research and Development in Education, 14*(1981), 30-39.

Yawkey, T., and Fox, F. Evaluative Intervention Research in Child's Play. *Journal of Research and Development in Education, 14*(1981), 40-57.

Yawkey, T., and Pellegrini, A. (Eds.) *Child's Play: Developmental and Applied.* Hillsdale, New Jersey: L. Erlbaum Associates, 1984.

Zervigon-Hakes, A. Materials Mastery and Symbolic Development in Construction Play: Stages of Development. *Early Child Development and Care, 17*(1984), 37-48.

Zubrowski, B. Play as Education in School-Age Day Care Programs. *Day Care and Early Education, 9*(1981), 17-19.

SUBJECT INDEX